Lecture Notes in Business Information Processing 114

Michael A. Cusumano
Bala Iyer
N. Venkatraman (Eds.)

Software Business

Third International Conference, ICSOB 2012
Cambridge, MA, USA, June 18-20, 2012
Proceedings

Springer

Volume Editors

Michael A. Cusumano
MIT Sloan School of Management
Cambridge, MA, USA
E-mail: cusumano@mit.edu

Bala Iyer
Babson College
Babson Park, MA, USA
E-mail: biyer@babson.edu

N. Venkatraman
Boston University
Boston, MA, USA
E-mail: venkat@bu.edu

ISSN 1865-1348 e-ISSN 1865-1356
ISBN 978-3-642-30745-4 e-ISBN 978-3-642-30746-1
DOI 10.1007/978-3-642-30746-1
Springer Heidelberg Dordrecht London New York

Library of Congress Control Number: 2012938679

ACM Computing Classification (1998): K.1, K.6, D.2

Typesetting: Camera-ready by author, data conversion by Scientific Publishing Services, Chennai, India

Printed on acid-free paper

Springer is part of Springer Science+Business Media (www.springer.com)

Preface

Change and progress in software and in computing and communications technology more broadly have had a substantial impact not only on productivity and economic growth around the world, but also on our daily work and lifestyles. The software business covers commercial activities in the software industry, aimed at generating income from the design, delivery, and maintenance of software products and information technology services to enterprises and individual consumers as well as from digital content. Although the software business shares common features with other knowledge-intensive businesses, it carries many inherent features making it a challenging domain for research. In particular, many software companies have to depend on one another as well as hardware companies and various service providers to deliver a unique value proposition to their customers. New developments like applications that run on pre-existing platforms have emerged as a major force and are creating what is being labeled "the App economy."

For this Third International Conference on Software Business, we received 60 research paper submissions from all over the world. The papers went through a thorough review process by at least two reviewers for each paper. The Program Committee deliberated with all the reviews and accepted 20 submissions to be presented as full papers for the conference (thus giving it an acceptance rate of 33%). In addition, ten papers were accepted as short research papers. The accepted papers follow diverse methodologies, and represent the diversity in research in our community. We have organized the papers according to the following categories: Software Development and Product Management, Software Platforms and Ecosystems, Organizational Transformation, Industry Transformation, and Emerging Trends and App Stores.

In addition to the full and short paper presentations, we opened the conference with a workshop on ecosystems and a tutorial on "Managing Project Value Throughout the Software Development Life Cycle: A Practical Approach" by Stefan Cedergren and Stig Larsson. The invited keynotes were given by: Jeremy Allaire (Brightcove, CEO and Founder), Brain Halligan (CEO and Co-founder), and Imran Sageed (NTT Data, CTO and senior VP, Global Development; senior lecturer at MIT Sloan). The 4th Software Ecosystems Workshop, held during the conference, was organized by Slinger Jansen, Jan Bosch, and Carina Frota Alves.

As chairs of the Program Committee, we would like to thank the Program Committee members for their time and dedication in providing feedback to the authors. Their input helped shape this conference and maintain a high quality of research. As has been the case in previous conferences, the Steering Committee was an invaluable source of organizational memory and provided valuable guidance at critical junctures.

June 2012

Michael Cusumano
Bala Iyer
N. Venkatraman

Organization

General Chair

Michael A. Cusumano	MIT Sloan School of Management, USA

Program Chairs

Bala R. Iyer	Babson College
N. Venkatraman	Boston University, School of Management, USA

Steering Committee

Kalle Lyytinen	Case Western Reserve,USA
Sjaak Brinkkemper	Utrecht University The Netherlands
Pekka Abrahamsson	University of Helsinki, Finland
Slinger Jansen	Utrecht University, The Netherlands
Pasi Tyrväinen	University of Jyväskylä, Finland
Björn Regnell	Lund University, Sweden
Inge van de Weerd	Utrecht University, The Netherlands

Website Management

Jaap Kabbedijk	Utrecht University, The Netherlands

Program Committee

Aybuke Aurum	University of New South Wales, Australia
Carliss Baldwin	Harvard Business School, USA
Jan Bosch	Intuit, USA
Peter Buxmann	Technische Universität Darmstadt, Germany
David Callele	University of Saskatchewan, Canada
Joao Falcao e Cunha	University of Porto, Portugal
Ernesto Damiani	University of Milan, Italy
Chris Dellarocas	Boston University, USA
Christof Ebert	Vector Consulting, Germany
Marko van Eekelen	Radboud University Nijmegen, The Netherlands
Samuel Fricker	Blekinge Institute of Technology, Sweden

Leah Goldin	Shenkar College of Engineering and Design, Israel
Volker Gruhn	Ruhr Institute for Software Technology, Germany
Thomas Hess	LMU München, Germany
Patrick Heymans	University of Namur, Belgium
Martin Höst	Lund University, Sweden
Marco Iansiti	Harvard Business School, USA
Slinger Jansen	Utrecht University, The Netherlands
Lena Johansson	Sony Ericsson, Sweden
Epaminondas Kapetanios	University of Westminster, UK
Marjo Kauppinen	Aalto University, Finland
Chris F. Kemerer	University of Pittsburgh, USA
Benn Konsynski	Emory University, USA
Olli Kuivalainen	Lappeenranta University of Technology, Finland
Patricia Lago	VU University Amsterdam, The Netherlands
Casper Lassenius	Helsinki University of Technology, Finland
Nazim Madhavji	University of Western Ontario, Canada
Rod McNaughton	University of Waterloo, Canada
Sten Minör	Software Innovation and Engineering Institute, Sweden
Oscar Pastor	Technical University of Valencia, Spain
Jan Pawlowski	University of Jyväskylä, Finland
Karl-Michael Popp	SAP, Germany
T. Ravichandran	Rensselaer Polytechnic Institute, USA
Camile Salinesi	University of Paris, France
Melissa Schilling	New York University, USA
Rick Selby	Northrop Grumman Corporation, USA
Kari Smolander	Lappeenranta University of Technology, Finland
Dan Stan	University of Cluj-Napoca, Romania
Pasi Tyrväinen	University of Jyväskylä, Finland
Tony Wasserman	Carnegie Mellon University, USA
Claudia Werner	Federal University of Rio de Janeiro, Brazil
Claes Wohlin	Blekinge Institute of Technology, Sweden
Stan Wrycza	University of Gdansk, Poland

Table of Contents

Full Papers

Software Product Management

Organizational Transformation

Industry Transformation 1

Software Platforms and Ecosystems

Emerging Trends

Industry Transformation 2

Short Papers

Software Product Management

Organizational Transformation

Industry Transformation

Emerging Trends

Pricing of Software as a Service – An Empirical Study in View of the Economics of Information Theory

Sonja Lehmann, Tobias Draisbach, Peter Buxmann, and Petra Dörsam

Technische Universität Darmstadt, Hochschulstraße 1,
64289 Darmstadt, Germany
{lehmann,draisbach,buxmann,doersam}@is.tu-darmstadt.de

Abstract. Software as a Service (SaaS) offerings are continuing to grow in importance. Due to this new form of software delivery, software vendors have to design appropriate pricing models for their SaaS offerings. This paper analyzes a) the disclosure of pricing information and b) the applied price metrics of SaaS business software building on the economics of information theory which recommends information activities (signaling and screening) in order to reduce uncertainty between providers and customers. By means of a content analysis, we investigate the websites of 300 SaaS solutions offered by 259 US-based providers. Our results reveal that especially small and young SaaS providers use their websites to communicate pricing information in terms of signaling. Regarding SaaS providers′ screening activities within the scope of this paper, we find that less than 10% of the offered SaaS solutions apply usage-dependent pricing metrics.

Keywords: Software as a Service, pricing, price metric, economics of information theory, signaling, screening.

1 Introduction

An increasing number of software vendors offer their products as Software as a Service (SaaS) – purchased and deployed via internet. This new software provisioning model is characterized by the provider's responsibility for operation and maintenance [1, 2].

In contrast to distribution models for on-premise software – which often involve customer-targeted sales activities – SaaS offerings are designed to be distributed without customer-specific marketing efforts. Therefore, SaaS providers need to communicate information on their offers via their websites in order to enable potential customers to seek relevant information – especially about the product and the corresponding pricing model.

Due to the new form of software provisioning, software vendors also have to redesign their existing revenue and pricing models which is of crucial importance in order to ensure both, revenue and profit. In theory and practice, usage-dependent pricing metrics are often claimed to be appropriate for SaaS solutions [3, 4] while software providers – at the same time – need to be able to conduct precise sales forecasts.

M.A. Cusumano, B. Iyer, and N. Venkatraman (Eds.): ICSOB 2012, LNBIP 114, pp. 1–14, 2012.

We take up these two aspects and apply the economics of information theory to answer the following research questions:

- To what extent do SaaS providers publish information about their pricing model and the applied metrics on their websites and in how far does the information disclosure depend on the providers´ characteristics size, age, and product category?
- What kinds of price metrics are currently being applied in the pricing models of SaaS providers and in how far do they depend on the providers´ characteristics?

We investigate the connectedness between the SaaS providers´ characteristics and the disclosure of pricing information on their websites (signaling activities) by means of a content analysis and chi-square tests for independence. Furthermore, we analyze the applied price metrics (screening activities) for SaaS solutions. Doing this, we focus on US-based providers since the US accounts for the largest SaaS market worldwide [5].

The topic we deal with in this paper is relevant for both, academia as well as practitioners. Since related work on SaaS pricing (in general) and the disclosure of pricing information (in particular) is sparse, we present an approach to the above-mentioned questions which can be seized and refined within future research. For SaaS customers, providers, and other software providers who plan the launch of a SaaS offer, we showcase insights into the current practice of SaaS pricing.

Our paper is organized as follows: In section 2 we present a possible design of price metrics for SaaS solutions. Section 3 introduces the theory of economics of information as a possible explanation for the activities performed by SaaS providers. In section 4 we present the results of our study based on the empirical data collected by means of a content analysis. The paper closes with a conclusion and outlines avenues for further research in section 5.

2 Price Metrics for SaaS

The pricing structure of SaaS offerings should reflect the individual value of software perceived by customers as well as the supplier's costs for the service provisioning [6, 7]. Among different design parameters of software pricing (for further reading see [8]) the price metric (which represents the unit that the price – as a monetary value – refers to) is of crucial importance [6]. Common price metrics that are applied in the software industry are *named user*, *concurrent user*, or a price *per machine or server.*

In practice, strategic aspects are oftentimes not considered when choosing a price metric although an additional margin with existing customers can be achieved and new customers can be gained by applying an appropriate price metric [6].

SaaS providers should also align their price metrics with the costs that arise by the software usage. A cost-based price metric enables the SaaS provider to offer lower prices to customers with low usage intensity while “power users” have to pay according to their usage [6]. Additionally, providers should take into account that significant efforts and – at least temporary – sales declines can be associated with the replacement of a price metric. Therefore, especially the initial pricing metric should be determined based upon elaborate analyses [4].

The price metric can either be directly linked to the actual software usage (*usage-dependent metric*: e.g., a price per transaction or minute) or represent a certain usage potential (*usage-independent metric*: e.g., a price per user or site; even if customers do not actually use the software they have to pay for it) [8]. Usage-dependent price metrics tend to be evaluated as fair pricing units because customers only pay for what they actually use. This aspect can ease the entry for potential customers with a low usage and therefore extend the provider's customer base [8]. Moreover, for SaaS it is likely that parts of the expenses are correlated with the usage of the software (such as storage capacities for example). Thus, applying a usage-dependent price metric can reduce the SaaS provider´s risk regarding operating costs. However, there are several disadvantages of usage-dependent price metrics from the provider's perspective. Usage-dependent pricing metrics cause additional administrative costs, e.g., for monitoring and billing [4, 6]. Even minor errors in the creation of bills can cause customer annoyance – possibly resulting in churns [9]. Furthermore, usage-dependent price metrics imply an increase of complexity for revenue forecast and determination of concrete prices per unit as the usage intensity and duration of use can hardly be predicted [4]. Concerning usage-independent price metrics customers are usually willing to pay more for the option of unlimited use [9]. An overestimation of their own usage intensity can often be observed which is referred to as the so-called flat-rate bias [10].

Empirical studies come to the conclusion that both, customers and software vendors show little interest in usage-dependent pricing metrics so far. A study of the Software and Information Industry Association [11] found out that only 5% of the respondents among business customers and 17% of the software providers prefer a usage-dependent pricing metric for software solutions. In the context of SaaS applications usage-dependent price metrics are frequently recommended (for example [4]). However, an empirical analysis investigating the applied price metrics in the German SaaS market did not find a wide-spread adoption of usage-dependent pricing metrics [12].

3 The Economics of Information Theory in the Context of SaaS

The economics of information theory (a part of the new institutional economics) is considered to be suitable for project-related cooperation and long term business relationships and widely applied to explain activities concerning price management [13]. In practice, most markets are characterized by asymmetric information. On the one hand, providers often have incomplete information about the needs, constraints, and expectations of customers [6]. On the other hand, buyers often have limited information about quality and prices of the offered products. The economics of information theory [14, 15] deals with these imperfect market conditions considering consequences of information asymmetries and how to overcome them. It aims to analyze the uncertainty created by asymmetric information between business partners [16]. Market participants have a strong interest in reducing these information asymmetries as they usually have a negative impact on economic efficiency. However, information search usually comes along with financial efforts. Moreover, information advantages can also be exploited opportunistically by one of the partners [17].

In order to reduce information asymmetries and the resulting uncertainty, the theory proposes two activities: screening by the uninformed partner and signaling by the informed partner [15, 18]. Both activities can be implemented either by providers or by customers.

Transferred to the situation of a SaaS business relationship, there is a lack of information on both sides – the SaaS providers as well as potential customers. The information asymmetry may be even stronger for SaaS applications (compared to on-premise software) as suppliers and customers have little experience with this new form of software provisioning and information on the providers´ websites (online marketing) replace direct, customer-specific marketing.

Hence, informational advantages can also exist on both sides: the customers´ as well as the providers´. For instance, the provider knows about the originating costs of his / her offer and the effect on the applied pricing model. Pricing details can either be communicated to or concealed from the customers. Customers can also have an information advantage. They know their requirements for the software as well as their willingness to pay. Moreover, customers can typically estimate their future usage intensity of the software (at least better than the provider).

In order to reduce the uncertainty between the business partners, the economics of information theory proposes signaling and screening activities. Signaling can be executed by making information accessible to customers. This is of crucial interest – especially regarding pricing information for the offered SaaS solutions. Screening can be accomplished by information acquisition conducted by the SaaS provider him / herself or through a third party [15]. A SaaS provider has to assure that the revenue exceeds at least the fixed costs of software development and the operating costs. To cover the costs, a reliable forecast of the expected turnover is essential. By choosing an easily predictable price metric, the provider can obtain the relevant information on future revenue [4]. The application of usage-dependent pricing metrics (such as prices per transaction) leads to an unpredictable sales volume. Consequently, the risk of misjudgments increases with usage-dependent price metrics as a result of a lack of accurate information. On the other hand, usage-independent price units (such as the number of users or a price per company) can easily and accurately be estimated (the total number of employees in client companies is often known to the SaaS provider and the potential user base can be derived). This is a possible explanation why SaaS providers mainly apply usage-independent pricing metrics [12] in order to reduce information deficits.

The purpose of this paper is to investigate whether SaaS providers apply signaling and screening activities to reduce information uncertainty. In order to investigate in how far the characteristics of a SaaS provider influence these information activities, we draft the research hypotheses stated in the next sections.

3.1 Signaling

From a customer's point of view, SaaS offerings are experience goods: the product can only be assessed by the customer once he / she has used it. Therefore, opportunistic options arise for software providers [17]. To reduce uncertainty, customers consult information substitutes, such as brand name, reputation of the SaaS provider or the price (e.g., [19]). Reputation describes the faith of a customer in the quality of a product without actually knowing it. On the one hand, customers are willing to pay a higher price for this information advantage [14]. Since high prices are – on the other hand – not in the interest of customers, vendors with an established reputation are likely to publish fewer details about their pricing models and rather stress other aspects of their products on their websites. Small and mid-size enterprises can usually not rely on a strong brand. Therefore, they need to reveal pricing information as an information substitute. Accordingly, we postulate the following dependencies:

- *H1a: The factors 'enterprise size' and 'disclosure of pricing information on the website' are statistically dependent.*
- *H1b: The factors 'enterprise size' and 'necessary search effort for price information on the website' are statistically dependent.*

Young SaaS providers need to establish reputation by means of positive customer experience over time. Hence, they are likely to publish more information about their pricing models than the established incumbents. This aspect is backed by the finding that customers prefer well-known providers in their purchase decision [20] which leads to the following hypothesis:

- *H2: The factors 'enterprise age' and 'disclosure of pricing information on the website' are statistically dependent.*

Customers for SaaS solutions often demand several solutions for different tasks. Presumably the decision whether a SaaS provider publishes pricing details on his / her website does not depend on the type of software offered. Hence, we assume:

- *H3: The factors 'product category of a SaaS solution' and 'disclosure of pricing information on the website' are statistically independent.*

3.2 Screening

As there are also other possibilities for SaaS providers to perform signaling activities than the disclosure of pricing details, a variety of possible screening activities exists as well. These market-oriented activities can be either competition-centered or customer-centered. Competitor intelligence (e.g., [21]) is an example for a competition-centered approach where an enterprise collects and analyzes data on its competitors from different sources. Market-driven requirements engineering (e.g., [22]) or the elicitation of the customers´ willingness to pay [12] are examples for customer-centered screening activities. In this paper, we focus on the SaaS provider's choice of the price metric as a screening activity in order to reduce information deficits (as described in section 2) and ease sales forecasts.

Regardless of the influence of product categories and reputation, all SaaS providers are interested in easily viable sales forecasts regarding their products [4]. Accordingly, we suppose that they prefer usage-independent pricing metrics. Hence, we do not assume a statistical dependency between the characteristics (size, age, and product category) of a SaaS provider and the applied price metric (as described in section 2):

- *H4: The factors 'enterprise size' and 'price metric' are statistically independent.*
- *H5: The factors 'enterprise age' and 'price metric' are statistically independent.*
- *H6: The factors 'product category of a SaaS solution' and 'price metric' are statistically independent.*

Figure 1 illustrates our research hypotheses that are directly linked to the research questions drafted in the introduction.

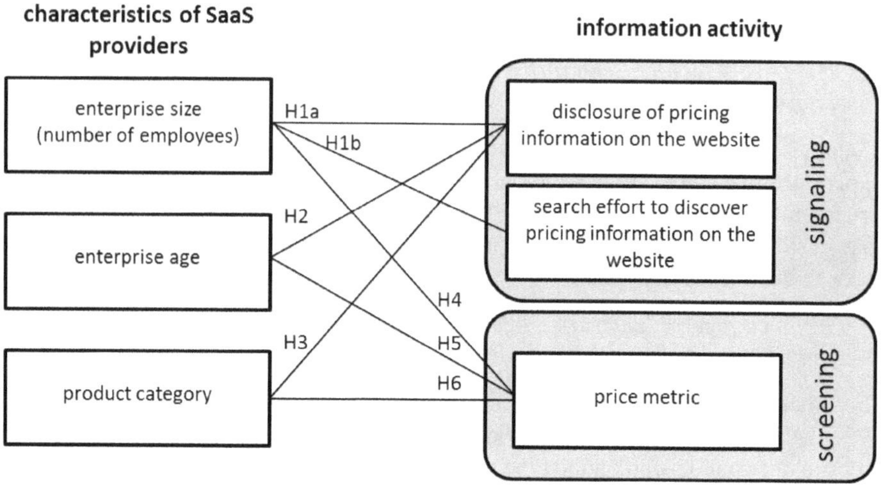

Fig. 1. Research Hypotheses

The enterprise size of a SaaS provider is measured in terms of the number of employees. Providers with 0-50 employees will be referred to as *small*, vendors with 51-250 employees will be called *mid-size* and those with more than 250 employees *large*. The age is measured in terms of *years since the enterprise foundation*. The product categories include *customer relationship management* (CRM), *enterprise resource planning* (ERP), *payroll/human resources* (HR), *accounting*, *marketing*, *e-commerce*, *supply chain management* (SCM) / *vendor management* and *project management*. The disclosure of pricing information is a binary variable and describes whether we could identify pricing information on the website (*yes / no*) whereas the search effort depicts how intuitively we gained that information. If the price model appears on the *homepage* or a button labeled *price* or *pricing* we call it *directly traceable*. Intuitive spots (like e.g., a *products* button) are called *easy to find*; any other position (e.g., *terms and conditions, FAQs,* or *news*) is referred to as *difficult to find*. For the applied price metrics we distinguish between *usage-dependent*, *usage-independent*, and *hybrid* (a combination of the latter two types) metrics.

4 Empirical Study: Information Activities of SaaS Providers

In order to answer our research questions concerning signaling and screening activities of SaaS providers, we first conducted a content analysis and used the acquired data to test the developed hypotheses. Wherever it is needed to go beyond the statistical tests to explain the results, we deliver descriptive interpretations.

4.1 Methodology and Sample

We conducted a content analysis (e.g., [23]) between February and May 2010. Therefore, we analyzed the websites of 259 US-based software providers offering 300 SaaS applications with regard to the disclosure of pricing information and the applied pricing metrics.

In order to identify our sample of SaaS providers, we utilized the "Software-as-a-Service Showplace" (http://www.saas-showplace.com) – an internet portal which lists more than 1,300 SaaS providers. According to the operators of the portal, it primarily lists US-based companies. Our study targets US-based software vendors with SaaS offers for enterprise customers which reduces the number of providers to 259.

Providers can register and categorize themselves according to application type and sector. The SaaS Showplace was chosen as a foundation for our study since it turned out to contain the most comprehensive and valid data when we compared different directories (e.g., http://www.saasdir.com). However, we cannot guarantee that the chosen sample is representative for all US-based SaaS providers since the registration process by the providers' own hands may potentially cause a bias (e.g., larger firms may be more secretive and reluctant to be on the SaaS Showplace). Since there is no other source known to the authors that eliminates these problems and it represents the most extensive listing, we decided to employ the SaaS Showplace as the best available alternative. Additionally, the structure of the sample resembles the one we found in a comparable setting (SaaS offerings within the German market [12]).

As representatives of the SaaS providers' characteristics we additionally gathered data on the enterprises' size, age, and the product categories of the offered SaaS solutions. This data originates from provider profiles from the SaaS Showplace as well as the providers' websites and / or other open web sources such as external business databases (e.g., crunchbase.com or spoke.com).

In order to assess a provider's signaling activity, we analyzed the websites for a) the availability of pricing information and b) the search effort to find pricing information. With regard to screening activity, we collected data about the applied price metrics. Our research hypotheses were checked by means of a two-sided chi-square-test.

56% of the SaaS providers in our sample are small companies (as defined above), 25% are mid-size and 13% large companies. 6% of the analyzed SaaS vendors did not provide information on the number of employees.

4.2 Results

Due to our second research question regarding the distribution of usage-dependent pricing metrics, the empirical analysis focuses on the metric. Therefore, the disclosure of pricing information refers to the availability of information on the price metric. 55% of the 300 analyzed SaaS-solutions' websites (166 applications) contain information about the price metric – the remaining 45% of the offers do not exhibit any information on the price metric. As described above, we could not gather the enterprise size for 15 providers. This results in an investigation of only 244 (out of 259) providers and 153 (instead of 166) applications with available pricing information for the analyses incorporating the enterprise size. In the screening section, we only consider those applications that disclose pricing information (166 or 153, respectively) because there is no information on the kind of applied price metric for all application that do not disclose any pricing information.

4.2.1 Signaling

We conducted the contingency analysis of the signaling activities by means of a chi-square test for independence according to Pearson. The results for hypotheses H1a, H1b, H2, and H3 are shown in the Tables 1, 2, and 3.

Table 1. Independence test between disclosure of pricing information and enterprise size

Independence test between "disclosure of pricing information on the website" and...		Pearson´s chi-square test		Cramér V	
		Value	Significance	Value	Significance
H1a	Enterprise size	8,271	0,016	0,184	0,016

From Table 1 it becomes visible that the independence hypothesis of the factors *enterprise size* (measured as the number of employees) and *disclosure of pricing information* on the website can be rejected for a significance level of 0.05. This result supports hypothesis H1a. In order to measure the strength of the association between enterprise size and disclosure of pricing information, we use the contingency measure Cramér V which provides values between 0 and 1 and does not depend on the number of dimensions. In the analyzed case, the Cramér V value of 0.184 suggests little statistical contingency. Since Cramér V does not allow an interpretation of the direction of the effect, we illustrate the association in Figure 2a.

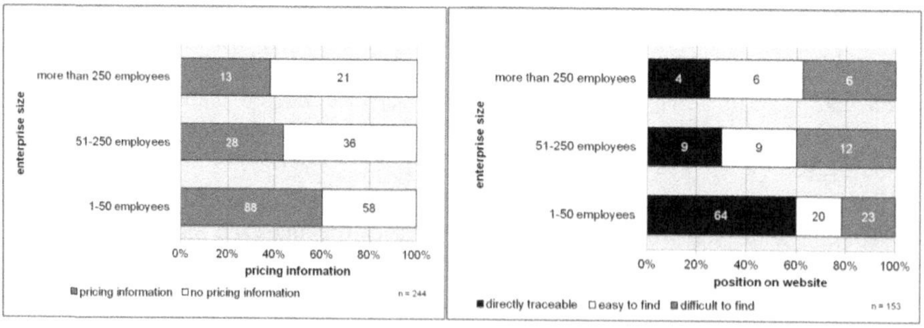

Fig. 2. Enterprise size and a) pricing information (left); b) position on website (right)

60% of the small SaaS providers disclose pricing information. Large vendors only provide information in 40% of cases. Looking at the small providers in detail, the tendency that small companies tend to disclose their information more often gets supported. Very small providers tend to publish pricing information to an even greater percentage than companies with about 50 employees.

Table 2. Independence test between search effort and enterprise size

Independence test between "search effort to discover pricing information on the website" and...		Pearson´s chi-square test		Cramér V	
		Value	Significance	Value	Significance
H1b	Enterprise size	13,154	0,011	0,207	0,011

Looking at the results of the statistical test, we can reject the independence hypothesis of the factors *enterprise size* and the necessary *search effort for pricing information on the website* for a significance level of 0.05 (see Table 2). One can assume that the search effort on the website and the provider's size are connected which supports hypothesis H1b.

Figure 2b presents the descriptive results of our analysis. Pricing information is *directly traceable* for 60% of the small SaaS providers and for less than 25% of the large providers.

Table 3. Independence test between disclosure of pricing information and characteristics

Independence test between "disclosure of pricing information on the website" and...		Pearson´s chi-square test		Cramér V	
		Value	Significance	Value	Significance
H2	Enterprise age	16,573	0,002	0,255	0,002
H3	Product category	21,257	0,003	0,266	0,003

Table 3 presents the results of the analysis of a potential association between the provider's age and the disclosure of pricing information (H2). The null hypothesis (both factors are statistically independent) can be rejected for a significance level of 0.05 which supports hypothesis H2. This result is not unexpected with regard to the probable correlation between enterprise size and enterprise age. One can assume a dependency between the disclosure of pricing information on the website and the SaaS provider's age with little to medium contingency (Cramér V = 0.255).

Figure 3a shows that primarily young companies publish pricing information on their websites. However, it is remarkable that SaaS providers founded before 1998 oftentimes publish pricing information as well. A possible explanation for this phenomenon is that these companies may have just launched their SaaS offers. In contrast to already existing on-premise offers, the SaaS solution might not yet be established in the market.

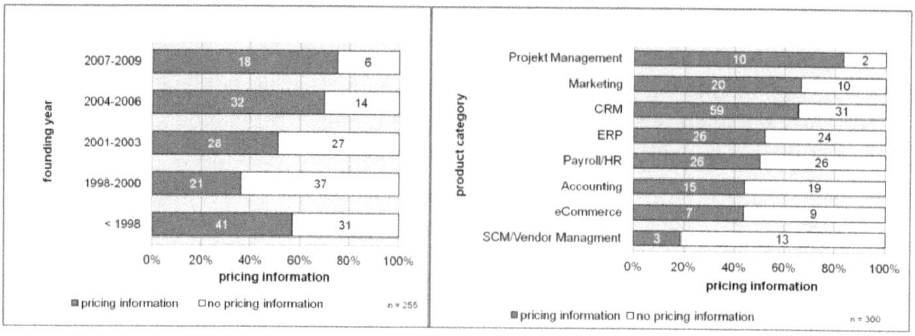

Fig. 3. Pricing information and a) founding year (left); b) product category (right)

Another statistically significant dependency (for a significance level of 0.05) could be found between the availability of pricing information and the product category of the SaaS-solution (see Table 3). Hence, hypothesis H3 does not get supported. The Cramér V-value of 0.266 indicates a medium contingency. Figure 3b illustrates the fractions of each product category. SaaS solutions for *project management* offer pricing information in 80% of cases while less than 20% of the *supply chain management* (SCM) and *vendor management* software vendors disclose pricing information for their applications.

Summing up the results for signaling activities of US-based SaaS providers, we conclude that small and young providers make use of the possibility to communicate their pricing model to potential customers by means of their websites. Further, we could identify a dependency between the product category and the availability of pricing information.

4.2.2 Screening

Besides signaling the economics of information theory also proposes screening activities – i.e., information acquisition by the uninformed partner. In the case of a SaaS provider, screening can be interpreted as precise information seeking concerning sales forecasts which can be eased by an appropriate price metric (as described in section 2 and 3.2).

In order to test the hypotheses H4 to H6 we also planned to conduct chi-square-tests. Due to the sparse application of usage-dependent price metrics the expected absolute frequencies per cell are partly below the threshold of 5 given in literature. Since this occurs in more than 20% of cases, the findings of the independence tests are not conclusive [24]. Nevertheless, the following descriptive discussion shall serve as an insight into the acquired data.

Regarding the applied price metrics for SaaS solutions of US-based software providers, we observed that exclusively usage-dependent pricing metrics are rarely applied (15 of 166 SaaS applications). The majority (114 of the analyzed 166 SaaS solutions) uses strictly usage-independent price metrics. 37 SaaS applications utilize hybrid price metrics.

The available data cannot provide a statistically significant answer to the research question whether the usage of a specific *price metric* is predominant for a specific *enterprise size* (H4). Usage-dependent pricing metrics can rarely be found for all company sizes (Figure 4a). The comparison of the SaaS provider's *age* with the applied *price metric* (H5) does not reveal an association either (Figure 4b). However, it is noteworthy, that those companies in our sample that were founded between 2007 and 2009 (the youngest ones) do not use exclusively usage-dependent pricing metrics at all.

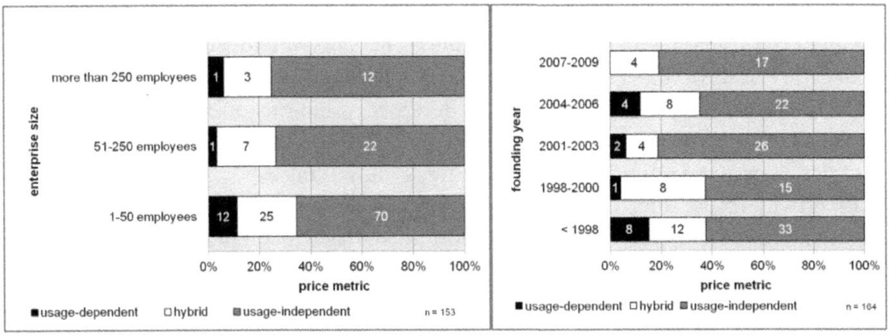

Fig. 4. Price metric and a) enterprise size (left); b) founding year (right)

The comparison of different *product categories* reveals an interesting distribution of the applied *price metrics* (see Figure 5). Exclusively usage-dependent pricing metrics are being applied for SaaS solutions in the categories *project management, marketing, payroll/human resources, customer relationship management,* and *enterprise resource planning* – despite representing only a small fraction of solutions in these categories.

Our analysis regarding the choice of a price metric as a screening activity of SaaS providers has shown that exclusively usage-dependent pricing metrics are rarely used by US-based SaaS providers. This supports the assumption that companies primarily

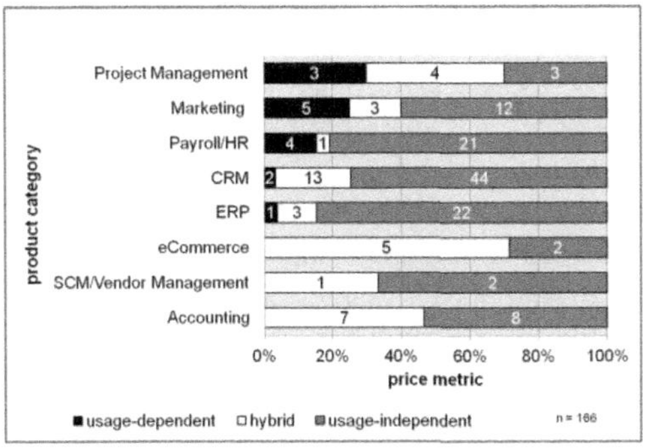

Fig. 5. Price metric and product category

rely on usage-independent pricing metrics for their information acquisition (e.g., for sales forecasts). Neither *enterprise size* nor *age* indicates an effect on the choice of a price metric. This can be interpreted as a hint for the support of hypotheses H4 and H5 despite lacking statistical evidence. An association between *product category* and *price metric* (H6) is imaginable though also not being statistically tested.

5 Conclusion and Avenues for Future Research

We analyzed signaling and screening activities of SaaS vendors concerning their price models in view of the economics of information theory. By means of a content analysis, we investigated the websites of 300 SaaS solutions offered by 259 US-based providers.

Our results concerning signaling activities show that especially small and young SaaS providers use their websites to communicate pricing information. Large and established providers may perhaps be able to reduce uncertainty by means of their reputation instead of having to utilize pricing information. Regarding the search effort to find pricing information on the website, we found that especially small providers present their pricing information in a way that can easily get accessed by potential customers. Furthermore, we identified a connectedness between the product category and the availability of pricing information.

We also investigated screening activities of SaaS providers – exemplarily in terms of currently applied price metrics as an approach to reduce information uncertainty and ease sales forecasts – and found that less than 10% of SaaS solutions utilize exclusively usage-dependent price metrics. The available data cannot provide a statistically significant answer to the research question whether the usage of a specific price metric is predominant for a specific enterprise size, age or product category due to statistical requirements concerning the data. However, we found that usage-dependent pricing metrics are rarely applied – regardless of the enterprise size or age of the SaaS provider. This supports the assumption that SaaS vendors prefer usage-independent pricing metrics in order to attain better results for sales forecasts and their revenue management.

Moreover, there may be a connectedness between product categories and the applied price metrics which we could not show statistically because the low amount of usage-dependent price metrics infringed some conditions of the conducted chi-square-tests for independence. Therefore, it might be promising to apply other statistical methods (also to comparable data sets; e.g., from other markets) in order to refine the conducted study and prove the insights presented in this paper. Furthermore, the conducted contingency analysis does not allow statements about the causality between the investigated variables. There is no guarantee that maybe a third variable exerts an influence on both variables which – again – warrants further research in this field.

Another limitation of the present study results from the chosen sample. As discussed above there may potentially be a bias due to the self-dependent registration procedure. However, we believe that our sample can be seen to be characteristic for the target group.

Other valuable research approaches concern the impact of different price metrics (e.g., on economic key figures of SaaS providers) or the reasons and conditions under which SaaS providers choose specific price metrics.

References

1. Cusumano, M.A.: The Changing Labyrinth of Software Pricing. Communications of the ACM 50(7), 19–22 (2007)
2. Weinhardt, C., Anandasivam, A., Blau, B., Borissov, N., Meinl, T., Michalk, W., Stößer, J.: Cloud Computing – A Classification, Business Models, and Research Directions. Bus. & Inf. Syst. Eng. 1(5), 391–399 (2009)
3. Choudhary, V.: Software as a Service: implications for investment in software development. In: Proc. 40th Hawaii International Conference on System Sciences (HICSS 2007), Hawaii (2007)
4. Kittlaus, H.B., Clough, P.N.: Software product management and pricing. Key success factors for software organizations. Springer, Berlin (2009)
5. Gartner: Market Trends: Software as a Service, Worldwide, 2009-2013 (May 7, 2009)
6. Nagle, T., Hogan, J.E.: The Strategy and Tactics of Pricing, 4th edn. Pearson/Prentice Hall, Upper Saddle River (2006)
7. Bontis, N., Chung, H.: The evolution of software pricing: from box licenses to application service provider models. Electronic Networking Applications and Policy 10(3), 246–255 (2000)
8. Lehmann, S., Buxmann, P.: Pricing Strategies of Software Vendors. Bus. & Inf. Syst. Eng. 1(6), 452–462 (2009)
9. Sundararajan, A.: Nonlinear pricing of information goods. Management Science 50(12), 1660–1673 (2004)
10. Lambrecht, A., Skiera, B.: Paying too much and being happy about it: existence, causes, and consequences of tariff-choice biases. Journal of Marketing Research 43(2), 212–223 (2006)
11. SIIA, Macrovision, SoftSummit: Key trends in software pricing and licensing (2008), `http://www.softsummit.com/library/reports/2008KeyTrendsSurvey.pdf` (accessed March 17, 2011)
12. Lehmann, S., Draisbach, T., Buxmann, P., Koll, C.: Pricing models of Software as a Service providers: usage-dependent versus usage-independent pricing models. In: Proc 8th Conference on Information Science Technology and Management (CISTM 2010), Tampere (2010)
13. Nagle, T.: Economic foundations for pricing. Journal of Business 57(1), 3–26 (1984)
14. Stigler, G.J.: The economics of information. Journal of Political Economy 69(3), 213–225 (1961)
15. Hirshleifer, J.: Where are we in the theory of information? The American Economic Review 63(2), 31–39 (1973)
16. Wankhade, L., Dabade, B.: Quality uncertainty and perception: information asymmetry and management of quality uncertainty and quality perception. Springer, Berlin (2010)
17. Molho, I.: The economics of information: lying and cheating in markets and organizations. Wiley-Blackwell, Oxford (1997)

18. Spence, M.: Job market signaling. The Quarterly Journal of Economics 87(3), 355–374 (1973)
19. Homburg, C., Kuester, S., Krohmer, H.: Marketing Management: a contemporary perspective. McGraw-Hill Higher Education (2008)
20. Scarpi, D., Dall'Olmo, R., Manaresi, A.: The role of service type, familiarity, contact and internet experience. In: Evanschitzky, H., Iyer, G. (eds.) E-Services: opportunities and threats. DUV, Wiesbaden (2007)
21. Fuld, L.M.: Competitor intelligence: How to Get It; How to Use It. John Wiley & Sons, USA (1985)
22. Regnell, B., Höst, M., Dag, J., Beremark, P., Hjelm, T.: An Industrial Case Study on Distributed Prioritisation in Market-Driven Requirements Engineering for Packaged Software. Requirements Engineering 6(1), 51–62 (2001)
23. Neuendorf, K.A.: The content analysis guidebook. Sage, Thousand Oaks (2002)
24. Bryman, A., Cramer, D.: Quantitative data analysis for social scientists. Routledge, London (1990)

Comparison of Software Product Management Practices in SMEs and Large Enterprises

Andrey Maglyas, Uolevi Nikula, and Kari Smolander

Department of Information Technology, Faculty of Technology Management,
Lappeenranta University of Technology,
P.O. Box 20, FI-53851 Lappeenranta, Finland
{andrey.maglyas,uolevi.nikula,kari.smolander}@lut.fi

Abstract. The aim of this interpretive qualitative study was to understand how software product management (SPM) activities differ in SMEs (small and medium-sized enterprises) and in large enterprises (LEs). We studied thirteen software organizations representing various types of software products and analyzed the collected data by applying the grounded theory method. As a result, we summarized the observations, explaining the main differences between SMEs and LEs and identified SPM activities that are size-dependent, size-independent, and specific for SMEs and LEs only. Our results indicate that the company size affects goals and activities of SPM. Therefore, companies of different size require different approaches in the adoption of SPM activities.

Keywords: Software product management, qualitative study, large enterprises, SMEs, grounded theory.

1 Introduction

Software product management (SPM) can be defined as "the discipline and role, which governs a product (or solution, or service) from its inception to the market or customer delivery in order to generate biggest possible value to the business" [1]. An empirical investigation of the projects in the industry suggested that focus on SPM allows the company to reduce cycle time in their business by 36%. SPM has also a major positive impact on quality [1]. From the business perspective, SPM plays a critical role in managing and achieving business goals by providing practices for the winning strategy in the market [2].

The existing software product management frameworks [2, 3] present a synthesis of SPM practices from observations and studies of companies regardless of their size. In general, organizational practices in enterprises of different sizes differ. For example, the studies [4–6] report on the differences in business activities between small and medium-sized enterprises (SMEs) and large enterprises (LEs). Similarly SPM practices are most probably different in organizations of different sizes. Understanding of these differences in the adoption of SPM practices by different kind of companies can offer a new viewpoint on further adoption of SPM practices.

M.A. Cusumano, B. Iyer, and N. Venkatraman (Eds.): ICSOB 2012, LNBIP 114, pp. 15–26, 2012.

In this study, our specific objective is to identify the differences in the adoption of software product management practices in SMEs and LEs. We analyze the difficulties that product managers and organizations face in their day-to-day activities and how these difficulties vary depending on the company size. Another goal of this study is to identify activities related to software product management in different sizes of organizations. To achieve these goals, we chose the grounded theory research method introduced by Glaser and Strauss [7] and extended by Strauss and Corbin [8]. The grounded theory method allowed us to develop and verify our findings iteratively and identify new issues that have not been reported earlier [8].

The paper is organized as follows: we introduce the related work in Section 2. The research process and grounded theory method are described in Section 3. The developed categories and findings are presented in Section 4, following by discussion of the results in Section 5. Finally, Section 6 concludes the paper.

2 Related Work

Software product management is a complex discipline. There are many frameworks that identify its key areas [1–3]. These frameworks have overlapping parts, but their structure and terminology vary. For example, software product management components have been defined as functions [2] and process areas [3] in different frameworks.

The Software Product Management Framework suggested by Kittlaus and Clough [2] presents the major functions involved in product management with tasks to participate in or to orchestrate. The tasks are divided into two levels: corporate level and product (family) level that are differentiated by the level of authority and strategic impacts to the company business [2]. Another framework is the reference framework for software product management [3], which defines four main process areas with their inputs and outputs. These process areas are portfolio management, product roadmapping, requirements management, and release planning [3]. Other authors have proposed that activities such as finance [9], defect management [3], and software configuration management [10] should be considered as parts of SPM, too.

Both frameworks were developed empirically by interviewing and working with experienced product managers from the companies of different sizes worldwide [3]. Therefore, the frameworks are a result of synthesis of product management practices at these particular companies. However, goals, strengths, weaknesses, and other factors in SMEs and LEs are different [4] and therefore they may require different kinds of frameworks and approaches of SPM.

A study of software enterprises of the different sizes in Austria [4] compared strengths, weaknesses, opportunities and threats faced by the companies and concluded that "every identified discriminating endogenous success factor is viewed more negatively by managers of micro-enterprises compared to larger firms" [4]. The study also concluded that one of the main competitive advantages of SMEs is the ability to adapt rapidly to external changes. The main problem faced by SMEs is financial support, because their ability to attract venture investments decreases with the company size. For large companies, the study identified three main strengths: financial resources, internationalization capabilities, and the business process of the organization. At the same time, the global business environment and competition in the global market were the barriers to further growth [4].

From the organizational viewpoint, SMEs seem to be more flexible and agile in reaction to the turbulent market changes. Large companies have all necessary resources including adequate human capital assets but they are unable to react effectively to external changes [11]. As the company grows, organizational processes and business model become well-defined. Christensen and Overdorf [11] discuss that changes in business models, values, and especially culture, are difficult, or even impossible, for large established companies. In contrast, smaller organizations are more flexible and their organizational structure can be easily tailored to achieve an advantage over larger organizations.

Overall, the studies on comparison of SMEs and LEs show the differences between these two types of enterprises. Most of these differences are related to business processes and activities [4, 11]. Thus a better understanding of the effects of company size to SPM practices is needed.

3 Research Method

Our goal is to identify common characteristics of software product management in the SME software companies in comparison with large software companies. We chose the grounded theory method because it allowed us to develop a study iteratively, without any assumptions in the beginning. The study is an interpretative qualitative study based on two critical assumptions [12]. The first assumption was that every software company has some kind of software product management, even if there is no special role of product manager in smaller organizations. In spite of this missing role, the tasks of a product manager must be handled and they are distributed to other roles. Our second assumption was that software product management processes in the companies are naturally progressing from chaos in SMEs to repeatable formal processes in LEs.

3.1 Grounded Theory

The grounded theory method was initially developed by Glaser and Strauss [7] as a pragmatic approach for conducting social science research [13]. Then, this method was divided into several branches. In this study we followed the Strauss and Corbin version of grounded theory [8], which relies on systematic codification and categorization process for observations. This approach is built upon two main concepts: *constant comparison* and *theoretical sampling*. The first concept is based on the idea that every piece of new information is compared with collected data to find similarities and differences. Therefore, data are collected and analyzed simultaneously. The concept of theoretical sampling shows an iterative process of theory building in which the next data sample is chosen based on the analysis of the previous samples.

The grounded theory approach contains three data analysis phases: Open, Axial, and Selective coding. During Open coding we coded the interviews with different aspects of software product management. Later we merged some of the identified categories and developed new categories. At the end of this phase we had 257 codes in 42 categories. In Axial coding, our focus was on the relations between the existing categories. We compared categories with each other and established relationships between them. These included associations, cause-effects, contradictions, and part–of relationships. At this stage, observations and codes became more focused on the phenomena under observation and we were able to continue with the identification of the core category. The purpose of Selective coding is finding the core category and explaining it [8, 14]. It may be one of the existing categories or a new category which has not been identified earlier. In our analysis we observed that most of our categories were grouped into four super categories. These super categories unite SPM activities in the context of company size as follows: *SME-specific activities, size-independent activities, size-dependent activities, and LE-specific activities.* Therefore, we identify the core category as *Effect of company size to the adoption of SPM activities*. Each of the super categories explains a part of the theory.

3.2 Research Sample

The companies in our study range in size from 15 employees to more than 10,000 employees and come from different business domains (Table 1). Nevertheless, all the companies were software companies developing commercial software products and systems for external stakeholders. We divided all the companies into two sample sets depending on their size. The first sample set represents LEs, while the second sample set consists of the SMEs. In this division we used the definition which classifies software companies as SMEs if they have less than 500 employees [15].

The interviews were conducted mainly in Moscow and Saint-Petersburg, Russia, but all the companies are international. The key informants were product managers and product marketing managers, but we also interviewed four technical specialists. Most of these companies have research and development departments in Russia and only two of them have local marketing and sales office only. In this study we did not collect information about the product management and development teams separately. Although our units of analysis [16] were product management and processes that support the product lifecycle, we did not provide any formal definition of software product management during the interviews. It allowed us to conduct flexible interviews with a focus on the interviewee's understanding of what product management means. Each interview started with asking the interviewee's view on the definition of software product management. Based on this definition, the interview continued with additional questions regarding these activities to identify activities which were perceived to belong to SPM.

The semi-structured interviews lasted from 40 to 80 minutes with an average of 52 minutes. The selection of interviewees was guided by our existing contacts and snowballing [8] in which the next interviewee was a referral from the previous one. The interviews were recorded and transcribed manually. The analysis of the collected data was performed with a special tool for qualitative research, ATLAS.ti [17].

Table 1. Company profile and interviewee role

Com pany	Business domain, type of product	Size (people)	Foun ded	Role of interviewee
Sample set 1: LEs				
A	Business and operational support systems	10,001+	1982	Product manager
B	International developer and supplier of a wide range of software, integrated solutions and hardware technologies	1,001-5000	1990	Deputy managing director for R&D
C	Internet applications	1,001-5000	1997	Two product managers
D	Security solutions	1,001-5000	1997	Product manager
E	Storage management solutions	501-1,000	2002	Product manager
F	Developer and provider of telecommunication solutions, software and hardware	501-1,000	2007	Department manager
Sample set 2: SMEs				
G	Date security and storage management	101-500	1994	Product manager
H	Integrator and developer of software for SME	101-500	1994	Deputy director of software development
I	In-house development of IT solutions	101-500	2000	Senior business analyst
J	Developer of software tools	101-500	2000	Product marketing manager
K	Provider and developer of interactive media solutions	101-500	2002	Team lead, project manager
L	Banking software	101-500	2004	Two product managers
M	Developer of software products for servers	11-50	2009	Sales director, technical director

4 Results

The main feature of grounded theory is that findings are tested and revised during the research, so at the end of research these findings are verified by new observations [18]. We compared our observations of the SMEs and LEs with each other and developed the results based on the constant comparison guidelines [14].

4.1 Categories

We focused on the comparison of software product management practices in SMEs and LEs. This resulted to four super categories with subcategories (Figure 1) showing how company size affects on SPM activities.

Size-independent activities, which include *development, lifecycle management, business analysis, product requirements*, and *sales,* were done similarly in both SMEs and LEs. Both types of companies knew these activities and implemented them similarly taking into account their own specific characteristics.

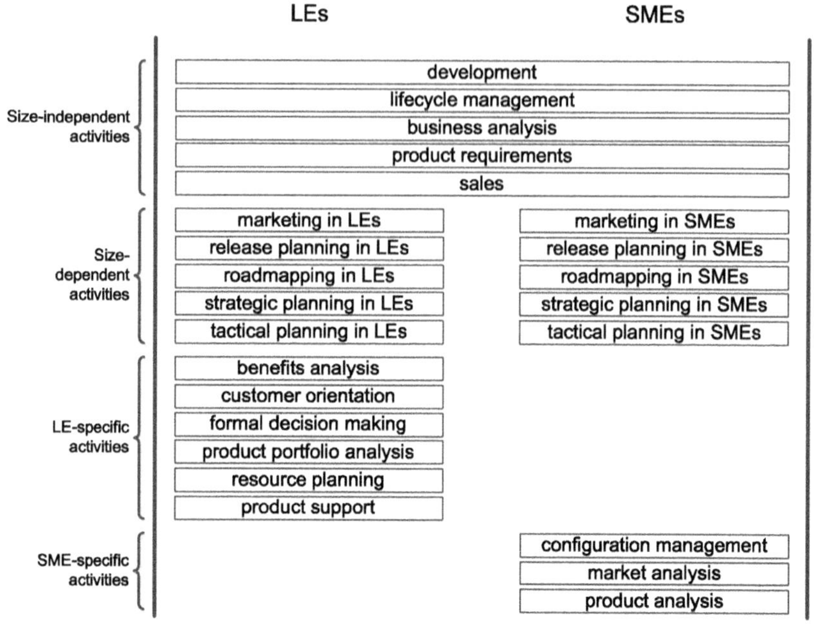

Fig. 1. Central categories explaining the differences and similarities in the activities of SMEs and large enterprises (LEs)

SME-specific activities such as *configuration management, market analysis,* and *product analysis* were typical for SMEs only. Although configuration management has been described as a necessary part of SPM [10, 19], recent frameworks [2, 20] do not separate this activity from *development.* We observed that when talking about SPM activities product managers in SMEs concentrated on technical aspects of product development rather than on business aspects. They described *development, configuration management, product requirements* and *release planning* as the central parts of SPM. Business oriented activities such as *market analysis* and *product analysis* were not considered as important as technical details of the product development. All interviewees in SMEs mentioned *market analysis* as a part of SPM but this activity was sporadic and informal. We also found out that SMEs are focused on *product analysis* in comparison with *product portfolio analysis* observed in LEs. SMEs have a limited number of products, usually only one product, so *product analysis* defines the company revenue and the possibility for further growth. This explains why our interviewees paid so much attention to talking about revenue as a result of *product analysis.* LEs usually have a large portfolio of products, so they conduct *product portfolio analysis* to analyze the total balance. Even if some products were unprofitable, the companies had other products and, in the end, the company balance was positive.

LE-specific activities include *benefits analysis, customer orientation, formal decision making, product portfolio analysis, resource planning,* and *product support.* In comparison with SMEs that concentrated on development issues, LEs were different. Product managers in LEs were focused on the *benefits analysis* and *customer orientation* with much less emphasis on *development*. They considered *development* as a black-box with a specification as the input and the new version of product as the output. In comparison with SMEs, which seem to be more technically oriented, LEs practiced customer oriented approach with the focus on *benefits analysis,* which the product provides to the customers. The product managers in LEs were responsible for the identification of customers' needs, collaboration and communication with the customers rather than for technical details of product implementation. *Resource planning* in the LEs was also considered as an important activity for product management. Usually this was supported by Enterprise Resource Planning (ERP) systems that helped to distribute resources between existing products [21]. Another specific characteristic of SPM in the LEs was the increasing role of *product support*. SMEs did not pay much attention to *product support* because the number of products and versions was limited and the products were not very old. LEs had to support all products and versions they had launched for a long period of time. Therefore *product support* had become an activity requiring deep analysis and attention. Another characteristic of the LEs was that because of broad responsibilities, the top management had to delegate their power and authority to product managers and other roles. Therefore, product managers in the LEs had power and authority for making decisions without consulting with higher management. Moreover, the procedure of decision making was formal in comparison with SMEs with their informal procedures of decision making. *Product portfolio analysis* in *LEs* consisted of many formal procedures and methods such as Quality Function Deployment (QFD) [22], Porter Five Forces analysis [23], and Delta model [24]. In addition, all studied LEs had a separate department that conducted market and customer analyses and provided necessary data to product managers. Overall, LEs were more advanced and sophisticated in adoption of SPM practices. They also used more formal techniques and methods than SMEs.

Finally, *size-dependent activities* unite five SPM activities: *marketing, release planning, roadmapping, strategic* and *tactical planning*. The adoption of these activities was significantly different in different-sized organizations. *Marketing* in LEs consisted of global, local and product marketing. In SMEs this kind of division was rarely observed and their understanding of marketing resembled closely to public relations (PR) [25]. SMEs did not make a difference between *release planning* and *roadmapping* because their number of products was limited and they did not have enough resources for long-term planning. Therefore, they typically created a release plan for one to three iterations. This issue was related to lack of investments and additional resources for long-term planning. In LEs *roadmapping* included all products for a period from one to three years. This roadmap was the outcome of *strategic planning* representing tactical steps for achieving the defined business goals. *Release planning* in LEs was seen in a frame of one product. In SMEs we also observed poor *strategic planning*. It was explained by these companies as a high level of uncertainty in the market environment. SMEs were market-driven and tried to adjust to the existing conditions. In opposite, LEs developed their strategic and tactical plans according to internally defined vision and goal. External conditions did not play as important role as for SMEs because LEs usually had enough resources for ignoring transient fluctuations in the market. As a result, SMEs were more flexible than LEs, but LEs had an advantage of concentrating in *strategic planning*.

4.2 Findings

Based on the described categories and analysis of observations we summarized them as three findings that generalize and explain the main differences and similarities between SMEs and LEs.

Finding 1: LEs are customer-oriented while SMEs are technically oriented
LEs consider their customers as the central part of their business. Their product management activities are customer focused that means close collaboration with the customers from requirements to support. Moreover, LEs pay more attention to usability issues than SMEs. In LEs software product managers are eager to talk about customers, their needs and wishes and how the company is satisfying these needs.

"I would like to tell you about our customers, because they are important to us. We have several channels to collaborate with them. First of all, our support is responsible for the rapid feedback to simple questions. The more complex issues they redirect to me. The second channel is an analysis of user actions, i.e. maps of their movements at the website, requests, and actions. A lot of analytical information that helps us to understand what is wrong and should be improved." - Product Manager A, Organization C

SMEs seem to be more technically oriented. They consider their technologies as the core competence in the business. Therefore, software product management in these companies is focused more on managing product development than strategic planning and collaboration with customers. Many software companies have grown from small technological companies run by engineers and technical people, which possibly explain this behavior.

"I think it is important to start by describing our product. Our product is a system consisting of hardware and software. The hardware is a standard server, which is mounted in a rack full of hard drives. This server runs our special software that implements algorithms for reliable preservation of data. So, let me briefly describe the technical side of our solution..." - Sales Director, Organization M

Our observations suggest that customer orientation is a must for LEs while SMEs can survive in the market by concentrating on technical excellence in their products.

Finding 2: LEs have strong and powerful product managers while in SMEs product managers have a limited authority
LEs have a multitude of products, projects and other issues to manage. Therefore the top management must delegate their power and authority in management of products to product managers who usually act as a product "mini-CEO" [1]. Sometimes the top management limits decisions of product managers to small tactical decision only, but despite of that the power and authority of product managers are much stronger in LEs when compared to SMEs.

"Product manager should be a director of a small enterprise within the company. It is a small independent company with its own budget and resources. After all, the most efficient scheme is when the responsibility and authority are not shared between people. The worst thing that can happen in a software company, in any company, is when the people who use resources and the people who are responsible for product management are different. Moreover, a product manager should have power of

decision making. Otherwise, he is not a product manager." – Product Manager B, Organization C.

The roles of product managers in SMEs are often unclear because they are not allowed to make decisions and their influence on strategic planning, product roadmapping and other activities related to the product is limited. Therefore, their role varies from being an adviser to a facilitator who orchestrates activities between departments.

"No results of our work are obligatory for implementation. We are just doing some research and recommend things, explaining what is wrong and providing solutions on how it should be done. The final decisions are made by the top management or an engineering team." – Product Manager, Company G

The limited role of product managers in SMEs is usually an outcome of lack of delegation from the top management. It seems that SMEs hire product managers too early, when the top management is not ready to delegate their own power and authority to product managers who are responsible for the product. This makes the role of a product manager in the company unclear.

Finding 3: LEs rely on strategic planning while SMEs are tactically oriented

Even several unprofitable years may not be a problem for LEs, but for SMEs they can be critical. LEs also have their long history of product releases that makes it necessary to concentrate on long term support as well.

"There is a big difference between releasing once and creating a product, which will get 4-5 service packs and 10-11 patches in the future. Therefore, we cannot rely on the short term cost cutting actions. We always think strategically, sometimes we skip possibilities to get easy money now, because we understand that it affects our long term strategy." – Product Manager, Organization D.

SMEs are more vulnerable to external conditions. Therefore their market environment requires more reactive orientation. SMEs must pay more attention to new technologies and trends in the markets. This leads to more tactical orientation and a shorter-term view on strategic planning where the horizon is rarely longer than one year.

"Roughly speaking, product management is not concerned with planning, but with the feedback from our users, our plans depend on what they want and need... We operate on this basis meeting their needs, using a problem-oriented approach. In our case, the risks are much greater than if we did planning. I mean that our competitive advantage is to react to the users requests as fast as possible, so planning is useless..." - Project Manager, Organization K

"This is a very specific company. We are the worldwide leader in the production of [Product] so the company employs the best people in the field, including marketing and development. Planning does not work well here, because we are a very specific company and our best people know better what they do and how they do it without any written plans." – Product Marketing Manager, Organization J

SMEs try to be agile and flexible in the turbulent market and, therefore, long strategic planning may be reduced in this type of companies. The strategic and tactical planning are tightly coupled together, but the main problem is the balance between them. Strategic planning provides a bird-eye view to the company business in the future, while tactical planning suggests steps in achieving this strategic vision. We observed that all the companies faced difficulties in finding the right balance between strategic and tactical planning, but SMEs are in a worse position because their resources are limited and they have to react to changes faster.

5 Discussion

The results of this study consist of activities and three findings that describe the differences between software product management practices in SMEs and LEs. In this study we identified empirically the activities related to software product management. We concluded that the viewpoints to software product management activities are different for SMEs and LEs. For example, SMEs considered configuration management as a part of SPM in contrast to LEs. The idea about close relationships between configuration management and SPM has already been suggested by Kilpi [10], who also studied small companies. Other identified activities specific to LEs as well as activities common to both SMEs and LEs have also been mentioned in existing frameworks [2, 20].

We observed that SMEs have a tendency to be more technically oriented in their product development processes than LEs, which are more customer oriented. This finding fits well with the Christensen and Overdorf claim [11] that lack of resources in SMEs is not so important because their organizational structure allows managers to proceed intuitively and "every decision need not be backed by careful research analysis" [11]. The technical excellence for SMEs is a must for competing with LEs. We identified that three activities *configuration management, market analysis* and *product analysis* are specific for SMEs only. As company grows, these activities shift to other departments such as development and marketing.

Literature on software product management describes a product manager as a "mini-CEO" [1, 2, 26, 27] of the product. In this study, we found that this is possible in LEs only. In LEs, top management must delegate part of its power and authority to product managers. In SMEs this did not happen. The product managers in SMEs are responsible for operational and tactical activities rather than for strategic activities and decision making. Another study [28] shows that in SMEs decisions about strategy and plans regarding to the product are done by the top management or in a close collaboration with the top management. Our study supports this with new observations from software companies.

In [4] it was shown that LEs have a better position for attracting capital, including venture capital, than SMEs. In addition, LEs have a long-term product portfolio generating a steady cash flow. This allows LEs to think strategically and to plan their roadmap for the next three to five years. Moreover, LEs usually have internal resources allowing them to survive during unprofitable periods. This is not possible for SMEs, which are more dependent on a short term external turbulent situation in the market [28].

There are several threats to the validity of this study [29]. Strauss and Corbin [18] emphasized the fact that using a grounded theory approach we create a theory, which is dynamic rather than static and can be extended by adding new data. Therefore, by increasing the number of the studied companies, we could reveal more details. However, already this number of companies enabled us to identify the differences based on company size. In addition, we noticed that the coding started to saturate – the late interviews did not bring any essential new details to the analysis. We did not have a goal to identify all possible differences but to show that these differences exist. Our study also has a territorial bias because we conducted the interviews in Russia only. We tried to decrease this bias by choosing international companies with offices in Russia. The snowballing is an additional risk for the external validity but in this study only three of seventeen interviewees were referrals. Grounded theory tends to produce credible results, because the theory development is based on the method of constant comparison in which categories and concepts repeatedly emerge and guide the continuous research [7].

6 Conclusion

The objective of this study was to understand how SPM practices differ in SMEs and LEs. Based on the empirical observations, we identified and verified three findings, which represent these differences between SMEs and LEs.

We found that LEs are more customer oriented and pay more attention to strategic planning. SMEs are more technically oriented and they rely on tactical planning. Their plans depend on the external conditions and on the situation in the market. We also observed strong and powerful product managers in LEs who acted as the products "mini-CEO". In comparison, their colleagues from SMEs did not have authority to make decisions. In SMEs most decisions were made by top management and product managers acted as advisors and facilitators in solving problems arising between departments.

We also identified activities related to software product management. Although there are several activities that are common to all companies regardless of their size, there are also SPM activities that are specific for SMEs and LEs only.

The results of this study show that SPM activities and goals are different for the companies of different sizes. Therefore, product management cannot be implemented in the same way in every company. There are specific characteristics, such as size in our case, which should be taken into account in the adoption of software product management.

References

1. Ebert, C.: The impacts of software product management. Journal of Systems & Software 80, 850–861 (2007)
2. Kittlaus, H.-B., Clough, P.: Software Product Management and Pricing. Key Success Factors for Software Organizations. Springer (2009)
3. van de Weerd, I., Brinkkemper, S., Nieuwenhuis, R., Versendaal, J., Bijlsma, L.: On the Creation of a Reference Framework for Software Product Management: Validation and Tool Support. In: International Workshop on Software Product Management (IWSPM), pp. 3–12 (2006)
4. Edward, B.: Factors in SWOT Analysis Applied to Micro, Small-to-Medium, and Large Software Enterprises: an Austrian Study. European Management Journal 20, 562–573 (2002)
5. Karlsson, C., Olsson, O.: Product innovation in small and large enterprises. Small Business Economics 10, 31–46 (1998)

6. Blili, S., Raymond, L.: Information technology: Threats and opportunities for small and medium-sized enterprises. International Journal of Information Management 13, 439–448 (1993)
7. Glaser, B., Strauss, A.: The Discovery of Grounded Theory: Strategies for Qualitative Research. Aldine Transaction (1967)
8. Strauss, A., Corbin, J.: Basics of Qualitative Research: Techniques and Procedures for Developing Grounded Theory. SAGE Publications (2008)
9. Konig, S.J.: Finance as a Stakeholder in Product Management. In: Third International Workshop on Software Product Management, IWSPM 2009, pp. 15–22 (2009)
10. Kilpi, T.: Improving software product management process: implementation of a product support system. In: Proceedings of the Thirty-First Hawaii International Conference on System Sciences, pp. 3–12 (1998)
11. Christensen, C., Overdorf, M.: Meeting the Challenge of Disruptive Change. Harvard Business Review 78, 66–72 (2000)
12. Isabella, L.: Evolving Interpretations as a Change Unfolds: How Managers Construe Key Organizational Events. The Academy of Management Journal 33, 7–41 (1990)
13. Suddaby, R.: From the editors: What Grounded Theory is not. Academy of Management Journal 49, 633–642 (2006)
14. Charmaz, K.: Constructing Grounded Theory: A Practical Guide through Qualitative Analysis. Sage Publications (2010)
15. U.S. Small Business Administration: Table of Small Business Size Standards Matched to North American Industry Classification System Codes (2010), `http://www.sba.gov/sites/default/files/Size_Standards_Table.pdf`
16. Yin, R.: Case Study Research: Design and Methods. Sage Publications (2002)
17. ATLAS.ti: Qualitative Data Analysis (2011), `http://www.atlasti.com/`
18. Corbin, J., Strauss, A.: Grounded Theory Research: Procedures, Canons, and Evaluative Criteria. Qualitative Sociology 13, 3–21 (1990)
19. Kilpi, T.: Choosing a SCM-tool: a framework and evaluation. In: Eighth Conference on Software Engineering Environments, pp. 164–172 (1997)
20. van de Weerd, I., Brinkkemper, S., Nieuwenhuis, R., Versendaal, J., Bijlsma, L.: Towards a Reference Framework for Software Product Management. In: 14th IEEE International Conference on Requirements Engineering, pp. 319–322 (2006)
21. Tsai, W.-H., Lee, P.-L., Shen, Y.-S., Lin, H.-L.: A Comprehensive Study of the Relationship between Enterprise Resource Planning Selection Criteria and Enterprise Resource Planning System Success. Information and Management (article in Press)
22. Haag, S., Raja, M.K., Schkade, L.L.: Quality function deployment usage in software development. Communications of the ACM 39, 41–49 (1996)
23. Porter, M.: How Competitive Forces Shape Strategy. Harvard Business Review 57, 137–145 (1979)
24. Hax, A.C., Wilde, D.L.: The Delta Model: Adaptive Management for a Changing World. Sloan Management Review 40, 11 (1999)
25. Broom, G.M., Lauzen, M.M., Tucker, K.: Public relations and marketing: Dividing the conceptual domain and operational turf. Public Relations Review 17, 219–225 (1991)
26. Dver, A.: Software Product Management Essentials. Meghan Kiffer Pr. (2003)
27. Gorchels, L.: The Product Manager's Handbook: The Complete Product Management Resource. McGraw-Hill (2000)
28. Westerberg, M., Singh, J., Häckner, E.: Does the CEO matter? An empirical study of small Swedish firms operating in turbulent environments. Scandinavian Journal of Management 13, 251–270 (1997)
29. Onwuegbuzie, A.J., Leech, N.L.: Validity and Qualitative Research: An Oxymoron? Quality & Quantity 41, 233–249 (2006)

Building Products as Innovation Experiment Systems

Jan Bosch

Chalmers University of Technology, Department of Computer Science,
Gothenburg, Sweden
Jan@JanBosch.com

Abstract. Traditional software development focuses on specifying and freezing requirements early in the, typically yearly, product development lifecycle. The requirements are defined based on product management's best understanding. The adoption of SaaS and cloud computing has shown a different approach to managing requirements, adding frequent and rigorous experimentation to the development process with the intent of minimizing R&D investment between customer proof points. This offers several benefits including increased customer satisfaction, improved and quantified business goals and the transformation to a continuous rather than waterfall development process. In this paper, we present our learnings from studying software companies applying an innovation experiment system approach to product development. The approach is illustrated with three cases from Intuit, the case study company.

Keywords: Product development approach, experiment systems, case study.

1 Introduction

The Internet has brought many changes and, as a society, we have barely started to exploit the possibilities that it brings. Over the last two decades, developments ranging from online commerce to open-source software to social networks have either been created or accelerated with orders of magnitude. In addition to the changes to products, services and communities, there is also a quite fundamental shift underway in how products and services are developed and deployed. This shift is driven by several fundamental differences between traditional licenses, on-premise software or embedded software and software-as-a-service solutions in a cloud-computing environment. These differences are driven by several factors, including the prevalent business models on the web, the deployment infrastructure, customer expectations, the network connectivity of increasingly many products and the real-time nature of online solutions.

The aforementioned factors have lead to the evolution of a new software development model that is different from development approaches for traditional software. First, it is focused on continuously evolving the software by frequently deploying new versions. Second, customers and customer usage data play a central role throughout the development process. Third, development is focused on innovation and testing as many ideas as possible with customers to drive customer satisfaction and, consequently, revenue growth. Stepping back, we can recognize that R&D in this context is best described as an "innovation experiment system" approach where the development organization constantly develops new hypothesis (ideas) and tests these with groups of customers.

M.A. Cusumano, B. Iyer, and N. Venkatraman (Eds.): ICSOB 2012, LNBIP 114, pp. 27–39, 2012.

Although the first area of application of this approach can be found in SaaS and cloud computing, the techniques can be applied to any product that is able to collect and provide data about its usage and performance to the R&D organization. This includes software-intensive embedded systems.

In the management literature, apply experimentation to business is a well-established concept, e.g. Davenport [4], though not practiced consistently and broadly in industry. Also, in innovation, the role of experimentation is broadly recognized, e.g. [9]. Finally, the notion of experimentation in online software is not novel. For instance, in response to Ray Ozzie's call to arms [6] to the Microsoft organization, Kohavi et al. [5] have developed an experimentation platform.

In practice, however, experimentation in online software is often limited to optimizing narrow aspects of the front-end of the website through A/B testing and in connected, software-intensive systems experimentation, if applied at all, is ad-hoc and not systematically applied.

In this paper, we take a broader perspective and address the scope ranging from optimization to new features and products. Consequently, the contribution of this paper is as follows. First, we present a first systematization of this innovation experiment system approach to software development for connected systems. Second, we illustrate the model using an industrial case study, Intuit.

The remainder of the paper is organized as follows. The next section discusses the key differences between traditional software development and the "innovation experiment system" (IES) approach increasingly found in cloud-based SaaS solutions as well as in other connected solutions. Subsequently, we present a first systematization of the "innovation experiment system". Then, we present the Intuit case study. Finally, we conclude the paper with a discussion of related work, conclusion and exploration of future work.

2 Traditional versus IES Development Approach

For decades, software development was a very structured and sequenced activity. First, the organization would figure out what to build, then the product would be developed and finally the software would be deployed. For embedded systems, the software would be deployed as part of the overall product, including mechanics and hardware. In the case of licensed software, the product is installed at the customer site on hardware owned and provided by the customer. The traditional software development process applies to both embedded and licensed software.

Over the last years, cloud computing and Software-As-A-Service (SaaS) solutions are rapidly becoming the norm and enjoy enormously rapid growth. The key reasons for this include the lower cost for the customer, the simplicity associated with not having to own hardware and the freedom from long-term constraints associated with most licensed software solutions.

Interestingly, these benefits extend in part also to software-intensive embedded systems and increasingly companies building connected embedded systems, from mobile phones to cars, are starting to exploit the advantages of frequent, post-deployment updating of software and the collection of usage and other performance data from systems in the field.

Common for SaaS software and software in connected embedded systems is that allows for an approach where instead of freezing the requirements before starting product development, the requirements constantly evolve and also affect already deployed systems that are actively used by customers. Consequently, requirements evolve in real-time based on data collected from systems in actual use with customers instead of being frozen early based on the opinions of product management about the likely customer needs 12, 18 or 24 months from now.

There are several important differences between traditional and this alternative approach to development. Below we discuss the most important differences and use these as context for a first systematization of the IES model of software development in the next section.

Business Model of SaaS and Other Frequently Updating Products Tends to Be Conducive to Continuous Deployment of New Functionality

Most SaaS offerings use a subscription model or a freemium model, where the basic solution is free, but the more advanced solution is paid for by the customer. Also in software-intensive embedded systems, the trend is to transition to providing products in a service-model. This means that the customer does not acquire the product, but rather engages in a subscription-model based service agreement. A subscription model, which typically allows a customer to leave after a brief notification period, requires a constant monitoring of customer satisfaction. Also, it typically requires a continuous flow of new functionality and redesign of existing functionality. Contrast this with licensed software, where customers are typically resistant against taking in new solutions because of the cost of integration in their IT infrastructure, or traditional embedded software, where upgrading is hard if not impossible for unconnected systems, and the difference in business drivers becomes obvious.

Customer Expectation of Continuous Evolution of the System

Due to the approach that companies like Google have taking concerning “perpetual beta”, customers expect a continuous evolution of product functionality. A similar example is provide by Apple’s frequent updating of its iOS software for its phone and tablets products. This is quite different from traditional licensed software where customers expected upgrades with a low frequency, perhaps once per year, in return for their maintenance fee. Customers are becoming increasingly accustomed to frequent, trouble-free updates that provide relevant additional value and consequently this is increasingly an expectation.

Interestingly, cases exist where SaaS product companies failed to provide continuous evolution of the system that created the impression of the product being stale. In combination with a subscription model that allows customers to leave the franchise at any moment, is a dangerous situation.

Cost of Deployment Much Lower for Connected, Prepared Products

Traditional on-premise software and unconnected embedded software is exceptionally expensive to upgrade and brings all kinds of risks, ranging from incompatibilities in the unique configuration at some customers to the complexities of rolling back new versions once deployed.

One of the key characteristics especially in SaaS environments but also in well designed connected embedded systems is that the cost of deploying a new version of the software in negligible. In a SaaS environment, a typical deployment starts by one of the many servers starting to run the new version under close monitoring by the deployment team. If this is successful, gradually more servers are configured with a new version of the software until all servers are successfully running the new version of the software. At any point in time, the deployment can be rolled back in response to problems starting to appear. The highly controlled environment lowers the cost of deployment with several orders of magnitude. In connected, embedded systems a similar approach is employed, but instead of servers, the deployed products are the destination point for new software.

A final aspect is the avoidance of versioning of software. Traditionally, for many companies, every customer would ultimately have a unique configuration of the product with different versions of components making up the system. This adds a whole new layer of complexity to the already costly process of deploying new versions. In an IES environment, there is only one version: the currently deployed one. All other versions have been retired and play no role.

Cost of Active and Passive Customer Feedback and Usage Data Collection

A perhaps less obvious but very important advantage of connected products is that the cost of collecting active and passive information from and about the customer is much lower. Active customer feedback is concerned with surveys and other mechanisms where the customer is aware that he or she is providing feedback. Passive feedback and usage data is collected while the customer is using the system. Examples include the amount of time a user spends using a feature, the relative frequency of feature selections, the path that the user takes through the product functionality, etc. The low cost and ease of data collection leads to the next major difference between IES-based and traditional software.

In connected, embedded systems, in addition to usage data, several kinds of other performance data can be collected. For example, connected cars can collect fuel consumption data whereas telecom equipment can collect real-time bandwidth data. In many systems, this data is already collected for operational management purposes, but hardly used in evolution of already deployed systems.

Real-Time Connection between Business Goals and Operational Metrics

The ease of collecting customer feedback and usage and other performance data leads to another important benefit of connected and SaaS products: it becomes feasible to build a real-time connection between the quantified business goals of the organization and the operational metrics collected from the installed base. This allows the organization to respond rapidly and dynamically to any changes to the use of its deployed products. For example, SaaS offerings driven by advertising revenue often use the metric of unique user growth as the driver for operational metrics. This gives the team working on the SaaS offering a real-time goal and metric to strive for and provides focus for the work.

From Opinion- to Data-Based Decision-Making

Everyone involved with a software product has many ideas about how to make it better. Conventionally, these ideas were collected and prioritized during the roadmapping and requirement management process as part of the yearly release cycle. The selection of the ideas to include was based on opinions by leaders in the organization with significant weight put on the opinions of those higher in the organizational hierarchy and often turned into a rather politicized process. These opinions formed the basis of dozens or hundreds of person years of R&D effort and the confirmation of the correctness of these opinions would only take place after the finalized product has been deployed, if at all.

A connected or SaaS product provides the invaluable ability to run experiments with the installed base and customer population. Rather than committing many person years of effort, an idea can be translated into a hypothesis, the hypothesis can be tested by investing a few weeks of R&D effort and deploying the solution to some segment of the customer population. Data comparing the base product and the product extended with experimental software can be collected and if the hypothesis holds, i.e. there is a positive correlation to the business goals, more R&D effort can be invested to fully develop the concept that tested successfully. This approach allows for a much more effective investment of R&D resources as one has confirmation that the resources are spent on value for customers.

3 Connected Products as Innovation Experiment Systems

Innovation is lifeblood of any organization, but notoriously hard to get right in many companies. Innovation in large organization is often characterized by an enormous imbalance between the number of ideas that, informally or formally, exist in the organization and the number of concepts that are in fact tested with customers. The ratio, depending on the attention the organization puts towards idea generation by its employees, can range from one in a hundred to one in thousands. With that strict a selection process and the high cost associated with testing, the importance of selecting the most promising ideas, turning these into concepts and then designing a (prototype) product to test the concept with customers becomes such that it receives significant attention by senior management and many other functions and layers in the organization.

The selection process is, unavoidably, driven by the earlier experiences and beliefs of the people in the selection process. In most organizations, it is the opinions of the more senior persons in the organization that tend to weigh the heaviest. The challenge with this approach is twofold. First, opinions are a very poor substitute for real customer data and the innovation literature has many examples of successful innovations that were resisted for years inside the organization before made successful by a small "skunk works" team working under the radar. Second, even if the organization is sufficiently open minded to explore more innovative ideas and concepts, there is a natural risk avoidance that causes organizations to settle on the safe bets. Human psychology, as has been studied extensively in behavioral economics, experiences a loss much more strongly than it experiences a win, causing a selection process where losses are as much as possible avoided, resulting in mundane innovations.

The solution is, obviously, to find ways to decrease the dependence on opinions and to increase reliance on real customer or other data. Traditional metrics such as the

Net Promoter Score [8] have been used for the last decade or more, but often fail to provide timely feedback during the development process as these are backward looking and focus on the entire product. To collect customer or performance data early in the innovation process, the organization needs to find mechanisms to test more ideas and concepts with customers and in the installed base in real-time and obviously at a much lower cost than earlier. This requires new behaviors at the business level, i.e. involving customers in feature and product concept validation without an, initially clear, business model. Also, it requires changes to the R&D processes as customers need to be involved much earlier and deeper in the R&D process. Finally, this requires changes to the architecture of the products and platforms to facilitate testing versions of screens, components, subsystems and entire products in order to determine customer preference and interest. The mechanisms used for achieving customer involvement and the efficient execution of experiments on the deployed product base depends heavily on the type of experiments, system, stage and purpose.

Cloud-based SaaS products as well as connected, software-intensive embedded systems offer a particularly well-suited context for building an innovation experiment system. As we discussed in the previous section, connected systems allow for the rapid and low-cost deployment of new functionality. In addition, the collection of customer feedback as well as usage and other performance metrics is simple and the connection to business goals is virtually real-time.

In figure 1, we present the concept of innovation experiment systems in R&D graphically. The loop between deploying new functionality, measuring usage and other performance metrics and subsequently using the collected data to drive development is the main process. The goal of an innovative product is to maximize the number of iterations that can be executed per time unit, e.g. per quarter. The rationale is that the faster the organization learns about the customer and the real world operation of the system, the more value it will provide and consequently the more successful it will be compared to its competitors.

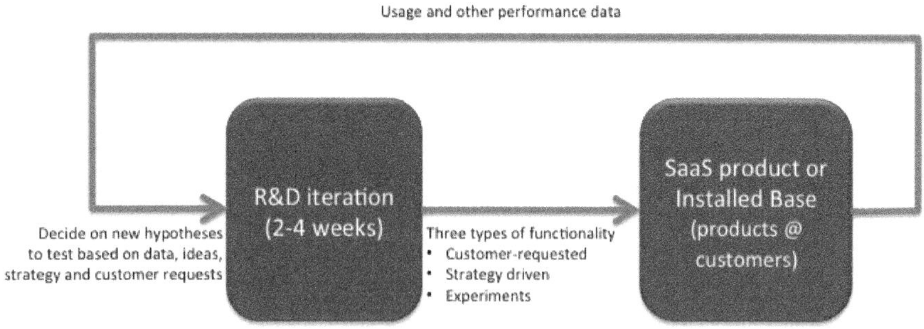

Fig. 1. Overview of R&D as an Innovation Experiment System

Development Approach

In this paper, we take the innovation experiment system as the basis for development. The approach recognizes three stages, i.e. pre-deployment, non-commercial deployment and commercial deployment. In addition, we distinguish between three scopes for experimentation, i.e. optimization, features and new products. Below, in figure 2, we provide an overview of these two dimensions and, for each combination, we mention one or more example techniques that can be applied to collect customer or product performance data.

Although there are obvious differences between product optimization, new feature development and new product creation, the basic principle is that we want to invest as little possible until deploying something to customers. For instance, for new product development, putting a minimal viable product as rapidly as possible in the hands of customers as quickly as possible is essential. Once we have a product that customers can use, the initial value is often such that it is not yet monetizable. However, it is still valuable to receive customer. Then the product development cycle starts and the company uses a non-commercial deployment approach. Once there is sufficient value, the product is commercially deployed using the selected business model. Even when the product reaches this stage, collecting customer feedback is still of immense importance to continue evolution of the product and to direct R&D investment to the most valuable features and functionality.

In the section below, we present each phase and describe the techniques that exist for obtaining customer feedback in each phase.

	Pre-Development	Non-commercial deployment	Commercial deployment
Optimization	Ethnographic studies	Independently deployed extensions	Random selection of versions (A/B testing)
New features	Solution jams	Feature alpha	Instrumentation/ collecting metrics
New Products	Advertising Mock-ups BASES testing	Product alpha Labs website	Surveys Performance metrics

Fig. 2. The scope of innovation experiments

Pre-deployment

The pre-deployment stage is concerned with, for a new product or a major new feature of an existing product, to involve the customer in the prioritization process to the extent possible. As there is no working implementation, only active customer feedback can be collected. Consequently, in this section we focus on techniques that can be applied to obtain customer feedback before development of a feature or new product is initiated. The purpose of these techniques is to collect customer feedback before any R&D effort has been expended. In figure 2, we mention several examples of techniques that are used during pre-development. In this section, we discuss three of the examples.

New product: BASES Testing
Originally introduced by Nielsen, BASES testing [7] is a technique for testing product concepts that do not have an associated implementation. Together with competing products or services, the concept is presented to a panel of customers. Often, detailed information is provided including pricing information and an assessment of the key differentiating features of the concept. The panel members are asked to rate the presented concept relative to competing offerings. For products addressing established markets and in mature product categories, BASES tests provide strong correlation with product success and hence are considered to be good predictors. In software product lines, BASES tests can be used to determine the viability of new members of the product family.

New product: Advertising
Several companies use online ads as a mechanism to test concepts. The ad is presented on sites visited by potential customers or inside existing products developed by the company. The goal of the advertisement is to evaluate the response (or click through rate) of customers. In addition, depending on the type of concept, customers can even be asked to complete an order form including payment information before being informed that the product currently not available. This provides significant information about the attractiveness of the concept and even allows for testing different presentations of the concept through A/B testing. Advertising can be used to test both new products and new (cross-platform) features.

New feature: Solution Jams
During the feature identification and selection process, a company can organize "solution jams" with engineers, designers, product managers and customers where employees can bring new ideas and work on turning these into concepts while getting feedback from customers. At the end of the jam, the most promising concepts can be selected for development. See [2] for more details.

Non-commercial Deployment

Once development has lead to an minimal viable SaaS or connected embedded product or implementation of a significant new feature of an existing product that can be put in the hands of customers, additional techniques for collecting customer feedback can be employed. The best techniques to use depend on the context. The team can be building an alternative implementation for an existing feature in the product, a significant new feature for an existing product, a new product adjacent to an existing product or set of products or a new product in an entirely new space for which no customer base exists inside the company.

In general, employing innovation experiment systems require extensive instrumentation of the product in order to be able to collect information about the usage and performance of the product. The collected and aggregated data is used by the development organization to determine whether the current implementation is optimal or, in the case of different alternatives being considered, which alternative is preferred. It also provides a feedback mechanism for those cases where during the pre-deployment stage decisions were made based on opinions. The data can be used to reflect on the accuracy of the original opinions.

In figure 2, we presented several examples of techniques to collect customer feedback during the non-commercial deployment stage. In the remainder of this section, we describe a few example techniques.

New feature: In-Product Surveys

Especially for SaaS products, though also applicable for connected embedded systems, it is very easy to create pop-up surveys at strategic locations in the product that allows for obtaining active customer feedback while the customer is in the process of performing a certain action. Although customers may experience this as an annoyance, when presented well, it can provide immensely valuable feedback that contains more semantic information than the purely passive data from product instrumentation.

New product: In-Product Marketing

A special case of advertising is in-product marketing of other products or of experimental features of the product currently in use. In this case, part of the screen real-estate is reserved for presenting marketing messages that preferably are as well aligned with the current context of use as possible. Similar to general advertising, this technique is often used for cross-sell and upsell purposes, but the technique can be used to determine the interest of customers during the pre-deployment stage or to draw attention to products or features in the non-commercial deployment phase.

New product: Labs website

Several companies have a separate "labs" website where prototypes and early versions of products can be made available free of charge with the sole purpose of collecting customer feedback. A labs website is especially valuable for companies that have an existing customer base that they can draw from for collecting feedback for new SaaS products that are under development. Existing, already deployed, products can then be used to encourage customers to try out the new product.

For connected, embedded systems this technique is less applicable. This type of experimentation requires the production of a set of prototype systems for the explicit purpose of collecting customer feedback during product development.

Commercial Deployment

Once the product is commercially deployed, the focus of the R&D investment shifts in two important aspects. First, as there now is a model of monetization, optimizing the actual use of the system, for instance through A/B testing of alternative feature implementations becomes an important part of development. Although the system will still be extended with new features, over time an increasing part of the R&D effort shifts to optimizing the existing features. Second, a new form of experimentation is often added to the equation: experimentation with alternative business models in order to drive revenue growth. The close, real-time alignment between business goals and operational metrics provides the basis for this.

Although most if not all of the aforementioned techniques can be used during this stage as well, there are some specific techniques exist that can be employed to drive the innovation experiment system specifically at this stage.

Similar to earlier sections, we discuss a few example techniques, based on the list shown in figure 2.

Optimization: Random Selection of Versions (A/B testing)

Possibly the most fundamental of mechanisms is the random selection of versions of use cases, features or other "chunks" of functionality and their subsequent presentation to customers. The versions are instrumented with data-collection functionality to capture the user behavior in a way that allows the team to select the preferred version. In online offerings, the notion of A/B testing is used extensively as a mechanism to determine the best web-page version. The metric for success differs based on the business goal. For instance, for websites that use advertising as a monetization mechanism, the user staying longer on the page is preferred, whereas a subscription-based web property offering productivity solutions would measure success in terms of the least amount of time spent on the page. Of course, a multitude of other metrics might constitute the definition of success.

Optimization: Ethnographic studies

Finally, ethnographic researchers, or for that matter, regular employees, can be sent out to meet with customers. Rather than interviewing the customer, the idea behind ethnography is to follow the customer in their daily life and study the use of the product or feature in context. This provides valuable information about the use of the product or feature in practice and is an important source for new work to be pursued. For example, at Intuit engineers collectively spend more than 10.000 hours in "Follow Me Home" sessions with customers.

4 Case Company: Intuit

Intuit is Fortune 1000 software product and services company that serves consumers, small businesses, accountants, financial institutions and healthcare providers with primarily finance and accounting related solutions. Intuit is organized in 10 business units that address different customer segments or provide solutions in specific domains. Although traditionally a licensed software company, over the last few years, more than half of Intuit's revenue has shifted to SaaS or SaaS related solutions and more than 70% of it's revenue now is pure SaaS or has a significant SaaS component.

As Intuit is a major SaaS company, there are numerous examples of SaaS offerings that are in one of the stages of the innovation experiment system model. However, for reasons of confidentiality, we can only share some aspects of each SaaS offering. During the time of the research, the author was an employee at Intuit and was indirectly involved with several SaaS initiatives. Consequently, the research underlying this case study is based on a participant-observer research method [1][3].

Pre-deployment

One of the products at Intuit with a significant SaaS component uses Solution Jams to prioritize the features to build even before investing any R&D budget. The solution jam is organized at the product development organization level. It is a full-day event where 10-15 customers are invited and all PM and PD staff currently not full-time assigned to development projects attends. Also, senior PM and PD management is present. Typically, somewhere between 20 and 50 Intuit staff attend the event. The customers invited to the solution jam are selected based on their potential interest in the areas addressed by the customer pain statements.

Before the solution jam, the coordinator connects with individuals and already created teams to facilitate the formulation of "customer pain" statements, i.e. hypotheses about areas that customers would prioritize development to take place in. During the solution jam, the team fleshes out the customer pain statement and starts to design a solution in terms of "mock-ups". Based on customer feedback, the team continues to iterate the design.

The customer feedback at this early stage in the process is invaluable for two reasons. Receiving customer feedback at the very start weeds out the well-intended but ill-conceived hypotheses of customer "pains" before any significant investment is made. Secondly, even if the customer pain is correctly identified and significant, engineers may still focus on the wrong aspects initially rather than fleshing out the design of the most important aspects.

During the final hour, all teams get the opportunity to present for a panel consisting of engineering and product management as well as customers. The panel decides which of the presented concepts are considered to be the most viable. For more details, see [2].

Non-commercial Deployment

About a year ago, Intuit introduced a new online solution to a new type of customer. Rather than immediately driving for commercialization, the business unit decided that it was most important to maximize the customer base and to achieve a significant network effect. The team followed the development process described in this paper and worked hard to get solution in the hands of customers within a few months.

Once the product was deployed (non-commercially) the team focused on growing the customer base as rapidly as possible as a proxy for future business success. The best way to drive growth of the customer base of free products is through word of mouth, i.e. through viral means. The team tracked the usage of the product and the satisfaction of the customer through product instrumentation and in-product surveys and drove development based on the active and passive customer feedback.

Commercial Deployment

Some of the SaaS properties of Intuit have been commercially deployed for several years already and have large customer bases. Over the last years, the team responsible for one of these properties has adopted a vigorous experimentation approach using A/B testing.

The team has adopted a weekly cycle of experimentation where it will decide which experiments to run early in the week, take one or two days to develop alternative implementations of aspects of the system, deploy the solution and start the experiment towards the end of the week, collect data over the weekend and decide early the week after which version (A or B) was more successful.

Every week, the team runs dozens of experiments and constantly improves the performance of the product and the customer satisfaction. Obviously, this affects the financial and business goals of the product quite positively as well.

5 Conclusion

Connected systems, be it SaaS solutions or software-intensive embedded systems, are affected by several important factors including the prevalent business models on the web and beyond, the deployment infrastructure, customer expectations, the network connectivity of increasingly many products and the real-time nature of online solutions. The aforementioned factors have lead to the evolution of a new software development model that is different from development approaches for traditional software. First, it is focused on continuously evolving the software by frequently deploying new versions. Second, customers and customer usage data play a central role throughout the development process. Third, development is focused on innovation and testing as many ideas as possible with customers to drive customer satisfaction and, consequently, revenue growth. Stepping back, we can recognize that R&D in this context is best described as an "innovation experiment system" approach where the development organization constantly develops new hypothesis (ideas) and tests these with groups of customers.

The innovation experiment system approach to software development that we present in this paper focuses on three phases, i.e. pre-deployment, non-commercial deployment and commercial deployment, as well as three scopes, optimization, new features and new products, and presents example techniques for collecting active and passive customer feedback in each phase.

In the management literature, apply experimentation to business is a well-established concept, e.g. Davenport [4], though not practiced consistently and broadly in industry. Also, in innovation, the role of experimentation is broadly recognized, e.g. [9]. Finally, the notion of experimentation in online software is not novel. For instance, in response to Ray Ozzie's call to arms [6] to the Microsoft organization, Kohavi et al. [5] have developed an experimentation platform.

In practice, however, experimentation in online software is often limited to optimizing narrow aspects of the front-end of the website through A/B testing and in connected, software-intensive systems experimentation, if applied at all, is ad-hoc and not systematically applied.

In this paper, we take a broader perspective and address the scope ranging from optimization to new features and products. Consequently, the contribution of this paper is as follows. First, we present a first systematization of this innovation experiment system approach to software development for connected systems. Second, we illustrate the model using an industrial case study, Intuit.

In future work, we intend to strengthen the validation of the development approach by studying other companies that employ similar principles to software development.

References

[1] Adler, P.A., Adler, P.: Observational Techniques. In: Denzin, N.K., Lincoln, Y. (eds.) Handbook of Qualitative Research, pp. 377–393. Sage, Thousand Oaks (1994)

[2] Bosch, J., Bosch-Sijtsema, P.M.: Introducing Agile Customer-Centered Development in a Legacy Software Product Line. Accepted for Software Practice and Experience (February 2011)

[3] Corbin, J., Strauss, A.: Basics of qualitative research, 3rd edn. Sage, Thousand Oaks (2008)

[4] Davenport, T.H.: How to Design Smart Business Experiments. Harvard Business Review (February 2009)

[5] Kohavi, R., Crook, T., Longbotham, R.: Online Experimentation at Microsoft. In: Third Workshop on Data Mining Case Studies and Practice Prize (2009)

[6] Ozzie, R.: Ozzie memo: Internet services disruption (October 28, 2005), http://news.zdnet.com/2100-3513_22-145534.html

[7] http://en-ca.nielsen.com/content/nielsen/en_ca/product_families/nielsen_bases.html

[8] Reichheld, F.F.: The One Number You Need to Grow. Harvard Business Review (December 2003)

[9] Thomke, S.H.: Experimentation Matters: Unlocking the Potential of New Technologies for Innovation. Harvard Business Review Press (2003)

Transforming to Product Software: The Evolution of Software Product Management Processes during the Stages of Productization

Wouter Leenen[1], Kevin Vlaanderen[1], Inge van de Weerd[2], and Sjaak Brinkkemper[1]

[1] Utrecht University, Department of Information and Computing Sciences, P.O. Box 80.007, 3508 TA, Utrecht, The Netherlands
waleenen@cs.uu.nl, {k.vlaanderen,s.brinkkemper}@uu.nl
[2] Vrije Universiteit Amsterdam, Faculty of Economics and Business Administration, De Boelelaan 1105, 1081 HV Amsterdam, The Netherlands
i.vande.weerd@vu.nl

Abstract. Within the software industry, one can recognize a strong trend towards productization, which is the transformation process from customer-specific software to a standard product. Organizations that originally focussed on building custom software regularly reorient towards a market. In order to grow into a mature product software company, an organization has to introduce and adapt its software product management processes. This paper presents a case study on how software product management processes evolve during the stages of productization at a small software company. We identify productization stages at the case company and describe the situational factors and implemented software product management capabilities during those stages. The paper provides a validation of the productization model, and insight into the development of SPM processes in relation to the productization stages.

Keywords: Software product management, productization, product software, process improvement.

1 Introduction

Software product management assists organizations in the governance of their software products during its whole life cycle in order to generate the biggest possible value to the business [17]. This discipline is essential in the product software industry with its big stress on time-to-market and pressure on market-driven development [15,5,10]. Product software companies must be dynamic and resilient in challenging the business environment, and the biggest challenges in company growth are (for a large part) management related [11].

The software industry is characterized by a strong trend towards "the transformation process from developing customer-specific software to developing standard product software", also known as productization [1]. Customer-specific

M.A. Cusumano, B. Iyer, and N. Venkatraman (Eds.): ICSOB 2012, LNBIP 114, pp. 40–54, 2012.

software refers to software that is specifically fitted to customer requirements, while standard product software refers to software products in an open market with many customers [14]. The stages of the productization model [1] describe the transformation of software companies, from the development of custom solutions to the development of a standard product for a larger market segment.

Deeper understanding of the changes in business orientation, defined as the focus towards either custom software development or market oriented software development, can assist in building theory for productization. The different stages of productization require certain changes made to the product management processes, which are highly dependent on the organizational context. This context can be described as a set of situational factors [3] and any changes in this context require a fitting adaptation by the case company. This can result in incremental changes to the original processes.

This paper presents a case study investigating the productization stages in a small-sized product software company in the service management industry in the Netherlands, with a specific focus on the influences it has on the company's software product management processes. The paper is structured as follows. Section 2 discusses the research context for the research performed in this paper. Section 3 describes the case study design. In Section 4, we analyze the evolution of the business orientation. Section 5 provides the main result of the case study linking SPM capabilities to the productization stages. Finally, Section 6 presents the conclusions and further research.

2 Research Context

A large share of software producing companies began with the development of custom software commissioned by customers. This way of working has evolved into the production of product software: products that are not developed for one specific customer, but for an entire market [8,20]. Mainly among SME's (small-to-medium enterprises), there are a lot of companies that focus on the development of product software. The change from custom software to product software requires significant adaptations in the management of business processes. Instead of dealing with one bidder and one delivery date, companies now have to cope with multiple stakeholders, and different releases and product configurations. In order to manage this effectively, implementing software product management processes in the organization is essential [7,6].

In both the software industry and scientific research, product software is receiving enhanced attention because of the apparent benefits of designing and developing software for larger markets [20], which show a much bigger potential for software companies [11]. Therefore, a relatively big part of produced software is offered to an open market instead of one specific customer [14]. Customer-specific software development and the development of product software have two main differences [15]: (1) the main stakeholder for customer-specific software is one organization, while the main stakeholder for product software is an entire market, consisting of multiple prospects and customers, and (2) product software has to deal with a high pressure on time-to-market while customer-specific software doesn't.

According to [11] the most important areas of improvement for software companies turning to the development of product software are the degree of productization and the competence level of the personnel. Productization refers to the conversion of a custom or incidental product to a standard product. The term is used for physical products [16], services [12,9], and software [1]. To measure the degree of productization in a software organization, [1] proposed a productization model with six different stages, shown in Figure 1. During these stages a software company initially offering customer-specific products can gradually transform its business to focus on product software.

Stage 1: ***Independent projects*** represents companies that only work with a portfolio of independent projects with few standard features or functions.

Stage 2: ***Reuse across projects*** represents companies that execute individual projects with the possibility of reusing features and functionalities.

Stage 3: ***Product recognition*** represents companies that start to reuse large parts of projects by identifying similarities of customers' wishes.

Stage 4: ***Product basis*** represents companies that created a product platform from which most of their software products are derived.

Stage 5: ***Product platform*** represents companies that increased the set of features and functionalities available through a product platform, and from which a stream of products is efficiently derived.

Stage 6a: ***Customizable product*** represent companies that chose to offer either a standard software package that can be customized and extended for specific customers.

Stage 6b: ***Standard product*** represent companies that produce a fully standard software product to be implemented as-is.

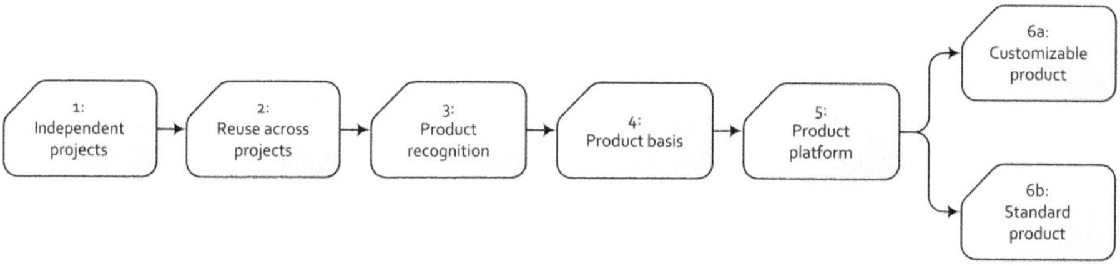

Fig. 1. Productization process proposed by Artz et al. [1]

In scientific literature very few publications are available that connect productization to the discipline of software product management. The stages of productization cause changes to SPM processes and management is responsible to guide these change processes as smooth as possible. Since the shift from developing customer-specific software to developing product software is considered highly profitable, more insight into the consequences of initiating such a productization process, mainly for the company's SPM processes, can be very helpful for companies considering this change.

Software companies take incremental steps to update and improve their management processes in order to adapt to the market they are entering. For product software companies specifically, product management requires skills and proficiency in several key areas. Therefore, [4] proposed a list of software product management capabilities that provide a way of focused process improvement. With the Situational Assessment Method (SAM) [2], a product manager is assisted in the task of updating and improving management processes in a timely and incremental manner. It provides assistance in determining what capabilities an organization has and has not currently implemented. During this process, the SPM Maturity Matrix provides an overview of all important capabilities in a best-practice order helping management to self-analyse its current situation. After analysis of this matrix, capabilities that should be implemented can be identified and suggestions for process changes can be made.

3 Case Study Design

3.1 Research Questions

An in-depth look at the stages of productization and the influenced SPM processes can be beneficial for successfully making the shift from customer-specific software to product software for a software company [11]. While moving through the productization stages, SPM processes require gradual changes. After assessing the original processes and the changes (i.e. incremental improvements) that were made to them, a clear understanding of the evolution of these processes can be obtained. In order to get an overview of the changes that occur to the SPM processes in a small software company during the stages of productization, we define the following general research question:

> **Main Research Question:** How do software product management processes evolve during the stages of productization in a small product software company in the service management industry?

As a starting point, we need a thorough description of the evolution of the case company's business orientation in the period between 2001 and 2011. This goal is summarized by **subquestion 1:** *How did the business orientation of the case company change in the period between 2001 and 2011?*

The situational context and the description of the evolution of the organizational focus allow us to analyze how we can map the history of the case company to the productization stages by [1]. This goal is reflected by **subquestion 2:** *Can we map the business orientation of the case company to the productization stages?*

Ultimately, we are interested in determining the relationship between SPM capabilities and the productization stages, leading to **subquestion 3:** *Which SPM capabilities were implemented during each productization stage?*

3.2 Case Company Selection

In this paper, we will obtain an answer to our main research question through the analysis of a case study at a small product software organization in the service management industry within the Netherlands. The case company was founded in late 2001 as a provider of fully custom software products. The organization now serves forty different customers spread over the Netherlands, Belgium, Germany, and the United Kingdom. It serves its customers with a small team of 7 FTE from one central location in the Netherlands. The organization sells its service management products largely through its own sales team directly to their customers; only ten percent of sales come in through three of their sales partners. Other partners include purchasing partners, hosting partners and hardware suppliers.

The company is an interesting subject for a case study, as it shows a clear path towards market driven product development. Over the last ten years, the company slowly changed its business strategy and gradually shifted towards the production of standard product software. In addition, the product manager has received training in the area of SPM, which has led not only to a higher coverage of SPM processes, but ensured that the organization was already familiar with the SPM capabilities defined by [4]. Based on our experience within the Dutch product software field, we believe that the case company represents a large group of software organizations that maintain a small product portfolio, aimed at the local or European market.

3.3 Data Collection and Analysis

Data collection has been performed on-site using semi-structured interviews and a document study. For the interviews, the company's two product managers (and co-owners) were selected because of their extensive knowledge of the history of the company. During the first interview session, the interviewees described their development focus and processes chronologically. The case company's situational context was described in terms of several situational factors [3], which were determined for several points in time. To summarize and link the company's evolution, a detailed timeline was created.

For this purpose, SPM maturity matrices were obtained for each productization stage showing what capabilities were implemented and what capabilities were not. A second interview session with the same interviewees was held to ask more detailed questions about the productization stages and the related SPM processes. During the interviews, snapshots were shown from internal company documents, presentations, applications and planning schedules. Upon finishing the interviews, more company documents were obtained to verify the statements made, identify omissions and details that were missed by the interviewees, and present insight into the SPM process deliverables implemented during the different stages of productization.

An answer to subquestion three is obtained by mapping the SPM activities at the case company to the identified productization stages. The resulting mapping was validated and corrected by the interviewees. This correction was based on detailed Process-Deliverable Diagrams [19], which described the companies' SPM-processes before and after implementation of SPM-capabilities.

3.4 Validity Procedures

In exploratory case studies, three types of validity criteria are relevant, namely construct validity, external validity and reliability [21,13]. To meet these criteria and ensure the rigor of this research, we followed several of the following validity procedures. First, in order to ensure construct validity, we used multiple sources of evidence (multiple interviewees and documents) and had key informants review the case study report. Secondly, the external validity concerns the generalizability of the results beyond the immediate case. In a single-case study this type of validity is often difficult to adhere to. Measures that can be taken are for example the use of rival theories within the case. However, due to the lack of theory on productization and the exploratory research of this research, this is not feasible. Although we cannot prove that the results are generalizable to the entire population, we do believe that the case company, based on its products, organization and sales, is a typical example of a product software company that went through the process of productization. Therefore, we do believe that the qualitative results are also to be found in other case studies in similar companies. Finally, in order to ensure the reliability of the research, we used a standard case study protocol [21] that is used and evaluated in earlier case studies.

4 Productization Stages at the Case Company

4.1 Evolution in Business Orientation

Within its first three years of existence, the case company worked largely different projects creating software entirely based on the customers' requirements. Development featured different platforms and programming languages used by employees that were working from the customers' site. The company custom developed four different software solutions, including service management software, risk assessment software, software for collection agencies, and credit management software. Within these three years the company only employed three full-time employees and only had one rather large but loyal customer for its service management product. Back then, the service management market already had 3500+ potential customers in Europe and showed a high variability in customer requirements. Due to the strictly custom approach there were only customer-specific releases and a high rate of customer involvement.

From 2005 to early 2006 the case company started identifying reusable software components of projects to reuse them in other customer projects; they started the development of Web Application Building Blocks (WABB), consisting of standard components from earlier projects that were suitable for reuse in future projects as well as tools and controls to integrate them. This toolkit was seen as a custom development accelerator and saw all employees working at the same location instead of at the customers' site. During this short period the case company saw only a marginal growth employing one additional full-time employee and growing its service management customers to five. Software was still produced solely custom and releases were still non-existent. Furthermore, the new yearly requirements rate and the amount of reported defects in the service management software also rose significantly, with the former mainly caused by a continued high rate of customer involvement.

In 2006 the WABB was implemented to help developers create custom software products based on the available components in the toolkit. All customers had their own code bases, requiring different maintenance approaches from the development team. Also, late 2006, the case company determined, based on client input and market research, that its service management product is its most promising software product and would be pursued for the future. The company's situational context saw some significant changes as well; even though they still only employed five full-time employees, the amount of customers rose again, the product was expanded to one additional country, and there was an aim to release a new customer-fitted product release every year. Furthermore, even though the amount of defects and new requirements increased, the customer satisfaction and loyalty improved as well.

In the period from early 2007 to 2010, the case company started focussing solely on producing standard service management software. To accompany this shift a separate Ltd. was registered and development of the other software packages was discontinued. From then on, they solely produced standard service management solutions consisting of four product lines that slightly deviated from the standard service management product. To support the shift, the customer's code bases were merged and product lines were developed from one single platform. From 2008, only standard customizations were performed for large customers. With all employees and resources focussed on its service management product, the increase in customer demand was continued, the product was expanded to two additional countries, and the variability of product feature customer wishes dropped. Then, a release frequency of seventy days was introduced while the amount of defects decreased, which can be attributed to the increasing reuse of software components within the case company. Finally, due to the dependency on customers' wishes, customer involvement was still considered high.

From 2010 the case company completed the switch to developing and maintaining service management software. Standard releases are presented to the whole customer base three to four times per year. However, larger customers still have the opportunity for a more customized product, and therefore releases can be delayed due to last-minute customer wishes. Looking at the situational factors, the case company still employs only seven full-time employees with significantly more customers than in the preceding stages. Due to the standard product the variability and the amount of defects decreased again, however, the steep increase in customers did cause an increase in new yearly requirements. Furthermore, because of the size of the company and the small but growing group of customers they're serving, customer involvement is still high. This is also reflected by the regular invitations of customers to the case company's offices to discuss the product.

Table 1. Applicable situational factors for each productization stage

Situational Factors	'01 - '05	'05 - '06	'06 - '07	'07 - '10	'10 - now
Employees	3FTE	4FTE	5FTE	6FTE	7FTE
Customer satisfaction	7/10	7/10	8/10	8/10	8/10
No. of customers	1	5	10	15	40
Localization demand	1	1	2	4	4
Release heartbeat	-	-	365 days	70 days	90 days
Feature req. variability	high	high	high	high	average
Defects per year	50	100	200	150	100
Annual new req. rate	25	50	75	150	200

Based on the presented data, we identified multiple time periods based on the company's strategy, development focus, and applicable situational factors. These time periods and the applicable situational factors are shown in Table 1.

4.2 Identification of Productization Stages

Figure 2 summarizes the case company's history by providing an overview of the evolution of the organizational focus as well as key developments and events during this period. Together with Table 1, containing the most important situational factors, we now have a detailed overview of the specific characteristics of the separate periods.

The shift towards product software was mainly initiated by the development and implementation of the WABB in 2005. By keeping an eye on technological developments and suggestions from its own clients, in 2006 the case company adopted its service management product as its sole focus while phasing-out its other software packages. In 2008, two important steps were made with the decision to base the service management product primarily (and almost solely) on market requirements (instead of customer requirements) while only providing standard customizations for select customers, and the decision to present releases of service management modules to the whole customer base. Since 2010 the company has been able to completely rely on the turnover generated by the sales and maintenance of the service management products.

Based on the timeline in Figure 2 and the time periods presented in the last paragraph, these time periods with were mapped to the productization model by [1]. Five different productization stages were identified that applied to these time periods. The period between the establishment of the case company and 2005 was mapped onto stage 1 (*Independent projects*) of the productization model. This stage fits well, since the case company's projects barely had common functions or features and were solely driven by the customers' requirements keeping a small physical distance between the customers and developers. Stage 2 of the productization model (*Reuse across projects*) fits the period between 2005 and early 2006, due to the company's reuse of previously developed features and functionality across projects, resulting in a basic set of standardized features and functionalities, while they still offered largely custom software. The period from early 2006 to early 2007 was identified with stage 3 of the productization model (*Product recognition*) because introduction of the WABB that caused a more structural reuse of software components, tools, and structural identification of similarities among development projects. Following this stage, the fourth stage of the productization model (*Product basis*) was found to be applicable to the period between early 2007 and 2010 at the case company. This is explained by the company's shift in focus to solely service management software, the identification of a product platform from which multiple products were build, and the planning of future releases and long-term product development. Finally, the period between 2010 and late 2011 was identified with stage 5 of the productization model (*Product platform*) because it represents the complete switch to service management software offering features to the full customer base, but still providing standard customization for larger customers.

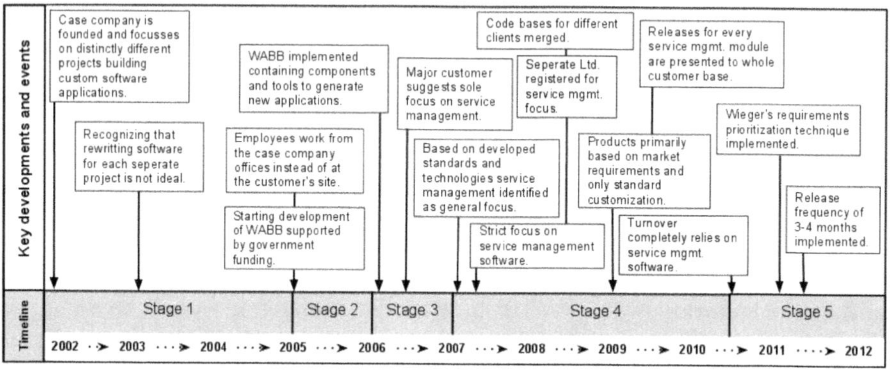

Fig. 2. Timeline indicating productization stages including key developments and events

We were not able to map any time period to the productization stages 6a (*Customizable product*) or 6b (*Standard product*). Even though identical software components of the service management product are released to all customers, the four product lines still need separate releases that also require separate delivery and installation. Moreover, occasionally projects with larger customer-specific parts are still performed. However, looking at the development through the five identified stages at the case company, reaching either stage 6a or 6b, would be a logical next step in de company's development.

4.3 Changes in the SPM Process

In order to obtain a more detailed overview of the SPM processes, we have described them using so-called process-deliverable diagrams [18]. These process-deliverables diagrams (PDDs) show detailed activities and deliverables as well as their interrelationships from the SPM-processes at the case company. Based on the gradual implementation of SPM capabilities as well as the situational factors and key developments pertaining to them, the focus of these PDD's lays on the release planning process.

For each identified productization stage a PDD for the company's processes surrounding release planning was created. An exception was stage 1, which had no implemented capabilities nor formal or informal release planning processes present within the case company, and therefore, no PDD was created for that stage. The PDDs were based on data from the interviews as well as the obtained company documents, and were later verified by the interviewees.

Figure 3 shows the PDD for the release planning process during productization stage 2. This stage marks the start of the case company's switch to a more structured approach towards custom software development. This switch also saw the case company's employees working collaboratively from a collective office instead of individually form the customer's offices.

For release planning, simple yet effective processes were put into place in order to validate and test customer-specific software builds. These implemented processes pertained to the SPM focus area of build validation and immediately followed the software development processes. To guide these processes, the case company tried to structure the activities as much as possible and simple technical and functional checklists were introduced to perform the technical and functional validation of the build to start with. The completion of these checklists was entirely based on the custom build software. Also, the case company introduced the development of an application test-environment with which the customer could validate the build together with the case company's project manager. Finally, a mandatory and formal completion agreement was introduced to get the approval for the installation of the custom software product at the customers.

5 Linking SPM Capabilities to the Productization Stages

Based on the data presented in the previous section, we linked the SPM capabilities to the stages of productization. The SPM-capabilities for each of the stages were determined according to the suggested Situational Assessment Method from [2], and are represented by the letters in Table 2. For explanation of the capabilities, we refer to [4]. The darker shadings represent capabilities implemented during the indicated stage, while the lighter shadings represent the capabilities that have been implemented in earlier stages.

During productization stage 1, software product management capabilities are almost non-existent because of the sole focus on customer-specific software. The only implemented capabilities are focussed on requirements gathering, registering, and validation from the *requirements management* business function, which are not necessarily linked to software product management because they can also apply to companies with a custom focus. Therefore, these capabilities can confidently be linked to this specific productization stage.

In comparison to stage 1, stage 2 presents a switch to a more structured approach towards custom software development. The software product management capabilities show the introduction of *release planning*, *product planning*,

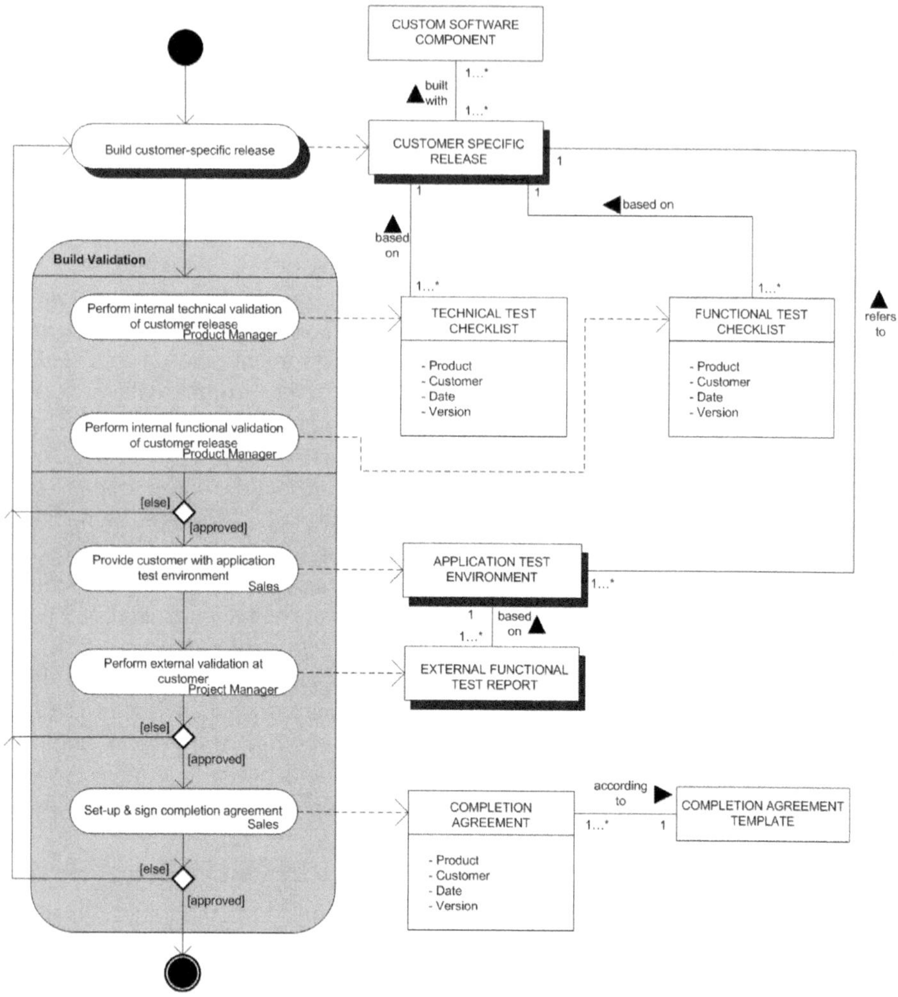

Fig. 3. Process-Deliverable Diagram for the release planning process during productization stage 2

and *portfolio management* capabilities. Capabilities for the validation of the software build are implemented to ensure the build quality and customer satisfaction. Furthermore, contractual documents are standardized, and the WABB urges the implementation of core asset roadmapping in order to identify and register reusable customer project components. By gradually implementing these capabilities a foundation for a future towards product software is in place. Productization stage three sees some very clear improvements in implemented SPM-capabilities. For *requirements management*, capabilities are implemented for the gathering of requirements through the implementation of a requirements sheet, and for constructing product requirements by rewriting customer requirements.

Table 2. Implemented SPM-capabilities for each productization stage

Capability Process	Stage 1	Stage 2	Stage 3	Stage 4	Stage 5
Requirements management					
Requirements gathering	A B C D E F	A B C D E F	A B C D E F	A B C D E F	A B C D E F
Requirements identification	A B C D	A B C D	A B C D	A B C D	A B C D
Requirements organizing	A B C	A B C	A B C	A B C	A B C
Release planning					
Requirements prioritization	A B C D E	A B C D E	A B C D E	A B C D E	A B C D E
Release definition	A B C D E	A B C D E	A B C D E	A B C D E	A B C D E
Release definition validation	A B C	A B C	A B C	A B C	A B C
Scope change management	A B C D	A B C D	A B C D	A B C D	A B C D
Build validation	A B C	A B C	A B C	A B C	A B C
Launch preparation	A B C D E F	A B C D E F	A B C D E F	A B C D E F	A B C D E F
Product Planning					
Roadmap intelligence	A B C D E	A B C D E	A B C D E	A B C D E	A B C D E
Coare asset roadmapping	A B C D	A B C D	A B C D	A B C D	A B C D
Product roadmapping	A B C D E	A B C D E	A B C D E	A B C D E	A B C D E
Portfolio management					
Market analysis	A B C D E	A B C D E	A B C D E	A B C D E	A B C D E
Partnering & contracting	A B C D E	A B C D E	A B C D E	A B C D E	A B C D E
Product lifecycle management	A B C D E	A B C D E	A B C D E	A B C D E	A B C D E
Total implemented capabilties	2 (3%)	7 (10%)	20 (29%)	30 (44%)	38 (56%)

Also, *product planning* capabilities for competitor product analysis and roadmap presentations are implemented, while *portfolio management* implements a market analysis to identify development opportunities and competitors. *Release planning* shows the most improvement, implementing activities for the creation of release tables, their validation, and the communication of the release. The fourth productization stage shows another large group of improvements for all business functions. *Requirements management* sees the implementation of capabilities for organizing requirements due to the introduction of a requirements management tool. For *release planning*, requirements prioritization is expanded, and release composition and description capabilities are added. *Product planning* sees the introduction of predictive plans, trend analysis, and short-term development plans. Finally, *portfolio management* implements review capabilities of the product portfolio, and protective measures for intellectual property by depositing these in a separate company foundation. All together, the case company is gradually growing into a mature but also structured software product company.

Since a majority of crucial SPM-capabilities were already implemented in the preceding stages, smaller changes over the four business functions are introduced during productization stage 5. *Requirements management* features the introduction of requirement status feedback to the submitting customer. *Release planning* sees the introduction of Wiegers' prioritization technique urging the case company to take costs, revenues and penalties into account when prioritizing requirements, and, for scope change purposes, key delivery dates in the development process are now determined and reviewed for internal clarity. *Product planning* sees the introduction of product roadmapping capabilities pertaining to the identification of release themes for product releases and the creation of release notes communicated to specific external stakeholders. At last, *portfolio management* introduces an external market research institution assisting in performing market analysis as well as a distribution channel analysis to identify possible improvements in the product distribution through sales partners.

6 Conclusions and Future Research

According to the results presented in this paper, a small software company can gradually improve its SPM capabilities, develop its software product, and grow its client base without losing appreciation for or requiring an exponential growth in number of employees. More specifically, the groundwork for successful software product management is built in the early stages of productization, while later productization stages provide fine-tuning and expansion of this groundwork applicable to the organization's context.

With this case study, we have further validated the productization model by Artz et al. [1]. The case company has moved through several phases with regard to its software development philosophy. We have successfully mapped these phases to five of the stages of the productization model by [1]. We argue that the organization has moved through the first five stages of the productization model, from the development of independent projects to the production of a product platform. The organization's business philosophy changed from being purely customer-oriented to being mainly market-oriented. However, we were not able to validate productization stages 6a (*Customizable product*) and 6b (*Standard product*). This can be explained by the fact that the organization is still changing. Even though some customer-specific parts are still being developed, it is very likely that this will stop in the near future.

In addition to the validation of the productization model, we were able to map SPM-activities to the productization stages by identifying the implemented SPM capabilities. Productization stages 1 and 2 mainly saw implemented SPM-capabilities that only have a weak connection to software product management, because these capabilities are also likely to apply to organizations with a custom approach. Looking at the meaning of those productization stages, those implemented capabilities show a strong link with those stages. Productization stage 3 had capabilities implemented that mainly provide the solid groundwork for a company's future as a product software vendor. Since this stage is characterized as the stage were an organization starts identifying its software as a standard product, the implemented capabilities found seem to show a strong connection with this. Lastly, productization stages 4 and 5 had capabilities implemented that provided fine-tuning of the available groundwork with a strong focus on the business functions of *product planning* and *portfolio management*. This also complies with the description of these stages in the productization model of [1].

Even though the conclusions from this case study are logical and accord with the available theory in this area, there is still a possibility that the results can be explained by factors that were not accounted for in this research. Therefore, for future research, we suggest to perform the same case study at similar software organizations in the same or similar industries. This can build on the conclusions in this report and imply theories on the evolution of a software company during the stages of productization. Furthermore, in order to assess the influence of company size on this evolution, we suggest performing similar case studies at one or more medium or large software companies.

References

1. Artz, P., van de Weerd, I., Brinkkemper, S., Fieggen, J.: Productization: Transforming from Developing Customer-Specific Software to Product Software. In: Tyrväinen, P., Jansen, S., Cusumano, M.A. (eds.) ICSOB 2010. LNBIP, vol. 51, pp. 90–102. Springer, Heidelberg (2010)
2. Bekkers, W., Spruit, M., van de Weerd, I., van Vliet, R., Mahieu, A.: A situational assessment method for software product management. In: Alexander, T., Turpin, M., van Deventer, J. (eds.) Proceedings of the European Conference on Information Systems, Pretoria, South-Africa, pp. 22–34 (2010)
3. Bekkers, W., van de Weerd, I., Brinkkemper, S., Mahieu, A.: The Influence of Situational Factors in Software Product Management: An Empirical Study. In: Proceedings of the International Workshop on Software Product Management, pp. 41–48. IEEE Computer Society, Washington, DC, USA (2008)
4. Bekkers, W., van de Weerd, I., Spruit, M., Brinkkemper, S.: A Framework for Process Improvement in Software Product Management. In: Riel, A., O'Connor, R., Tichkiewitch, S., Messnarz, R. (eds.) EuroSPI 2010. CCIS, vol. 99, pp. 1–12. Springer, Heidelberg (2010)
5. Berander, P.: Evolving prioritization for software product management. Ph.D. thesis, Blekinge Institute of Technology, Ronneby (2007)
6. Carmel, E., Becker, S.: A process model for packaged software development. IEEE Transactions on Engineering Management 42(1), 50–61 (1995)
7. Cusumano, M.: The Business of Software: What Every Manager, Programmer, and Entrepreneur Must Know to Thrive and Survive in Good Times and Bad. The Free Press, New York (2004)
8. Ebert, C.: The Impacts of Software Product Management. Journal of Systems and Software 6(80), 850–861 (2007)
9. Feller, J., Finnegan, P., Fitzgerald, B., Hayes, J.: From Peer Production to Productization: A Study of Socially Enabled Business Exchanges in Open Source Service Networks. Information Systems Research 19(4), 475–493 (2008)
10. Gorschek, T., Kittlaus, H.B.: International Software Product Management Association. In: Proceedings of the International Workshop on Software Product Management, Trento, Italy, pp. 1–2 (2011)
11. Hietala, J., Kontio, J., Jokinen, J.: Challenges of software product companies: results of a national survey in Finland (2004)
12. Jaakkola, E.: Unraveling the practices of "productization" in professional service firms. Scandinavian Journal of Management 27(2), 221–230 (2011)
13. Jansen, S., Brinkkemper, S.: Applied Multi-Case Research in a Mixed-Method Research Project: Customer Configuration Updating Improvement. In: Cater-Steel, A., Al-Hakimi, L. (eds.) Information Systems Research Methods, Epistemology, and Applications, pp. 120–139. IGI Global, Utrecht (2007)
14. Regnell, B., Brinkkemper, S.: Market-driven requirements engineering for software products. Engineering and Managing Software Requirements, 287–308 (2005)
15. Sawyer, S.: Packaged Software: Implications of the Differences from Custom Approaches to Software Development. European Journal of Information Systems 1(1), 47–58 (2000)
16. Suominen, A., Kantola, J., Tuominen, A.: Reviewing and Defining Productization. In: Proceedings of the XX ISPIM Conference (August 2009)
17. van de Weerd, I., Bekkers, W., Brinkkemper, S.: Developing a Maturity Matrix for Software Product Management. In: Tyrväinen, P., Jansen, S., Cusumano, M.A. (eds.) ICSOB 2010. LNBIP, vol. 51, pp. 76–89. Springer, Heidelberg (2010)

18. van de Weerd, I., Brinkkemper, S.: Meta-modeling for situational analysis and design methods. In: Handbook of Research on Modern Systems Analysis and Design Technologies and Applications, ch. III, p. 35. Information Science Publishing (2008)
19. van de Weerd, I., de Weerd, S., Brinkkemper, S.: Developing a Reference Method for Game Production by Method Comparison. In: Ralyté, J., Brinkkemper, S., Henderson-Sellers, B. (eds.) Situational Method Engineering: Fundamentals and Experiences. IFIP, vol. 244, pp. 313–327. Springer, Boston (2007)
20. Xu, L., Brinkkemper, S.: Concepts of Product Software. European Journal of Information Systems 16, 531–541 (2007)
21. Yin, R.K.: Case Study Research - Design and Methods. SAGE Publications (2003)

Consumer Value-Aware Enterprise Architecture

Eric-Oluf Svee, Jelena Zdravkovic, and Constantinos Giannoulis

Stockholm University, Department of Computer and System Sciences,
Forum 100, 16440 Kista, Sweden
{eric-sve,jelenaz,constantinos}@dsv.su.se

Abstract. To improve the alignment between business and IT, this paper explores how to make Enterprise Architecture (EA) aware of consumer values. Current proposals in enterprise modeling recognize the need for modeling user needs, or values. However they do not classify them nor do they provide means to obtain them. In our study, these are first introduced as basic values captured via Schwartz's Value Survey, a cross-culturally applicable tool from the world of psychology, which are mapped onto Holbrook's Typology of Consumer Values. Additionally, because formal models require inputs that are more concrete than abstract, and through this proposal, the indistinct values of consumers can be transformed and formalized to be incorporated into enterprise architecture, represented here by ISO/IEC 42010. The novelty of this work is found in the method for operationalizing consumer values for their alignment and utilization within information systems.

Keywords: Value, Consumer Value, Business-IT Alignment, Enterprise Modeling, Enterprise Architecture.

1 Introduction

An enterprise exists to fulfill both a business mission and a vision [1], and a key element necessary to complete those tasks is deemed the *value proposition*. This clarifies how the enterprise will create differentiated, sustainable value to specific customers [2].

The value proposition is part of a business's strategy and as such it is ultimately linked to the infrastructure that enables the business to provide value to its customers. Such support systems are often larger-scale enterprise systems that allow for provisioning of goods and services to customers as promised by the value proposition. What the value proposition generally addresses is an amount in goods, products, services or money, considered as a suitable equivalent for something else—a fair price or return for an investment [3] focusing primarily on the *economic value* exchanged. In counterpoise how a good, product, or service is delivered to, or perceived by, the consumer is described by *consumer values* [4].

Although how economic values relate and influence business IT systems is an area that has been addressed [5, 6, 7], it is not clear whether and how consumer values do so, in particular where they fit within the design of enterprise systems. However, perhaps more critical to this research is whether this is an important area to study at all.

M.A. Cusumano, B. Iyer, and N. Venkatraman (Eds.): ICSOB 2012, LNBIP 114, pp. 55–69, 2012.

Kotler [8] acknowledged the crucial role consumer values play in all marketing activity; as the key motivator behind, and the primary driver within, value exchanges, they both induce the consumer to seek solutions to fulfill their needs as well as catalyze their exposure to the marketing information presented to them. Therefore, enterprise systems should reflect consumer values as well.

But beyond the simple transfer of value objects, what is the relevance of consumer values and how does this affect enterprise systems? Using book selling as an example, one can illustrate the impact of consumer values on enterprise systems. *Borders* was the largest book store in the United States, but they missed the shift of the book selling business to e-sales. Shopping online became appealing to consumers in different ways than shopping at physical bookstores, for reasons such as convenience, while the core economic value involved remained money for books. However, a brick-and-mortar competitor, *Barnes & Noble*, did not overlook this shift in consumer values and extended its business online while preserving its book stores. *Amazon* set up its entire business around this shift and soon dominated online book sales, while *Borders* recently went out of business [9]. Additionally, to better compete with Amazon and Barnes & Noble, *Apple's* move into e-book sales necessitated either improving on the value of convenience or choosing other consumer values to attract consumers. As a consequence, Apple recently put forward the idea of providing books to consumers directly from the authors via its online delivery platform *iTunes*, aiming to attract consumers based on how acquiring books directly from the authors is perceived, thus aiming at consumer values different than convenience [10].

In both cases, aiming at particular consumer values suggested that the enterprise (re)designed their systems to support the provision of these consumer values. For example, to support different consumer values surrounding convenience, Amazon developed entirely new capabilities to purchase and deliver e-books, something for which its infrastructure for processing and shipping physical goods would not have been designed, leading Amazon to the top of book and e-book sales online. Similarly, to be capable to support their e-publishing idea, Apple had to not only leverage the wide popularity of their authoring tools among authors to allow them to publish and sell to their readers directly via iTunes, but also to undertake all the necessary changes in its existing products, as well as to introduce new ones. All of this necessitated changes to the underlying architecture of their online delivery platform.

Although the core value exchange remains money for books, the consumer values driving this vary greatly. These bookseller examples highlight that variability and show how it directly influences the success of the value proposition via the attendant value exchange. Success depends on an enterprise's capability to set up its IT systems to efficiently marshal and align its resources to aid in effectively presenting, and delivering upon, its value proposition to consumers.

Consequently, the aim of this study is to explore how consumer values fit within the design of enterprise systems. Attaining this goal relies on relating consumer values to enterprise systems. To accomplish this, there needs to be a means for obtaining and classifying consumer values on a common level, such that they can be related to enterprise systems. The proposal below describes just such a means—relating basic values captured through Schwartz's Value Survey [11] to Holbrook's Typology of Consumer Values [4]. For enterprise systems, the present work addresses them holistically through Enterprise Architectures (EA), these being the fundamental conception of an enterprise as captured by a set of elements, their relationships to each other and to the environment [12]. For the scope of this study a standard for architectures—ISO/IEC 42010, Architecture Description [12]—is used upon which the aforementioned value frameworks are mapped. This allows the extension of the proposed mappings towards EAs rooted in this standard, and thus constitutes mappings agnostic of any particular EA approach.

The paper is structured as follows: Section 2 presents a discussion on values, basic values, and consumer values, Section 3 presents the integrated consumer value framework that was developed, Section 4 presents how the integrated consumer value framework fits within enterprise architecture, and Section 5 presents the conclusions and directions for future research.

2 Conceptions of Value

The concept of *value* has a wide variety of accepted meanings, with the choice of usage primarily one of context. In business it is most commonly used in an economic sense to mean an object that can be offered by one actor to another [13] often where the worth or desirability of something is expressed as an amount of money [14]. In the Business-IT alignment discipline, a *value object* (also called a *resource*) is considered as something that is of *economic value* for at least one actor, e.g., a car, a book, Internet access, or a stream of music [15]. Henkel et.al. state that values can be psychological and social in nature, such as beauty, pleasure, health state, honor, and a feeling of safety [5]. According to Gordijn [6], a user experience is also recognized as having a value. To distinguish between these different kinds of values, Ilayperuma et.al. identified two categories of values—*economic* and *internal* [7] — where *internal value* could be a certain property attached to an actor, such as their beauty or health, or it could be a property of some enabling service, such as speedy delivery. In contrast to the present proposal, none of these works from Business-IT alignment attempt to capture such values, nor do they relate it to EA. The term for these adopted within this work is *consumer values*, as defined by Holbrook [4] (see discussion in §2.2).

2.1 Basic Values

Schwartz's Value Theory (SVT) adopts the definition of value from Rokeach, summarized as a belief that a specific mode of conduct or end-state is personally or socially preferable to its opposite [16]. Values serve as criteria for judgment, preferences, choice and decisions as they underlie the person's knowledge, beliefs, and attitudes [17]. According to Schwartz, all the items found in earlier value theories, in value questionnaires from different cultures, as well as religious and philosophical discussions of values, can be classified virtually into one of the following motivationally distinct *basic values* [11] (Table 1): *Power*, *Universalism*, *Achievement*, *Benevolence*, *Hedonism*, *Tradition*, *Stimulation*, *Conformity*, *Self-direction*, and *Security*.

SVT emphasizes the profound nature of values, but at the same time offers a new consumer research approach by concretely combining these value structures with an analysis of human motivation [18]. This integrated structure of values can be summarized with two orthogonal dimensions: *Self-enhancement* (the pursuit of self-interests) vs. *Self-transcendence* (concern for the welfare and interest of others); and *Openness to Change* (independence of action, thought, and feeling, and a readiness for new experiences) vs. *Conservation* (self-restriction, order, and resistance to change).

Table 1. Schwartz's Basic Values as per their Classifying Dimensions, with examples [11]

Dimension	Basic Value	Dimension	Basic Value
Openness to Change	Self-direction *(Creativity, Freedom)*	**Self-transcendence**	Universalism *(Equality, Justice)*
	Stimulation *(An exciting life)*		Benevolence *(Helpfulness)*
	Hedonism[1] *(Pleasure)*		Hedonism *(Pleasure)*
Self-enhancement	Achievement *(Success, Ambition)*	**Conservation**	Conformity *(Obedience)*
			Tradition *(Humility, Devotion)*
	Power *(Authority, Wealth)*		Security *(Social order)*

Thereafter, Schwartz developed the Value Survey (SVS) to measure the basic values [11]. SVS focuses on a universally applicable method for capturing and describing values across cultures and it has been applied in numerous places [19], including business strategy development support [20]. The Value Survey operationalizes the ten basic values with a set of 56 items, 30 of which were originally used in the work of Rokeach. The answers from the questionnaire can then be converted into a set of numerical results that can be used directly, or visualized via a value structure.

2.2 Consumer Values

Holbrook refines the value concept, focusing on those held by individuals during a value exchange, referring to them as *consumer values* and classifying them into a Typology of Consumer Values.

A consumer value is "an interactive, relativistic preference experience" [4] (Table 2); interactive entails an interchange between some subject and an object, relativistic refers to consumer values being comparative, preferential refers to consumer values embodying the outcome of an evaluative judgment, and experience refers to consumer

[1] Hedonism shares elements of both *Openness* and *Self-enhancement* [25].

values not residing in the product/service acquired but rather in the consumption experience. Holbrook's definition allows for a rather expansive view of value, because all products provide services in their capacity to create need- or want-satisfying experiences.

Holbrook identifies three dimensions in consumer values that are used as the basis for developing his typology [4]: *Extrinsic* vs. *Intrinsic*, *Self-oriented* vs. *Other-oriented*, and *Active* vs. *Reactive*.

Extrinsic is a means/end relationship wherein consumption is prized for its functional, utilitarian ability to serve as a means to accomplish some further purpose, aim, goal or objective, for example, purchasing from an online bookseller solely because it has the lowest prices. *Intrinsic* occurs when some consumption experience is appreciated as an end in itself—for its own sake, such as choosing to shop at a book store rather than an online retailer due to its comfortable reading room and pleasant ambience.

Self-oriented refers to occasions where some aspect of consumption is cherished, either selfishly or prudently, for the individual's sake; an efficient online book store saves time and effort when purchasing books. *Other-oriented* refers to occasions where the consumption experience or the product on which it depends is valued by others, either beyond the subject, for its own sake, for how they react to it, or for the effect it has on them. A consumer may be driven to buy a book from a local book store instead of Amazon in order to support the local economy.

Active entails a physical or mental manipulation of some tangible or intangible object, involving things done by a consumer to or with a product as part of some consumption experience: the experience of reading from a paper book versus an electronic one has great appeal to many people. *Reactive* results from apprehending, appreciating, admiring, or otherwise responding to an object, when the object acts upon the subject. Similar to the example given for intrinsic, the dream of reading in a book-filled space also be reactive, when the primary force behind the consumption experience is the object of consumption (the book) and not the subject (the consumer).

Based on these three dimensions, Holbrook's Typology of Consumer Values identifies eight archetypes that represent distinct types of value in the consumption experience [4] (Table 2): *Efficiency*, *Excellence*, *Status*, *Esteem*, *Play*, *Aesthetics*, *Ethics, and Spirituality*.

Table 2. Holbrook's Typology of Consumer Values, with examples [4]

		Extrinsic	**Intrinsic**
Self-oriented	**Active**	Efficiency (*Convenience*)	Play (*Fun*)
	Reactive	Excellence (*Quality*)	Aesthetics (*Beauty*)
Other-oriented	**Active**	Status (*Success*)	Ethics (*Virtue, Justice*)
	Reactive	Esteem (*Reputation*)	Spirituality (*Faith, Sacred*)

A final set of key concepts from Holbrook begins with *Market Space Dimension*. This represents those characteristics, attributes, or features of brands in the product class that provide consumer value. It contains within it the concept of *Ideal Point*, which indicates a position of maximum consumer value for the customer segment of interest. Taken together, these frame *Transactions*, or the exchange of interest, a process between two parties in which each party gives up something of value in return for something of greater value.

3 Mapping Basic Values onto Consumer Values

While various conceptual frameworks such as Holbrook's Typology, Maslow's Hierarchy of Needs [21] or McClelland's Trichotomy of Needs [22] can function as means for understanding consumers, they lack a method for the values' instrumentalization and operationalization. Beyond mapping such values to existing approaches to business strategy [23] or remaking another tool that contains the necessary functionality, such as SERVQUAL [24], there have been very few attempts for working directly within this field.

3.1 Mapping Schwartz's Basic Values onto Holbrook's Consumer Values

Schwartz claims his values are universal and are not designed for a particular application, but rather for broader, more general tasks. To provide them with a specific orientation—in this case consumer values—it is therefore necessary to map them to an applicable framework. While it is possible to relate both Schwartz and Holbrook individually to EA, such a solution would be lacking: applying Schwartz to EA provides only a means for capturing higher level values, and by introducing Holbrook's Typology into EA development one is given a framework for understanding consumer values without any means to obtain them. While in either approach a necessary side of the process is missing, in combination, Schwartz and Holbrook provide a way to capture and understand consumer values allowing them to be related with EA.

Values serve as criteria for judgment, preferences, choice and decisions as they underlie the person's knowledge, beliefs, and attitudes [17]. Schwartz applies this definition directly, basing his Value Theory on the fact that these values are desirable, trans-situational goals of variable importance that are applied as broader guiding principles by a person or social entity [11].

In summary, to Schwartz:

- Values are beliefs tied inextricably to emotion, not objective, cold ideas.
- Values are a motivational construct: they refer to the desirable goals people strive to attain.
- Values transcend specific actions and situations, and this abstract nature distinguishes them from concepts like norms and attitudes, which usually refer to specific actions, objects, or situations.
- Values guide the selection or evaluation of actions, policies, people, and events. That is, values serve as standards or criteria.
- Values are ordered by importance relative to one another. Peoples' values form an ordered system of value priorities that characterize them as individuals [25].

By extension, a customer's purchasing behavior reflects those actions which are based on a relationship between their values, desires, and actions. Recalling Holbrook's definition of consumer value as being "an interactive, relativistic preference experience" [4], it is apparent that there is significant overlap with Schwartz's Value Theory.

Schwartz's Value Survey (SVS) measures the ten basic values [11] found in the Value Theory with a set of 56 items. These results can then be mapped to the conceptual framework of Holbrook's Typology. Thus a tool widely used in the psychology community can provide quantitative data that can express formerly solely qualitative concepts. The converse—mapping Holbrook to Schwartz—would not provide any means to obtain and operationalize the values (Table 3).

To understand the mapping, it is necessary to reintroduce both the dimensions that Holbrook uses to define his archetypical consumer values (*Self-Oriented* vs. *Other Oriented*, *Extrinsic* vs. *Intrinsic*, and *Active* vs. *Reactive*) as well as those of Schwartz (*Openness to Change*, *Self-Enhancement*, *Self-Transcendence*, and *Conservation*).

These can in turn be mapped, with Holbrook's *Self-oriented* and Schwartz's *Self-enhancement* and Holbrook's *Other-oriented* relating to Schwartz's *Self-transcendence* due to their intended focus: the individual in the former or others in the latter. Holbrook's *Active* and *Extrinsic* relates to Schwartz's *Openness to Change* and Holbrook's *Reactive* and *Intrinsic* to Schwartz's *Conservation.* This also relates to intentional direction; *Active*, *Extrinsic*, and *Openness to Change* are directed outside the self while *Reactive*, *Intrinsic*, and *Conservation* entail processes internal to the individual.

Because these are the underlying concepts for each of the values, it is necessary to first relate them to each other before proceeding further. No direct, one-to-one relationships exist, and further complicating matters is the fact that the terms have similar names, but not definitions.

Table 3. Mapping Schwartz's Value Dimensions and Holbrook's Value Dimensions

Schwartz's Value Dimensions	***Holbrook's Value Dimensions***		
Openness to Change	Self-oriented	Active	Intrinsic
Self-Transcendence	Other-oriented	Active	Intrinsic
Conservation	Self-oriented	Reactive	Extrinsic
Self-Enhancement	Other-oriented	Active	Extrinsic

3.2 Reasoning Behind the Mapping

Now that the relationships between the dimensions have been established, mappings relating Schwartz's Basic Values onto Holbrook's Consumer Values (Table 4) are introduced and the reasoning behind them presented and explained.

Table 4. Schwartz's Basic Values Mapped onto Holbrook's Consumer Values [4]

		Extrinsic	Intrinsic
Self-oriented	**Active**	Efficiency (*Conformity, Security*)	Play (*Self-direction, Stimulation*)
	Reactive	Excellence (*Achievement*)	Aesthetics (*Hedonism*)
Other-oriented	**Active**	Status (*Power*)	Ethics (*Universalism*)
	Reactive	Esteem (*Power, Achievement*)	Spirituality (*Benevolence, Tradition*)

(*Italics=Schwartz's Basic Values*)

Conformity and Security *to* Efficiency. Schwartz's *Conformity* promotes cooperation in order to avoid negative outcomes for the self, and not necessarily out of altruism (self-orientation). Furthermore, it establishes and maintains such cooperation through actions unlikely to upset others or violate social norms, a classic means/end relationship which is the hallmark of the Extrinsic dimension. *Security* is quite similar and is based on the safety and harmony of society, of relationships, and of self, for the benefit of the individual. Holbrook's *Efficiency* is a utilitarian value that results from the active use of a product or consumption experience as a means to achieve some self-oriented purpose. Another view of *Efficiency*—convenience—is often a measure of utility derived versus time or energy expended [26]. Using the bookseller as an example, a consumer being able to efficiently and securely purchase a book through a website that is easy to use and conforms to a set of well-promulgated standards would be an example containing all three values.

Achievement *to* Excellence. The *Achievement* value is an internal, personal appreciation of success achieved through the demonstration of competence according to social standards. With *Excellence*, one admires some object or prizes some experience for its capacity to accomplish some goal or to perform some function. The consumer reactively apprehends their purchase, viewing it as a wise decision within their social structure. In the example, the bookseller would be able to satisfy both values by having a well-designed website that allows customers to easily make purchases.

Power *to* Status. For Schwartz, *Power* speaks directly to social status, prestige, and dominance over people and resources, matching Holbrook's definition nearly identically. It is also possesses a reactive quality, where self-apprehension of one attaining or preserving a dominant position within a more general social system. For Holbrook, *Status* is sought by adjusting consumption to affect those whom one wishes to influence: by consuming products or engaging in consumption experiences to project a particular type of image. Such values are most commonly met by offering exclusivity in some form, for example high-end products not available from other retailers. In the example, a bookseller could differentiate itself by having a special section that offered rare books for sale.

Power and Achievement *to* Esteem. Recalling *Power* (social status, prestige) and *Achievement* (an internal, personal appreciation of success), to satisfy such values the bookseller could offer multiple product options, such as physical books and e-books. Holbrook's *Esteem* is the reactive appreciation of consumption or lifestyle in a somewhat passive way as a potential extrinsic means to enhance ones' other-oriented public image. A consumer could be motivated to choose the e-book because of its more environmentally friendly delivery method, relishing "saving the planet" while also exercising their independent choice over delivery options.

Stimulation and Self-direction *to* Play. Holbrook's consumer value *Play* is a self-oriented experience, actively sought and enjoyed for its own sake, and as such, typically involves having fun. Schwartz's value for *Self-direction* is about creativity, freedom, independence, and being able to choose ones' own goals, while his value *Stimulation* is based on excitement and novelty directly experienced is related to *Play* via Holbrook's Intrinsic and Active dimensions. In the example, a new media-enabled tablet could provide the bookseller an opportunity to provide the instantaneous gratification of new and unique content, beyond a simple black-and-white e-book. Building such a delivery infrastructure however would entail an entire configuration of their enterprise systems, which were most likely designed around the delivery of physical products.

Hedonism *to* Aesthetics. In Schwartz's value *Hedonism*, pleasure and sensuous gratification are directed towards oneself. Similarly Holbrook's *Aesthetics* refers to an appreciation of some consumption experience enjoyed for its own sake, without a need for external justification. Through *Aesthetics*—an Intrinsic and Reactive value—the consumer apprehends and internalizes the consumption experience, making this broader than generally understood where only external attributes catalyze reactions. Returning to the example, the development of e-book readers took into account a number of factors, among them the pleasure derived from reading a physical book. A centuries-old technology, the book has been perfected over time and is difficult to improve upon: a superior form factor with text optimized for reading.

Benevolence and Universalism *to* Ethics. Schwartz's *Benevolence* attempts to enhance and preserve the welfare of those within a person's social group, while *Universalism* seeks to understand, appreciate, tolerate, and protect the welfare of all people and nature. There are undercurrents of Holbrook's Reactivity (appreciating the experience personally) but the differentiating factor here is that there is an externalized locus of intention: the basis for the action is not self-satisfaction, but is focused on helping or pleasing others. Similarly, Holbrook's *Ethics* involves doing something for the sake of others— that is, with a concern for how it will affect them or how they will react to it— where such consumption experiences are valued as ends in themselves. A bookseller could satisfy these concerns by implementing practices for an ethical supply chain, focusing on smaller scale publishers who utilize recognized fair trade and labor practices.

Tradition *to* Spirituality. In Schwartz's basic values this is most closely related to *Tradition*, or respect commitment, and acceptance of customers and ideas that traditional culture or religion provides the self. Holbrook's consumer value *Spirituality* entails an experience that is sought not as a means to an ulterior end but rather prized for its own sake, specifically by accessing an external Other or greater power.

Spirituality can be difficult to address directly due to the many sensitivities that exist around it; explicitly making spirituality a focus of an enterprise entails a great deal of difficulty. However, it has many indirect responses, as found in an example from the United States. Many localities ban certain products, such as pornography and alcohol, based on "community standards". The example bookseller, being unable to ship such items to customers, must have systems in place to either block their display on the website or to block the transaction at the time of purchase.

4 Consumer Value-Aware Enterprise Architecture

ISO/IEC 42010 [12] describes software system architectures through a set of generic concepts and terms of reference constituting an architecture description. Linking concepts from this standard to consumer values allows for the extension of enterprise architectures that are based on this standard, such as TOGAF [27], ArchiMate [28], etc., towards consumer value-awareness. This section presents how EA can be extended towards consumer values; the linkage is illustrated with the previously explored example of consumer-awareness in selling of e-books. The section concludes with a brief discussion on the impact of those extensions being used for TOGAF to become consumer value-aware.

4.1 Description of ISO/IEC 42010 Meta-Model

In ISO/IEC 42010 *Concerns* are interests relevant to one or more *Stakeholders* that drive a *System-of-Interest*. *Concerns* arise from requirements and can be shown for example as goals, needs, quality attributes, and architecture decisions. *Stakeholders* can be an individual, team, organization, or classes thereof, having an interest in a system. *System-of-Interest* is a facilitator of value exchange between enterprise and consumer. *Architecture Description* expresses the *Architecture* of a *System-of-Interest* related also to the stakeholder(s), and the concern. As the key artifact, it explains, on a high level the design components of the system-of-interest.

Architecture Rationale contains quantitative and qualitative evidence of the proposed architecture that records the reasoning behind chosen *Concerns*. *Correspondence* expresses relationships between elements of the Architecture Description and can be used to express, record, enforce, and analyze consistency and dependencies spanning more than a single model. *Correspondence Rule*, which enforces the application of *Correspondences* between elements of the *Architecture Description*. *Architecture Viewpoint* contains the conventions that frame an *Architecture* with respect to a set of *Concerns*. *Architecture View* expresses *Architecture* through a cohesive group of models, and is governed by an *Architecture Viewpoint*.

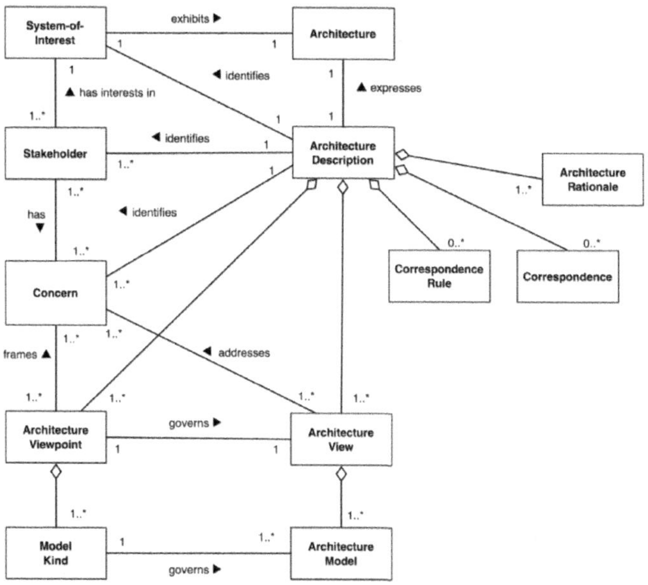

Fig. 1. Conceptual model of an architecture description within ISO/IEC 42010 [12]

4.2 Consumer Value-Awareness in ISO/IEC 42010

Below, consumer value awareness within ISO/IEC 42010 is demonstrated first by those consumer value concepts that relate directly to concepts found in ISO/IEC 42010's meta-model. Following this, the bookseller example is used to elucidate each concept from the meta-model to highlight how consumer value-awareness can be achieved.

For Holbrook, *consumer values* are preferences in a value exchange, and thus they map directly to *Concern* (Figure 1). In the example, Schwartz's ten basic values are quantified via his SVS, with one such value being *Stimulation*, which in turn maps to Holbrook's consumer value *Play*. This then becomes a *Concern*.

ISO/IEC 42010's *System-of-Interest* is the locus of a value exchange, in this example between the bookseller and the consumer. Recalling the concepts of *Market Space Dimensions*, and *Ideal Points* introduced in §2.2, *System-of-Interest* becomes where Holbrook's *Transaction* occurs. As parties with interests in that system *Stakeholders* map to *Consumers* in Holbrook's Typology.

Table 5. Concepts of ISO/IEC 42010 Related to Consumer Values

ISO Concept	Consumer Value
Concern	Consumer Value
Stakeholders	Consumers
System-of-interest	Transactions

Below in Table 6, concepts that lack a direct correspondence are grouped conceptually, and an example for each is provided.

Table 6. Relationships between ISO/IEC 42010 meta-model and Consumer Value Concepts

ISO Concepts and Descriptions	Example
Architecture Description expresses the *Architecture* of ISO's *System-of-Interest/* Holbrook's *Transaction* related to ISO *Stakeholder*/Holbrook's *Consumer*, as well as ISO's *Concern/*Holbrook's *Consumer Value*. As the key design artifact, it explains on a high level the design components of the system-of-interest. *Architecture Rationale* contains quantitative and qualitative evidence of the proposed architecture that records the reasoning behind chosen *Concerns*.	Summary results from Schwartz's Value Survey, mapped to Holbrook's Typology are populated here. It is because of this concept's constraints that, when deciding where to expend valuable resources, it would be important for the book seller to understand whether consumers valued efficiency in the form of cheaper prices and slower shipping times (Holbrook's *Efficiency* and Schwartz's *Security*), or higher prices and providing the product electronically for immediate gratification (Holbrook's *Play* and Schwartz's *Stimulation*).
To become consumer values-aware, the *Correspondence Rule*, which enforces the application of *Correspondences* between elements of the *Architecture Description*, should be handled similarly: each must utilize the results of the consumer-value aware survey based on Schwartz and Holbrook as found in the *Architecture Rationale*.	A rule could be that consumer interaction with a *System-of-Interest* (e-book reader) must implement the *Concern*, e.g., Holbrook's *Play*.
Architecture Viewpoint is captured as methods, heuristics, metrics, patterns, design rules or guidelines, and best practices. *Architecture View* expresses *Architecture* through a cohesive group of models, and is governed by an *Architecture Viewpoint*.	As the *Concern* in the example, the consumer value *Play* dictates the methods and patterns which will facilitate its design. This focuses how a concern is expressed by the *Architecture,* and structures models grouped within the *Architecture View*.

4.3 Consumer Value-Awareness in Other Enterprise Architectures

Enterprise architecture frameworks such as TOGAF [27], etc. are aligned with the concepts of the ISO/IEC 42010 architecture description model. Therefore, when considering an enterprise as a system-of-interest, thus aiming at an architecture description of an enterprise, relationships between consumer values and ISO/IEC/IEEE 42010 models can be identified for explicit consumer value-awareness within enterprise architectures.

For example, because TOGAF is closely related to ISO/IEC 42010 it carries forward concepts from that standard; for example, its definition of stakeholder is nearly identical— "people who have key roles in, or concerns about, the system" [27]. They also share a problem: both lack an explicit consumer value-aware orientation. Certain EA standards do address this issue, though not explicitly, containing concepts which can contain consumer values but which do not explicitly call for them.

TOGAF is an excellent exemplar, as its content meta-model supports extensions that allow for more in-depth consideration of particular architecture concerns. For example, several TOGAF concepts relevant to this research are *Motivation Extension* which contains *Drivers*, or external or internal conditions that motivate an organization to define its goals; *Goals*, or high-level statements of intent or direction for an organization that are typically used to measure success; and *Objectives*, which are time-bounded milestones for an organization used to demonstrate progress towards a goal. The logical progression is that the *Organization* is motivated by the *Driver*, which creates the *Goal*, which is realized through the *Objective*.

The consumer value—*Play* in the book seller example—can be mapped directly to TOGAF's *Driver*. Extending this, the book seller is motivated by *Play* to increase sales and develops a TOGAF *Goal* of increasing revenue derived from products intended to engage that consumer value. The TOGAF *Objective* supported by the TOGAF *Driver* and the TOGAF *Goal* is that within one fiscal year, revenues derived from the enhanced e-book reader will have increased 20% over previous levels.

5 Conclusions and Future Work

The aim of this study was to explore how consumer values can be linked to enterprise architecture to enrich business-IT alignment efforts. Its justification has been motivated using current, real-world examples about book selling, a consumer-value sensitive business where low profit margins and easy switching by consumers make for an extremely competitive environment. The value frameworks used in the study are Schwartz's [11] and Holbrook's [4], with Schwartz allowing for the elicitation of basic values while Holbrook allows for the classification of consumer values. The two frameworks have been integrated with a proposed set of mappings between the basic values of Schwartz, and the consumer values of Holbrook. The outcome is an integrated consumer value framework that includes both elicitation and classification of consumer values applicable to any line of business.

Enterprise Architecture provides the methods and models used to design and realize an enterprise's organizational structure, processes, and information systems. As such, the proposed integrated consumer value framework has been linked to ISO/IEC 42010 [12] to illustrate the explicit introduction of consumer values into core concepts of architecture, thus providing the following benefits:

- Linking consumer values with distinct EA concepts allows for the identification of system requirements coming from particular consumer values.
- Standards-based and independence from any particular EA.
- Propagates consumer values into EA frameworks based on ISO/IEC 42010, such as TOGAF.

Future research directions will focus on shifting from the generic level of ISO/IEC 42010 into distinct EAs rooted in the standard to demonstrate the practical applicability of the proposal. Additionally, links to known RE approaches such as GORE will be explored.

References

1. Kaplan, R., Norton, D.P.: Having trouble with your strategy? Then map it. J. Harvard Business Review 78, 167–176 (2000)
2. Kaplan, R., Norton, D.: Strategy Maps: Converting Intangible Assets into Tangible Outcomes. Harvard Business Review Press (2004)
3. McCarthy, W. E.: The REA Accounting Model: A Generalized Framework for Accounting Systems in a Shared Data Environment. The Accounting Review (1982)
4. Holbrook, M.B.: Consumer Value: A Framework for Analysis and Research. Routledge, London (1998)
5. Henkel, M., Johannesson, P., Perjons, E., Zdravkovic, J.: Value and Goal Driven Design of E-Services. In: Int'l Conf. on E-Business Eng. (ICEBE 2007). IEEE Press (2007)
6. Gordijn, J., Akkermans, H., van Vliet, H.: Business Modelling Is Not Process Modelling. In: Mayr, H.C., Liddle, S.W., Thalheim, B. (eds.) ER Workshops 2000. LNCS, vol. 1921, pp. 40–51. Springer, Heidelberg (2000)
7. Ilayperuma, T., Zdravkovic, J.: Exploring Business Value Models from the Inter-Organizational Collaboration Perspective. In: ACM Symposium on Applied Computing (SAC), pp. 99–105 (2010)
8. Kotler, P.J.: Marketing Management, 7th edn. Prentice-Hall, Englewood Cliffs (1991)
9. The Wall Street Journal (January 25, 2012), `http://online.wsj.com/article/SB10001424052702303661904577645435376855028O.html`
10. Apple (January 26, 2012), `http://www.apple.com/pr/library/2012/01/19Apple-Reinvents-Textbooks-with-iBooks-2-for-iPad.html`
11. Schwartz, S.H.: Universals in the Content and Structure of Values: Theoretical Advances and Empirical Tests in 20 Countries. In: Zanna, M. (ed.) Advances in Experimental Social Psychology, vol. 25, pp. 1–62. Academic Press, San Diego (1992)
12. International Organization for Standardization: ISO/IEC 42010 in: Systems and Software Engineering — Architecture Description (2011)
13. Wieringa, R., Gordijn, J., van Eck, P.: Value-Based Business-IT Alignment in Networked Constellations of Enterprises. In: 1st Int'l Workshop on Requirements Engineering for Business Need and IT Alignment, REBNITA (2005)
14. Weigand, H., Johannesson, P., Andersson, B., Bergholtz, M., Edirisuriya, A., Ilayperuma, T.: On the Notion of Value Object. In: Martinez, F.H., Pohl, K. (eds.) CAiSE 2006. LNCS, vol. 4001, pp. 321–335. Springer, Heidelberg (2006)
15. Afuah, A., Tucci, C.: Internet Bus. Models and Strategies. McGraw Hill, Boston (2003)
16. Rokeach, M.: The Nature of Human Values. The Free Press, New York (1973)
17. Rokeach, M.: Beliefs, Attitudes and Values. Jossey-Bass, San Francisco (1968)
18. Puohiniemi, M.: Values, Consumer Attitudes, and Behaviour: An application of Schwartz's value theory to the analysis of consumer behaviour and attitudes in two national samples, Research report, University of Helsinki (1995)
19. Schwartz, S.H., Melech, G., Lehmann, A., Burgess, S., Harris, M., Owens, V.: Extending the cross-cultural validity of the theory of basic human values with a different method of measurement. J. of Cross-Cultural Psychology 35(2), 519–542 (2001)
20. Epstein, M., Manzoni, J.F.: Implementing corporate strategy—from Tableaux de Bord to Balanced Scorecards. European Management J. 16(2), 190–203 (1998)
21. Maslow, A.H.: A Theory of Human Motivation. Psychological Rev. 50(4), 370–396 (1943)
22. McClelland, D.C.: Human Motivation. Cambridge University Press (1988)

23. Svee, E.O., Giannoulis, C., Zdravkovic, J.: Modeling Business Strategy: a Consumer Value Approach. In: Proceedings of Practice of Enterprise Modeling (PoEM 2011), Oslo, Norway, pp. 69–81 (2011)
24. Parasuraman, A., Zeithaml, V.A., Berry, L.L.: SERVQUAL: A multiple-item scale for measuring consumer perceptions. J. of Retailing 64(1), 12–40 (1988)
25. Schwartz, S.H.: Basic human values: Their content and structure across countries. In: Tamayo, A., Porto, J.B. (eds.) Valores e comportamento nas organizacões (Values and behavior in organizations), pp. 21–55. Vozes, Petrópolis (2005)
26. Leclerc, F., Schmitt, H.H., Dubé, L.: Waiting Time and Decision Making: Is Time Like Money? J. Consumer Research 22, 110–119 (1995)
27. The Open Group (October 31, 2011), `http://pubs.opengroup.org/architecture/togaf9-doc/arch/`
28. Jonkers, H., van Burren, R., Arbab, F., de Boer, F., Bonsangue, M.M., Bosma, H., ter Doest, H.: Towards a language for coherent enterprise architecture descriptions. In: 7th IEEE International EDOC Conference (EDOC 2003). IEEE Computer Society, Brisbane (2003)

Using Knowledge from End-Users Online for Innovations: Effects of Software Firm Types

Mikko O.J. Laine

Software Business Lab, Aalto University, Otaniementie 17, Espoo, Finland
mikko.laine@aalto.fi

Abstract. As firms need to persistently innovate, they search knowledge from sources external to the firm in order to aid their innovation processes. Firms, however, use the wide range of available types of external knowledge sources heterogeneously. In this paper we explore the factors that affect high-technology firms' utilization of end-users online as a source of knowledge for their innovations. Drawing data from a survey of the Finnish software industry, we find that several firm and environmental characteristics decrease and increase this propensity.

Keywords: open innovation, external knowledge source, online end-user, software firm.

1 Introduction

Firms need to innovate constantly, and even that may not be enough to guarantee survival [1, 2]. This need is especially prevalent in high-technology industries characterized by turbulence, short product life-cycles and global competition [3]. In order to achieve constant innovations, firms actively combine knowledge from within the boundaries of the firm with knowledge from external sources outside the firm [4–6]. The popular framework of "open innovation" promotes the usage of these rich flows of knowledge out from and into the firm, facilitated by engaging external actors [3, 7].

To draw new knowledge into the firm, there are various external sources available. End-users, for one, have been identified as productive innovators and influential potential contributors to firm innovation [8, 9]. With the proliferation of electronic communication medium in general and the Internet in particular, it has become easier and easier for firms to potentially reach millions of end-users. These end-users can be reached through alternatives ranging from simple discussion forums to online communities [10] in the social media. Correspondingly, the methods of engagement range from simple feedback forms to novel interaction possibilities such as crowdsourcing problems [11, 12] via innovation intermediaries like InnoCentive [13].

Still, not all firms utilize these or other available types of sources even in the high-technology industries. Despite the wide-ranging alternatives, reach, and potential benefits of engaging the end-users online, it is not yet well understood what firm and environmental characteristics affect a firm's propensity to draw knowledge from end-users in order to benefit their innovative activities. Therefore, in this paper we

M.A. Cusumano, B. Iyer, and N. Venkatraman (Eds.): ICSOB 2012, LNBIP 114, pp. 70–78, 2012.

ask: What types of high-technology firms draw knowledge from end-users online for their innovations? We employ data from a survey of the Finnish software industry, and explore a host of firm and environmental factors that may affect the above propensity. We find that firms that are international, operate in hostile environments or have open search strategies are more likely to utilize this knowledge source, whereas device manufacturers, older or larger firms are less likely to do so. Thus, our paper makes a contribution to open innovation literature by increasing our understanding of the open innovation practices and tendencies of firms in a high-tech industry. In particular, we shed light on the types of firms that use knowledge from end-users online to benefit their innovative processes.

The rest of the paper is structured as follows. In chapter 2 we give background for the study and define relevant concepts. In chapter 3 we explain the sample, data, measures and statistical analysis methods. We follow with results and discussion in chapter 4. Chapter 5 ends the paper with concluding remarks.

2 Background

Innovation in general is conventionally defined as "a process that begins with an invention, proceeds with the development of the invention, and results in the introduction of a new product, process or service to the marketplace" [14]. The open innovation framework posits that historically, innovations were concocted in firms' research and development (R&D) departments in "closed" operating models where all knowledge was kept strictly proprietary. This closed operating model for R&D is arguably not sufficient in modern hypercompetitive markets, and thus the concept of "open innovation" was coined by Chesbrough [3, 15, 16]. Open innovation is defined as "the use of purposive inflows and outflows of knowledge to accelerate internal innovation, and expand the markets for external use of innovation, respectively. [It] is a paradigm that assumes that firms can and should use external ideas as well as internal ideas, and internal and external paths to market, as they look to advance their technology" [7]. Thus, in open innovation, the boundaries of the firm become porous, enabling inflows and outflows of knowledge with other relevant external actors. In this study, we concentrate on the inflows of knowledge with which firms seek to benefit their innovative activities.

It must be noted that the above definition of openness in a firm's innovation process is centrally different from a related use, where openness is associated with all information about an innovation being a public good [17]. In this related conception, information about the innovation is thus "freely revealed" and all exclusive intellectual property rights to that information are given up [18, 19]. Innovators can also selectively reveal desired parts of the innovation information [20]. However, in our use of the term, openness only refers to the permeability of a firm's boundaries, while information about the innovations may or may not be kept proprietary between interacting agents.

There are several types of external knowledge sources available for firms to engage, such as suppliers, universities, consultants and even competitors, to name a few. End-users have been regarded as one potentially powerful source of innovation knowledge [8, 9, 21]. Especially the so-called lead users as are deemed to be influential in this regard [8]. Furthermore, the emergence of the Internet as a communication medium with its special characteristics [22] has made millions of end-users potentially accessible to firms. The combination of the special attributes of end-users and the medium may offer special benefits but also challenges for firms.

Previous studies on the external knowledge sources for open innovation have e.g. identified the various factors affecting the openness of a firm's search strategy [23] or openness' performance implications [24]. Studies concentrating on a specific external knowledge source are scarcer, but prior research has examined e.g. industry-university linkages [25]. To our knowledge, no studies have yet examined the specific factors affecting firms' usage of end-users online as an external knowledge source in the open innovation context.

3 Methods

3.1 Sample and Data

To explore which firms utilize end-users online as sources of knowledge for their innovations, we draw data for the analyses from a survey of the Finnish software industry in 2010 [26]. The software industry as a high-technology industry is a fitting setting for this study as firms need to engage in complex problem-solving to accomplish their innovations. Furthermore, the electronic operating medium highly present in the software industry offers opportunities for drawing knowledge from novel external sources and to utilize new external knowledge transfer and problem-solving methods such as crowdsourcing in general or tapping into open source software communities.

The data collection and general results of the survey are explained in greater detail in [26]. In short, the survey targeted all firms in the Finnish software industry, and aimed for the CEO or CTO as the informant. An initial list of 7578 firms was devised with broad oversampling of inactive firms or firms operating in a different industry to ensure appropriate coverage of the industry. The initial list was compiled based on public industry codes and lists from previous runs of the survey. The survey was then conducted in paper and online formats. Non-responding firms were contacted by multiple emails to ensure a response. The survey in paper format was 8 pages long and contained a wealth of questions about various aspects of the firms' offering, operations and structure, in addition to basic questions about the firm and the questions about innovations employed here. In total, 650 complete and 754 partial responses were received. We exclude one-person firms from the following analyses, and thus our subsample contains valid responses from 254 firms.

3.2 Measures

Dependent variable. To measure the extent of firms drawing knowledge for their innovations from end-users online, we utilize a question indicating how important a firm considers this particular source of knowledge to be for their innovation activities. A similar strategy has been used to e.g. measure firm-university relationships [25]. The utilized question is a part of a set of questions surveying the importance of a wide variety of external sources. This set of questions was adopted from the European

Community Innovation Surveys (CIS) that have been frequently utilized in (open) innovation research [24, 25, 27–29]. However, the set was modified to distinctively include end-users online and offline. In the questions, the firm rated the importance of a list of 11 knowledge source alternatives, such as suppliers, competitors, consultants and universities, on a 5-point Likert scale, where 1 indicated no use and 2 to 5 indicated "low importance" to "very important", respectively. For sensitivity analyses, we also employ another variation of the dependent variable, and hence use a dummy variable indicating any utilization of the source (responses from 2 to 5).

Independent variables. We use several independent variables to examine the factors affecting how a firm draws knowledge from end-users online. We constructed two variables reflecting a firm's openness similarly to [24, 25]. These constructs have been used widely in later research, e.g. [30, 31]. Search breadth was constructed by adding up the measures indicating any utilization (responses from 2 to 5) of an external knowledge source in the question set of 11 possible sources mentioned above. Search depth, then again, was constructed by adding up the measures indicating deep utilization (responses from 4 to 5) of an external knowledge source. Responses indicating usage of end-users online as a source were omitted when constructing these variables as it is used as the dependent variable. We also investigate the effects of firm age and size on the propensity to draw knowledge from end-users online. We use a natural logarithm of firm age, and natural logarithm of personnel count as firm size.

Control variables. The firm's internal revenue allocations to R&D may affect the available resources for engaging various external knowledge sources. We thus control for R&D intensity measured by R&D expenditure divided by personnel. Similarly we control for a firm's past performance by including profitability measured by profit divided by revenue as a proxy for firm performance. Although the data is from a single country, a firm's geographic location may influence its habits and possibilities of utilizing external sources, especially in a firm and resource rich environment. We thus control for whether the firm is based in the capital area. Comparably, we control for the firm being international, measured by whether it receives any revenue from abroad. Furthermore, if a firm is using open source software as a part of their offering, they are probably more likely to also draw knowledge from end-users online. We control also for this effect using a dummy variable. Although the data is from a single industry, there are still drastic differences in the firms and their offerings. In the survey, the respondents indicated which of five types their firm mostly is: software product firm, device manufacturer, software project contractor, consulting firm or reseller. We thus use a set of dummy variables to control for different firm types, with software product firm being the omitted category. Finally, in parallel with different types of firms operating in the software industry, we control for environmental dynamism and hostility perceived by these firms as it may affect their propensity to use end-users online for innovation knowledge. We use the environmental dynamism and hostility scales used e.g. in [32] and [33], respectively.

3.3 Statistical Method and Analyses

As the dependent variable is the degree of usage of end-users online as sources of knowledge for innovation, and is a discrete and ordered choice variable, we use an ordered logistic regression to estimate our model. For robustness, we also ran the analyses with an OLS and tobit regression for this dependent variable. We also employed the alternative dependent variable explained above and estimated it using logit and probit regressions. The results remain largely the same, with slight variations discussed in the results section. All analyses were carried out using Stata version 10.1.

Table 1 lists the descriptive statistics and correlations for all the variables used in the study. None of the correlations seem alarmingly high. In general, end-users online are not widely used as a source of knowledge, as indicated by the low to medium mean importance (2.32). It is also apparent that the Finnish software industry is characterized by very small and young firms.

4 Results and Discussion

Table 2 presents the results of the regression analyses for using end-users online as a knowledge source for the firm's innovation. Models 1-3 use the degree of source usage as the dependent variable, and for robustness check models 4 and 5 use the dummy variable of any usage of the source as the dependent variable. Models 1 through 3 employ ordered logistic regression, and for further robustness tobit and OLS regressions, respectively. Models 4 and 5 employ logit and probit regressions.

Because all of the models' variables come from a single self-reported cross-sectional survey, common method variance might be a problem. To investigate this, we used Harman's single factor test [34, 35]. All of the study's variables were entered into an exploratory principal component factor analysis. The analysis retained six distinct factors with the first factor explaining 12.7% of the variance, thus suggesting that common method variance is not of great concern.

In Table 2 we can observe some clear and strong effects across all models on firms' propensity to utilize end-users online as a source of knowledge. We find that device manufacturers tend to use online end-users less. This is likely due to the nature of knowledge available from end-users. Device manufacturing requires specific knowledge from specialized areas that may not be generally available to end-users, and thus firms rely less on them. When a firm pursues open search strategies and is more open especially in terms of breadth, it is also more likely to also use end-users online. The tendency for openness makes firms also utilize knowledge from these novel channels. This result parallels findings from industry-university linkages [25]. If the firm is international, it is more likely to draw knowledge from end-users online. International experience and operations drives the firm to utilize novel means to sustain and develop its competences and capabilities to compete in the global market. Due to the same reasons, a perceived hostile environment seems to make firms make use of end-users online.

Table 1. Descriptive statistics and correlations

	Mean	SD	Min.	Max.	1	2	3	4	5	6	7	8	9	10	11	12	13	14	15
1. Using end-users online	2.32	1.23	1	5															
2. Firm age	2.01	.82	.69	3.78	-.22														
3. Firm size	2.34	1.11	1.1	7.33	-.12	.37													
4. R&D/employee/1000	13.84	18.66	0	110	-.05	.07	.06												
5. Openness breadth	7.67	2.19	0	10	.34	.07	.28	.05											
6. Openness depth	2.99	1.79	0	10	.32	-.08	.1	.12	.5										
7. OSS importance	3	1.51	1	5	.29	-.24	-.1	-.06	.07	.14									
8. Capital area firm	.44	.5	0	1	-.11	.26	.28	.07	0	-.06	-.07								
9. Firm: Devices	.04	.18	0	1	-.01	-.01	.04	-.01	.07	.1	-.01	-.02							
10. Firm: Project contractor	.4	.49	0	1	.1	-.11	.05	-.05	.01	-.07	.14	-.1	-.1						
11. Firm: Consulting	.08	.27	0	1	-.04	-.09	-.24	0	-.12	0	.06	-.06	-.06	-.23					
12. Firm: Reseller	.03	.18	0	1	-.09	-.01	0	-.01	-.02	-.04	-.15	-.02	-.02	-.09	-.06				
13. Revenue from abroad	.48	.5	0	1	.06	.16	.26	.05	.14	.07	-.05	.16	.12	-.08	-.02	.02			
14. Environmental dynamism	2.76	.57	1.2	5	-.17	.11	-.03	.09	-.04	0	-.19	-.04	.04	-.09	.09	-.03	.05		
15. Environmental hostility	2.85	.6	1	4.8	.18	-.11	-.05	-.08	.03	.04	.12	-.03	.01	-.04	-.01	.1	-.05	-.28	
16. Firm performance	0.00	0.46	-4.04	0.84	-0.01	0.02	-0.08	0.02	-0.16	-0.07	-0.05	-0.10	-0.03	0.08	0.10	0.00	-0.03	0.10	-0.11

Some effects seem to be apparent in the models 1 through 3, but disappear in the robustness check models 4 and 5. First, an interesting result is with firm size. Larger firms seem to utilize end-users online less than smaller firms. This effect is likely due to the commitment and resource constraints relaxed by e.g. nature of the medium used to engage this particular knowledge source, when compared to others. As firms need to engage external sources of knowledge to accomplish their innovations, sources that can be easily utilized and have a high perceived cost to benefit ratio become attractive. Engaging end-users online is relatively easy due to the familiar operating medium for software firms, the medium's speed and cost-effectiveness, lack of required commitment and the source's potential to access masses of end-users. Similar effect is observed with age. Younger firms may be more aware of this relatively fresh knowledge source, and also more willing and able to engage it. Finally, depth of a firm's search strategy seems to have a slight positive effect. The rest of the variables do not seem to have an effect on the firms' propensity to draw knowledge from end-users online.

Table 2. Results of regression analyses for using end-users online as a knowledge source

Variable	Model 1	Model 2	Model 3	Model 4	Model 5
Firm age	-0.30*	-0.19*	-0.19**	-0.26	-0.16
Firm size	-0.27**	-0.17**	-0.16**	-0.20	-0.12
R&D/employee/1000	0.00	0.00	0.00	-0.00	-0.00
Openness breadth	0.35***	0.16***	0.15***	0.51***	0.31***
Openness depth	0.12*	0.08*	0.08*	0.04	0.02
OSS importance	0.16*	0.08	0.08	0.11	0.06
Capital area firm	-0.22	-0.18	-0.16	-0.36	-0.21
Firm: Devices	-2.49***	-1.35***	-1.31***	-2.20**	-1.31**
Firm: Project contractor	0.32	0.24	0.22	0.51	0.35
Firm: Consulting	0.09	0.11	0.09	0.14	0.10
Firm: Reseller	-0.75	-0.32	-0.31	-1.05	-0.63
Revenue from abroad	0.77***	0.37**	0.37**	0.94***	0.55***
Environmental dynamism	-0.26	-0.11	-0.12	-0.42	-0.24
Environmental hostility	0.39*	0.23*	0.22*	0.72**	0.44**
Firm performance	-0.02	-0.03	0.01	0.29	0.12
Observations	254	254	254	254	254
R^2			.259		
Pseudo R^2	.114	.090		.243	.244

* $p < 0.10$, ** $p < 0.05$, *** $p < 0.01$

5 Conclusions

In this paper we have started to explore the firm and contingency characteristics that affect high-technology firms' propensity to draw knowledge from end-users online to benefit their innovations. Utilizing data from a survey of the Finnish software industry, we found strong evidence that openness in terms of breadth in the firm's search strategy, the firm being international and it operating in a hostile environment all contribute positively to the likelihood of a firm drawing knowledge from end-users online. Device manufacturers were found less likely to do this. In addition, evidence was found that firms that are smaller, younger and have deeper open search strategies are more likely to utilize end-users online.

Several limitations apply to this study. As this is an exploratory study, in the short theoretical background examination literature was not extensively reviewed to develop testable hypotheses. This is something to be taken upon by further research. In addition, the study employed data from a single country and a single industry. Further research could expand these considerations to data on other industries and countries to give a richer view of the characteristics of firms and other contingencies that affect firms drawing innovation knowledge from end-users online.

References

1. Henderson, R.M., Clark, K.B.: Architectural innovation: The reconfiguration of existing product technologies and the failure of established firms. Administrative Science Quarterly 35, 9–30 (1990)
2. Cohen, W.M., Levinthal, D.A.: Absorptive capacity: A new perspective on learning and innovation. Administrative Science Quarterly 35, 128–152 (1990)
3. Chesbrough, H.W.: Open Innovation: The New Imperative for Creating and Profiting from Technology. Harvard Business School Press, Boston (2003)
4. Katila, R., Ahuja, G.: Something old, something new: A longitudinal study of search behavior and new product introduction. Academy of Management Journal 45, 1183–1194 (2002)
5. Cassiman, B., Veugelers, R.: In search of complementarity in innovation strategy: Internal R&D and external knowledge acquisition. Management Science 52, 68–82 (2006)
6. King, A.A., Lakhani, K.R.: The contingent effect of absorptive capacity: An open innovation analysis. Harvard Business School Working Paper (2012)
7. Chesbrough, H.W.: Open innovation: A new paradigm for understanding industrial innovation. In: Chesbrough, H.W., Vanhaverbeke, W., West, J. (eds.) Open Innovation: Researching a New Paradigm, pp. 1–14. Oxford University Press, New York (2006)
8. von Hippel, E.: Lead users: A source of novel product concepts. Management Science 32, 791–805 (1986)
9. von Hippel, E.: The Sources of Innovation. Oxford University Press, New York (1988)
10. von Hippel, E.: Innovation by user communities: Learning from open-source software. MIT Sloan Management Review 42, 82–86 (2001)
11. Howe, J.: The rise of crowdsourcing (2006), `http://www.wired.com/wired/archive/14.06/crowds.html`
12. Afuah, A., Tucci, C.L.: Crowdsourcing as a solution to distant search. Academy of Management Review 37 (2012)
13. Pisano, G.P., Verganti, R.: Which kind of collaboration is right for you? Harvard Business Review 86, 78–86 (2008)
14. Edwards, K.L., Gordon, T.J.: Characterization of Innovations Introduced on the U.S. Market in 1982. The Futures Group and U.S. Small Business Administration, Washington, DC (1984)

15. Chesbrough, H.W.: The era of open innovation. MIT Sloan Management Review 44, 35–41 (2003)
16. Chesbrough, H.W.: The logic of open innovation: Managing intellectual property. California Management Review 45, 33–58 (2003)
17. Baldwin, C.Y., von Hippel, E.: Modeling a paradigm shift: From producer innovation to user and open collaborative innovation. Organization Science 22, 1399–1417 (2011)
18. Harhoff, D., Henkel, J., von Hippel, E.: Profiting from voluntary information spillovers: How users benefit by freely revealing their innovations. Research Policy 32, 1753–1769 (2003)
19. von Hippel, E., von Krogh, G.: Free revealing and the private-collective model for innovation incentives. R&D Management 36, 295–306 (2006)
20. Henkel, J.: Selective revealing in open innovation processes: The case of embedded Linux. Research Policy 35, 953–969 (2006)
21. von Hippel, E.: Democratizing Innovation. MIT Press, Cambridge (2005)
22. Afuah, A.: Redefining firm boundaries in the face of the Internet: Are firms really shrinking? Academy of Management Review 28, 34–53 (2003)
23. Lichtenthaler, U.: Open innovation in practice: An analysis of strategic approaches to technology transactions. IEEE Transactions on Engineering Management 55, 148–157 (2008)
24. Laursen, K., Salter, A.: Open for innovation: The role of openness in explaining innovation performance among U.K. manufacturing firms. Strategic Management Journal 27, 131–150 (2006)
25. Laursen, K., Salter, A.: Searching high and low: What types of firms use universities as a source of innovation? Research Policy 33, 1201–1215 (2004)
26. Rönkkö, M., Ylitalo, J., Peltonen, J., Parkkila, K., Valtakoski, A., Koivisto, N., Alanen, L., Mutanen, O.-P.: Software Industry Survey 2010, Espoo, Finland (2010), http://www.softwareindustrysurvey.org/ReportFinland2010.pdf
27. Leiponen, A., Helfat, C.E.: Innovation objectives, knowledge sources, and the benefits of breadth. Strategic Management Journal 31, 224–236 (2010)
28. Leiponen, A., Helfat, C.E.: Location, decentralization, and knowledge sources for innovation. Organization Science 22, 641–658 (2011)
29. Mol, M.J., Birkinshaw, J.: The sources of management innovation: When firms introduce new management practices. Journal of Business Research 62, 1269–1280 (2009)
30. Chiang, Y.-H., Hung, K.-P.: Exploring open search strategies and perceived innovation performance from the perspective of inter-organizational knowledge flows. R&D Management 40, 292–299 (2010)
31. Keupp, M.M., Gassmann, O.: Determinants and archetype users of open innovation. R&D Management 39, 331–341 (2009)
32. Miller, D., Dröge, C.: Psychological and traditional determinants of structure. Administrative Science Quarterly 31, 539–560 (1986)
33. Slevin, D.P., Covin, J.G.: Strategy formation patterns, performance, and the significance of context. Journal of Management 23, 189–209 (1997)
34. Podsakoff, P.M., Organ, D.W.: Self-reports in organizational research: Problems and prospects. Journal of Management 12, 531–544 (1986)
35. Podsakoff, P.M., MacKenzie, S.B., Lee, J.-Y., Podsakoff, N.P.: Common method biases in behavioral research: A critical review of the literature and recommended remedies. Journal of Applied Psychology 88, 879–903 (2003)

Comparison of Visual Business Modeling Techniques for Software Companies

Garm Lucassen, Sjaak Brinkkemper, Slinger Jansen, and Eko Handoyo

Department of Information and Computing Sciences, Utrecht University,
Princetonplein 5, 3584 CC Utrecht The Netherlands
{g.lucassen,s.brinkkemper,slinger.jansen,eko.handoyo}@uu.nl

Abstract. Despite the widespread adoption of business modeling techniques in academic research and business, no research has been done into how efficient and effective business modeling techniques document and communicate business models. This paper compares three visual business modeling techniques with a visual approach and identifies the strong and weak points of each modeling technique, based on applying the techniques to three startups and interviews with industry experts. With this comparison, visual business modeling technique developers can improve their own techniques and software companies can determine which technique to apply in their specific case.

Keywords: Visual Business Modeling Techniques, Software Business Models, Software Business Analysis.

1 Introduction

According to Gordijn, Akkermans and van Vliet[1], a business model presents the business essentials of the business case to be developed and is seen as a first step in requirements engineering for any e-commerce information systems. Based on an elaborate literature study of business model definitions, Osterwalder et al. [3] defined the term business model as:

"A conceptual tool that contains a set of elements and their relationships and allows expressing the business logic of a specific firm. It is a de- scription of the value a company offers to one or several segments of customers and of the architecture of the firm and its network of partners for creating, marketing, and delivering this value and relationship capital, to generate profitable and sustainable revenue streams."

In order to create business models, dozens of scientists have done research into universally applicable techniques. In the past ten years this has resulted in as many different techniques with varied approaches and results [1,4,5,6,7,8,9,10,11,12]. But it was not until the introduction of Osterwalder's business modeling ontology [12] and corresponding book [2] that business models have become a frequently discussed topic and widely adapted tool in science and all forms of

M.A. Cusumano, B. Iyer, and N. Venkatraman (Eds.): ICSOB 2012, LNBIP 114, pp. 79–93, 2012.

business. According to Google Scholar, Osterwalder's thesis outlining the business modeling ontology has been cited 475 times to date. Furthermore, the Business Model Canvas is currently being deployed by larger consultancy firms. All technique creators argue that they have identified essential concepts which any given business model is made up of. It can be argued that no single business modeling technique successfully reached this goal. All techniques take widely diverging approaches, none of which have been fully accepted in business nor academics. Of all these techniques, some provide visual elements that can be used to create a business model, we refer to these as *visual business modeling techniques*. Three visual business modeling techniques: The Business Model Canvas [2], Software Ecosystem Model [4] and Board of Innovation [5] will be studied in this paper. We expect that these techniques are more effective and efficient when communicating the business models than non-visual business modeling techniques.

Yet, despite the widespread adaption of the Business Model Canvas, no research has been done into how effectively and efficiently different business modeling techniques document and communicate business models. In this paper we address this hiatus by asking the research question "What business modeling technique documents and communicates the business model of a software business most effectively and efficiently?". In section 2 the research method we used to formulate an answer to this question is introduced. Section 3 will identify the required concepts that modeling techniques should include. Following, section 4 introduces the business modeling techniques that will be examined in this paper more elaborately. Section 5 compares the aforementioned techniques' conceptual adherence to a list of requirements based on literature research and documenting and communicating effectiveness and efficiency based on application of the business modeling techniques to three software start-ups and interviews with industry experts. In this context effectiveness is regarded as to what extent the business modeling technique successfully captures and communicates the entirety of the business model, whereas efficiency is defined as how flexible and adaptable the business model capturing process is and how comprehensible and explicit all modeled information is communicated to the reader. To conclude, in section 6 the (dis)advantages extracted from the comparison of each model will be discussed and compared in order to formulate the recommended approach. The paper ends with a conclusion and future research possibilities in section 7.

2 Research Method

In this research several visual business modeling techniques (BMTs) are discussed and compared. In order to be able to generate a scientifically accountable list of requirements a literature study was conducted. Google Scholar and ACM Digital Library searches were performed with combinations of *business model, business modeling, technique, e-business,* as keywords. Business model definitions based on 16 authors and 10 relevant modeling techniques were accumulated this way. Furthermore, the studied BMTs were applied to three high-tech startups in order to investigate the effectiveness and efficiency of the documenting process. This part of the research was conducted using Yin's case study method [13]. First the startups were modeled based on information extracted from the products. Afterwards a meeting with a founder of the startups took place where the modeling process was repeated. Upon completion the models were compared and discussed with the entrepreneur. Ultimately the digital models were redesigned and confirmed by the entrepreneurs via email. Last but not least, structured interviews with industry experts consisting of six (ex-)entrepreneurs, two network partners and one venture capitalist were conducted in order to examine the effectiveness and efficiency of communicating the business models. The experts were asked what concepts they saw as essential, to evaluate several business models presented in each BMT, discuss (dis)advantages and articulate their preferred technique. After conducting the interviews and startup modeling lists of (dis)advantages were extracted within 24 hours of the interviews.

3 Identification of Core Concepts

Osterwalder's definition of business models [3] as presented in the introduction corresponds with our perception of business models and contains the foundation of what concepts we expect the BMTs to include:

1. Customer Value Proposition
2. Partnerships
3. Architecture of the firm
4. Revenue streams
5. Logic of earning money

To confirm whether this list of concepts is still viable, we reiterated upon Shafer et al.'s [14] research into essential business model concepts for business modeling techniques. In the paper, 12 business model definitions in academic articles, originating between 1998-2002, are dissected in order to find one list of essential business model concepts. We reiterated upon this study in Table 1 by adding 4 more definitions by different authors between 2000-2008 [7,8,9,15]. Among these definitions, 9 concepts were observed significantly more frequently than others. Descriptions of these concepts can be found in Table 2.

1. Customer
2. Value Proposition
3. Revenue
4. Costs
5. Activities
6. Partners
7. Distribution Channels
8. Resources
9. Competencies

When applied to software companies, two of these concepts are considered unnecessary. First, analysis of business models made with the Business Model Canvas revealed that the most important resources are the result of activities of the company. Explicitly specifying resources displays redundant information to the reader. Secondly, information concerning competencies compared to the

Table 1. All observed concepts

Concepts	Timmers (1998)	Hamel (2000)	Linder and Cantrell (2000)	Afuah and Tucci (2001)	Amit and Zott (2001)	Weil and Vitale (2001)	Dubosson-Torbay et al. (2002)	Margretta (2002)	Rayport and Jaworski (2002)	Van Der Vorst et al. (2002)	Hoque (2002)	Chesbrough (2003)	Hedman and Kalling (2003)	Morris et al. (2003)	Osterwalder et al. (2004)	Johnson et al. (2008)	Total
Customer		X		X			X	X	X		X	X		X	X	X	10
Partners & Channels	X	X	X			X	X			X	X	X	X		X		10
Revenue/pricing	X	X	X	X			X				X	X		X	X	X	10
Value Proposition			X	X			X	X	X	X		X		X	X	X	10
Activities		X	X	X			X			X			X		X	X	8
Competencies		X		X	X		X						X	X	X		7
Cost			X				X	X				X		X	X	X	7
Resources/assets		X			X		X		X		X		X			X	7
Strategy		X	X								X	X					4
Customer relationship		X					X								X		3
Differentiation		X									X			X			3
Information flows	X				X	X											3
Output (offering)					X				X				X				3
Product/service flows	X				X	X											3
Branding							X				X						2
Competitors									X				X				2
Create value					X									X			2
Customer information		X					X										2
Financial aspects							X		X								2
Management													X	X			2
Mission		X									X						2
Profit							X	X									2
Business opportunities					X												1
Cash flows						X											1
Culture											X						1
Customer benefits									X								1
Customer interface		X															1
Economic logic								X									1
Environment											X						1
Firm identity											X						1
Firm reputation											X						1
Fulfillment and support		X															1
Functionalities										X							1
Implementation				X													1
Infrastructure-applications										X							1
Infrastructure-management							X										1
Product innovation							X										1
Specific characteristics										X							1
Sustainability				X													1
Transaction content					X												1
Transaction governance					X												1
Transaction structure					X												1

competitors does not fit the scope of a business model. A business model specifically provides information about the business being studied. Not its competitors. Considering that Osterwalder's definition includes all 7 remaining concepts, we conclude that his definition is viable for the scope of our research.

However, interviews with industry experts identified only 4 essential concepts that are relevant in their position. They mainly use business models to communicate the business its potential to investors in a visually pleasing way. In order to reach this goal a wide variety of concepts that should be included were identified, varying between backgrounds, experience with BMTs and role specific needs. After extensive analysis of recordings of all interviews, 4 concepts were found to be essential: (1) Value proposition, (2) Identification of customers, (3) Logic of earning money, consisting of costs and revenues in concrete figures and (4) Activities. These concepts encapsulate the diversifying aspects of a business, which are the defining factors for investors according to the experts. These required concepts conform to the concepts identified by the literature study excluding channels and partners. Although experts acknowledged that channels and partners are important, they were deemed inessential due to their often replaceable nature and limited added value when communicating a unique value proposition.

In order to effectively compare all BMTs in section 5, one uniform list of required concepts needs to be formulated. The five concepts identified through interviews with experts and supported by the literature study form the foundation. All BMTs include partners and two out of three BMTs include channels in their approach extensively. Not including channels and partners in the comparison would mitigate the use of both the Software Ecosystem Model and Board of Innovation extensively. Therefore, both channels and partners are added. The final list of required concepts, shown in Table 2, effectively mirrors the 7 concepts identified in the literature study.

Table 2. Final list of required concepts for visual business modeling techniques

Concepts	Description
Customer	Which customer segments are targeted? [16]
Value proposition	What bundle of products and services creates value for a specific customer segment? [12]
Revenue	How much money can be made by price x volume? [8]
Partners	Who are the partners that provide the key resources to the company? [13]
Activities	What makes the profitable delivery of the value proposition repeatable and scalable? [8]
Resources	What are the most important assets required to make the business model work? [13]
Costs	How are costs allocated? [8]

4 Introduction of Business Modeling Techniques

In this section three BMTs will be introduced by discussing their approach. Specifically visual business modeling techniques were used for this research because the resulting models incorporate visually distinguishable elements that facilitate easy and fast communication of the business model. More specifically these three techniques were selected because of three different factors. The Business Model Canvas was chosen because of its widespread acceptance among business and academics. The Software Ecosystem Model is used in several courses and developed at Utrecht University, where this study took place. Lastly, the Board of Innovation was adopted because it is the latest visual BMT and generating publicity quickly.

Business Model Canvas [2] is derived from Osterwalder et al.'s research [12] into a business model ontology. His research identified four areas with nine building blocks that a business model should address to create a complete visual representation which displays the links between all business segments. Modeling starts on the right side of the canvas by clearly formulating the customer and value proposition. The remaining seven building blocks, consisting of Key Partners, Key Activities, Key Resources, Customer Relationships, Channels, Revenue Streams and Cost Structure, are derived from the needs and requirements of the customer segments and value proposition. Figure 1 in the next section provides an example of a completed Business Model Canvas.

Software Ecosystem Model [4] is based on Weil and Vitale's supply networks [16] and specifically aimed at modeling product software businesses. The approach combines two models. (1) A Product Deployment Context (PDC) provides a simple, quick overview of the architecture and dependencies of a software product in its running environment by describing the context in which the product operates. The stacking order of the elements defines the hierarchy between different products and components. (2) The accompanying Software Supply Network (SSN) displays all parties that facilitate the company to provide a value adding product. The diagram shows asset, knowledge and software transactions between the different parties in the company's network. Examples of both the SSN and PDC are shown in Figure 2 in the next section. Modeling starts by defining all entities and flows. Company of interest, customers, potential intermediaries are connected by product, service, finance and content transactions between the entities. Afterwards all suppliers are listed and transactions with the company of interest added. Based on the list of suppliers the PDC is modeled of how the technology of the product is made up.

Board of Innovation [5] is a technique that aims to provide users an easy way to create a visual representation of transactions within any company. The scope of this technique is limited to visually representing concrete activities and asset transaction that take place in the context of the business. Intangible information such as customer relationships, positioning and strategy are left out. By using 16 distinctive icons a comprehensive image of the business model takes shape. 6 Actor icons represent the business, companies and suppliers in the value network, consumers, non-profits and government. The 10 remaining icons represent product, service, experience, exposure, reputation, money, less money, data, right and credit transactions. Icons can easily be moved around to facilitate business model innovation. The Board of Innovation is used as a whiteboard kit with magnets that represent the actors and transactions. Modeling starts by identifying all actors in the ecosystem, followed by defining the initial transaction with the customer. Afterwards all transactions with suppliers, partners and stakeholders related to the initial transaction are added. An example is presented in Figure 3 in the next section.

5 Comparison of Business Modeling Techniques

This section will compare the BMTs introduced in the previous section. First we will research whether the BMTs theoretically include all required concepts introduced in section 3. Afterwards, an assessment will be done concerning to what extent the required concepts are effectively and efficiently communicated and documented based on experiences with the documenting process of three software startups and interviews with industry experts. The next section will present the recommended BMT based on (dis)advantages of each technique, which are in turn based on the findings of this section.

5.1 Comparison on Concepts

As seen in Figure 1 the Business Model Canvas explicitly provides segments for each required concept. The technique also includes key resources, which we considered to be inessential in section 3 because it displays redundant information. In this example you can see that all the resources can be derived from the key activities segment. Thanks to the flexibility of this technique redundant segments, such as key resources, can be ignored when necessary.

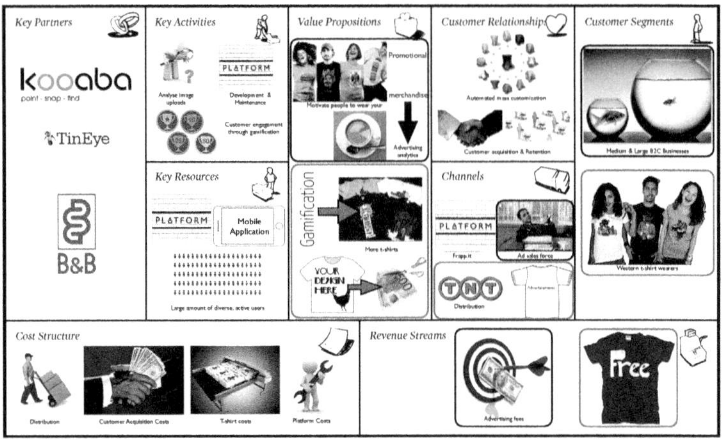

Fig. 1. Business Model Canvas - Software Startup 1

Figure 2 shows an example of a Software Ecosystem Model for a fictitious software company. The SSN uses light (yellow) and dark (orange) labels for customers and suppliers respectively. Transaction flows with labels map the value proposition, cost and revenue. Internal processes and activities are not explicitly identified, instead the model exclusively focuses on the product by modeling what architectural elements the product comprises of in the PDC. Channels are occasionally included when the customer is reached through an intermediary, but more often than not the model assumes customers are being reached without specifying how.

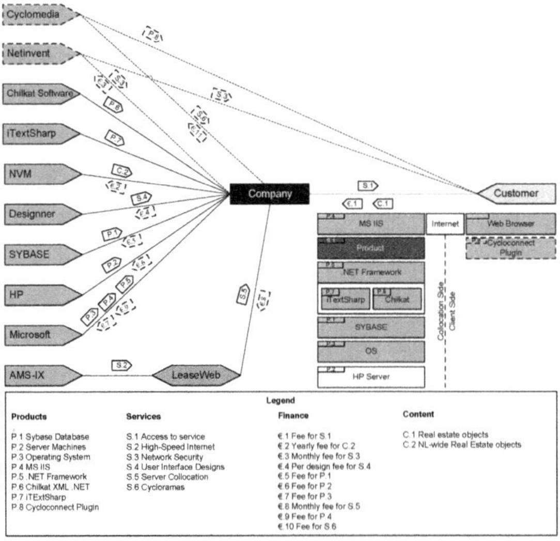

Fig. 2. SSN & PDC - Example Software Company [17]

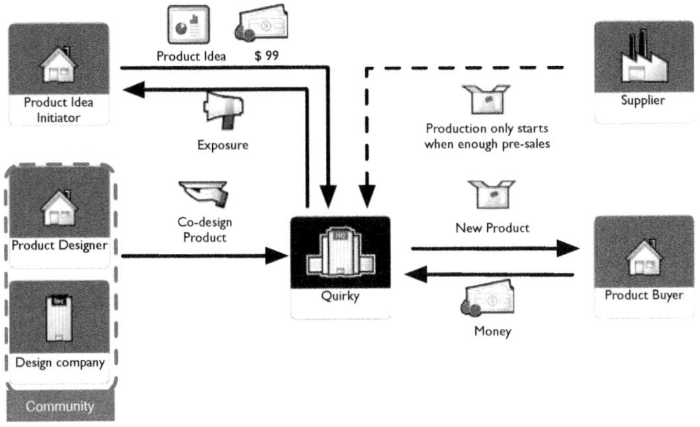

Fig. 3. Board of Innovation - Quirky [5]

The Board of Innovation uses distinct icons clarified by text to identify between different types of customers and partners. Flows with transactions represented by smaller icons model the value proposition, processes, activities and revenue flows. Costs are left out, although including them is possible. The model assumes customers are reached without concretely specifying how, as can be seen in Figure 3.

5.2 Effectiveness and Efficiency Comparison

As mentioned in the introduction, in the context of this research effectiveness is regarded as to what extent the business modeling technique successfully communicates and captures the entirety of the business model. Efficiency, on the other hand, is defined as how comprehensible and explicit all modeled information is communicated to the reader and how flexible and adaptable the business model capturing process is. To be able to effectively assess these four aspects, each is broken down into a number of elements that will be compared. Both definitions and all elements were extracted from the interviews with industry experts.

Communicating effectiveness

1. **Acceptance:** of the technique in business and academics.
2. **Internal Cohesion:** the elements of the model are related to one another.
3. **Number Concreteness:** concrete numbers are shown in the model.

Capturing effectiveness

1. **Explicit Modeling Method:** instructions explicitly defining the approach are provided.
2. **Method Efficacy:** instructions are easily translated into practice.
3. **Absence of Redundancy**, the resulting models contain no redundant information.

Communicating efficiency

1. **Accessibility and Understandability:** accessible and understandable at first encounter of a model resulting from the modeling technique.
2. **Value Proposition**, External Process, Internal Process, Transaction and Partner Explicitness: explicit representation of aforementioned elements in the model.

Capturing efficiency

1. **Evolvability:** modeling approach can be changed without redesigning the entire approach.
2. **Flexibility:** inclusion of concepts can be adapted to the modeler's needs.

With the evaluation of the preceding section in mind, we expect the Board of Innovation and Software Ecosystem Model will be least effective and efficient in documenting and communicating business models of software companies, whereas the Business Model Canvas will have a negligible amount of complications.

Business Model Canvas. Modeling the startups appeared to be easy thanks to the collaborative, iterative and segmented style of the business Model Canvas. In practice modelers struggled with the individual segments and considered them unclear concepts. The provided discussion questions for each segment that are supposed to provide thinking guidelines turned out to be a double edged sword. More often than not the questions lead to considering the segment completed after answering the questions or provoking discussion on semantics of the segments instead of the segments themselves. Moreover, although including arrows is encouraged in order to clarify relationships between segments this often results in cluttered models with reduced communication value. Lastly, it is difficult to determine when a model is satisfyingly correct and/or complete thanks to the flexibility of the technique. Regardless of these inconveniences all entrepreneurs preferred the Business Model Canvas for documenting the business model because it contained the most explicit information on both tangible and intangible aspects of the business and communicated the information in a highly accessible manner.

Opinions regarding communicating effectiveness and efficiency were varied among industry experts. Most stated the Business Model Canvas is a great tool because it provokes modelers to actively think about all required aspects of a business model and has a strong emphasis on clearly communicating the value proposition. At the same time they thought the technique still had room for improvement when it comes to explicitly presenting crucial aspects of business models. Instead of using vague, general terms such as customer retention and acquisition, segments should clarify how the business aims to achieve these goals. Furthermore, although the Business Model Canvas identifies the cost factors, revenue streams, key partners and key activities, no information is given on concrete figures of costs factors and revenue streams, what the role of these partners is, nor what concrete processes the key activities entail. According to the experts this information is crucial to communicate the differentiating factors of the business. Lastly, the experts stated that the ambiguous discussion questions lead to a confusing documenting process. One entrepreneur experienced with using the technique in project groups reiterated that many people resort to strictly filling in the discussion questions. Seven out of eight experts preferred the Business Model Canvas for their communication needs, although three out of seven stressed that it was important to include a process focused model such as the Board of Innovation.

Software Ecosystem Model. Modeling the startups on a whiteboard was easy compared to the digital modeling process. The Software Ecosystem Model comes with templates for use with modeling software such as Microsoft Visio or Omnigraffle, which do not facilitate automatically formatting the individual elements. Instead these software products require modelers to carefully align every single element by hand, resulting in a large amount of tedious tasks. Moreover, whenever changes are necessary to maintain an up to date model, all numbers on the labels and in the legend need to be changed manually. This discourages keeping the model current and results in a particularly painful modeling experience. Furthermore, although modelers are instructed to include *all* software suppliers, the questions was raised to what extent *all* reaches. Software products which are built with Ruby, should theoretically include 31 gems by 21 different developers when deploying the core Ruby on Rails framework. Including all the tiniest suppliers will inevitably lead to a confusing SSN, cluttered by dozens of suppliers. Regardless of these inconveniences, the main objection for the entrepreneurs not to prefer this model was its incapability of including intangible elements of a business such as good-will, status or customer relationships. Last but not least is the high level of entry for non-technical modelers. Without extensive technical knowledge the model turned out to be inapplicable.

All experts considered the Software Ecosystem Model to be ineffective and inefficient at communicating a business model. Although the extensive inclusion of supplier details received praise, the model was deemed too technical, inaccessible and unattractive to be used as a communication tool towards potential investors. All experts said that they were not provoked to study the transactions due to the use of text instead of images. Moreover the priority of suppliers was impossible to discern because their transactions are not linked to the customer, caused by the congregating lines at both sides of the model. Another implication of this disadvantage is that internal software and business logic can not be included, which the entrepreneurs regard as an essential concept as identified in section 3. Similar to the Business Model Canvas no concrete figures or profitability estimates are provided. One entrepreneur with extensive experience with this technique did mention that the Software Ecosystem Model is the only technique that is capable of effectively communicating money flow nuances such as the difference between kick-back fees and license fees.

Board of Innovation. Modeling the startups was easy because of concrete guidelines as to what information is expected to be included. Moreover the whiteboard kit that facilitates collaboration was considered to be particularly useful when discussing details of the company with colleagues. On the other hand, entrepreneurs regarded the model to be too simplistic for extensive internal briefing on the business due to its lack of freedom concerning intangible elements. Equivalent to the Software Ecosystem Model, this was the main objection for the entrepreneurs not to prefer this model.

Expert opinions on the Board of Innovation were divided in two camps. Half of the experts appreciated the clear, synoptic approach and lauded the technique's inclusion of strictly essential aspects. The other half claimed the presented models were *too* simplistic while still requiring to be extensively studied to completely understand the business model and discover what aspects are essential. A frustration all experts agreed on was that the relation between transactions of different actors was unclear. Again, missing information on core internal activities was a source of criticism.

6 Discussion of Advantages and Disadvantages

Table 3 was created by assessing the (dis)advantages identified in the preceding section for each element introduced in section 5.2. Considering the results of the theoretical comparison of BMTs and preference of entrepreneurs and industry experts we expected the Business Model Canvas to have a negligible amount of disadvantages in comparison with the Software Ecosystem Model and Board of Innovation. Although the Business Model Canvas is the strongest BMT when it comes to communicating effectiveness and capturing efficiency, the Board of Innovation is superior in efficiently communicating and effectively capturing a business model. Moreover the Board of Innovation has a larger absolute number of positive aspects (7 versus 10). Therefore, we were inclined to think that the Board of Innovation is the most effective and efficient BMT.

However, industry experts specifically stressed that the most important aspect of a BMT is to be able to include all differentiating factors of a business and effectively communicate those factors to potential investors. This are the exact aspects the Business Model Canvas accomplishes best, while the Board of Innovation has a weaker approach. Furthermore, all negative aspects of the capturing effectiveness are caused by the ambiguous guidelines presented in the handbook. These aspects can easily be improved by explicating what is expected of the modeler, providing concrete modeling guidelines and updating the examples to include more explicit information. Although this simultaneously solves the partner inexplicitness and number inconcreteness, explicit process information remains absent. This is where the Board of Innovation comes in. The flexibility allows modelers to painlessly incorporate internal processes by modeling the internal logic in a large business icon, perfectly complementing the Business Model Canvas. In practice the Business Model Canvas can then be used as a first, general overview, while the Board of Innovation provides a more elaborate insight concerning role of the partners, the internal and external processes of the business. What BMT is best applicable in a specific use case depends on

Table 3. Comparison of all business modeling techniques

			Business Modeling Techniques		
			BMC	**SEM**	**BoI**
Effectiveness	Communicating	Acceptance	+ +	- -	0
		Internal Cohesion	+	-	-
		Number Concreteness	-	- -	-
	Capturing	Explicit Modeling Method	-	+ +	+ +
		Method Efficacy	- -	- -	+ +
		Absence of Redundancy	-	+ +	+ +
Efficiency	Communicating	Accessibility and Understandability	+	-	+ +
		Value Proposition Explicitness	+ +	+	+ +
		External Process Explicitness	-	+ +	+ +
		Internal Process Explicitness	- -	- -	- -
		Transaction Explicitness	+	+	+
		Partner Explicitness	-	+ +	+ +
	Capturing	Evolvability	+ +	- -	+ +
		Flexibility	+ +	- -	-

Legend: + + Perfect; + Acceptable; 0 Neutral; - Suboptimal; - - Unusable

the working context, but with the knowledge presented in this section we recommend modelers to adopt both the Business Model Canvas and the Board of Innovation when modeling a software business.

7 Conclusions and Future Work

This paper discussed the effectiveness and efficiency of three visual business modeling techniques and presented concrete advantages and disadvantages of each technique. After conducting a literature study and interviews with experts a list of seven essential concepts was identified which each technique should include in their framework. Based on theoretical inclusion of the essential concepts we expected the Business Model Canvas to be most effective and efficient at communicating and documenting business models, whereas the Software Ecosystem Model and the Board of Innovation were expected to garner a considerable amount of criticism.

The documenting process and interviews with experts concerning communication of the business modeling techniques revealed that the Business Model Canvas is the preferred method because it effectively models explicit information of both tangible and intangible aspects of the business and communicates this information in a highly accessible manner to parties unfamiliar with the modeling technique. However the technique still has room for improvement concerning its unclear modeling process and inexplicit representation of certain crucial aspects, such as the provided discussion questions and how to determine when a model is satisfyingly correct. The heaviest criticism was reserved for the Software Ecosystem Model, which was considered unpractical to work with, too technical for non-technical readers and to produce unattractive and inaccessible business models. The Board of Innovation, on the other hand, received acclaim for its pleasant documenting process. Half of the experts praised the clear, synoptic modeling approach which results in accessible and efficient models. However, the other half of the experts considered the resulting models to be too simplistic for most of their needs. In the discussion we analyzed the strong and weak points of each technique and concluded that the Business Model Canvas is the most effective communicating and efficient documenting technique because of its acceptance and internal cohesion, and evolvability and flexibility respectively. These aspects are considered to be the most important aspect of a business modeling technique by the industry experts. The Board of Innovation is considered as the most effective documenting and efficient communicating technique due to its extremely simple approach when both capturing and modeling. The Business Model Canvas and Board of Innovation complement each other on communication of the entire business model. This resulted in the recommendation of adopting both business modeling techniques when modeling a software business.

Future work includes validating the (dis)advantages through quantitative research consisting of more case studies and interviews with experts. Furthermore improvements based on the identified (dis)advantages need to be incorporated into the business modeling techniques. For example, the Software Ecosystem Model requires a complete overhaul of the modeling approach and a graphical redesign in order to become relevant and accessible for non-technical readers.

References

1. Gordijn, J., Akkermans, H.: Designing and Evaluating E-business Models. IEEE Intelligent Systems 16, 11–17 (2001)
2. Osterwalder, A.: Business Model Generation: A Handbook for Visionaries, Game Changers, and Challengers. Wiley, Hoboken (2010)
3. Osterwalder, A., Pigneur, Y., Tucci, C.L.: Clarifying Business Models: Origins, Present and Future of the Concept. Communications of the Association for Information Science 16, 1–25 (2005)
4. Brinkkemper, S., Soest, I., Jansen, S.: Modeling of Product Software Businesses: Investigation into Industry Product and Channel Typologies. In: 16th International Conference on Information Systems Development, pp. 307–325. Springer, Boston (2009)
5. de Mey, N., de Ridder, P.: Board of Innovation, `http://www.boardofinnovation.com`

6. Chesbrough, H., Rosenbloom, R.S.: The role of the business model in capturing value from innovation: evidence from Xerox Corporation's technology spin off companies. Industrial and Corporate Change 1, 529–555 (2002)
7. Morris, M., Schindehutte, M., Allen, J.: The Entrepreneur's Business Model: Toward a Unified Perspective. Journal of Business Research 58, 726–735 (2005)
8. Johnson, M.W., Christensen, C.M., Kagermann, H.: Reinventing Your Business Model. Harvard Business Review 12, 50–59 (2008)
9. Linder, J., Cantrell, S.: Changing Business Models: Surveying the Landscape. Accenture Institute for Strategic Change, Cambridge (2000)
10. Lagha, S.B., Osterwalder, A., Pigneur, Y.: Modeling e-business with eBM. In: 5th International Conference on Management of Networked Enterprises (CIMRE), Mahdia, pp. 1–14 (2001)
11. Pateli, A.G., Giaglis, G.M.: A Framework For Understanding and Analysing e-Business Models. Eur. J. Inf. Syst. 13, 302–314 (2004)
12. Osterwalder, A.: The Business Model Ontology - a proposition in a design science approach. Unpublished doctoral dissertation, HEC Lausanne (2004a)
13. Yin, R.K.: Case Study Research - Design and Methods. SAGE Publications, Newbury Park (2003)
14. Shafer, S.M., Smith, H.J., Linder, J.C.: The Power of Business Models. Business Horizons 48, 199–207 (2005)
15. Osterwalder, A., Pigneur, Y.: Investigating the Use of the Business Model Concept through Interviews. In: 4th International Conference on Electronic Business, pp. 568–573. Academic Publishers/World Publishing Corporating, Beijing (2004b)
16. Weill, P., Vitale, M.: Place to Space: Migrating to Ebusiness Models. Harvard Business Press, Boston (2001)
17. Boucharas, V., Jansen, S., Brinkkemper, S.: Formalizing software ecosystem modeling. In: 1st International Workshop on Open Component Ecosystems, pp. 41–50. ACM, New York (2009)
18. Penker, M., Eriksson, H.: Business Modeling With UML: Business Patterns at Work. Wiley, Hoboken (2000)

IP Modularity in Software Ecosystems: How SugarCRM's IP and Business Model Shape Its Product Architecture

Josef Waltl[1], Joachim Henkel[1], and Carliss Y. Baldwin[2]

[1] Technische Universität München
TUM School of Management
Arcisstr. 21, 80333 Munich, Germany
[2] Harvard Business School
Soldiers Field, Boston, MA 02163

Abstract. We provide a case study of the concept of "IP modularity," analyzing the case of SugarCRM. The modular architecture of this platform software is aligned with its intellectual property structure in such a way that the firm can derive, from the same code tree, an open source community version and a proprietary version. The software's IP modular structure also facilitates the development of complements by distributed and anonymous complementors and simplifies downstream customizations, thus enhancing the platform's attractiveness. We find that SugarCRM implements IP modularity on three different levels of the architectural hierarchy, in some cases down to the source code level. Our study thus extends the concept of IP modularity to comprise the notion of hierarchy levels.

Keywords: Intellectual Property, Modularity, Platforms, Software Ecosystems.

1 Introduction

This paper provides a case study of the concept of "IP modularity" introduced by Henkel and Baldwin [1,2] in a software ecosystem. A system is called "IP modular" if its module boundaries are drawn in such a way as to separate parts of the system that the architect desires to, or needs to, treat differently with respect to intellectual property (IP). For example, the architect may create separate modules for code that the firm owns and desires to keep secret, for proprietary code that it wants to disclose to select customers, and for open source code that it needs to license according to the GPL. Thus, designing an IP modular system requires managing the system's IP rights and its modular structure in conjunction. Importantly, the module boundaries imposed by considerations of IP may differ from those that are optimal from a technological or organizational perspective.

The goal of IP modularity is to optimize the system with respect to the firm's business model, and in particular to reconcile distributed value creation and value appropriation. These goals are often conflicting, and particularly so in the management

M.A. Cusumano, B. Iyer, and N. Venkatraman (Eds.): ICSOB 2012, LNBIP 114, pp. 94–106, 2012.

of platform ecosystems. Relinquishing control typically increases adoption and outside contributions, but makes it harder for the platform owner to realize profits and maintain differentiation [3]. To analyze if and how the concept of IP modularity can be applied in such a case, we study a platform product that is particularly interesting in this respect, SugarCRM. This paper is the first in a series of cases studies we currently conduct in three of the main fields of enterprise application software.[1]

The goals of this paper are threefold. First, we explore SugarCRM as a concrete realization of IP modularity. The firm faces the conflicting goals of openness toward users and complement developers for the purpose of distributed value creation, and of maintaining exclusivity of essential modules in order to appropriate value [1]. IP modularity is of highest strategic relevance for SugarCRM and its ecosystem:

> "I would say it's one the most fundamental aspects of our entire business model strategy that we purposely keep the modularity in such a way that we can easily create different [open source and proprietary] editions. What we sell is based on IP modularity." (Clint Oram, co-founder and CTO)

Second, we juxtapose our case to propositions derived by Henkel and Baldwin [1]. Analyzing the reasons behind and the effects of SugarCRM Inc.'s adoption of an IP modular architecture, we find them fully in line with theoretical predictions.

Third, based on our case analysis we link the notion of IP modularity to that of hierarchy levels. Modules form hierarchies, and a high-level module may contain heterogeneous IP while its constituent low-level modules are homogeneous with respect to IP. Thus, the system would be IP modular on the low level but not on the high level. In this sense, a system that is IP modular on both levels would be IP modular to a higher degree.

Taking our findings together, we show how the identified effects resulting from an IP modular platform design influence both the platform and product attractiveness as well as the competitive position toward other platforms.

In the following sections we provide a short literature review, describe our method and data, present our results, and conclude with a discussion and outlook.

2 Literature Review

2.1 IP Modularity

A software system is IP modular when its technical module boundaries coincide with the boundaries of parts defined by homogeneous IP rights [1,2]. These IP rights not only comprise formal IP like patents, copyright and licensing contracts, but also informal IP like secrecy (realized, e.g., by not disclosing a program's source code). Of particular interest in the present context is "outgoing IP modularity," where the focal firm owns the IP related to an artifact and defines the artifact's modular structure and each module's IP rights (i.e., licensing conditions) in conjunction.

---

[1] Our research covers CRM software with SugarCRM Inc. as research partner, ERP software with SAP AG as research partner, and PLM software.

Henkel and Baldwin [1] analyze theoretically under which conditions IP modularity is beneficial and thus, assuming rational behavior on the part of system architects, most likely to be observed. In particular, they derive the following propositions (numbered 2 and 4 in [1]):

> *Proposition 1: [Distributed Co-Creators] The more distributed, numerous, and anonymous the co-creators of value, the more advantageous is outgoing IP modularity.*
>
> *Proposition 2: [Customization] The greater and more varied the need for downstream adaptations, the more advantageous is outgoing IP modularization. The module boundaries should separate the IP that serves as the basis for modification from the IP supporting the proprietary "core" modules.*

Analyzing the rationales behind SugarCRM Inc.'s architectural decisions we find that they are fully captured by these propositions. Our research thus provides the first in-depth empirical test of the concept of IP modularity.

2.2 Platforms

Proposition 2 on customization links IP modularity to the rich theoretical basis on technological platforms, where the development of "core modules" and the downstream adaptations are shared between platform providers and ecosystem partners. Technological platforms have extensively been researched in the last years (Cusumano and Gawer 2002 [4], West [5], Gawer and Henderson [6], Baldwin and Woodard 2008 [7], Cusumano 2010 [8] and Boudreau [3]).

Our understanding of "platform" draws on the work by Cusumano and Gawer [4], who define an industry platform as a product that provides a core technology that can be reused in different product variations that are likely to come from different companies. In addition, Baldwin and Woodard [7] define a "platform architecture" as a modularization which partitions a system into a set of components the design of which is stable and a complementary set of components which are allowed — indeed encouraged — to vary.

Opening up an industry platform to a wide set of potential complementors implies that the platform provider has to cede some control. However, doing so may boost the development of complements, as Boudreau [3] shows for the case of handheld computing systems. There is a broad consensus in the literature that the management of IP is a key lever for platform providers to manage the cooperation with other firms that provide complementary products.[2] Cusumano [8] points out the connection of platform modularity and openness (through accessibility of the interfaces and intellectual property) as a major lever for platform leadership. These interfaces are

[2] Eisenmann, Parker and Van Alstyne [9] name these companies "supply-side users" and the product's end-users "demand-side users." For simplicity, we will use the terms "complementors" and "end-users." Furthermore, they differentiate between "platform sponsor" and "platform provider." Since both are the same in our case, we use the latter term.

typically implemented as Application Programming Interfaces (APIs) as a means to control openness of proprietary platforms.

2.3 Hybrid OSS Business Models

A similar tension between openness and control as for platforms exists for commercially developed open source software (OSS). If an OSS project is organized on a public platform, with code coming from a large number of contributors, then the potential for distributed value creation is maximized. Downsides are that in such a case a product-based business model is difficult or impossible, and the original owner of the code may even lose control over its further development.

Various approaches have been proposed, and implemented in practice, to harness the power of community-based OSS development while still running a product-based business model. Hecker [10] and Raymond [11] suggest various ways to profit indirectly from OSS, by selling complements. West [5], Bonaccorsi et al. [12] and Lindman et al. [13] study "hybrid" business models empirically, which combine open source and proprietary elements or make use of dual licensing. Riehle 2012 [14] comprehensively presents the properties of this hybrid approach referred to as "single vendor commercial open source business model"[3].

Our study relates to this literature as SugarCRM Inc. licenses a community edition of its software under an open source license while selling the commercial edition under a standard proprietary license. However, their approach goes beyond simple dual licensing by creating two distinct versions out of the same IP modular code tree.

To our knowledge this study is the first to link research on hybrid OSS business models with that on modular product architectures.

3 Method and Data

We explore unchartered territory by combining the concept of IP modularity with research on platforms and software business models. For such nascent field research qualitative methods to generate theory based on empirical evidence are most appropriate [15,16]. Whereas qualitative research has proven advantages in new field research, it also has limitations. During our research we implemented a number of measures to ensure case study rigor.

Our research draws on nine in depth interviews with SugarCRM Inc. executives in technical, business and legal roles and executives of complementors (see the Appendix for an interviewee overview). The interviews with platform provider executives were all in person and took place at the headquarters in Cupertino, CA as well as the firm's office in Munich, Germany. The interviews with the complementary good providers were conducted by telephone. The average interview time was 56 minutes; the interviews were semi-structured based on an interview guideline.

---

[3] Industry experts also refer to this type of business model as "open core" approach: `http://alampitt.typepad.com/lampitt_or_leave_it/2008/08/open-core-licen.html`

To triangulate our data, we complement the interviews with information from extensive field notes, analyst reports [17, 18] and data from the company's open source community website.[4]

All interviews were recorded and transcribed. The information was coded using the software package NVivo 9, with a theory based coding scheme that was extended and adapted during the analysis.

4 Results

4.1 SugarCRM's Software Platform and Business Model

SugarCRM Inc. was founded in 2004 and provides an open source Customer Relationship Management (CRM) software platform product as well as commercial editions[5] with extended functionality. This software platform is the object of our study.

The business model built around it differs from that of other open source companies in how IP and source code ownership are managed. The company maintains all source code for its products in one proprietary code tree and licenses parts of it for the open source community edition, under the GNU Affero General Public License (see www.gnu.org/licenses). The commercial product editions are sold to customers under proprietary license terms[6]. So SugarCRM combines an open source approach with a proprietary software product business model.

SugarCRM also opened up the platform to enable complementors to create additional extension modules for end-users and build-up a whole software ecosystem.

4.2 The IP Modular Platform Architecture

Our research shows that SugarCRM's platform architecture and its business model are inseparably linked. The business model is enabled by a product architecture that separates the IP elements for the community edition from the elements required for the commercial editions. Fig. 1 depicts the basic architecture in an schematic representation for selected platform functionality and extension modules.

[4] `www.sugarforge.org`

[5] At the time of this research four commercial editions exist that add further functionality. For our study we do not differentiate between them. However, a detailed look across the versions in further research would add an additional dimension to our findings.

[6] Sugar CRM is implemented in PHP technology, which does not allow to keep source code secret for it is interpreted at runtime and not compiled. Following this technical conditions SugarCRM operates on a combination of Open Source Software (OSS) and open code software.

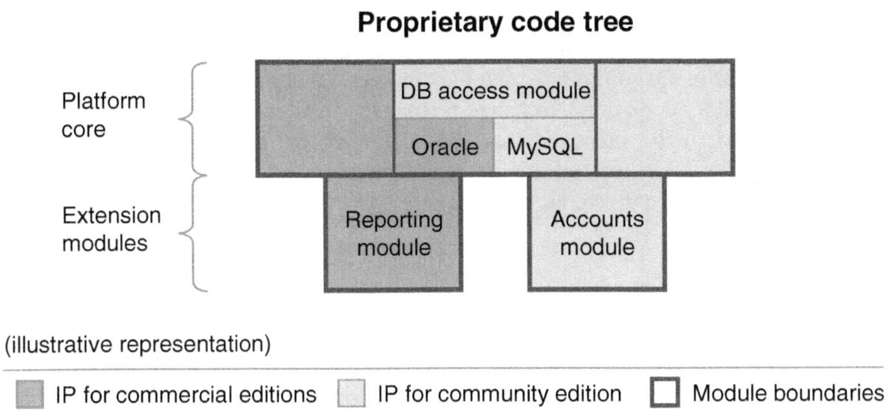

Fig. 1. Schematic Architecture Overview

Nick Halsey, chief marketing officer and executive vice president of corporate development, explains the link between Sugar's product architecture and the company's business model as follows:

> "Our business model would not be possible without an IP modular architecture. If we solely had an open source product and sold consulting services around it, we would probably do very well, but we wouldn't have the same kind of explosive growth[7] we're experiencing with our commercial product."

The goal of SugarCRM is to reach clear IP modularity between the open platform core and the extension modules. This is the case when a certain business functionality that is to be included into one of the commercial editions can be fully implemented in one extension module.

However, if this is not possible for some cases, since some functionalities for the commercial edition cannot solely be implemented in an extension module, but also require modifications in the platform core. If possible, such IP for commercial editions is then encapsulated in separate modules within the platform. In the worst case, the code for the commercial editions cannot be split into different modules within the platform as (named components). Lila Tretikov, vice president of engineering states:

> "We try to keep the platform IP modular as well, but there are some historical things that are there from before. An example of this would be our general database component that has code to connect to MySQL that goes into our community edition and code to connect to Oracle that goes into our commercial editions."

To overcome this problem and reach IP homogeneity in the released editions, the code is tagged in the proprietary code tree when it is only to be included in one of the

[7] To give an example: In North America the billings for the first quarter in 2011 showed a 63% growth over the same quarter in 2010 [17].

proprietary editions. As shown in Fig. 2 a special build process takes out the IP for the commercial editions from the code that is released under the AGPL license. So IP homogeneity within the community and the commercial editions can be achieved with only one proprietary code tree that has to be managed. Alternatively two parallel code trees would have to be managed that only differ in the parts for the commercial editions. This would require additional maintenance effort and increase the risk of incompatibility between the versions.

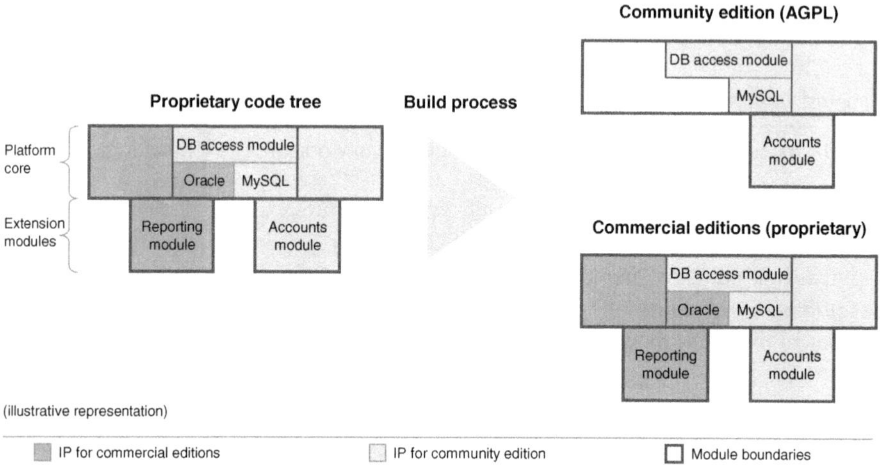

Fig. 2. Build process to separate IP

Based on these findings, we can extend the concept of IP modularity to include the notion of hierarchy levels. In our case, we identified three IP modularity levels. On the first and highest level, the relevant elements are the platform and the extension modules on an architectural level. The second level is within the platform itself in a way that its sub-modules are IP homogenous. On the third level, the modules have to be split on a source code level to reach IP homogeneity in the end products.

Table 1 provides a detailed description of the identified hierarchy levels of IP modularity and their implications for platform strategy, governance mechanisms, and implementation. According to Clint Oram the overall aim is to keep the IP separation at the platform architecture and module level since the implementation of IP modularity on the source code level implies higher technical complexity and implementation cost.

In the case of SugarCRM the need for IP modularity on the source code level is given for three different reasons. First, the SugarCRM platform is a constantly evolving product and the focus towards IP modularity has increased over time. So for historical reasons there is still code that has not been designed with the principle of IP modularity in mind, as Nick Halsey explains:

> "Now we are 100 percent committed to IP modularity. In the early days our main focus was to bring our product to the market."

Table 1. Hierarchy Levels of IP Modularity

	Platform architecture level	Module level	Source code level
Characteristics	• Modularity between between architectural elements	• Modularity between modules within one architectural element	• Modularity between source code sections within one module
Strategic rationale	• Split open platform from proprietary extension modules • Fundamentally enabling "open core" business model	• Separation of proprietary and open modules	• Separation of proprietary and open code segments
Governance	• Architectural design committee defines general design rules	• Product management guides engineers	• Product management guides engineers
Implementation	• Platform API • Module builder toolset	• Assignment of IP status to modules	• Assignment of IP status to code segments
Cost of implementation	Low	Low	High

Second, there are modules that cannot be split due to technical or architectural reasons, for example the DB access module as shown in Fig. 2. Here the need for technical optimality justifies the additional cost of implementing IP modularity on the source code level.

Third, the further down IP modularity is implemented in this layer model, the more granular the balance between openness and value appropriation can be managed as CEO, Larry Augustin, explains:

> "With our IP modular architecture, we have more flexibility and can draw that line in a more granular place. For example, parts our open platform can be proprietary. [...] I think we have more flexibility to choose what is free versus what is not free."

This highly granular possibility to control the IP even on the source code level for commercial versions is a core enabler for increased openness, since modules that only partly consist of proprietary elements do not have to be kept proprietary as a whole. On the other hand these mechanisms to separate IP down to source code level can lead to higher cost at least initially, as Nick Halsey accounts:

> "If you take just a little bit of extra time up front to determine the right IP modular design that fits your business needs, it might mean higher costs up front, but in the end, you will wind up saving time, saving money and having increased productivity over time."

To sum-up our findings we conclude that, when IP modular platform design is fundamentally linked with a company's business model it has to be decided to which level IP modularity is implemented to be beneficial from an overall strategic perspective. This may – and in the present case does – outweigh higher cost in R&D and/or technical drawbacks.

4.3 Implications for the Software Platform Ecosystem

Besides enabling SugarCRM's business model, the IP modular platform design entails a whole set of additional effects on company performance and the entire platform ecosystem, as depicted in Fig. 3.

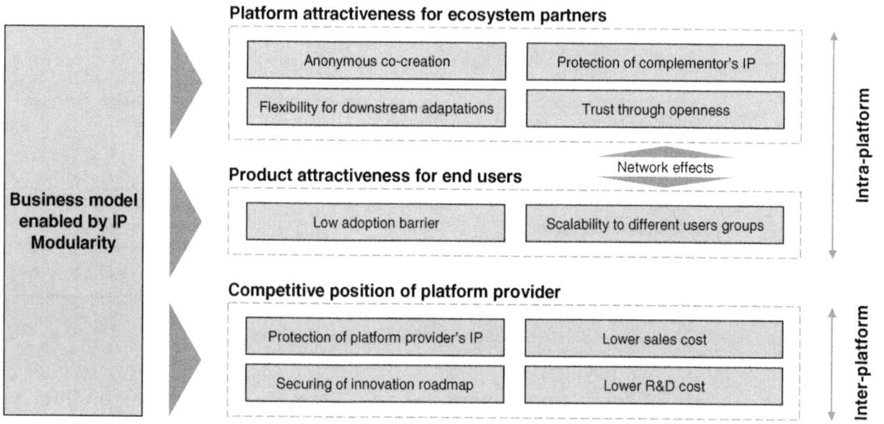

Fig. 3. Intra- and inter-platform effects

Within intra-platform effects, we further split between effects that increase the platform attractiveness for complementors and those that increase the product attractiveness for end users. Not surprisingly and in line with existing research, our data indicate a network effect between those two. Our interviews show that executives devote particular attention to the platform attractiveness for ecosystem partners, as Nick Halsey testifies:

> "By taking the IP modular architecture approach, we have made it easier for our partner ecosystem to develop add-ons and extensions to our product that they can build businesses around. As a result, that means we have a much larger ecosystem with better solutions that are easier to implement and upgrade."

Furthermore, for anonymous co-creation (see Proposition 1 above) the specific platform architecture that enables the highly open strategy eliminates the need for complementors to directly interact with the platform provider. CEO, Larry Augustin, illustrates why this fosters innovation in the entire ecosystem:

> "There are many third parties that show up and say: We have a product that works with SugarCRM, and they try to sell to our customer base. Many third parties created those integrations using our open source tools, and they don't have to talk to us at all to develop a useful solution. We may not have supported them if they had chosen to talk to us."

In addition, we found out that the low entry barrier and the possibility for anonymous co-creation paved the way for strong partnerships with complementors. Mirco Müller, CEO of InsignioCRM (one of SugarCRM's largest partners in Europe) describes this process as follows:

> "In the beginning we did our business only based on the community edition. SugarCRM did not know us. We started to partner when we acquired our first big customers – still we did not interact much with SugarCRM. We were able to solve our problems on our own since we had access to all source code for the community and commercial editions. That changed when Sugar opened an office in Europe and we now do interact very closely, especially in marketing."

These findings on the rationales for and effects of IP modularity are perfectly in line with, and thus support, Proposition 1 above [1] regarding the distribution, number, and anonymity of potential value co-creators. Similarly, the following findings on customization and downstream adaptations lend support to Proposition 2. As Clint Oram explains:

> "The reason why our ecosystem partners come to us is because we reduce risk for them. They have more control over the building of products because they have full visibility into the source code, and they understand exactly how the product works."

Also, the ecosystem partners appreciate the flexibility for adoption and customization on the platform core to implement end-customer requirements. The core benefits were best described by Clemens von Dinklage, CEO of Gold-Partner MyCRM GmbH:

> "We don't have to ask SugarCRM when we customize the product, since we can open the engine hood ourselves and implement customer requirements directly without additional communication overhead towards the platform vendor."

Overall the identified framework of intra-platform and inter-platform effects shows that IP modular platform design has a variety of strategic implications far beyond the basic business model mechanics.

5 Discussion and Outlook

Our findings on the implementation and the effects of IP modularity in one particular software ecosystem may provide insights beyond that particular case and encourage additional research as well as provide insights for industry practitioners.

We found that the IP modular platform architecture is the key enabler for the company's hybrid OSS business model. SugarCRM separates components that it licenses under an OSS license from those that it puts under a proprietary license in a single code tree, and in this way manages to combine the benefits of open source licensing with those of a proprietary product-based business model.

With a detailed analysis of SugarCRM's software platform we identified three hierarchy levels for the application of IP modularity: the architectural level, the module level and the code level. IP modularity is easiest to implement on the architectural level, but hybrid architectural components may remain. These, in turn, can be made IP modular through a clear separation on the module level. Still there may remain modules with a hybrid IP status that require differentiation on the source code level. The further down in this hierarchy IP modularity is implemented the higher is the related cost, but also the better is the strategic control of value appropriation in a hybrid OSS business model.

We also identified a set of secondary effects that can be clustered into effects that increase the platform attractiveness for end-users and effects that increase the competitive position towards other platform providers. Analyzing the effects on platform attractiveness for ecosystem partners we found them fully in line with propositions derived in earlier work [1].

As stated in the introduction this research is the first in a series of in-depth case studies of IP modular software systems. Especially the comparison of this case with the more proprietary SAP NetWeaver platform ecosystem may further enrich our findings. Also interesting should be a study that focuses on the attractiveness of SugarCRM's platform compared to other platforms in the same industry but without a hybrid OSS business model, such as that of salesforce.com.

References

1. Henkel, J., Baldwin, C.Y.: Modularity for Value Appropriation - How to Draw the Boundaries of Intellectual Property. Harvard Business School Finance Working Paper, No. 11-054 (2010), http://papers.ssrn.com/sol3/papers.cfm?abstract_id=1340445
2. Baldwin, C.Y., Henkel, J.: The Impact of Modularity on Intellectual Property and Value Appropriation. Harvard Business School Finance Working Paper No. 12-040 (2011), http://papers.ssrn.com/sol3/papers.cfm?abstract_id=1971203
3. Boudreau, K.: Open Platform Strategies and Innovation: Granting Access vs. Devolving Control. Management Science 56(10), 1849–1872 (2010)
4. Gawer, A., Cusumano, M.A.: Platform leadership. How Intel, Microsoft, and Cisco drive industry innovation. Harvard Business School Press, Boston (2002)
5. West, J.: How Open Is Open Enough? Melding Proprietary and Open Source Platform Strategies. Research Policy 32(7), 1259–1285 (2003)
6. Gawer, A., Henderson, R.: Platform Owner Entry and Innovation in Complementary Markets: Evidence from Intel. Journal of Economics and Management Strategy 16(1), 1–34 (2007)
7. Baldwin, C.Y., Woodard, C.J.: The Architecture of Platforms: A Unified View. In: Gawer, A. (ed.) Platforms, Markets and Innovation, pp. 19–44. Elgar, Cheltenham, U.K. (2009)
8. Cusumano, M.A.: Staying power. Six enduring principles for managing strategy and innovation in an uncertain world (lessons from Microsoft, Apple, Intel, Google, Toyota and more). Oxford University Press, Oxford (2010)

9. Eisenmann, T.R., Parker, G., van Alstyne, M.: Opening Platforms: How, When and Why? In: Gawer, A. (ed.) Platforms, Markets and Innovation, Cheltenham, U.K. and Northampton, pp. 131–162. Elgar, Mass (2009)
10. Hecker, F.: Setting up shop: The business of open-source software. IEEE Software 16(1), 45–51 (1999)
11. Raymond, E.S.: The cathedral and the bazaar. Musings on Linux and Open Source by an accidental revolutionary, Rev. edn. O'Reilly, Beijing (2001)
12. Bonaccorsi, A., Giannangeli, S., Rossi, C.: Entry Strategies Under Competing Standards: Hybrid Business Models in the Open Source Software Industry. Management Science 52(7), 1085–1098 (2006)
13. Lindman, J., Rossi, M., Puustell, A.: Matching Open Source Software Licenses with Corresponding Business Models. IEEE Software 28(4), 31–35 (2011)
14. Riehle, D.: The single-vendor commercial open course business model. Information Systems and e-Business Management 10(1), 5–17 (2012)
15. Edmondson, A.C., McManus, S.E.: Methodological fit in management field research. Academy of Management Review 32(4), 1155–1179 (2007)
16. Eisenhardt, K.M.: Building Theories from Case Study Research. Academy of Management Review 14(4), 532–550 (1989)
17. Band, W.: The Forrester Wave^{TM}: CRM Suites For Midsized Organizations. In: Q2 2010, Cambridge, Mass (2010)
18. Dow Jones Company Report - SugarCRM Inc. (2011)

Appendix – Interviewee Overview

Interviewee	Larry Augustin	Clint Oram	Jay Seirmaco	Lila Tretikov	Nick Halsey	Christian Knoll	Mirco Müller	Clemens v. Dincklage
Company	SugarCRM					KINAMU Business Solutions AG	Insignio CRM GmbH	MyCRM GmbH
Company description / type	Platform provider					Complementor		
Job title	CEO	CTO and co-founder	General legal counsel	Vice president of engineering	Chief marketing officer and executive vice president of corporate development	CEO	CEO	CEO
Job description	Responsible for the whole business involving product, but also for sales, marketing and all the other aspects	Leads product strategy, product management and community. Is one of the original architects.	As attorney he oversees legal, facilities and IT functions	Responsible for engineering and technology operations, including engineering development and managing cloud services technology	Manages the company's overall go-to-market strategy	Founder and CEO	Founder and CEO	Founder and CEO
Interview date	Sep 23, 2011	Aug 19, 2011	Sep 19, 2011	Sep 19, 2011 and Jan 24, 2012	Sep 9, 2011	Dec 7, 2011	Dec 12, 2011	Dec 16, 2011
Interview location	In person: SugarCRM Munich Office (GER)	Via telephone: Cupertino (US) and Munich (GER)	In person: Sugar HQ Cupertino (US)	In person: Sugar HQ Cupertino (US)	In person: Sugar HQ Cupertino (US)	Via telephone: Schwechat (AUT) and Munich (GER)	Via telephone: Kassel (GER) and Munich (GER)	Via telephone: Plochingen (GER) and Munich (GER)

Is Perceived Domestic Market Attractiveness a Growth Impediment? Evidence from the German Software Industry

Christian Hoerndlein[1], Michel Schreiner[1], Alexander Benlian[2], Thomas Hess[1], and Arnold Picot[1]

[1] Munich School of Management, LMU Munich, Germany
{hoerndlein,schreiner,thess,picot}@bwl.lmu.de
[2] Chair of Information Systems & Electronic Services, TU Darmstadt, Germany
benlian@ise.tu-darmstadt.de

Abstract. The German software industry is vital to the German economy's success. However, it has missed some current trends where software companies lack broader international activity. Existing models that take domestic market size into account can only partially explain the different degrees of internationalized companies *between* different countries. In addition, they are unable to explain individual companies' internationalization *within* a specific country. In our empirical study, an online survey of 869 German software companies, we examined the impact of perceived domestic market attractiveness as an impediment to internationalization. We found that it accounts for a considerable share of companies' variation in their internationalization activities. Based on our findings, we discuss policy and management implications.

Keywords: Software industry, internationalization, market size, market attractiveness, perception.

1 Introduction

Information and communication (ICT) technologies drive more than 80% of the innovations in important industries, such as the German automotive industry, medical technology and logistics sector [1]. However, both the international ICT market in general and the software market in particular are dominated mainly by non-German companies (see e.g. [2]). Only few German software companies, among them particularly SAP, have managed to grow considerably to be considered among the world's largest software companies [2, 3].

When German software companies manage to reach a certain size and expand internationally, these companies are usually so-called "hidden champions" [4], operating in niches in the fields of business-to-business software and business-to-business services [5]. The fact that there are no internationally known German companies in recent consumer software markets like social networks (e.g. Facebook, LinkedIn), search engines (e.g. Google), content platforms (e.g. YouTube, Flickr), social news (e.g. Twitter), or consumer-to-consumer auctions (e.g. eBay) also fits this trend.

M.A. Cusumano, B. Iyer, and N. Venkatraman (Eds.): ICSOB 2012, LNBIP 114, pp. 107–113, 2012.

The tendency of a nation's companies not to expand internationally can have severe negative consequences; they might miss out on growth opportunities and market leadership. This is especially true in the software industry: The software market is characterized by network effects[1] [7], which often cause the emergence of a "winner-take-all market" [8, p. 177]. We hence argue that internationalization can be a strategic imperative for software companies that do not want to be swept away by their international competitors.

Extant research has analyzed the factors that have an impact on individual companies' internationalization in general and aspects like market selection and market entry forms in particular. The factors that have been considered in the literature can be grouped broadly into the following categories[2]:

- Company-specific (e.g. the company's networks [9], market orientation [10], or business model [11])
- Product-specific (e.g. the specifity of the software offered [12])
- Economic-environmental (e.g. the market size of the target market or geographic distance [13])
- Institutional (e.g. tax system and government support in the home country [14])
- Cultural (e.g. cultural distance between software vendor and client [13])

These factors, however, cannot explain evidence in the software market that both countries with a relatively small (e.g. Scandinavian countries like Sweden, Norway, or Finland [3]) and large (e.g. USA [2]) domestic market generally tend to have a higher degree of internationalized companies, compared to countries with a medium market size such as Germany.

The remainder of this paper is structured as follows: In the next section, we will describe the effect of domestic market size and market attractiveness on a software firm's international business activities. Subsequently, we describe the research design and the data collection approach we applied. The fourth section will provide the results of the statistical analysis, before we conclude this study with pointing out policy and management implications as well as potential areas for further research.

2 Domestic Market Size and Internationalization

Literature suggests that, in general, there is a U-shaped relationship between a country's market size and its degree of internationalized companies: Firms in small markets might be forced to expand internationally to achieve economies of scale, scope, and learning [15, 16]. A large domestic market, on the other hand, can cause companies to use these advantages to primarily meet domestic demand, as foreign demand can seem more uncertain and local firms enjoy endowed advantages in their home markets [17]. However, very large markets are more competitive, which might cause companies to expand internationally to sustain growth or fill capacity [17, 18].

---

1 Network effects, or network externalities, are defined as "*(...) the utility that a given user derives from the good depends upon the number of other users who are in the same 'network'* " [6, p. 424].

2 This categorization does not claim to be exhaustive or mutually exclusive. It is solely meant as one possible approach to cluster the research conducted so far on this topic. Besides, the studies may also analyze more than one factor at a time.

Still, a very large market size does not necessarily translate directly into a high degree of internationalized companies in a nation's software industry: In a qualitative study, Burzynski et al. [14] identify the high demand within the domestic market as one of the major factors inhibiting Brazilian software companies' internationalization. Although this finding might sound counterintuitive at first, the authors conclude that *"(...) new markets are sought out when they are needed. If there is no need, considering that a company may already operate close to its maximum capacity, the search for new markets becomes a secondary concern. Although the entrepreneurs consider that the external market is a promising one, they prefer to focus on the internal market because so many unexplored opportunities there remain*" [14, p. 510].

These results indicate that it might rather be a company's subjective perception of the attractiveness of its domestic market than merely its home country's objective market size that contributes to a country's software industry's degree of internationalization: If software firms within a country consider their domestic market to exhibit sufficient opportunities, there might be no immediate need to expand internationally. As it is the subjective rather than the objective environment that explains behavior [19], different perceptions of the same "objective" reality could therefore explain different internationalization behaviors by companies' managers.

In summary, the U-curve that we described above can explain the general predisposition of a certain country's software companies to internationalize if the objective and subjective attractiveness of the domestic market are in accordance. However, as Brazilian companies' hesitation to internationalize shows, the U-curve cannot explain the degree of internationalized companies in countries where objective and subjective attractiveness of the domestic market seem to differ. Besides, the U-shaped relationship cannot explain which software companies internationalize *within* the same market, as some successful internationalizations of German software firms show. Therefore, it is our study's goal to shed more light onto this aspect and to answer the following research question:

How does a software company's perception of the domestic market attractiveness affect its decision to expand internationally?

3 Research Design and Data Collection

We collected data through a web-based survey and invited managers of software companies via e-mail to participate as key informants; the managers' contact data had been extracted from the Hoppenstedt database (www.hoppenstedt.de). The survey was online from September 19, 2011 through October 18, 2011. After about two weeks, we sent out an e-mail reminder to those participants who had not participated yet. The variables were operationalized as follows:

- The dependent variable "share of international revenue" was measured by asking respondents to indicate the percentage of their company's revenue outside the domestic (German) market for the last business year. This corresponds to the operationalization of "international diversification" in Li and Yue [15].
- The independent variable "perceived domestic market attractiveness" was measured by asking participants to indicate on a 5-point Likert-scale to what degree they agree with the following statement: *"The German market is profitable enough not having to internationalize (any further)."*

- In addition, we measured the two independent control variables "company size", which was measured as number of employees, and "age of the company", which was calculated based on the company's founding year.

4 Data Analysis and Results

The survey showed a response rate of about 11% and a retention rate of about 21%. We excluded those datasets from further analysis that had more than 25% of missing values and where participants dropped out completing less than 80% of the pages of the questionnaire. This resulted in a cleansed set of 869 datasets. Table 1 shows the distribution of the companies' size and the average share of international revenue per category of company size. The categorization was based on the classification provided by the European Commission (http://ec.europa.eu/enterprise/policies/sme/).

Table 1. Distribution of Companies' Size and Share of International Revenue

Employees	Companies in %	Share of International Revenue in %
<= 9	17.8	12.3
>= 10 and <= 49	53.3	13.0
>= 50 and <= 249	20.4	17.7
>= 250	7.5	30.1
n/a	1.0	32.8
	100.0% ***(n=869)***	**14.9%** ***(n=721)***

We first divided the datasets in two groups: companies conducting business internationally (more than 5% international revenue) and companies that had not internationalized yet (a maximum of 5% international revenue); we considered it adequate to call companies non-international even if they earned a minor fraction of their revenue abroad. Subsequently, we performed a non-parametric (Mann-Whitney-U) test to analyze whether the two groups differed regarding the value of the variable "perceived domestic market attractiveness". International companies showed a significantly *lower* value for perceived domestic market attractiveness. To check for robustness, we performed the test with a threshold of 10% international revenue. The results were basically the same. An overview of the results is shown in Table 2.

Table 2. Group Comparison of Perceived Domestic Market Attractiveness

	Internationalization Threshold 5%		**Internationalization Threshold 10%**	
	Non-int'l	Int'l	Non-int'l	Int'l
Perceived Domestic Market Attractiveness	ø 3.39 *(n=382)*	ø 2.46 *(n=310)*	ø 3.31 *(n=452)*	ø 2.34 *(n=240)*
	Z = -9.803***		Z = -9.808***	

*** $p < 0.001$; Non-int'l: Non-international; Int'l: International.

Subsequently, we checked whether the results could possibly be due to differences in company size or age by running a binary logistic regression. As shown in Table 3, only perceived domestic market attractiveness has a significant impact.

Table 3. Results of Binary Logistic Regression

	Internationalization Threshold 5%		**Internationalization Threshold 10%**	
	b	**Wald**	**b**	**Wald**
Variables				
Perceived Domestic Market Attractiveness	–0.643***	78.795	–0.670***	77.092
Number of Employees	$0.000^{n.s.}$	1.219	$0.000^{n.s.}$	1.587
Age of Company	$0.004^{n.s.}$	0.793	$0.008^{n.s.}$	3.338
Nagelkerke's R^2	0.189		0.204	
Correct Classification	68.5%		70.1%	

n.s.: not significant; *** $p < 0.001$; n=682.

We tested for non-response bias, which we found to be unlikely, as a chi-square test showed no significant differences in the distribution of the variables for the first and last 25% of the respondents. In addition, we checked for multicollinearity of the independent variables, which we found not to be an issue (Kendall's Tau $|b| <= 0.145$).

In summary, the results show that one single variable can contribute significantly to predict which companies will not internationalize, only based on their perception of perceived domestic market attractiveness. Company size and age, one the other hand, turned out not to be significant predictors.

5 Implications and Further Research

Our findings indicate that perceived market attractiveness can account for some of software companies' hesitation to expand internationally. For countries that want to promote their software industry's international expansion, this has important policy implications which might appear paradoxical at first sight: By stressing that the domestic market is not as profitable in the long run as it might seem, politicians could possibly nudge software companies to step out of their "comfort zone" and expand internationally. Besides, managers of software companies could ask themselves whether their decision not to internationalize is based on their perception of the profitability of their domestic market, which could hurt their company in the long run. Therefore, managers should critically reflect on their own subjective perception of market attractiveness and compare it with objective market data, such as domestic market growth rates or profit margins, to avoid making the wrong strategic decisions.

Although we contributed to the understanding of the internationalization of German software companies, there are two aspects of our study that would require further research regarding the generalizability of the results: First, our study would have to be replicated in other countries to analyze whether our findings are specific to the German market. In addition, further studies have to show whether the findings are specific to the software sector or also apply to other industries. Moreover, our study incorporates only three variables to predict whether a company has internationalized. Further research should incorporate additional variables, such as access to growth capital or managers' attitude towards risk, to increase the model's predictive power.

Acknowledgments. We are thankful for the financial support from the Federal Ministry of Education and Research that made this research possible.

References

1. Federal Ministry of Education and Research: ICT 2020 – Research for Innovations, http://www.bmbf.de/pub/ict_2020.pdf
2. Top 100 Research Foundation, http://www.softwaretop100.org
3. Truffle Capital, http://www.truffle100.com/downloads/2011/Truffle Europe-2011-v7.pdf
4. Simon, H.: Hidden Champions of the 21st Century – Success Strategies of Unknown World Market Leaders. Springer, Heidelberg (2011)
5. Leimbach, T.: Software und IT-Dienstleistungen: Kernkompetenzen der Wissensgesellschaft Deutschland. In: Leimbach, T., Kestermann, C. (eds.) Software-Monitor Deutschland 2010, pp. 35–67 (2010)
6. Katz, M.L., Shapiro, C.: Network Externalities, Competition, and Compatibility. The American Economic Review 75(3), 424–440 (1985)
7. Buxmann, P., Diefenbach, H., Hess, T.: Die Softwareindustrie: Ökonomische Prinzipien, Strategien, Perspektiven. Springer, Heidelberg (2011)
8. Shapiro, C., Varian, H.R.: Information Rules: A Strategic Guide to the Network Economy. Harvard Business School Press, Boston (1999)
9. Ruokonen, M., Nummela, N., Puumalainen, K., Saarenketo, S.: Market Orientation and Internationalisation in Small Software Firms. European Journal of Marketing 42(11/12), 1294–1315 (2008)
10. Moen, Ø., Gavlen, M., Endresen, I.: Internationalization of Small Computer Software Firms. European Journal of Marketing 38(9/10), 1236–1251 (2004)
11. Ojala, A., Tyrväinen, P.: Business Models and Market Entry Mode Choice of Small Software Firms. Journal of International Entrepreneurship 4(2), 69–81 (2006)
12. Winkler, J.K.: International Entry Mode Choices of Software Firms – An Analysis of Product-Specific Determinants. Peter Lang, Frankfurt am Main (2009)
13. Ojala, A., Tyrväinen, P.: Market Entry and Priority of Small and Medium-Sized Enterprises in the Software Industry: An Empirical Analysis of Cultural Distance, Geographic Distance, and Market Size. Journal of International Marketing 15(3), 123–149 (2007)
14. Burzynski, O.R., Graeml, A.R., Balbinot, Z.: The Internationalization of the Software Market: Opportunities and Challenges for Brazilian Companies. Journal of Information Systems and Technology Management 7(3), 499–516 (2010)

15. Li, J., Yue, D.R.: Market Size, Legal Institutions, and International Diversification Strategies: Implications for the Performance of Multinational Firms. Management International Review 48(6), 667–688 (2008)
16. Kogut, B.: Designing Global Strategies: Comparative and Competitive Value-Added Chains. Sloan Management Review 26(4), 15–28 (1985)
17. Porter, M.E.: The Competitive Advantages of Nations. The Free Press, New York (1990)
18. Arora, A., Gambardella, A.: Domestic Markets and International Competitiveness: Generic and Product-Specific Competencies in the Engineering Sector. Strategic Management Journal 18(S1), 53–74 (1997)
19. Simon, H.A.: Theories of Decision-Making in Economics and Behavioral Science. The American Economic Review 49(3), 253–283 (1959)

The Emergence of an International New Software Venture from an Emerging Economy

Romeo V. Turcan[1] and Norman M. Fraser[2]

[1] Department of Business and Management, Aalborg University, Fibigerstraede 10, 9220 Aalborg, Denmark
rvt@business.aau.dk
[2] Henley Business School, Whiteknights, Reading, RG6 6UD, United Kingdom
n.m.fraser@henley.reading.ac.uk

Abstract. This study is positioned at the intersection of legitimation and international entrepreneurship theories. It is a longitudinal ethnographic case study that explores the process of emergence of an international new software venture from an emerging economy and the effect this venture has on the process of industry creation in that economy. Data were collected over a two year period, 2010-2011, via in-depth interviews, observations, and unobtrusive data. Data analysis reveals three different contexts in which legitimation took place: legitimation of the new venture domestically and internationally, and legitimation of the new industry. To acquire cognitive legitimacy and socio-political legitimacy and successfully internationalize, an international new venture needs to design a robust business model targeting both internal and external stakeholders, engage in persuasive argumentation invoking familiar cues and scripts, promote and defend incentives and operating mechanisms in political negotiations, and overcome the country-of-origin effect by pursuing a technology legitimation strategy.

Keywords: Internationalization, legitimation, software, new venture, emerging industry, emerging economy, ethnography.

1 Introduction

In this longitudinal ethnographic case study we explore the process of emergence of a software international new venture (INV) from an emerging economy and the effect an INV has on the process of industry creation in that economy. More specifically, drawing on institutional theory, we focus on *how* an emerging economy INV acquires legitimacy and how this INV contributes to the legitimation of the new industry within which it operates.

With this study we aim to contribute to the advancement of the growing international entrepreneurship research field [1]. To achieve this aim, we address herein a number of criticisms of the field. The extant international entrepreneurship research suffers from coverage bias [2] by focusing mostly on high-technology INVs from developed economies [3]. It also suffers from theoretical paucity [4] and needs

M.A. Cusumano, B. Iyer, and N. Venkatraman (Eds.): ICSOB 2012, LNBIP 114, pp. 114–127, 2012.

to borrow more actively from other disciplines in order for a robust international entrepreneurship theory to emerge [2]. To this criticism, we may add that research on legitimation in international business and research in international entrepreneurship are, respectively, in an embryonic stage [5] and virtually non-existent [4].

We define an INV as a new venture that aims to derive profits from international activities right from their inception or immediately thereafter [6]. The emergent nature of the INV and of the new industry suggests that both initially lack legitimacy and credibility [7]. Moreover, uncertain decision-making settings characterize a new industry in which decisions are made under conditions of technology and market uncertainty, as well as goal ambiguity [8]. As to the emerging nature of an economy, the most important criterion defining an emerging economy is how well it helps buyers and sellers to come together, implying that an emerging economy falls short to varying degrees in providing the institutions necessary to support basic business operations [9].

We explore the legitimation process of MDsoft[1], an INV in an emerging economy, the Republic of Moldova. MDsoft is in the business of custom software development. Data collection took place over the period of two years: 2010-2011. Data were collected using several methods: in-depth interviews with the top management team and founders of MDsoft as well as a number of key stake-holders; observations, since one of the authors is the co-founder of MDsoft; and unobtrusive data.

2 Theoretical Background

The process of new venture emergence can be understood and predicted by viewing it as a quest for legitimacy [10]. From the institutional theory perspective, legitimacy plays a key role in overcoming the liability of newness [11] and the liability of foreignness [12] that shape the behavior of INVs in the early years of their existence [13]. We define legitimacy as "a generalized perception or assumption that the actions of an entity are desirable, proper, or appropriate within some socially constructed system of norms, beliefs, and definitions" [14, p574]. In the early stages of their emergence, new ventures lack cognitive legitimacy, defined as knowledge about the new activity and what is needed to succeed in an industry, and socio-political legitimacy, defined as the value placed on the new activity by cultural norms and political authorities [15].

To acquire these types of legitimacy, new ventures seek various legitimation strategies in order to enhance their survival and facilitate the transition to other forms of organizing activities [16]. Several theoretical perspectives related to new venture legitimation strategies can be identified. For example, new ventures may seek legitimacy via *conformance* strategy [14] that aims at achieving conformity within the demands and expectations of the existing social structure in which the venture is currently positioned; in other words, it means to follow the rules [17]. New ventures may also pursue s*election* strategy [14] that allows them to select a favorable geographic location where there are organizations that conform to similar rules, norms, values and models and may provide a new venture with legitimacy. An

[1] The name of the company and the names of interviewees are disguised throughout the paper.

example would be for a software new venture to locate its operations in Silicon Valley, California, US or Silicon Glen, Scotland [18]. Through a *manipulation* strategy [14] new ventures may make changes in the environment to achieve consistency between the venture and its environment.

When an industry is in the early years of its formation [19], it poses additional challenges and pressures on INVs' quest for legitimacy as there are no or few precedents for the kind of activities they want to found [7; 20]. In such context, new ventures may pursue *creation* legitimation strategy that "...involves developing something that did not already exist in the environment" [21, p425], such as, new operating practices, norms, values, beliefs, expectations, models, patterns of behavior, and networks. It is theorized that this strategy is especially evident during the introductory stage of new industries [21].

The extant empirical research on legitimation of new ventures and new industries highlights a number of symbolic legitimation strategies available to new ventures, such as *credibility*, defined as personal capability and personal commitment to the venture; *professional organizing*, defined as professional structures and processes; *organizational achievement*, defined as partially working products and technologies, venture age and number of employees; and *quality of stakeholder relationships*, defined as prestigious stakeholders, and personal attention [22]. To the above, INVs may pursue *technology* legitimation strategy to validate a technology or know-how; *market* legitimation strategy to better understand the market; *operating* legitimation strategy to have an optimal organizational gestalt; *locational* legitimation strategy to overcome the disadvantages of foreignness; *alliance* legitimation strategy to mitigate the risk of newness and smallness; and *anchoring* legitimation strategy to intentionally misrepresent the facts [23].

As to the legitimation strategies related to the introduction of an institutional change or the creation of new organizational form or practice, the extant research suggests that in order for a new form or activity to become more of a taken-for granted practice, or for an institutional change to be instilled, they have to be theorized [24; 25]. The key steps of the process of theorization are problem specification by framing the problem and justification by invoking professionals' values [24]. If the irregularities are not problematized, then extant theory will not be challenged, and rogue activities will wane or persist in a marginalized fashion [25]. Theorizing is thus not a momentary act but, one that requires sustained repetition to elicit a shared understanding of the problem [24]. In relation to the above, three sets of critical legitimation strategies may be available to new ventures: *bridging* diverse stakeholders; *theorization* of new practices (framing problems and justifying new practices and political negotiations); and *institutionalization* of new practices (by attaching them to preexisting organizational routines and reaffirming their alignment with stakeholder values on an ongoing basis) [26].

When 'innovations meet institutions', robust design mediates between institutionalized design and technical innovation [27]. An innovation's design is defined as robust "...when its arrangement of concrete details are immediately effective in locating the novel product or process within the familiar world, by invoking valued schemas and scripts, yet preserve the flexibility necessary for future evolution, by not constraining the potential evolution of understanding and action that follows use" [27, p479]. The robust design reduces the uncertainty linked to the new activity, and ensures that the main stakeholders would consider the new activity legitimate.

When the venture and the industry are in their early stage of formation, the challenge ultimately lies in finding familiar cues that locate and describe new ideas without binding users too closely to the old ways of doing things [27]. That is, as new technologies emerge, entrepreneurs and innovations must find the balance between novelty and familiarity, between impact and acceptance. Furthermore, new venture conformity to norms and practices will legitimate only to the extent that those norms and practices are themselves legitimate, credible, and valued [28]. It may be thus argued that in order to successfully legitimatize the new venture in an emerging, new industry, the entrepreneur will have to change and/or create new "structural meaning" [29, p158] of norms, practices and values at macro, mezzo, and micro levels. It could be further argued that successful attainment of the legitimacy threshold "below which the new venture struggles for existence and probably will perish and above which the new venture can achieve further gains in legitimacy and resources" [21, p427] will depend on the success of transformations that entrepreneurs will induce at the macro, mezzo, and micro levels. This challenge is further amplified by the emergent nature of the economy within which the new venture emerges. In this study we explore how entrepreneurs of new ventures change and create new structural meaning not only at the macro, mezzo, and micro levels, but also at the international level in an attempt to gain cognitive and socio-political legitimacy in an emerging industry.

3 Method

Given the scarcity of empirical work regarding the internationalization and legitimation of INVs from emerging economies [3], we use a single, longitudinal ethnographic case study in line with a theory-building research design [30].[2] Our interest in this study is to explore the process of legitimation of an emerging economy INV and its impact on the process of industry creation within which it emerges, aiming to advance international entrepreneurship theory.

The case company was purposefully selected following sampling strategies pertinent to inductive, theory building research. We followed the intensity sampling strategy, the logic and power of which lies in selecting information-rich cases that manifest the phenomenon intensely, but not extremely [32] and in which the phenomenon of interest is transparently observable [33]. The selected case also had to resemble an INV as defined earlier [6], and be located in an emerging economy.

Based on the above sampling criteria, we selected for studying in depth MDsoft as an INV from an emerging economy, the Republic of Moldova. MDsoft started-up in 2000 with 4 people and grew over the span of 10 years to a medium-sized company with more than 500 employees, reaching an operating turnover of approximately 28

[2] Examples of extant longitudinal, ethnographic field work could be found in [25] and [31] that examine the construction of legitimacy and identity during the life cycle of an entrepreneurial Internet firm [31] and how innovation in activities lead to the establishment of a new practice via institutionalization [25].

million Euros. According to various rating agencies [34; 35; 36],[3] Moldova is considered as an emerging, factor-driven economy making marginal progress in fostering sound macroeconomic management and enhancing the entrepreneurial climate, scoring low on business freedom, investment freedom, corruption and labor freedom, as well as on protecting investors and enforcing contracts.

Our data collection and analysis occurred over a period of two years: 2010-2011. Data were collected using several methods: in-depth interviews, participant observation and unobtrusive data collection. We interviewed the top management team and founders of MDsoft who were driving the start-up process (six interviews). We also interviewed key stakeholders of MDsoft, e.g., the director of the industry association; the deputy minister of ICT; and two academics from the Technical University who were actively involved at that time (2000-2001) in the process of industry creation. We also collected observational data since one of the authors of this study was the co-founder of MDsoft.

Unobtrusive data [37] were collected at length to contribute further to the triangulation of the data that were emerging from the interviews. The unobtrusive data consisted of (i) running records, such as legislative initiatives and bills, and (ii) episodic and private records, such as company sales, financial and organizational records, industrial and institutional records.

We followed inductive theory-building strategies to analyze the data. We created a data-base for the case to organize and document all collected data, thus contributing to the enhancement of the reliability of the study. To ensure further reliability, the following key activities of the case study protocol were adopted in the present study: negotiating access; writing the history of the case and highlighting the phenomenon of interest by exhausting all secondary sources prior to interviews; validating the history of the company at the first interview; negotiating access to the stakeholders of the company; and negotiating access for follow-up interviews.

Transcribed interviews were sent back to interviewees for review and comments that were incorporated for further analysis. Along with such multiple sources of evidence (for the purpose of triangulation), the interviewees' feedback contributed to the construct validity of the study. Explanation-building was conducted by describing and exploring the case in narrative form and constantly comparing emergent constructs and theory with the extant literature, thus contributing to internal validity. According to Dubin [38], the very essence of description is to name the properties of things, and the more adequate the description, the greater the likelihood that the concepts derived from the description will be useful in subsequent theory building.

The within-case analysis [32] was the basis for developing early constructs surrounding legitimation of MDsoft and of the industry within which MDsoft operated. We then further theorised in an attempt to move to a higher level of (analytical) generalizability, thus contributing to the external validity. During this process of data analysis we employed theoretical coding [39] to conceptualize the emerging patterns within the case, and middle-range theorizing [40] to help manage the complexity of the emergent patterns. The sampling strategy adopted, as well as the sampling criteria developed also contributed to external validity of the study.

[3] Note that the Republic of Moldova started being included in the ranking calculations from 2004/2005.

4 Findings

Analysis of the data collected reveals three different contexts in which legitimation took place. The credibility of MDsoft needed to be established in Moldova, as did the wider software sector it played a key role in pioneering. A different set of challenges was faced by the sales arm of the business in the UK market, UKsoft. Some of the strategies deployed in legitimating the business in these contexts were found in the data collected; these are presented below.

4.1 Legitimating MDsoft in Moldova

The British investor (the "Investor") had previously co-founded a technology business that had achieved a successful IPO on the London Stock Exchange and, by the year 2000, was performing strongly in the dynamic dot.com economy. Before and concurrently with that he had held academic posts in the UK and published his work in international journals. The accessibility via the Internet of a corpus of research output and positive media coverage provided a vital source of independent validation for the member of MDsoft's founding team who would otherwise have been hardest to evaluate in Moldova.

The three Moldovan founders were also able to demonstrate significant prior credibility as managers and technologists in the local context. For example, the Chairman had been a co-author of the Moldovan Declaration of Independence from the USSR and had served for almost a decade as a Member of Parliament and respected public figure; by background, he was a professor of computer science and holder of a number of technology patents. The CTO had formerly held the same post in the country's leading ISP business.

The Silicon Valley vision of startup technology companies being founded in garages by college drop-outs with nothing more than drive and ingenuity was completely alien to Moldova in 2000. In a culture that requires serious ventures to be led by serious people, referenceable accomplishments of the founders contributed to a bedrock of credibility from which MDsoft could begin to build its institutional legitimacy.

The quest for seriousness continued in MDsoft's approach to human resources. To begin with, in the absence of competition, it was possible to hire – literally – the smartest young engineers and mathematicians in the country. In the words of the Chairman, a former professor:

> "*With the support of my friends from local universities, we were able to find very quickly a team of talented young Moldovans, many of them participants and winners of International Olympiads.*"

The founders consciously set out to promote a culture of excellence in the new venture. They embraced the idea, famously espoused by Steve Jobs of Apple, that "A players like to work with A players" [41, p363]. Employees were encouraged to suggest and help recruit the programmers they most admired. Several respected university professors of computer science were among the early hires.

In its third year the business established a new department dedicated to education and training. Courses were taught in new technologies and project management, and all staff was required to learn English up to specified standard. Each member of staff had a personal development plan with clear objectives and regular monitoring.

In addition to investment in staff excellence, a quality system and set of operating processes was developed for the business. It its fourth year the company achieved ISO-9001 certification, and quickly added many other technical and business accreditations.

The company's conspicuous commitment to excellence became a prominent feature of its identity and helped to legitimate it, not just to the current and potential staff but also to the wider community. This was reinforced in its fourth year when the business sponsored the creation of the country's first university Chair of Software Engineering.

In pursuit of socio-political legitimacy, the Investor and Chairman devoted considerable time and effort to articulating the vision and purpose of the business in the Moldovan media and with prominent figures in business and politics.

A more mundane, but hugely important, contribution to the company's legitimacy resulted from its policy of proactively paying all legitimate taxes and never paying any illegitimate taxes, i.e., bribes. When the company was founded, rates of tax recovery in Moldova were extremely low, both from businesses and individuals. Against the general pattern, MDsoft kept only one set of accounts and promptly paid all taxes. By this simple means it established an identity with the authorities almost overnight as one of the best corporate citizens in the country. In the year after the business was established the Investor and the Chairman were summoned to see the Deputy Prime Minister who was struggling to understand how it could be that a new business was already contributing more tax per month than any single county in Moldova. As the Chairman explained:

> "*From the very beginning we set three major goals – to have offices in Moldova and Romania, provide competitive salaries, and work transparently. These goals helped us to build a reliable and competitive company. During the first four years [MDsoft] continuously doubled its staff; by the end of 2005 we had around 145 employees.*"

In the context of the country's developing institutions it was not always possible simply to obey the law; sometimes it was necessary to help define it. For example, in its third year the company was presented with a large tax bill in respect of VAT (i.e. purchase tax). By law this had to be levied on all goods and services sold in Moldova. The software that MDsoft developed was sold outside of Moldova, chiefly in the UK, but no physical goods were transported out of the country, so the law was somewhat vague with respect to VAT. According to the Chairman:

> "*It was very difficult to demonstrate to [the Government] that we indeed export our services, and to argue and use relevant data on how software services can be delivered via Internet without any customs approvals.*"

Tax officials privately agreed with the company that software exports should be VAT-exempt, but none dared to implement their opinion for fear that their decision in the absence of legal clarification would be interpreted as resulting from receipt of bribes. Thus MDsoft was required to pursue a legal action all the way to the Supreme Court, which decided in its favor and established the interpretation of VAT law relied upon by the country's software industry to this day.

The existence of MDsoft, a British-backed company, was acknowledged to be one of the factors that led the British government to open an embassy in Moldova for the first time. Formally opening the embassy, a member of the British Royal Family delivered a speech before the President, Prime Minister, assembled VIPs and media, in which he warmly eulogized MDsoft's vision and achievements, thereby effectively putting the company's socio-political legitimacy beyond doubt.

4.2 Legitimating the Software Sector in Moldova

In the year 2000 the idea that Moldova could address global markets with knowledge products, such as custom software, could easily be dismissed as foolish [6]. Speaking about the first time the idea of software development for foreign markets was presented to him, MDsoft's Chairman reflected:

> "*When I met one of my former students who told me that he and one of his friends were planning to launch a software company together with a British investor, I expressed my eagerness to join them, but it was like a joke – a joke I wanted to be a reality.*"

The existence of successful analogous models was used as a resource, first by the British Investor and subsequently by the wider founding team, to argue for the plausibility of a software sector that initially seemed little more then fantasy. Specifically, the success of the Indian offshore software development sector was used to inspire optimism. Most people were willing to concede that some of the challenges of poverty and underdevelopment in India surpassed even those of Moldova. Most were also willing to concede that *a priori* India was an even less likely location than Moldova to give birth to a software industry with global reach. And yet, the facts spoke for themselves – India provided a clear existence proof that a well-conceived export-oriented software industry could emerge from the midst of economic despair to conquer global markets.

MDsoft's founders appealed to the Indian example often over the first few years, but they were also able to reference comparable small scale, but still encouraging initiatives in the immediate neighbors Romania and Ukraine, and in other countries of the region, such as Russia, Czech Republic and Hungary.

Many Moldovans were justifiably proud of the country's heritage of Soviet technical education,[4] so the idea that Moldovan software engineers could stand shoulder-to-shoulder with international competitors was not completely implausible, even if it was hard to envisage how organizational structures could be financed and realized. Within its first two years, MDsoft itself came to be cited as a Moldovan existence proof in media and public policy discussions that the dream of a Moldovan software sector was not completely foolish.

Around four years after MDsoft launched, the Moldovan government introduced a package of generous tax reliefs specifically targeting the IT sector to encourage

[4] During the Soviet Union era, Moldova was promoted externally as an agricultural country in an attempt to disguise the presence of a dozen large high-technology enterprises and R&D centers that were involved in full-scale and component production and R&D activities mainly for the naval and aerospace Soviet war military complex. One of the co-authors worked for one of these companies and had access to four other enterprises.

inward investment. This legislated incentivization played an important role in driving the expansion of existing software businesses and the establishment of new ones.

In 2008 the Moldovan Association of Private ICT Companies was formed as a forum for larger businesses in the sector; at the time of writing, it has 37 corporate members [42] According to government figures there are now more than 1,500 ICT companies in the country, contributing approximately 10% of GDP, with 70% of the production of software companies being exported.

4.3 Legitimating UKsoft in the UK

UKsoft is MDsoft's sales, marketing and customer relationship partner in the UK within the same corporate group. UKsoft was the first business to sell software development services from Moldova into the UK. In a context where most potential customers had never heard of Moldova, the company initially sought to legitimate itself for purposes of selling on a combination of the founders' track records and pricing that was "*too cheap to ignore*". As the Investor, who was initially also the sole member of UKsoft's staff, recalls:

> "*When I started to go out selling I had to say to companies, 'Please send your mission critical software development projects to a country you have never heard of, to a company that has no track record, contracting with a one-person British company – and you have no way of verifying any of my claims.*' "

Initial sales were small, non-strategic for the customer, and with deeply discounted pricing. This created a number of modest case studies of successful delivery. The first significant enterprise sale was to develop an online portal providing pay-per-view access to a video library of high culture stage events, such as opera, ballet and theatre. The sale was closed largely on the strength of the Investor's prior standing with the customer's CTO. The project proved to be highly demanding for MDsoft, encompassing major learning steps in technology and business. However, the end result was a visually striking, richly functional media portal that compared favorably with systems developed by global leaders.

Because of this, MDsoft came to the attention of a global technology company, BIGsoft,[5] which was planning to test the consumer appetite for pay-per-view live streaming media events. They organized a concert starring an A-list pop performer as their test event. When they began looking for a supplier to develop an online payments solution to process potentially very large numbers of ticket sales immediately before the start of their concert they drew a blank. As the Investor and the Chairman explain:

> "*When BIGsoft went to all of the usual suspects, i.e., the market leaders in online payments, none of them would touch this project; they wouldn't have come anywhere near it. When BIGsoft asked us what experience we had, ultimately the answer was 'None, but what options have you got?'... Eventually, the most robust stable...part of the whole system was our payment solution.*"

[5] BIGsoft is one of the largest software companies in the world.

> *"It was a very ambitious project because it had to be run on a new BIGsoft ... server platform that at the time was a beta version. We did not have enough experience in the area of project management and in working with foreign partners. Nevertheless, our work was well received by BIGsoft as we successfully implemented their first industrial solution."*

Orders followed from the credibility this won, and with them came further positive references and case studies. The necessity to justify the location of UKsoft's production center (MDsoft) in an "exotic" location receded. In the UK market, where the concept of off-shore and near-shore sourcing of software development was already thoroughly legitimate, only the specific choice of Moldova needed to be justified, and referenceable success proved to be sufficient to achieve legitimation.

5 Theoretical Reflections

MDsoft faced the challenge of establishing both cognitive legitimacy and socio-political legitimacy [15]. That is, the company had to frame and communicate its own identity and mission in such a way that interested parties could understand it as a rational and coherent enterprise. It also needed to position itself socio-politically as an initiative that was appropriate and valid in the Moldovan context. Strategies of cognitive legitimation centered on establishing the credentials of the founders and the business model, and on framing the company's mission, in part at least, as the pursuit of excellence.

The above challenge was amplified by the emerging state of the industry and of the economy within which MDsoft started operating. Related to the new sector of the economy, as theorized elsewhere [21], MDsoft pursued the creation legitimation strategy thus contributing to the creation and legitimation of new laws and norms, new values and expectations, as well as new business models and operating practices. As to the emerging state of the economy, MDsoft had to overcome the country-of-origin effect in order to mitigate the liability of foreignness [43].

In this quest for legitimacy, the data reveal several legitimation strategies adopted by MDsoft. First, MDsoft designed a robust business model targeting internal (employees) and external stakeholders. MDsoft did so, for example, by providing competitive salaries and continuous professional education for its employees, paying all taxes and complying with all laws and norms, achieving internationally recognized certification, and engaging in community/charity activities. In contrast to earlier findings according to which entrepreneurs in their pursuit of robust design shall decide, among other things, which details to hide from view altogether [27], MDsoft decided from the start to operate openly and transparently.

Second, MDsoft engaged in theorizing its business model. More specifically, it engaged in persuasive argumentation [26] invoking familiar cues and scripts, such as referring to the success of Indian and Central European software companies. At the same time, it engaged in political negotiations [26] promoting and defending incentive and operating mechanisms aimed to make the sector of the economy efficient and eventually successful. Being integral to institutional change [24], our data suggest theorizing is also integral to institutional experimentation when an industry emerges and tries to achieve its legitimacy threshold.

At the same time, MDsoft aggressively pursued a technology legitimation strategy [23] in order to overcome the liability of foreignness, especially with reference to the country-of-origin effect. Of all the other internal and external legitimation strategies available to international new ventures [23], the data point to technology legitimation strategy as *the* strategy that contributes to rapid and successful internationalization of the new venture.

The above legitimation strategies were aimed at establishing both cognitive legitimacy and socio-political legitimacy. Although these legitimation strategies were pursued concurrently, their effect on the acquisition of cognitive legitimacy and socio-political legitimacy is path-dependent. According to our data, there is a time-lag of three or four years between the acquisition of cognitive legitimacy and socio-political legitimacy. The data also suggest a cause-effect relationship between the two legitimacies, with cognitive legitimacy leading to socio-political legitimacy. We thus conjecture that the relationship between cognitive legitimacy and socio-political legitimacy is inherently temporal and that the acquisition of socio-political legitimacy is positively associated with the acquisition of cognitive legitimacy.

We further argue that the acquisition of socio-political legitimacy is prerequisite to the acquisition of legitimacy threshold. Nationally, according to the data, MDsoft reached legitimacy threshold when it won its legal battles on the disputes over VAT and exporting software products. At the international level, MDsoft reached legitimacy threshold when it won and successfully delivered a software solution for one of the largest software companies in the world. Drawing on estimates of new venture survival after three years [44], we argue the acquisition of socio-political legitimacy is critical for passing that survival threshold.

The above mentioned strategic legitimation efforts by MDsoft were also directed towards changing and creating new structural meanings [29] that helped the new, emerging sector of the economy reach what we call *industry legitimation threshold.* The data suggest the industry legitimation threshold was achieved when the lawmakers made the ICT sector one of the country priority sectors and introduced a long-term tax relief package for software companies. In contrast to earlier findings [28] according to which industry norms and practices ought to be legitimate, credible and valued before a new venture can conform to them and eventually legitimate, our data suggest that the new venture may actually drive the process of industry legitimation by legitimating, achieving legitimacy threshold first nationally at meso and micro levels as well as internationally.

From the social construction of reality point of view [45], the emergence of a new industry or sector of the economy could be seen as a process whereby legitimation and institutionalization alternate each other and during which the bonds between the two are created or loosened up. In this context, we define legitimation as a process during which structural meanings are changed and/or created at micro and meso levels in order to achieve cognitive legitimacy and forge strong bonds with institutionalization. We define institutionalization as a process during which new structural meanings have strong traction at the macro level, making the bonds between legitimation and institutionalization loosen up, eventually leading to socio-political legitimacy.

6 Conclusion

To achieve cognitive legitimacy and socio-political legitimacy in an emerging industry located in an emerging economy, and successfully internationalize, an INV shall (i) design a robust business model targeting both internal and external stakeholders, (ii) engage in persuasive argumentation invoking familiar cues and scripts, (iii) engage in political negotiations promoting and defending incentive and operating mechanisms, and (iv) overcome the country-of-origin effect by pursuing technology legitimation strategy. We advocate for more theory-building research at this intersection of legitimation and INVs within emerging and established industries as well as emerging and established economies in order to advance international entrepreneurship theory.

References

1. Coviello, N., McDougall, P., Oviatt, B.: The Emergence, Advance and Future of International Entrepreneurship Research - An Introduction to the Special Forum. J. Bus. Venturing 26, 625–631 (2011)
2. Turcan, R.V., Mäkelä, M., Sørensen, O., Rönkkö, M.: Mitigating Theoretical and Sampling Biases in the Design of Theory-Building Research in International Entrepreneurship. Int. Ent. Manage. J. 6, 399–417 (2010)
3. Yamakawa, Y., Peng, M., Deeds, D.: What Drives New Ventures to Internationalize from Emerging to Developed Economies? Ent. Theory Practice 32, 59–82 (2008)
4. Jones, M., Coviello, N., Tang, Y.: International Entrepreneurship Research (1989-2009): A Domain Ontology and Thematic Analysis. J. Bus. Venturing 26, 632–659 (2011)
5. Turcan, R.V., Marinova, S., Rana, M.: Empirical Studies on Legitimation Strategies: A Case for International Business Research Extension. In: Devinney, T., Pedersen, T., Tihanyi, L. (eds.) Institutional Theory in International Business, Advances in International Management, vol. 12 (forthcoming, 2012)
6. Oviatt, B., McDougall, P.: Toward a Theory of International New Ventures. J. Int. Bus. Stud. 24, 45–64 (1994)
7. Aldrich, H., Fiol, M.: Fools Rush In? The Institutional Context of Industry Creation. Acad. Manage. Rev. 19, 645–670 (1994)
8. Turcan, R.V.: Entrepreneur-Venture Capitalist Relationship: Mitigating Post-Investment Dyadic Tensions. Int. J. Entr. Finance 10, 281–304 (2008)
9. Khanna, T., Paleru, K.: Why Focused Strategies May Be Wrong for Emerging Markets. Harvard Bus. Rev. 75, 41–51 (1997)
10. Tornikoski, E., Newbert, S.: Exploring the Determinants of Organizational Emergence: A Legitimacy Perspective. J. Bus. Venturing 22, 311–335 (2007)
11. Stinchcombe, A.: Social Structure and Organizations. In: March, J. (ed.) Handbook of Organizations. Rand McNally, Chicago (1965)
12. Zaheer, S.: Overcoming the Liability of Foreignness. Acad. Manage. J. 38, 341–363 (1995)
13. Zahra, S.: The Theory of International New Ventures: A Decade of Research. J. Int. Bus. Stud. 36, 20–29 (2005)
14. Suchman, M.: Managing Legitimacy: Strategic and Institutional Approaches. Acad. Manage. Rev. 20, 571–610 (1995)

15. Ranger-Moore, J., Banaszak-Holl, J., Hannan, M.: Density-Dependent Dynamics in Regulated Industries: Founding Rates of Banks and Life Insurance Companies. Admin. Sci. Q. 36, 36–65 (1991)
16. Delmar, F., Shane, S.: Legitimating First: Organizing Activities and the Survival of New Ventures. J. Bus. Venturing 19, 385–410 (2004)
17. North, D.: Institutions, Institutional Change and Economic Performance. Harvard University Press, Cambridge (1990)
18. Turcan, R.V.: External Legitimation in International New Ventures: Toward the Typology of Captivity. Int. J. Ent. Small Bus. 15, 262–283 (2012)
19. Santos, F., Eisenhardt, K.: Constructing Markets and Shaping Boundaries: Entrepreneurial Power in Nascent Fields. Acad. Manage. J. 52, 643–671 (2009)
20. Navis, C., Glynn, M.A.: How New Market Categories Emerge: Temporal Dynamics of Legitimacy, Identity, and Entrepreneurship in Satellite Radio, 1990-2005. Admin. Sci. Q. 55, 439–471 (2010)
21. Zimmerman, M., Zeitz, G.: Beyond Survival: Achieving New Venture Growth by Building Legitimacy. Acad. Manage. Rev. 27, 414–431 (2002)
22. Zott, C., Huy, Q.: How Entrepreneurs Use Symbolic Management to Acquire Resources. Admin. Sci. Q. 52, 70–105 (2007)
23. Turcan, R.V.: How International New Ventures Acquire Legitimacy. Paper presented at the European International Business Academy, Bucharest, Romania, December 08-10 (2011)
24. Greenwood, R., Suddaby, R., Hinings, C.: Theorizing Change: The Role of Professional Associations in the Transformation of Institutionalized Fields. Acad. Manage. J. 45, 58–80 (2002)
25. Lounsbury, M., Crumley, E.: New Practice Creation: An Institutional Perspective on Innovation. Org. Stud. 28, 993–1012 (2007)
26. Maguire, S., Hardy, C., Lawrence, T.: Institutional Entrepreneurship in Emerging Fields: HIV/AIDS Treatment Advocacy in Canada. Acad. Manage. J. 47, 657–679 (2004)
27. Hargadon, B., Douglas, Y.: When Innovations Meet Institutions: Edison and the Design of the Electric Light. Admin. Sci. Q. 46, 476–501 (2001)
28. Glynn, M., Marquis, C.: When Good Names Do Bad: Symbolic Illegitimacy in Organization. Res. Sociol. Org. 22, 147–170 (2004)
29. Abbott, A.: Time Matters: On Theory and Method. The University of Chicago Press, Chicago (2001)
30. Dyer, G., Wilkins, A.: Better Stories, Not Better Constructs, to Generate Better Theory: A Rejoinder to Eisenhardt. Acad. Manage. Rev. 16, 613–619 (1991)
31. Drori, I., Honig, B., Sheaffer, Z.: The Life Cycle of an Internet Firm: Scripts, Legitimacy, and Identity. Ent. Theory and Practice 33, 715–738 (2009)
32. Miles, M., Huberman, M.: Qualitative Data Analysis: An Expanded Sourcebook. Sage, London (1994)
33. Pettigrew, A.: Longitudinal Field Research on Change: Theory and Practice. Org. Sci. 1, 267–292 (1990)
34. Doing Business in a more Transparent World, `http://www.doingbusiness.org`
35. The Heritage Foundation, `http://www.heritage.org`
36. The World Economic Forum, `http://www.weforum.org`
37. Webb, E., Campbell, D., Schwartz, R., Sechrest, L.: Unobtrusive Measures. Sage Publications, Thousand Oaks (2000)
38. Dubin, R.: Theory Development. Free Press, New York (1978)
39. Glaser, B.: Theoretical Sensitivity. Sociology Press, Mill Valley (1978)

40. Merton, R.: Social Theory and Social Structure. Free Press, New York (1957)
41. Isaacson, W.: Steve Jobs: The Exclusive Biography. Little Brown, London (2011)
42. Moldovan Association of Private ICT companies, `http://www.ict.md`
43. Cuervo-Cazurra, A., Maloney, M., Manrakhan, S.: Causes of the Difficulties in Internationalization. J. Int. Bus. Stud. 38, 709–725 (2007)
44. Storey, D.: Understanding the Small Business Sector. Routledge, London (1994)
45. Berger, P., Luckmann, T.: The Social Construction of Reality. Doubleday, New York

Topics in Software Industry Transformation Research: A Topic Analysis of Major IS Conferences

Anton Pussep, Markus Schief, Benedikt Schmidt, Florian Friedrichs, and Peter Buxmann

Technische Universität Darmstadt, Chair of Information Systems, Hochschulstraße 1, 62849 Darmstadt, Germany
{pussep,schief,buxmann}@is.tu-darmstadt.de,
florian.friedrichs@stud.tu-darmstadt.de
SAP Research, Bleichstraße 8, 64283 Darmstadt, Germany
benedikt.schmidt@sap.com

Abstract. As the information load grows, it becomes increasingly difficult to follow-up new trends in business and management. However, new developments in technologies and markets pose threats and open up opportunities to firms. Especially the software business changes continuously and profoundly. It is therefore necessary for researchers and practitioners to follow up recent developments and to cope with the information overload. We suggest the application of a data mining technique in order to automatically identify topics: Latent Dirichlet Allocation (LDA). Using a sample of 13,799 publications from ICSOB and major conferences on Information Systems, we identify topics relevant to industry transformation research and review their development on a timescale. As proof of concept, we conduct a short case study using Green IT in order to demonstrate that topic analysis can yield relevant results for literature search beyond the results that can be obtained through a simple keyword search.

Keywords: topic analysis, latent dirichlet allocation, LDA, industry transformation, software industry.

1 Introduction

IT and software are fast changing businesses. The last decade has seen the rise of Google and Facebook from small startups to the most valuable firms on the planet. While Google made its business with internet search engines, Facebook became the biggest social network. Both businesses engaged in early markets and current technologies, profiting by the first-mover advantage. In presence of network effects, it can be argued that the first-mover advantage could be even more beneficial in the software business [1], [2].

As information grows, it becomes increasingly hard to follow-up important trends and to hence identify sweet spots yielding great business potential. For instance, in our sample the number of sources doubled in the period 2000-2011 and even fourteen-fold in 1993-2011. In research, meta-analysis studies are becoming increasingly popular in order to cope with the information load: A search in titles in

M.A. Cusumano, B. Iyer, and N. Venkatraman (Eds.): ICSOB 2012, LNBIP 114, pp. 128–140, 2012.

the Business Source Premier database indicates a continuous growth in the period 1990-2010 from 23 to 96 sources per year. State of the art works solely attempt to sum up the current body of knowledge on a particular topic. However, meta-analysis and state of the art analysis is costly, as all work needs to be reviewed manually. A solution can be found in assisting methods from Data Mining, such as the Latent Dirichlet Allocation (LDA). LDA is an unsupervised learning algorithm which can automatically extract topics from a large dataset. In this paper, we suggest the application of LDA to: (1) overview the topics in IS in order to identify relevant topics for software business and management; (2) assess the development of topic relevance over time; and (3) support literature search and review through the unsupervised identification of relevant sources.

Consequently, the research question that we address in this paper is: Which recent topics in IS and software business research are relevant to the field of software industry transformation? Our main contribution to software business and management research is the identification of relevant topics and their development over time. We further demonstrate how the method can support literature search on large datasets beyond a keyword search.

Researchers will find the topics presented here useful to overview their respected fields and assess the current relevance of the topics. Whereas the identified topics are inherent to IS research, they either deal with software directly or can be used as a starting point for software-specific research. Furthermore, the method used in this paper proved to be useful for the identification of relevant sources. We therefore suggest it as an assisting tool for literature search and review. Practitioners will find the results and methods useful for tracking developments in their respective industries, thereby supporting the identification of threats and opportunities to their businesses.

The remainder of the paper proceeds as follows: Section 2 provides an overview on applied topic analysis demonstrating its potential. We proceed with the presentation of the data and method used in this paper in section 3. Next, an overview of relevant topics is presented in section 4, followed by an analysis of how the topic relevance evolved over time in section 5. Finally, section 6 concludes the paper and provides avenues for further research.

2 Literature Review

Topic analysis is a useful tool for the identification of structures in large textual datasets. A set of approaches exists that is based on Bayes methods and enables topic analysis. In the following, we present different applications of topic analysis to datasets and motivate why an approach to software business and management research appears to be promising.

Steyver and Griffiths analyze the proceedings of the national academy of sciences (PNAS) to get insight into the content [3]. They identify topics that show meaningful aspects of the structure of science and show relationships between different science disciplines. By analyzing documents separated by the year of their publication they demonstrate research trends. A similar study with a focus on the time evolution of documents is performed by Blei and Lafferty on the archives of the journal Science for the period 1880-2000 [4]. Another specialization of topic extraction for time series is topics over time. The method has performed well on 17 years of NIPS conferences, 21 decades of presidential state-union-addresses, and 9 months of email [5].

Wang et al. [6] use the group topic model to analyze voting data to the senate dataset (voting records of Senators in the 101st-109th US Senate) and the UN dataset (voting records of the UN general assembly). They identify topic groups that show the voting attitude of groups with respect to different topics.

Topic models are applied by Schmidt et al. [7] to analyze the text which knowledge workers interact with while executing a set of tasks. The emerging topics give hints about the task types and are able to be used to identify structures in the work process.

Despite the work on particular topic modeling methods for specific applications (e.g. time series data), accompanied by a dedicated example, few work exists that shows a general acceptance of these techniques in the scientific communities. Ramage suggests that topic analysis provides valuable support for social scientists, as textual datasets grow in size and scope [8]. The adaptation is complex: on the one hand, the corpora for analysis need to be transformed to specific data formats which can be tedious task for large collections of data. On the other hand, the application of topic modeling techniques requires theoretical background, as long as no "out of the box tool" exists. Recently, libraries like the Stanford Topic Modeling Toolbox (TMT) emerged that support the general application of topic modeling.

Talking about industry transformation indicates a very broad scope that implies large sets of text documents that may be considered relevant. Existing work focuses on specific industries [9, 10] or takes a system perspective [11]. An application of topic modeling approach to literature in the domain of software industry transformation does not exist to our best knowledge.

3 Data and Method

This paper aims at identifying scientific topics relevant to industry transformation research in software business and management. As this is a very broad theme, we used the description provided by the ICSOB 2012 call for papers description in order to identify issues relevant to the overall theme. By this, we obtained nine issues relevant to industry transformation: (1) increasing verticalization of software; (2) software industry evolution and technological change; (3) empirical research issues; (4) security; (5) user experience; (6) green software; (7) internationalization; (8) outsourcing; (9) open source. However, we acknowledge that further issues can be relevant to industry transformation research.

The method applied in this paper relies on unsupervised learning to identify topics from a large dataset. As there is only one relevant conference directly targeted at software business and management, we extended the dataset by major IS conferences. The IS field is relevant as software is part of IS, while having distinguishing characteristics as well [12]. Furthermore, the IS field inherently deals with topics issues on the intersection between IT and business. Arguably, conferences are more suitable to track current topics as there are large IS conferences with up to twenty different tracks per conference. Thus, in addition to the International Conference on Software Business, our sample comprises six conferences from the Association for Information Systems (AIS): AMCIS, Conf-IRM, ECIS, ICIS, MCIS, PACIS. From those, we collected all publications dating back to 1993, resulting in a total of 14,077 documents for the period 1993-2011.

We downloaded all documents as PDF files using a crawler which is based on the Apache httpclient library. Before the PDF files could be converted to text files readable by the topic analysis tool, we had to apply Optical Character Recognition (OCR) to the PDF files that were saved as pictures and not as text. For that, we used the Adobe Acrobat Professional 9. For conversion to text we used the Apache pdfbox library. As three files could not be processed with this library, we manually copied the text from those files. 278 documents could not be converted to text files due to bad image quality or were recognized as documents not written in English. This left us with 13,799 text files usable for topic analysis.

To identify topics in the document corpus, we use Latent Dirichlet Allocation (LDA) [13]. Deerwester [14] has empirically shown that the latent structure of topics can be recovered based on the co-occurrence structure of terms in text documents. For this, bags of words for document sets are created as input. LDA creates a generative probabilistic model of a text corpus using Bayesian methods. For LDA, documents are random mixtures over topics and each topic is a distribution over words. In the following, we specify this idea and describe the method application. A good introduction is also given in [15] and [16].

In LDA, a word is generated by a convex combination of topics z. The probability that a word is chosen from a sampled topic-word distribution, i.e. the sum of the probabilities that a word belongs to a topic and that a topic belongs to a document:

$$P(w_i) = \sum_{j=1}^{T} P(w_i|z_i = j)P(z_i = j)$$

By setting $P(w|z=j)= \Phi^{(j)}$ and $P(z)= \Theta^{(j)}$ we get the following equation:

$$P(w_i) = \sum_{j=1}^{T} \Phi^{(j)}\Theta^{(j)}$$

The distribution referring to Φ is the multinomial distribution over words for topic j and indicates which words are important for which topic. Θ says which documents are important for a specific topic.

The following definitions hold for LDA:

- D is the document corpus
- N is the total amount of word tokens
- d is a document
- d consists of N_d word tokens
- the distributions in the equation above Θ, Φ and the topics z are latent variables

A good overview of the LDA algorithm can be given based on the plate notation (see Figure 1). The outer plate represents documents. The inner plate stands for repeated choices of topics and words within a document. Blei uses a Dirichlet prior on Θ with a single hyperparameter α. As described by Heinrich [15] the process can be seen as follows: LDA generates observable words w, partitioned by documents D. For each word, a topic proportion Θ is drawn. This is used to sample z. By this, a relation between words and documents can be identified for z. Then the corresponding topic-specific term distribution Φ(z) is used to draw a word. The topics Φ are sampled once for the entire corpus. After finalizing the process, the relevance of a word to a topic and the relevance of a topic to a document have been quantified.

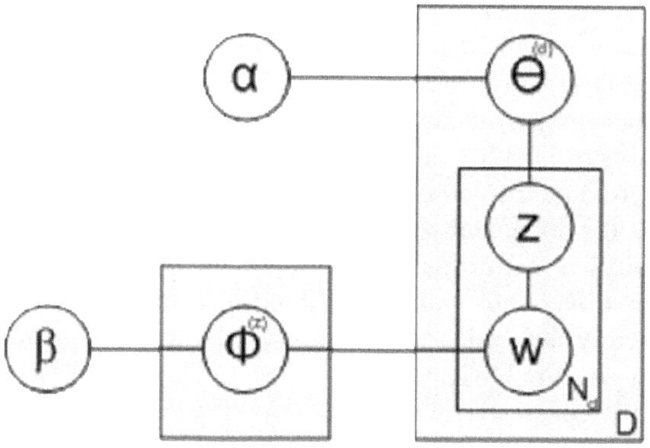

Fig. 1. Latent Dirichlet Allocation in plate notation

An important aspect is the need of the definition of the amount of topics to be sampled by LDA. It assumes that the number of topics is given. As the actual number is unknown, an optimal number of topics can be estimated using an objective function, such as the perplexity. The perplexity "is monotonically decreasing in the likelihood of the test data, and is algebraically equivalent to the inverse of the geometric mean per-word likelihood" [13]. The lower the perplexity score, the better the generalization performance for the given number of topics. The perplexity curve is U-shaped, where the minimum indicates the optimal number of topics.

To improve the results, different operations can be performed on the text data, before the bags of words per documents that are input to LDA are created. A language detection based on language specific n-grams helps to focus on one language, if the corpus contains documents in several languages. Stemming and part-of-speech tagging help to standardize the used words and filter those word types considered meaningful, e.g. verbs and nouns. Stopword lists help to filter words that are considered as not meaningful.

Table 1. Sample distribution over the sample period

Year	1993	1994	1995	1996	1997	1998	1999	2000	2001	2002	2003	2004	2005	2006	2007	2008	2009	2010	2011
Documents	2	3	4	2	84	82	34	11	19	23	42	65	60	69	63	68	92	78	90

As we focus on topics relevant to industry transformation research and the calculations are very intense, we reduced the sample by papers that appeared not to be relevant. For that, we computed 120 LDA topics. The value of 120 was selected using an optimal perplexity value. Out of these topics, 30 topics could be mapped to the issues in industry transformation research. The final document sample comprises documents that are at least 50% relevant to these 30 relevant topics, leaving us with a sample of 891 documents. The sample distribution is shown in Table 1.

4 Topics in Industry Transformation Research

Within this section, we present and discuss the results of the topic analysis. As described above, the topics have been extracted from the 891 documents that appeared to be relevant to the ICSOB 2012 track "Industry Transformation".

In order to obtain the optimal number of topics, we calculate the perplexity value for 20 to 1,000 topics (using steps of 20). The results are depicted in Figure 2. From this graph it can be seen that the optimal number of topics is around 160. Thus, we run LDA with 160 topics to retrieve the actual topics.

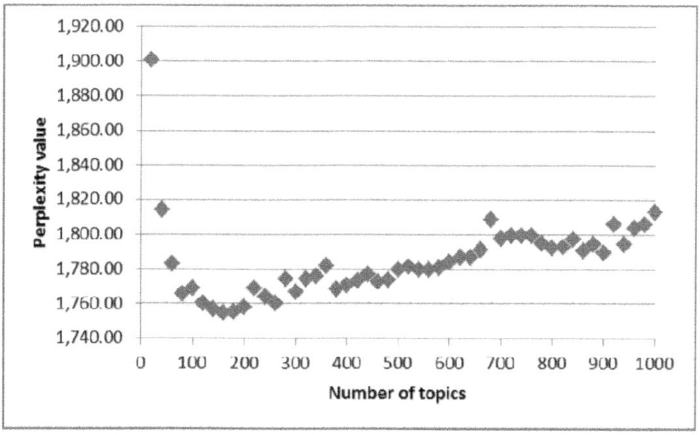

Fig. 2. Perplexity value for different numbers of topics

As the obtained number of topics is too large to be reviewed here individually, we map those to the industry transformation issues first and analyze them on this aggregated level further on. The mapping was done by two authors in three steps: (1) exclusion of "noisy" topics; (2) individual expert mapping of topics to track issues; and (3) detailed analysis of mismatches. The main result is shown in Table 2.

The noisy topics could be easily identified by both authors individually as they contained nonsense words or conference names and locations. Further, some automatic rules have been applied to identify irrelevant topics: (1) at least three documents must have a relevance of at least 1%; (2) at least one source must have a relevance of at least 50%; (3) total topic relevance must be at least 100 (this is a low value, as the average relevance is 11,000); (4) the term with the maximal relevance must attribute for at least 1% of the total topic relevance. This left us with 101 topics.

Within the separate mapping both authors assigned each topic to exactly one track issue. 70 mappings have been assigned consistently by both. For the remainder, both authors reviewed them together and either excluded the topics or assigned them to an issue. Where no decision was possible, the relevant documents were briefly reviewed in order to make a decision. Finally, this process resulted in 74 relevant topics.

Given the association of LDA topics to conference issues, we identified the documents relevant to the conference issues. For that, we assigned each document to the most relevant issue, where the relevance was bigger than 1%. As a result, we obtained an association of 701 documents to the given conference issues.

The results in Table 2 show the topics per industry transformation issue and the document numbers associated with them. In the following paragraphs, all issues are briefly reviewed. Further, as a detailed example, we provide a profound review of the topics related to industry transformation issue Green IT.

It becomes apparent that the issue of verticalization in software markets is not associated with any topics or sources. In general, this result confirms our feeling that verticalization is not a major issue in software business and IS research yet.

The issue of empirical research in software business has a cross-cutting role as it focuses on a method that is applicable to all other issues. Naturally, we find topics there, which explicitly deal with measurement and data collection. Another stream is related to stock market studies, as those are empirical in nature and not associated with the other issues. Thus, in order to identify sources applying particular methods, both relevance measures should be analyzed: the relevance to the method and the particular field.

The largest issue deals with industry evolution and technical change as it spans multiple streams. The main streams can be divided in technology adoption and diffusion, social networks and web 2.0, and ICT development of countries. Furthermore, we find four topics associated with cloud computing representing 29 documents: application service providing (ASP) and software as a service, cloud computing and pricing, as well as service level agreements (SLA). Two topics with 26 documents represent the mobile technology.

The second-largest issue is user experience. By far the largest topic deals with the technology acceptance model. Interestingly, it appears that terms are used especially consistently in this stream, as 134 documents are associated with one topic. This is different for the stream related to the IS success model, which comprises various LDA topics. Another stream in this issue deals with the design and usability of systems and interfaces.

The issue security encompasses 85 documents, covering diverse streams. Those include privacy, trust, anonymity, and policies in organization. Rather technical streams are vulnerability of systems and encryption. Minor streams cover Bluetooth and home security.

Conference issue	LDA topic	Sour-ces	LDA topic	Sour-ces
Verticalization	*no topics and no sources*			
Impact of industry evolution and technological change(e.g. mobile, on-demand, cloud)	adopt innov diffus technolog roger	9	network access cost wireless technolog	12
	adopt organ organiz technolog institut	10	phone countri 0 readi network	3
	asp risk applic vendor saa	5	platform open develop applic technic	1
	broadband adopt consum research internet	13	resist inhibitor adopt non-adopt belief	5
	cloud price resourc comput revenu	12	rfid tag technolog reader retail	7
	commun social presenc virtual interact	2	site answer wikipedia portal q&a	2
	countri develop industri econom sector	7	social movement polit media twitter	3
	develop ict countri access africa	15	social network user facebook onlin	14
	ict countri develop fdi corrupt	6	technolog micro-blog social commun http	2
	ict develop countri econom sustain	5	telecommun broadband industri polici monopoli	2
	invest telecom econom economi countri	0	vol attitud smart control meter	3
	mobil servic phone consum devic	23	web 2.0 applic content share	5
	mobil wireless commerc solut applic	3	web workflow execut leas sla	6
	model workload oper instanc sla	6	wireless mobil network user devic	24
	nation countri diffus technolog develop	10		
				215
Open-source software business and management	softwar sourc open oss product	9		
				9
Empirical research issues in software business and management	breach market event return announc	7	model measur construct research item	63
	market futur index predict stock	3	qualiti dimens servic measur user	18
	market invest stock announc reaction	7	web-bas survei respons web mail	3
	measur success model dimens survei	10		
				111
Issues in user experience	aesthet color websit design usabl	3	usabl develop user oss cost	0
	bank risk phone cell perceiv	0	usabl qualiti web design instrument	4
	continu satisfact perceiv user intent	15	usag behavior organiz implement user organ	7
	enjoy motiv intrins perceiv activ	5	user design devic interfac task	9
	internet onlin user usag access	0	user profession percept satisfact congruenc	1
	satisfact expect user factor perform	9	user visual input access error	9
	success user satisfact qualiti model	14	virtual world life second user	0
	technolog perceiv model accept intent	134		
				210
Issues in security	concern secur factor trust dimens	3	protect threat password secur cost	4
	kei secur authent network encrypt	9	secur bluetooth comput respond health	3
	osn privaci user trust provid	6	secur home comput behavior practic	2
	person data concern privaci user	5	secur polici employe comput organ	10
	polici user privaci wap site	3	tag user anonym tor latenc	5
	privaci concern person control trust	26	vulner patch attack vendor time	5
	privaci protect polici iso control	4		
				85
Issues in "green" software	green environment motiv technolog sustain	5	grid cost energi power server	5
				10
Internationali-zation of software firms	cultur organiz organis technolog internet	4	cultur valu nation countri dimens	20
				24
Outsourcing	offshor distanc outsourc term nearshor	4	outsourc risk bpo deal market	4
	outsourc cost decis relationship develop	7	outsourc success cost benefit organ	13
	outsourc relationship contract manag govern	9		
	37			
Number of issues: 9	**Number of LDA topics: 74**		**Number of sources: 701**	

37 documents cover the issue outsourcing. The topics appear to be quite indicative with regard to the stream discussed. Those include (1) the definition of terms; (2) the outsourcing decision; (3) the contract management; (4) the risk associated with outsourcing; and (5) the success of outsourcing.

Two rather small issues are open source software and internationalization of software firms. The open source issue includes just one topic. However, a closer look indicates that the included documents are quite diverse. It appears that they have been summarized under this topic due to their high relevance to open source, but they also deal with other topics such as usability and security. The issue internationalization subsumes two cultural topics, whereas the bigger stream deals with cultural differences in different countries. The smaller stream deals with cultural differences on the organizational level.

The issue green software is discussed in more detail here. The comprising topics and associated documents are shown in Table 3. We combine the detailed view with a short case study, in order to evaluate if the topic analysis yields useful results for literature search.

Table 2. Documents associated with Green IT

Terms	Relevance	Title	Year	Conference	"Green IT" in title
green environment motiv technolog sustain	0.35	Testing Multimedia for Ecological Sustainability	1998	AMCIS	no
	0.62	Green IT Adoption: A Motivational Perspective	2011	PACIS	yes
	0.72	Organizational Motivations for Green IT: Exploring Green IT Matrix and Motivation Models	2009	PACIS	yes
	0.68	IT and Eco-sustainability: Developing and Validating a Green IT Readiness Model	2009	ICIS	yes
	0.04	Solving the Traffic Problem by Using A Simulation Model	2008	Conf-IRM	no
grid cost energi power server	0.72	Does Green IT Matter? Analysis of the Relationship between Green IT and Grid Technology from a Resource-Based View Perspective	2009	PACIS	yes
	0.37	Reducing datacenter energy usage through efficient job allocation	2011	ECIS	no
	0.76	A multi-model algorithm for the cost-oriented design of the information technology infrastructure	2003	ECIS	no
	0.69	The Impact of MIS Software on IT Energy Consumption	2010	ECIS	no
	0.38	Grid Technology as Green IT Strategy? Empirical Results from the Financial Services Industry	2010	ECIS	yes

In order to analyze the applicability of LDA to literature identification, we run a benchmark test on the defined document sample. By searching for "green IT" within the titles of all 701 documents, we retrieved five documents, which are also included in the LDA results list. Further, we searched for the term "green" only and identified one further paper "Why are consumers going green? The role of environmental concerns in private green-IS adoption" [17]. In our approach, this paper was not assigned to the green IT topics as its content is more related to an industry evolution topic (smart meters) than to a Green IT topic (only 5%).

While the benchmark validation by standard term search confirms that our topics do not omit any documents, our Green IT topics, notably, cover five further documents that do not contain "green IT" within their title. Thus, content-wise related papers appear in our search result. These documents would be hard to find with predefined keywords as their titles are very heterogeneous, whereas a search on the full text of all articles would most likely yield too many unrelated results.

We further examined the content of the retrieved documents in order to evaluate if the selected documents fit to the proposed topics. In general, our findings confirm the logical soundness of the topics. While the first topic mainly comprises documents dealing with an organizational perspective (motivation and readiness for green IT as well as adoption) of green IT, the second topic primarily consists of documents focusing on technical matters (energy consumption and costs of IT infrastructure such as grid technology). However, the relevance of the assigned documents may not be neglected. For instance, the paper "Solving the Traffic Problem by Using a Simulation Model" [18] has only a 4% relevance and is hence only partially related to the other papers' content. The proposed optimization algorithms of the traffic domain do relate in certain aspects to green IT (e.g. reduce carbon emissions or transfer optimization approach to the ones in datacenters), but not to the full extent. Consequently, the relevance values for each document need to be considered.

5 Topic Evolution

Figure 3 shows the development of the conference issues over the sample period. The values reflect the relevance of the issues. Whereas the absolute altitude is not indicative, the changes in time and relative differences between the values reflect relative differences in relevance. We excluded the issues empirical research and internationalization of firms in order to make the figure more readable. Whereas the issue internationalization was too unimportant, the empirical research issue deals with a particular method. Thus, we decided to focus on the other issues.

For each year and each issue, the relevance is calculated using the associated LDA topics. For each topic, each of the 891 documents has a relevance value for the topic. The sum of all these relevancies is the topic relevance. The issue relevance is the sum of all relevancies from associated topics. Interestingly, nearly the same results were obtained by looking at the absolute number of documents and associating each

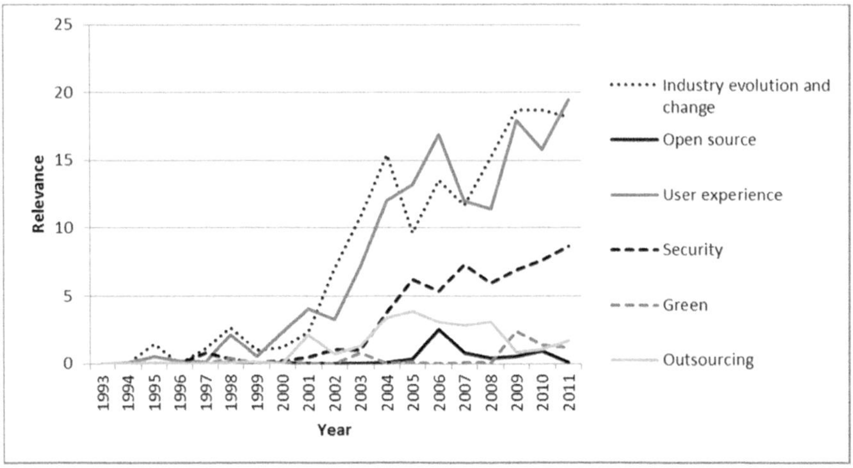

Fig. 3. Evolution of the industry transformation issues over time

document with just one topic, as we did in section 4. As working with these fragment-relevancies is the common procedure [13] and is provided directly through Stanford TMT, we use this representation form in this section.

The results indicate that the largest issues being industry evolution and user experience continue to increase in relevance. However, as those are quite broad issues, comparisons with more specific topics such as open source and green software are less meaningful.

Security appears to be of continuous interest. Whereas it only came up around the year 2000, it soon became more important than outsourcing and continuously grew in relevance faster than all the smaller issues.

Outsourcing shows a similar behavior to security until the year 2003. The following five years, outsourcing reaches its highest attention, before the interest even declines. It appears that the relevance starts to stabilize again, even though it is hard to conclude on a change from the last two years.

Open source displays a similar development as outsourcing, but with a lower relevance over the entire period. Also, there is no indication of a change in the trend downwards.

Apart from two small occurrences, one publication in 1998 and one in 2003, Green IT is a very recent topic. Eight out of ten relevant documents have been published since 2008. These figures go along with the observation by Molla et al. [19], concluding that despite increased attention from business and government, the interest from IS researchers is a more recent phenomenon. It hence can be assumed that more publications are yet to come with increasing scientific interest.

6 Conclusion

Topic analysis can be useful for overviewing the topics in a particular field and their relevance in time. Furthermore, it helps to identify sources relevant to particular topics and can therefore support literature search.

In this paper, we identified topics relevant to industry transformation research in software business and management. For that, we performed a topic analysis of scientific publications in IS research using the LDA approach. Our sample comprised 13,799 documents from seven conferences: ICSOB, AMCIS, Conf-IRM, ECIS, ICIS, MCIS, and PACIS. We assigned the topics identified by LDA to the various issues in software industry transformation research. Thus, indicating the particular topics within the broad issues and their development in time. A short case study on the issue Green IT confirmed that topic analysis can be used to identify relevant sources beyond the possibilities of mere search engines. An overview of the development of the topics in the sample period in general confirmed our impression, e.g. the diminishing interest in outsourcing, steady increase of security topics, and the recent rise of Green IT.

We contribute to the software business and management research by identifying topics relevant to industry transformation, as well as through the analysis of their development over time. Furthermore, we demonstrate how topic analysis can be used for literature search and evaluation. Researchers in the area of software business and management will find the results useful in order to overview topics relevant to their field. The results on source identification further suggest a powerful method for assisted literature search and review beyond search engines. Practitioners can use our results in particular and the method in general in order to identify threats and opportunities to their businesses. The sample can be easily switched to other data sources such as social networks or company wikis, as the input documents are mere text files.

There are certain limitations to this paper. Due to the large sample, we could not process the raw data manually. Also, we could not review all final sources in detail. Furthermore, as no sufficient dataset is available on the software business and management field in particular, we focused on the larger set of IS research. Finally, the evaluation of topics can be greatly improved by applying a structured approach such as systematic mapping. In our further research we attempt to extend the sample by major journals, include publications from the software and business field, apply the topic analysis to issues beyond industry transformation, and provide a software tool for literature search that incorporates our method and findings.

Acknowledgments. This work was supported by the Software-Cluster and partially funded within the Leading-Edge Cluster competition by the German Federal Ministry of Education and Research (BMBF) under grant "01IC10S05". The authors take the responsibility for the contents.

References

1. Lieberman, M.B., Montgomery, D.B.: First-mover advantages. Strategic Management Journal 9, 41–58 (1988)
2. Katz, M.L., Shapiro, C.: Network Externalities, Competition, and Compatibility. American Economic Review 75, 424–440 (1985)

3. Griffiths, T.L., Steyvers, M.: Finding scientific topics. Proceedings of the National Academy of Sciences of the United States of America 101, 5228 (2004)
4. Blei, D.M., Lafferty, J.D.: Dynamic topic models, pp. 113–120 (2006)
5. Wang, X., McCallum, A.: Topics over time: a non-Markov continuous-time model of topical trends, pp. 424–433 (2006)
6. Wang, X., Mohanty, N., McCallum, A.: Group and topic discovery from relations and text, pp. 28–35 (2005)
7. Schmidt, B., Stoitsev, T., Mühlhäuser, M.: Analysis of Knowledge Work Execution at Computer Workplaces. In: Proceedings of 12th European Conference on Knowledge Management (2011)
8. Ramage, D., Rosen, E., Chuang, J., Manning, C.D., McFarland, D.A.: Topic modeling for the social sciences (2009)
9. Berger, A.N., Kashyap, A.K., Scalise, J.M., Gertler, M., Friedman, B.M.: The transformation of the US banking industry: What a long, strange trip it's been. Brookings Papers on Economic Activity, 55–218 (1995)
10. De Vany, A., David Walls, W.: Natural gas industry transformation, competitive institutions and the role of regulation: Lessons from open access in US natural gas markets. Energy policy 22, 755–763 (1994)
11. Dennis, D., Meredith, J.: An empirical analysis of process industry transformation systems. Management Science, 1085–1099 (2000)
12. Messerschmitt, D.G., Szyperski, C.: Software Ecosystem. MIT Press, Cambridge (2003)
13. Blei, D.M., Ng, A.Y., Jordan, M.I.: Latent dirichlet allocation. The Journal of Machine Learning Research 3, 993–1022 (2003)
14. Deerwester, S., Dumais, S.T., Furnas, G.W., Landauer, T.K., Harshman, R.: Indexing by latent semantic analysis. Journal of the American Society for Information Science 41, 391–407 (1990)
15. Heinrich, G.: Parameter estimation for text analysis. Fraunhofer Technology Report (2009)
16. Steyvers, M., Griffiths, T.: Probabilistic topic models. Handbook of Latent Semantic Analysis 427, 424–440 (2007)
17. Kranz, J., Picot, A.: Why Are Consumers Going Green? the Role of Environmental Concerns in Private Green-is Adoption. In: Proceedings of ECIS 2011 (2011)
18. Yang, C.-L., Wen, W.W.: Solving the Traffic Problem by Using A Simulation Model. In: Proceedings of CONF-IRM 2008 (2008)
19. Molla, A., Cooper, V.A., Pittayachawan, S.: IT and Eco-sustainability: Developing and Validating a Green IT Readiness Model. In: Proceedings of ICIS 2009 (2009)

Platform Substitution and Cannibalization: The Case of Portable Navigation Devices

Francesco Novelli

SAP Research Darmstadt, Bleichstr. 8,
64283 Darmstadt, Germany
francesco.novelli@sap.com

Abstract. Platform competition may engender a substitution process whereby customers and complementors drift from one platform to another. For example, as the aftermath of a competitive race between a general-purpose platform and a single-purpose rival. A case in point is how sales of personal navigation devices (PND) have allegedly been sapped by GPS-enabled smartphones with comparable turn-by-turn navigation functionalities. Using a structural-break unit-root econometric model, the impact of smartphones on the quarterly volume sales of two leading PND manufacturers can be statistically assessed. Such an econometric analysis reveals a significant shift in the level of the underlying stochastic processes and dates the structural change at the third quarter of 2008, when the iOS and Android ecosystems were launched.

Keywords: platform competition, technologic substitution, sales cannibalization, structural break.

1 Introduction

Leading information technology (IT) vendors have thoroughly embraced platform design principles as the foundation of their product strategies [1] and have been incentivizing complementary innovation in the surrounding ecosystems [2]. As a consequence, the competitive game can now be played within the same platform (inside competition) or between platforms (outside competition) [3]. This has turned skirmishes among few competitors within homogeneous product categories into vast confrontations engaging whole ecosystems across the product space. The outcome of such platform wars may be platform substitution by both customers and complementors, and – in what I judge an intriguing instance – the trailing vendor might even be induced to cannibalize its own platform.

Such a competitive landscape is epitomized by the recent developments in personal computing devices, where smartphones and tablets have been catalysts for radical change in several markets. Among the affected incumbents, portable navigation devices (PND, also called personal navigation devices), supposedly displaced by GPS-enabled smartphones offering turn-by-turn navigation [4]. PND manufacturers have themselves developed smartphone applications which replicate the navigation

M.A. Cusumano, B. Iyer, and N. Venkatraman (Eds.): ICSOB 2012, LNBIP 114, pp. 141–153, 2012.

functionalities of their own standalone devices[1], thus running the risk of cannibalization.

Using state-of-the-art time-series econometrics, I intend to provide *significant evidence* of whether smartphones affected PND sales. In particular, this paper investigates the presence of structural changes in the underlying sales processes of two leading PND manufacturers and verifies whether these changes can be ascribed to the phenomena of platform substitution and cannibalization. Methodologically, I arrange the study in the two phases of exploratory and confirmatory data analysis [5], i.e., I first look for qualitative clues of the afore-mentioned structural changes and then employ rigorous statistical techniques (econometric models and test procedures) to identify them formally.

The existence of a structural shift in the sales-generating stochastic processes can be detected early in the exploratory stage. By means of an appropriate test procedure [6], it is subsequently dated at the third quarter of 2008, that is, the quarter in which the iOS and Android marketplaces were launched. Taken alternative explanations into account, this finding confirms, I believe, that the PND manufacturers' predicaments have started with the rise of the most recent smartphones ecosystems. Instead, although the potential for sales cannibalization inherent in the navigation "apps" offered by PND manufacturers cannot be neglected, no significant cannibalization effects could be identified in terms of structural shifts in the sales-generating processes.

The present work is organized as follows: I first review the multidisciplinary literature relevant to the topic and sketch the historical development of the personal navigation market; I subsequently proceed with the data analysis and illustrate the main empirical results; eventually, I discuss the meaning and limitations of my findings and conclude.

2 Related Work

In this paper I assess the impact of an innovative technologic artifact (smartphone) on the sales of an incumbent (PND). Therefore, it represents an addition to the multidisciplinary array of studies about the race for technological dominance – the process by which a technology attains market ascendancy [7]. However, since both the considered artifacts can be categorized as computing platforms, I judge the platform competition stream to be the most relevant.

The term platform has commonly two purports: with an engineering connotation, the core components shared by a set of products [8]; with a microeconomic connotation, a multisided market serving groups of interacting agents [3]. These perspectives can overlap for, on the one hand, a modular product platform may naturally lend itself to the creation of a multisided market whereas, on the other hand, a multisided market may require an underlying product platform.

[1] According to TomTom 2010 annual report (p. 25), the offered iPhone app is based on the same navigation application embedded in dedicated standalone devices.

Competition between platforms ("outside competition") is inherently multidimensional, for it involves competition on both sides along the dimensions of pricing, service differentiation, agent differentiation, network size, and the possibility of multihoming [3]. From a dynamic perspective, the chances for a late entrant to successfully take over a platform market (or for an incumbent to defend it) depend on the relative quality and network size, mediated by the level of indirect network effects and consumers' expectations for future applications [9].

The form of platform competition which most closely relates to the present work is that of platform envelopment, whereby a platform functionality is incorporated by a rival in a multi-platform bundle [10]. The occurrence of an envelopment scenario is determined by a vendor decision to alter its platform boundaries. Plasticity of platform boundaries can be interpreted as a response to the tension between the conflicting inclinations to integrate or to outsource components depending on the coordination complexity and network effects they may generate [11].

Owing to the already stated aim of detecting platform substitution and cannibalization, the two phenomena need to be clearly defined. Substitution is the process by which a product or service supersedes another in performing a particular function or set of functions for a buyer [12]. The displacement may be the result of competition between different implementations of the same base technology or between successive generations of that base technology. In the latter case, technologic substitution is properly defined as the mechanism by which adopters and potential adopters of preceding generations of a base technology opt for a successive one [13].

A recent study investigated the relationship between the pace of substitution among competing technologies and the respective challenges or opportunities in building an ecosystem around them [14]. The rate of substitution is found to be the highest when the ecosystem emergence challenge for the new technology is low and the extension opportunity for the old technology is low as well.

I define cannibalization an *intra-organizational* substitution process, i.e., the phenomenon by which buyers and potential buyers of an item in a company's product portfolio opt instead for another item in the same portfolio. Cannibalization measurement endeavors can be categorized depending on the type of model they rely on: descriptive models (e.g., [15]), where no response function is identified, or econometric models, which mathematically formalize the sales response of a product item, either the cannibal, the victim, or both. An overview of state-of-the-art econometric models for the measurement of cannibalization can be found in [16].

The sales cannibalization study closest to my work is [17], where a Dickey-Fuller unit-root test is extended by the authors and employed to assess whether the revenues of a national newspaper are negatively affected by launching a web companion. However, the research issue is different in that I consider both substitution and cannibalization. Moreover, the structural-break date with regard to the former phenomenon is endogenous (i.e., unknown), and I, therefore, adopt a different test: the Zivot-Andrews unit-root test [6]. As far as I know, this represents one of the first microeconomic applications of such a test.

3 The Personal Navigation Market

The U.S. military began testing a satellite-based navigation system in the 60s, conceived the now commonly called Global Positioning System (GPS) in the successive decade, and completed it in 1995. The system was open to nonmilitary uses from the beginning, but it was not until the year 2000 that a civilian GPS market could surge, since the military henceforth ceased to guard the higher quality signal for security purposes [18]. This, coupled with the industry ride down the experience curve[2], has fueled the explosive growth of the world GPS market: from $4 billion in 1998 [19] to the current $110 billion [20].

The focus of this study lies in the personal navigation segment, represented by handheld devices with navigation functionalities based on a GPS-positioning capability. This set of electronic products comprises dedicated devices – so-called personal (or portable) navigation devices (PND) – and GPS-enabled phones equipped with a software application offering comparable navigation functionalities.

If we consider dedicated devices alone, the market structure has been relatively stable since 2006, with the PND manufacturers Garmin and TomTom dueling for market primacy. According to industry estimates[3], Garmin has a 40-50% market share in North America and TomTom follows with 20-30%. The opposite is true in Europe, where TomTom takes the largest market share. The PND segment enjoyed notable growth rates until 2008, when sales started to plateau. As already mentioned in the introduction, this slowdown is explained by some analysts as the result of smartphones with equivalent navigation functionalities becoming more appealing than a standalone PND [4].

In fact, Java-based mobile phones started offering turn-by-turn navigation in 2003 already, with so-called off-board solutions (i.e., data were downloaded on the phone at each route request) tied to the network carrier by specific extra-fees. Standalone software applications (on-board solutions) for the then most popular mobile operating systems followed suit. However, the impact on the PND market apparently became disruptive only with the most recent generations of smartphones.

Apart from the technologic evolution (and a certain fad, one may claim) which made such phones intrinsically more attractive to consumers, two other factors can be mentioned. First, coherently with the scenario sketched in the introduction, today's successful smartphone platforms are the pivot of rich and innovative software application marketplaces, in which navigation is indeed a renowned segment. Second, Google and Nokia have dropped the price floor for turn-by-turn navigation to 0 by respectively releasing Google Maps Navigation and Ovi Maps (now Nokia Maps) free-of-charge. Smartphone-related events relevant for the evolution of the PND market are listed in Table 1.

---

[2] The cost of a commercial GPS receiver, for instance, has dipped from $150,000 in 1983 [19] to less than $50 today.

[3] Figures based on estimates by the independent market research company NPD, from quarterly TomTom earnings presentations.

Table 1. Chronology of the events which marked the PND/smartphone clash

Date	Event	Platform
9 January 2003	Televigation launches North America's first mobile navigation service	Java
29 June 2007	Apple releases the iPhone	iOS
10 July 2008	Apple opens the iTunes AppStore	iOS
28 August 2008	Google announces the Android Market	Android
22 October 2008	Google opens the Android Market	Android
17 August 2009	TomTom releases its iPhone navigation app	iOS
4 November 2009	Google releases Google Maps Navigation (free-of-charge)	Android
22 January 2010	Nokia releases Ovi Maps 3.03 (free-of-charge)	Symbian, Windows Phone 7
5 January 2011	Garmin releases its iPhone navigation app	iOS

4 Data

I gathered quarterly unit sales figures from the publicly available financial reports of the PND manufacturers Garmin and TomTom. Such reports span the period up to the third quarter of 2011, starting from the first quarter of 2000 (47 observations) in the case of Garmin, and from the first quarter of 2004 (31 observations) for TomTom.

Sales figures reported by Garmin refer to total unit sales regardless of business segments and therefore include, alongside handhelds, aviation products, which are supposedly immune to the phenomena targeted in my study. However, a closer look at the financial results reveals that the consumer segment has historically constituted between 70% and 90% of the company's overall net revenues. Hence, I consider these observations representative. Figures reported by TomTom only include sales of portable navigation devices.

5 Methodology

I use an array of state-of-the-art statistical techniques to analyze the data at my disposal and assess whether GPS-enabled smartphones produced a statistically significant structural change in the PND vendors' underlying sales-generating process.

Following [5], I arrange my study into the two phases of *exploratory* and *confirmatory* data analysis. The exploratory stage consists of detective work to reveal the main statistical characteristics of the time series under screening and to suggest the orders for the ARIMA models to be tentatively estimated [21]. Therefore, this phase encompasses instruments, such as time-plots, smoothers, autocorrelation and partial autocorrelation functions, which do not assume an underlying formal model fitted to the sample.

In the confirmatory data analysis I rigorously verify the clues identified by the exploratory procedures and provide statistically significant evidence thereon. In qualitative terms, the underlying model can be written as

response variable = nonstationary component + autocorrelated noise

where the nonstationary component may entail a deterministic trend, a stochastic trend, and structural breaks, while the autocorrelated noise is a stationary component which can be modeled using the Box-Jenkins methodology [22].

In the last decades, scholars at the forefront of econometric research have been relentlessly extending the concepts and procedures to model and test nonstationary components. Structural breaks, in particular, are a topical field of research. On the one hand, their presence biases the various Dickey-Fuller unit-root tests towards nonrejection of the nonstationarity hypothesis [23]; on the other hand, they pose challenging research issues of their own, such as testing for a structural change of unknown date and estimating it.

Zivot and Andrews [6] proposed a unit-root testing procedure in the presence of a potential structural break. They allowed the date of the change to be unknown and showed that the endogenous determination of this breakdate reduces the aforementioned bias. Following their notation, the null hypothesis to be tested is $y_t = \mu + y_{t-1} + e_t$, that is, an integrated process without structural break. The regression equation used in the test procedure (in its less restrictive form, which allows for a change in both intercept and trend) is the following:

$$y_t = \hat{\mu} + \hat{\theta} DU(\hat{T}) + \hat{\beta} t + \hat{\gamma} DT(\hat{T}) + \hat{\alpha} y_{t-1} + \sum_{j=1}^{k} \hat{c}_j \Delta y_{t-j} + \hat{e}_t \tag{1}$$

where DU and DT are dummy variables to respectively control the changes in level and trend from the breakdate $\hat{T}$ onwards. DU is a step dummy variable which equals 1 if $t > \hat{T}$, 0 otherwise. DT assumes the value $t - \hat{T}$ if $t > \hat{T}$ and 0 beforehand. $\hat{\alpha}$ is the coefficient whose significance determines the rejection of the null hypothesis. The summation component preceding the error term, eventually, tackles the serial correlation in the residuals. The test endogenously estimates the breakdate by running equation (1) sequentially and selecting the point in time less favorable to the null hypothesis.

6 Empirical Results

6.1 Exploratory Data Analysis

The first step in the exploratory phase is the perusal of the time-series plots (Fig. 1). The behavior of the two processes over time exhibits a strong resemblance. Clearly, the two time series share some fundamental attributes: both are nonstationary (in level and variance), show evidence of seasonality, and rise until 2008/2009, where they level off. Garmin unit sales are higher in magnitude (remember, however, that the TomTom time series only includes consumer PND unit sales) and in variance.

In order to investigate the time series further, I applied a robust locally weighted regression smooth (also known as LOESS) and added its trace (the dashed lines in Fig. 1) to the plots. The smoothed curve highlights the trend component and a decline in sales which was not so obvious in the time-series plot alone. The noise left by the smoother (not reported here) also confirms the higher variance of the Garmin time series. Moreover, I invite the reader to notice that it is not possible to unequivocally identify any structural change based on this visual inspection alone.

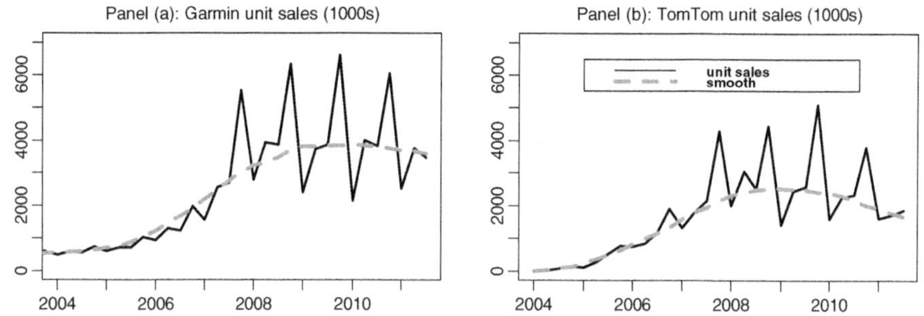

Fig. 1. Time plots of quarterly unit sales

Before proceeding, a Box-Cox transformation (with $\lambda = 0$ and $c = 0$) is applied to the Garmin series to tame its variance[4], and both time series are differenced with lag 4 (i.e., quarterly) in order to eliminate the seasonal persistence. The seasonally differenced time series now reveal some interesting facets of nonstationarity (Fig. 2). In fact, a drop in sales can be detected clearly, at least visually, and seems to have impacted the two sales-generating processes somewhere between 2008 and 2009.

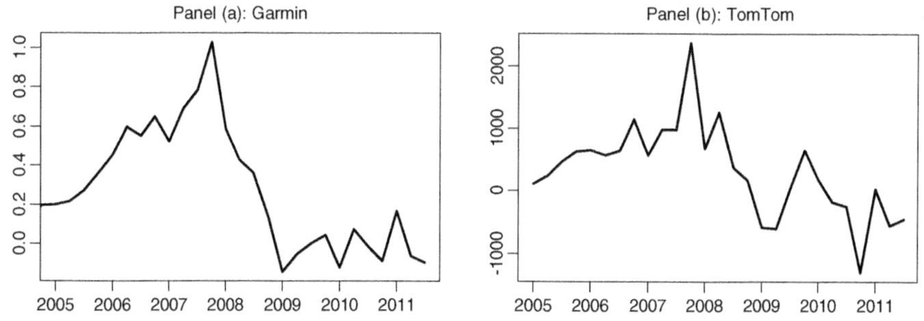

Fig. 2. Seasonally-differenced time series (Panel (a): also transformed)

[4] This Box-Cox transformation was applied following the detection of heteroscedasticity in the residuals during the diagnostic checks at the end of a first round of estimations in the confirmatory phase.

The last step of the explanatory phase is the analysis of the sample autocorrelations (ACF) and partial-autocorrelations (PACF) in order to identify candidate p, d, and q orders for the ARIMA(p,q,d) models to be fitted in the confirmatory phase. Examining the autocorrelogram of the original series (Panels (a) and (d) in Fig. 3), the similarities between the two stochastic processes are highlighted once again, although the ACF for the Garmin series seems to tail off more slowly. Once the seasonal persistence is removed (and the Garmin series is transformed), ACF and PACF for both series display an oscillating decay (Panels (b) and (e)). The Garmin series has a rather significant PACF at the first lag and significant ACF for the first 4 lags, while the TomTom series exhibits an ACF which truncates after lag 2 and a significant PACF at lag 1. Given these clues, we may presume ARMA(p,q) models where both p and q are positive and small. The ACF and PACF of the first-differenced series provide some additional insight (Panels (c) and (f)). In fact, the seasonally differenced Garmin growth series appears to be white-noise, thus supporting the claim that this could rather be a difference-stationary process, while the TomTom differenced series exhibits some new autocorrelations, a possible signal of overdifferentiation.

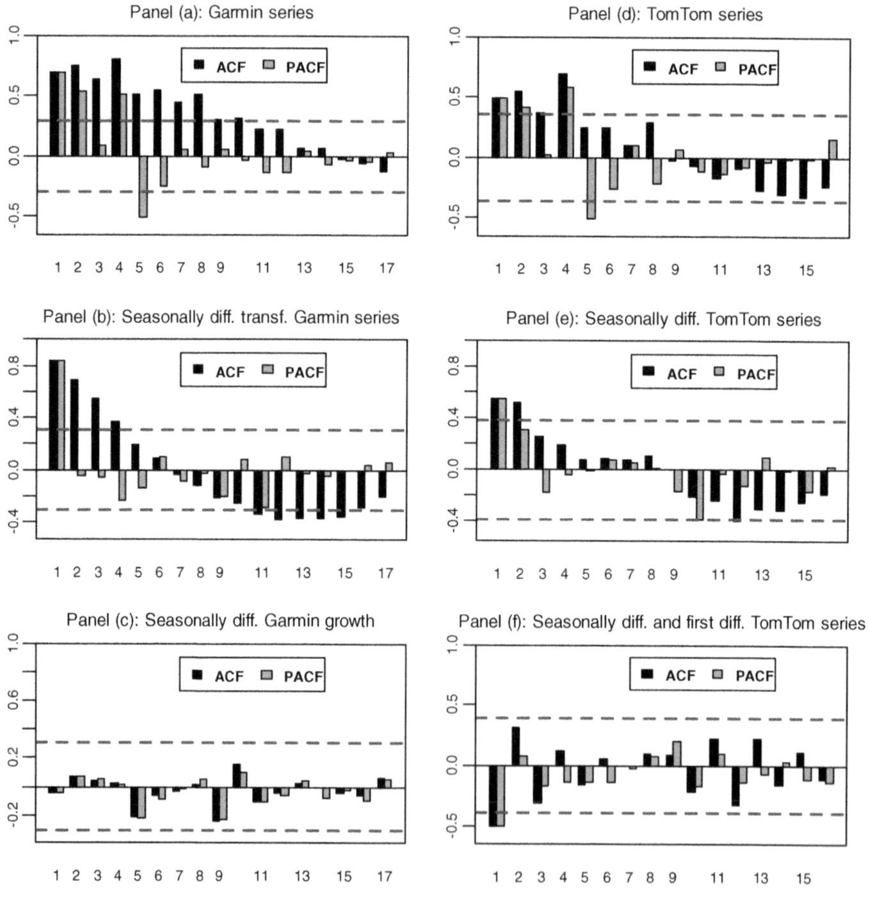

Fig. 3. Sample autocorrelations and partial-autocorrelations

6.2 Confirmatory Data Analysis

From a formal point of view, two are the interrelated facets of nonstationarity whose presence needs to be ascertained: stochastic trends and structural changes of unknown timing.

To illustrate the first aspect, I fit some autoregressive moving-average models with the classical Box-Jenkins methodology. Following the hints given by the exploratory phase on the AR and MA orders, and based on information criteria (both Akaike and Bayes) and standard errors of the estimated coefficients, the best models I can indentify are an AR(2) for the TomTom seasonally differenced series and an AR(1) for the Garmin growth series, both without intercept term.

However, a closer examination of the fitted models reinforces the suspicion of unit-root nonstationarity already arisen in the exploratory phase. Exemplarily, this proximity with a difference-stationary process can be seen in the AR(1) model fitted to the Garmin growth series, $y_t = .917_{(.0613)} y_{t-1} + \hat{e}_t$ (in parenthesis the corresponding estimated standard error). The coefficient .917 is less than 1.4 standard deviations from unity. As a matter of fact, the Augmented Dickey-Fuller unit-root test (ADF) does not reject the null hypothesis (presence of a unit root) for either the Garmin series or the TomTom one. The complication here is the possible dependency of the ADF results on the presence of a structural break, for the latter would bias it towards nonrejection [23].

The Zivot-Andrews test procedure allows tackling both issues simultaneously. I conducted tests for the two most plausible scenarios on the basis of the exploratory analysis, that is, a change in the intercept only or a simultaneous change in intercept and slope. All four tests, whose results are gathered in Table 2, identify the third quarter of 2008 as the most plausible breakdate. Three of them deliver an estimate for

Table 2. Results of the Zivot-Andrews unit-root tests

Series	Garmin growth	Garmin growth	TomTom	TomTom
$\hat{T}$	2008 Q3	2008 Q3	2008 Q3	2008 Q3
$\hat{\mu}$	-.0003981 (.0538270)	-.014260 (.057169)	842.9 ° (403.6)	233.289 (379.4213)1
$\hat{\alpha}$	.5259470 *** (.1347699)	.465224 ** (.157577)	.0535 (.2789)	-0.9427 * (0.3852)
$\hat{\beta}$	.0097486 * (.0040730)	.011732 * (.004865)	-.4134 (31.82)	150.4013* (53.7704)
$\hat{c}_1$	.1168423 (.1518068)	.158732 (.162456)	.008261 (.2376)	0.7361 * (0.2984)
$\hat{c}_2$	N/A	N/A	.2625 (.1957)	0.6984 ** (0.2094)
$\hat{\theta}$	-.3866350 ** (.1236079)	-.378184 ** (.124851)	-1047 ° (528.3)	-1817.1279 ** (492.3040)
$\hat{\gamma}$	N/A	-.010112 (.013373)	N/A	-291.9066 ** (91.2364)
Unit root	Non-rejected	Non-rejected	Non-rejected	Rejected °

NOTE: the symbols °, *, **, and *** indicate that the value is significant at the 10%, 5%, 1%, and .1% levels respectively.

the change in intercept significant at the 1% level, the other one at the 10% level. On the other hand, one of two gives significant evidence of a change in slope. Eventually, the null hypothesis of difference-stationarity can be rejected only for the model of simultaneous change in intercept and slope applied to the TomTom series, where the test statistic assumes a value of -5.044 (with critical values -5.57, -5.08, and -4.82 for the 1%, 5%, and 10% levels of significance).

The last step of the confirmatory data analysis consists in a series of diagnostic checks on the residuals from the calibrated models. These checks are designed to verify if the residuals are independent, normal, and homoscedastic – in other words, to assess whether all the relevant information was extracted from the data. Appropriate tests (respectively the Ljung-Box, the Shapiro-Wilk, and the Breusch-Pagan) confirm that residuals are roughly white, normal, and homoscedastic. Normality and lack of autocorrelation allow us to qualify them as independent as well.

7 Discussion

7.1 Interpretation of the Empirical Results

In the previous section I obtained some statistical evidence that the underlying sales processes of the leading PND manufacturers Garmin and TomTom have been affected by a structural shift, and dated it at the third quarter of 2008. Now the question is to determine whether this shift can be ascribed to the phenomena of substitution and/or cannibalization, which the appearance of GPS-enabled smartphones could have engendered.

If we look at the chronology reported in Table 1, we find a pivotal event which took place exactly in that quarter: Apple launched the AppStore – the online marketplace for software applications running on the iOS platform. Google concurrently announced the Android Marketplace, due to open in the successive quarter. These events testify the rise of a new generation of smartphones which, on the one hand, introduced a form factor more suitable for navigation functionalities (in fact, similar to most PND) and, on the other, were surrounded by an ecosystem allowing the development and distribution of advanced mobile software applications.

However, two competing explanations to the slowdown in PND sales exist: the effects of the late-2000s financial crisis on consumer spending and a saturation of the PND market. On the basis of my statistical result, I rule out the saturation hypothesis for we would otherwise see a different, more gradual change pattern in the stochastic processes – and not a structural break, which represents by definition a change materializing rather instantaneously, at least from an approximate point of view.

It is more complicated to assess the alternative hypothesis of a generalized effect on consumers due to the deteriorating economic climate, which would have affected PND sales just as much as other consumer durables or electronic devices. As a matter of fact, Lehman Brothers filed for bankruptcy in the same quarter the AppStore was opened.

To evaluate this alternative hypothesis, I decided to conduct a Zivot-Andrews test on a time series representing consumers' confidence, under the hypothesis that, should this be the actual driving factor in the PND sales slowdown, the test procedure would lead to results analog to those for the Garmin and TomTom series. I employed the consumer confidence index published monthly by Thomson Reuters and the University of Michigan, from which I extracted a quarterly time series over the same horizon as the Garmin time series. The Zivot-Andrews test rejects the unit-root hypothesis at the 1% level, finds a significant change in slope, and identifies a different breakdate than the one derived previously. Therefore, I conclude that a change of consumer behavior due to the financial crisis was not the driving factor in the PND sales slowdown, and that technologic substitution is a more plausible explanation.

My interpretation is also coherent with the most recent findings on platform competition. As hypothesized in [14], a relationship between the pace of technology substitution and the development in the surrounding ecosystems emerges: although smartphones have offered some navigation functionalities since 2003, it is only with a more mature ecosystem around them that the rate of substitution eventually took off at the expense of standalone navigation devices. At present, smartphones ecosystems are among the most innovative and successful ones. Contrariwise, PND manufacturers struggle to find differentiating extension opportunities in their ecosystems, for they are forced to replicate every innovation (e.g., live traffic services) in their smartphone applications as well – thus stuck in a vicious cycle where they cannot provide any sustainable advantage to their standalone devices.

Considering the threat of sales cannibalization, the release dates for the Garmin and TomTom iPhone apps become candidate dates for a structural change in the respective sales-generating processes. In fact, neither release date matches the structural-break timing identified by the Zivot-Andrews test for the two series. TomTom released a first navigation app in the third quarter of 2009 while Garmin did it at the beginning of 2011, so that the identified structural shift anticipates these events by at least one year. Since the diagnostic checks on the residuals confirmed that the calibrated regressions fit the data well, I may conclude that, with the observations at my disposal, it was not possible to detect a significant cannibalization effect.

This does not mean that the potential for sales cannibalization should be neglected. TomTom declares 189,000 and 500,000 downloads of its iPhone navigation app for the years 2009 and 2010[5]. Since in the same two years the company experienced a decrease in PND sales of about 0.5 million and 1.5 million units, this translates to a hypothetical cannibalization rate of at most 30-38%. However, we can reasonably assume that TomTom smartphone offerings drew some customers from the competition as well, amounting to a yet lower impact – just not high enough to be distinguishable from the overall substitution effect in my econometric analysis.

[5] These are the only publicly available figures on the sales volume of either TomTom or Garmin on the iTunes AppStore (from the TomTom Annual Report 2009 and 2010).

As a final remark, the PND manufacturers' launch of applications (but also car kits and subscription services) for the most popular smartphone platforms might be read as a first step towards the redefinition of their platform boundaries in response to a mutated competitive landscape, as described in [11]. Perhaps the initial phase of a transition to become – shedding skin – suppliers of best-of-breed navigation solutions for mobile computing platforms.

7.2 Limitations

The econometric approach I employed has some obvious limitations. First of all, it tries to identify a unique shift materializing itself at a discrete point in time whereas such a change would rarely manifest itself instantaneously. Moreover, the explanation behind the sales drop could actually be a combination of all the factors mentioned above, and the presented model cannot verify this assumption, nor it can disentangle the individual effects.

Eventually, every test procedure was based on a relatively limited number of observations, and it may be argued that more data points are needed for a representative realization of such stochastic processes. In particular, the quarterly time series do not contain enough information to significantly distinguish the sales cannibalization effect from the overall substitution effect. If sales data with a lower sampling interval were available, a test procedure for a structural change of known date (such as [23]) might have allowed a more accurate analysis of cannibalization.

8 Summary

A fascinating aspect of contemporary IT markets is the occurrence of platform wars which shape the involved ecosystems through platform substitution and platform cannibalization. These dynamic processes, however, represent a maturing field of study, where empirical work is still needed in order to understand them thoroughly.

By means of a Zivot-Andrews unit-root test, I obtained evidence of the impact of smartphones in the quarterly volume sales of two leading PND manufacturers. My econometric analysis reveals a significant shift in the level of the underlying stochastic processes which can be dated at the third quarter of 2008, when the iOS and Android ecosystems were launched. This substantiates a causal relationship between the PND sales slowdown and the rise of the most recent generation of GPS-enabled smartphones.

References

1. McGrath, M.E.: Product strategy for high technology companies: accelerating your business to web speed. McGraw-Hill (2001)
2. Gawer, A., Cusumano, M.A.: Platform leadership: how Intel, Microsoft, and Cisco drive industry innovation. Harvard Business School Press (2002)

3. Roson, R.: Two-Sided Markets: A Tentative Survey. Review of Network Economics 4, 142–160 (2005)
4. O'Brien, K.: Smartphone Sales Taking Toll on G.P.S. Devices, http://www.nytimes.com/2010/11/15/technology/15iht-navigate.html
5. Tukey, J.W.: Exploratory data analysis. Addison-Wesley Pub. Co. (1977)
6. Zivot, E., Andrews, D.W.K.: Further Evidence on the Great Crash, the Oil-Price Shock, and the Unit-Root Hypothesis. Journal of Business & Economic Statistics 10, 251 (1992)
7. Suarez, F.F.: Battles for technological dominance: an integrative framework. Research Policy 33, 271–286 (2004)
8. Meyer, M.H., Lehnerd, A.P.: The power of product platforms: building value and cost leadership. Free Pr. (1997)
9. Zhu, F., Iansiti, M.: Entry into Platform-based Markets. Strategic Management Journal 106, 88–106 (2012)
10. Eisenmann, T., Parker, G., Van Alstyne, M.: Platform envelopment. Strategic Management Journal 1285, 1270–1285
11. Boudreau, K.: The boundaries of the platform: Vertical integration and economic incentives in mobile computing (2006)
12. Porter, M.E.: Competitive advantage: creating and sustaining superior performance. Free Press (1985)
13. Norton, J.A., Bass, F.M.: A diffusion theory model of adoption and substitution for successive generations of high-technology products. Management Science 33, 1069–1086 (1987)
14. Adner, R., Kapoor, R.: Innovation Ecosystems and the Pace of Substitution: Re-examining Technology S-curves (2010)
15. Lomax, W., Hammond, K., East, R., Clemente, M.: The measurement of cannibalization. Journal of Product and Brand Management 6, 27–39 (1997)
16. van Heerde, H.J., Srinivasan, S., Dekimpe, M.G.: Estimating Cannibalization Rates for Pioneering Innovations. Marketing Science 29, 1024–1039 (2010)
17. Deleersnyder, B., Geyskens, I., Gielens, K., Dekimpe, M.G.: How cannibalistic is the Internet channel? A study of the newspaper industry in the United Kingdom and the Netherlands. International Journal of Research in Marketing 19, 337–348 (2002)
18. Feanny Corbis, N.: A Brief History of GPS, http://www.time.com/time/magazine/article/0,9171,1901500,00.html
19. Global Positioning System: Market Projections and Trends in the Newest Global Information Utility. The International Trade Administration (U.S. Department of Commerce) (1998)
20. Dee Ann, D.: GPS Community Confronts Light Squared Move into L1 Spectrum, http://www.insidegnss.com/node/2508
21. Hipel, K.W., McLeod, A.I.: Time series modelling of water resources and environmental systems. Elsevier (1994)
22. Enders, W.: Applied econometric time series, 3rd edn. John Wiley and Sons, Inc., New York (2010)
23. Perron, P.: The great crash, the oil price shock, and the unit root hypothesis. Econometrica: Journal of the Econometric Society 57, 1361–1401 (1989)

Cooperative Advertising in Video Game Software Marketing: A Game Theoretic Analysis of Game Software Publisher – Platform Manufacturer Dynamics

Gozem Guceri-Ucar and Stefan Koch

Department of Management, Faculty of Economic and Administrative Sciences, Bogazici University, 34342 Bebek, Istanbul, Turkey
gozem.guceri@gmail.com,
stefan.koch@boun.edu.tr

Abstract. We aim to model and analyze possible cooperative advertising strategies in the context of a gaming platform manufacturer and a game software publisher in the video game industry. The analysis takes on a game theoretic approach in understanding the impact of a video game's total advertising budget and the co-op advertising sharing policy on each player's preferred strategy and corresponding payoffs. Non-cooperative schemes have been demonstrated in which Stackelberg and Nash equilibriums were identified. These were compared with a cooperative Pareto efficient scheme to understand under which conditions both players would be willing to cooperate. Results show that a non-cooperative simultaneous-move game is never preferred by either player, and there exists at least one Pareto efficient solution where both players are better off than at the Stackelberg equilibrium. However, in order to reach this solution, both parties should be willing to negotiate over the co-op advertising sharing policy.

Keywords: Cooperative advertising, Video games, Game software, Game theory.

1 Introduction

Cooperative advertising schemes in manufacturer-retailer dynamics have been a popular topic for economists, marketers and operational researchers ever since the 1950s: [1], [2], [3], [4], [5], [6]. Co-op advertising is defined as the advertising budget contribution of a manufacturer to a retailer's local advertising expenditures, in order to induce sales of a product close to the point of purchase at the local level [7]. The traditional co-op advertising business model was consolidated and formalized in Hutchins' book Cooperative Advertising [8]. In this model, the major motivation behind a manufacturer's use of co-op advertising is to increase the advertising budget a retailer could allocate to his product's advertising at the local level, which is also assumed to increase the effects of the manufacturer's national brand name investments in generating a stronger sales response. Recent studies have shown that cooperative advertising strategies are more efficient when decided and applied by the coordinated efforts of both parties [7], [9], [10].

M.A. Cusumano, B. Iyer, and N. Venkatraman (Eds.): ICSOB 2012, LNBIP 114, pp. 154–167, 2012.

Although academic studies are only focused on manufacturer-retailer interactions, the notion of cooperative advertising is not specific to supply chain dynamics between a manufacturer and a retailer, and certainly not specific to a single industry. Joint marketing and advertising schemes among vertically integrated companies are common in many industries and among different parties within the supply chain, yet analyses of specific industries or corporate interactions are rare in literature. This study contributes to extant literature in the following ways: First, co-op advertising studies mainly focus on manufacturer-retailer dynamics, without any emphasis on cooperative marketing strategies between other players, like companies offering complementary products. Second, extant cooperative advertising literature takes on a generalist approach without considering industry-specific cases. Therefore, although the video gaming industry is a great candidate for game theoretic analyses of competition and cooperation, there is a lack of academic studies that investigate cooperative strategies within this industry from a game theory perspective.

In the context of video game software marketing, cooperative advertising may be redefined as the advertising budget contribution of a video gaming platform (game console) manufacturer to the advertising expenditures undertaken by a game software publisher, to support the launch of a new game. We investigate possible cooperative advertising strategies that can be applied in the simplified case of a single platform manufacturer and a single game software publisher when launching a game published exclusively for the manufacturer's proprietary gaming platform. Our analysis takes on a game theoretic approach in understanding the impact of game advertising budget and co-op advertising sharing policy for a platform-exclusive game.

2 The Video Game Industry

Several studies investigate the structure of the video game industry and provide detailed descriptions of the interactions that take place among existing players: [11], [12], [13], [14], [15], [16]. As a result, an in-depth elaboration will not be presented here except for some definitions that relate to the current study.

The production network and industry dynamics of the video game industry has been outlined in detail by Johns [12]. Accordingly, the production network can be divided into two interrelated parts, hardware and software production. Hardware production refers to the production and distribution of video gaming platforms (consoles), and currently there are three major players in this arena: Nintendo (Wii), Sony (Playstation 3) and Microsoft (Xbox 360). Software production, on the other hand, refers to the development, publishing and distribution of video game software. In this section of the industry, the strongest players are generally the publishers, since they control the financing of the software production network. Although some platform manufacturers are vertically integrated to perform software production tasks as well (e.g. Nintendo), the game development and publishing divisions are organized as separate companies within the group. Hence, the supply chain dynamics between software and hardware production entities do not differ greatly from those that are not vertically integrated within the same organization.

Johns [12] reports that "Empirical evidence suggests that the manufacturer is able to capture 20% of the total retail value of a console game; developer and publisher (combined), 40%; distributor, 10% and retailer, 30%. These figures are estimates and represent an average distribution of value across the production network as negotiations between actors will vary between games." (p. 163). Revenue sharing models have been subject to empirical analyses through the public availability of sales numbers and retail price information, yet it is more difficult to empirically analyze the marketing budget sharing strategies due to the discreteness of agreements between companies. However, this is not an obstacle against game theoretic analyses based on the 'new empirical industrial organization' (NEIO) approach, which relies on the assumption that firm decisions are based on profit maximization and are interdependent on the decisions of competing (and/or cooperating) firms [17]. This is the approach we have adopted throughout this study.

3 Assumptions

In order to construct the basic model, the case of a single platform manufacturer and a single video game publisher has been chosen as the focus of this study. The game, which will be promoted cooperatively by the platform manufacturer and the game publisher, is assumed to be exclusively designed and published for being played on the platform manufacturer's proprietary platform. No contribution is present from other players in the supply chain such as distributors or retailers. Our analysis focuses on stationary gaming platforms such as the XBOX 360, Nintendo Wii and Playstation 3, as well as portable platforms, such as Nintendo DS or Sony PSP, for which the video game supply chain operates in a similar fashion to what has been described in Section 2. Games designed for mobile devices such as mobile phones or tablets are not within the scope of this analysis.

Game publishers usually advertise individual games, while not making additional brand name investments. On the other hand, platform manufacturers invest heavily on their platform's brand name, while providing support for the publisher's advertising expenditures allocated to the promotion of games published exclusively for their platform. Lee [18] states that "...console manufacturers have primarily relied on internal development, integration, or favorable contracting terms to third party developers or publishers (e.g. lump sum payments or marketing partnerships) in order to secure exclusive titles. More recently, as development costs for games have been increasing and porting costs have fallen as a percentage of costs, most third-party titles have chosen to multi-home in order to maximize the number of potential buyers; in turn, console providers have become more reliant on their own first-party titles to differentiate their platforms" (p. 7). This statement summarizes the motivation of console manufacturers to provide advertising budget contributions to publishers of potentially blockbuster games. Exclusivity may also be a publisher's preference under certain circumstances. Several scenarios are summarized in The Guardian Games Blog: "Sometimes, the exclusives are for specific platforms: Modern Warfare 3 will feature DLC that will be available only on Xbox 360 for a short period. Other deals are cut with retailers – the Battlefield 3: Physical Warfare pack, which features exclusive weapons and maps, will only be available when the full game is pre-ordered through Game and Gamestation in the UK. However, it arrives as a DLC add-on for everyone else later. For the game publisher, payments and joint-marketing deals can be the incentive, for the retailer or platform-holder, the hope is that they're able to capture a larger amount of the initial release rush" [19].

Games are assumed to be advertised most heavily right at the time of their initial launch. Co-op advertising is generally used to induce advertising activity near the time of market entry in order to attract the attention of customers. As a result, it is assumed to stimulate short-term sales. The sales response function of the video game, S, is assumed to be affected mainly by the game's advertising budget, a, and the manufacturer's national brand name investments, q, which include brand name investments for the platform and control of implementing co-op advertising agreement between the platform manufacturer and the game publisher. The brand name investments, q, by the platform manufacturer to promote its proprietary platform are assumed to directly affect the sales potential of a game exclusively published for this platform. In sum, a and q serve as different, but complementary functions that have positive effects on the overall game software sales.

The advertising budget allocated to promoting an exclusive game serves as a stimulant to maximize the sales of the game itself, as well as acting as an indirect contribution to game platform promotion. In order to direct our focus to video game software sales only, the latter is excluded from this analysis. In addition, due to our focus on the sales response function of the video game only, we exclude any assumptions or variables that relate to platform (hardware) sales for the sake of simplicity.

Since co-op advertising is intended to generate short-term sales, we may consider one-period expected sales response volume as:

$$S(a,q) = \alpha - \beta a^{-\gamma} q^{-\delta} \tag{1}$$

where $\alpha > 0$ is the sales saturate asymptote, and β, γ, δ are positive constants [10].

This sales response function is consistent with industry reports that show a diminishing hype cycle and visible seasonality for individual and overall video game sales [20], [21]. According to these reports, the sales of a video game sharply peak during the time of its launch, which is generally executed in line with the holiday season in the United States. This peak is followed by a steep fall for 1 to 2 months, then levels back up to a moderate level and follows a smoother pattern for the remainder of its relatively short life cycle. In support of these industry reports, Calantone et al. [22] also state that the product life-cycle of games is similar to that of movies, which they have defined as "short product life-cycle products." (p. 1)

The platform manufacturer's marginal profit from unit sales of an exclusive game is ρ_m, and the game publisher's marginal profit is ρ_p. The marginal profit is defined as the profit gained from the single unit sales of a video game software CD or DVD. Accordingly, the platform manufacturer can be assumed to have no costs associated with the production of a single game unit, meaning that his marginal profit will be replaced by his revenue share from unit sales of a game CD/DVD, which is the unit price of a video game multiplied by the revenue share fraction that the publisher agrees to share with the platform manufacturer.

The unit price of a game is denoted by p_g. The revenue share fraction that the game software publisher agrees to share with the platform manufacturer is assumed to be a constant which has already been agreed upon, and is denoted by $0 < \tau < 1$. The fraction of total advertising expenditures for an exclusive game which the platform manufacturer agrees to share with the game publisher is t. This fraction is the platform manufacturer's co-op advertising reimbursement policy.

The profit functions of each player and the system are then given as follows:

$$\pi_m = p_g \tau(\alpha - \beta a^{-\gamma} q^{-\delta}) - ta - q \,. \tag{2}$$

$$\pi_p = \rho_p(\alpha - \beta a^{-\gamma} q^{-\delta}) - (1-t)a \,. \tag{3}$$

$$\pi = \pi_m + \pi_p = (p_g \tau + \rho_p)(\alpha - \beta a^{-\gamma} q^{-\delta}) \,. \tag{4}$$

4 Sequential (Leader-Follower) Game

In this section, we model the relationship between the platform manufacturer and the video game publisher as a sequential-move non-cooperative game, where the platform manufacturer is the stronger player (leader) and the game publisher is the weaker player (follower). This analysis demonstrates the general structure of a non-cooperative game model in which one of the players strictly dominates the other. In order to maintain simplicity of this paper and allocate more space to alternative models, the case of a strong publisher and a weak platform manufacturer will not be demonstrated due to its similarity to the present analysis.

The solution of a non-cooperative sequential game is called Stackelberg equilibrium. This game model is based on the assumption that a game publisher wants to promote his video game more strongly than what would be possible by his existing marketing budget, and asks for support from the platform manufacturer. In this scenario, the determination of the level of advertising expenditures depends on how much the platform manufacturer is willing to subsidize the publisher, where he can also have some requirements on the co-op advertising spending strategy such as the type, length and frequency of the advertisements, the display of the platform's brand name, or the marketing channels through which the ad will be serviced.

The platform manufacturer, as the leader, first declares the level of brand name investments for its proprietary platform, and the co-op advertising sharing policy. The publisher, as the follower, then determines the number of game units to be published at launch, taking into consideration the total advertising expenditures to be spent. The publisher takes the Stackelberg equilibrium of the game's advertising expenditures into account in deciding the volume of product to be published. Therefore, we first solve for this stage of the game:

$$\frac{\partial \pi_p}{\partial a} = \gamma \rho_p \beta a^{-(\gamma+1)} q^{-\delta} - (1-t) = 0 \,. \tag{5}$$

This results in

$$a = \left(\frac{\gamma \rho_p \beta}{(1-t)q^{\delta}}\right)^{1/(\gamma+1)}. \tag{6}$$

In Eq. (6), we can also observe the effects of changes in t and q on the video game's advertising budget:

$$\frac{\partial a}{\partial t} = \frac{1}{\gamma+1}\left(\frac{\gamma \beta \rho_p}{q^{\delta}}\right)^{1/(\gamma+1)}(1-t)^{-(2+\gamma)/(\gamma+1)} > 0\,. \tag{7}$$

Eq. (7) tells us that the more the platform manufacturer is willing to share the cost of the game's advertising, the more the publisher will be willing to spend on advertising the game. This demonstrates the signaling effect of the platform manufacturer's co-op advertising sharing policy on the publisher's budget allocation intentions for the game's launch strategy. The platform manufacturer can use this signaling effect to manipulate the publisher into increasing advertising expenditures for the game, at a level that the platform manufacturer expects. The ultimate result of an increase in platform manufacturer's co-op advertising sharing policy is an increase in the game's overall advertising budget, which will generate more overall sales of the product.

$$\frac{\partial a}{\partial q} = -\frac{\delta}{\gamma+1}\left(\frac{\gamma \beta \rho_p}{(1-t)}\right)^{1/(\gamma+1)} q^{-(\delta+\gamma+1)/(\gamma+1)} < 0\,. \tag{8}$$

From the publisher's perspective, Eq. (8) demonstrates the importance of capitalizing well on the platform manufacturer's brand name investments, which may lead to a reduced need for advertising expenditures for the individual game. If the platform manufacturer increases the brand name investments for its proprietary platform, the publisher will be inclined to spend less on the game's advertising. Hence, the platform manufacturer's brand name investments also have a signaling effect on the publisher's advertising expenditures for the launch of an exclusive game.

We next determine the optimal values of q and t by maximizing the platform manufacturer's profit function:

$$\underset{q,t}{\text{Max}}\, \pi_m = \rho_m\left(\alpha - \beta a^{-\gamma} q^{-\delta}\right) - ta - q = p_g \tau\left(\alpha - \beta a^{-\gamma} q^{-\delta}\right) - ta - q \tag{9}$$

s.t.

$0 \le t \le 1,\ q \ge 0\,.$

Substituting Eq. (6) into Eq. (9) results in:

$$\begin{aligned}\text{Max}\, \pi_m = {} & p_g \tau\left[\alpha - \beta\left(\gamma \rho_p \beta\right)^{-\gamma/(\gamma+1)}(1-t)^{\gamma/(\gamma+1)} q^{-\delta/(\gamma+1)}\right] \\ & -\left(\gamma \rho_p \beta\right)^{1/(\gamma+1)} t(1-t)^{-1/(\gamma+1)} q^{-\delta/(\gamma+1)} - q\end{aligned} \tag{10}$$

s.t.

$0 \le t \le 1,\ q \ge 0\,.$

This yields the Stackelberg equilibrium point, (a^*, t^*, q^*) of the sequential game:

$$a^* = \left[\delta^{-\delta}\beta\gamma^{\delta+1}(p_g\tau - \gamma\rho_p)\right]^{1/(\delta+\gamma+1)}, \tag{11}$$

$$t^* = \begin{cases}(p_g\tau - (\gamma+1)\rho_p)/(p_g\tau - \gamma\rho_p), & p_g\tau/\rho_p > \gamma + 1, \\ 0, & otherwise,\end{cases} \tag{12}$$

$$q^* = \left[\delta^{\gamma+1}\beta\gamma^{-\gamma}(p_g\tau - \gamma\rho_p)\right]^{1/(\delta+\gamma+1)}. \tag{13}$$

Based on Eqs. (11)-(13), we can conclude that the platform manufacturer's sharing policy depends on the unit sales price p_g of a game, the publisher's marginal profit ρ_p, and the influence parameter γ. If the publisher's marginal profit is relatively high with respect to the sales price of the video game, he has strong incentive to spend more on the game's advertising to stimulate a higher sales volume, and this advertising spend is likely to be in line with the platform manufacturer's optimal amount. In this case, the platform manufacturer is not likely to share advertising expenditures with the publisher. Another observation is that since γ has a positive effect on sales volume, an increase in γ such that $p_g\tau / \rho_p < \gamma + 1$ will cause the video game sales to increase, which will give the publisher incentive to advertise more without the platform manufacturer's support. Finally, the higher the publisher's marginal profit (or the lower the video game's unit price), the lower the platform manufacturer's advertising support for the publisher. This may be due to the fact that costs associated with a blockbuster game are generally higher than regular games, resulting in a relatively low marginal profit for the publisher. However, if advertised correctly and sufficiently, such games generate more sales in volume and hence more revenue for the platform manufacturer (as well as indirect network effects for console sales). As a result, he will have more incentive to contribute to the advertising budget of these games when compared to games with lower cost and higher marginal profit for the publisher.

After determining the Stackelberg equilibrium values of our variables of interest, we now look at how changes in each player's marginal profit affects the co-op advertising sharing policy of the platform manufacturer. Since there is no cost for the platform manufacturer that is associated to the production of one unit of game software, we can write $\rho_m = p_g\tau$. Hence, we have

$$\frac{\partial t^*}{\partial \rho_m} = \frac{\rho_p}{(\rho_m - \gamma\rho_p)^2} = \frac{\rho_p}{(p_g\tau - \gamma\rho_p)^2} > 0, \tag{14}$$

$$\frac{\partial t^*}{\partial \rho_p} = \frac{-\rho_m}{(\rho_m - \gamma\rho_p)^2} = \frac{-p_g\tau}{(p_g\tau - \gamma\rho_p)^2} < 0. \tag{15}$$

If the unit price of a video game is high, it is important to show to consumers that this is a game worth paying a premium for. The only way to show this is through marketing communications, meaning that the platform manufacturer should contribute significantly to the advertising expenditures of the product, especially if the publisher's budget is not as high as the optimal level targeted by the platform manufacturer. On the other hand, if the publisher's marginal profit is high when compared to the video game's unit price (or the platform manufacturer's revenue from unit sales), the publisher has strong incentive to spend advertising money in order to attract consumers to buy the game, even if the manufacturer's contribution to the marketing budget is low.

5 Non-cooperative Simultaneous-Move Game

In the previous section, we assumed that one of the players (platform manufacturer) held extreme power and control over the behavior of the other (video game publisher). Such a scenario is not very common in today's industry environment where each player has different competitive advantages, and it is usually difficult to determine which player has more control over the movements of the other. A video game publisher may have a blockbuster game in its hands, which could create a shift in the sales figures of game consoles if it were to be released exclusively for a specific platform. A platform manufacturer, on the other hand, could be leveraging strongly on a large installed base, technological superiority, or strong marketing budget, which could cause video game publishers to compete against each other to gain exclusivity for their upcoming games. Although the platform manufacturer's brand name investments can form the customer base of a platform-exclusive video game, the publisher's game-specific advertising expenditures is what determines the actual sales figures in the end.

In this section, we assume a symmetric relationship between the platform manufacturer and the video game publisher. In such a scenario, both players simultaneously and non-cooperatively maximize their profits with respect to any possible strategies applied by the other member in the system. The solution for this simultaneous-move non-cooperative game is called Nash equilibrium.

The platform manufacturer's optimal problem can be stated as follows:

$$\underset{t,q}{\text{Max}}\, \pi_m = p_g \tau\left(\alpha - \beta a^{-\gamma} q^{-\delta}\right) - ta - q \tag{16}$$

s.t.

$0 \le t \le 1,\, q \ge 0.$

The video game publisher's profit maximization problem is:

$$\underset{a \ge 0}{\text{Max}}\, \pi_p = \rho_p\left(\alpha - \beta a^{-\gamma} q^{-\delta}\right) - (1-t)a\,. \tag{17}$$

To find the Nash equilibrium, we simultaneously solve the following two equations:

$$\frac{\partial \pi_m}{\partial q} = \beta\delta p_g \tau a^{-\gamma} q^{-(\delta+1)} - 1 = 0\,, \tag{18}$$

$$\frac{\partial \pi_p}{\partial a} = \beta\gamma\rho_p a^{-(\gamma+1)} q^{-\delta} - (1-t) = 0\,. \tag{19}$$

When we solve for a, t and q, we obtain the following Nash equilibrium advertising scheme:

$$a^{**} = \left[(1/(\delta p_g \tau))^{\delta} \beta (\gamma \rho_p)^{\delta+1}\right]^{1/(\gamma+\delta+1)}\,, \tag{20}$$

$$t^{**} = 0\,, \tag{21}$$

$$q^{**} = \left[\left(\delta p_g \tau\right)^{\gamma+1} \beta (\gamma \rho_p)^{-\gamma}\right]^{1/(\gamma+\delta+1)}\,. \tag{22}$$

Eqs. (20)-(22) tell us that regardless of other parameters' values, the platform manufacturer will not be willing to commit to any co-op advertising schemes in a non-cooperative simultaneous-move game structure. The platform manufacturer will always prefer the leader-follower game model rather than the simultaneous-move structure. On the other hand, the publisher will prefer the simultaneous-move game model if $\gamma\rho_p/p_g\tau + (\rho_p/p_g\tau)^{\gamma/(\gamma+1)} \geq 1$. Otherwise, he will prefer the leader-follower game structure.

Under these circumstances, it is not logical to launch a video game exclusively for the manufacturer's proprietary gaming platform since he will not be willing to contribute to its promotion. This result shows that if both players hold equal power, then they should consider cooperative strategies instead of a non-cooperative simultaneous-move game structure when planning the advertising scheme for a platform-exclusive video game, since such cooperative schemes have the potential to yield higher profits for both parties. It also demonstrates that a non-cooperative simultaneous-move strategy is not a preferable advertising strategy for a platform-exclusive game.

6 An Efficiency Co-op Advertising Model

In extant cooperative advertising literature, it is generally assumed that the players which utilize co-op advertising sharing policies are vertically separated, causing effective cooperative game models to be unfeasible. The video game industry is an exception due to high levels of cooperation between players within the supply chain, especially between platform manufacturers and game publishers. This cooperation reaches maximum efficiency when both parties have to cooperate in the launch of a platform-exclusive game. In such a setting, the co-op advertising sharing policy becomes an extension of the platform manufacturer's console brand name investments and a contributor to the video game publisher's reputation.

In this section, we will take an approach that is closer to real-life interactions between the platform manufacturer and the video game publisher. We investigate the efficiency of a vertical co-op advertising agreement. A similar approach has been elaborated on by Huang and Li [10] in the context of vertically integrated (cooperative) manufacturer-retailer supply chain dynamics.

As a starting point in efficiency analysis, we need to define Pareto efficient advertising schemes in cooperative advertising agreements. A scheme (a_0, t_0, q_0) is called Pareto efficient if one cannot find any other scheme (a, t, q) such that neither the platform manufacturer's nor the video game publisher's profit is less at (a, t, q) but at least one of the platform manufacturer's and publisher's profits is higher at (a, t, q) than at (a_0, t_0, q_0) [10]. In other words, (a_0, t_0, q_0) is Pareto efficient if and only if $\pi_m(a, t, q) \geq \pi_m(a_0, t_0, q_0)$ and $\pi_p(a, t, q) \geq \pi_p(a_0, t_0, q_0)$ for some (a, t, q) implies that $\pi_m(a, t, q) = \pi_m(a_0, t_0, q_0)$ and $\pi_p(a, t, q) = \pi_p(a_0, t_0, q_0)$.

π_m and π_p are quasi-concave functions, therefore the set of Pareto efficient schemes corresponds to points where their iso-profit surfaces are tangent to each other:

$$\nabla\pi_m(a,t,q) + \mu\nabla\pi_p(a,t,q) = 0\,, \tag{23}$$

for some $\mu \geq 0$ (see [10]), where

$$\nabla\pi_m = \left(\frac{\partial\pi_m}{\partial a}, \frac{\partial\pi_m}{\partial t}, \frac{\partial\pi_m}{\partial q}\right)$$

stands for the gradient of π_m.

Effectively, the collection of Pareto efficient schemes is described by the set below:

$$Y = \{(\bar{a}^*, t, \bar{q}^*): 0 \leq t \leq 1\}\,, \tag{24}$$

where

$$\bar{a}^* = \left[\delta^{-\delta}\beta\gamma^{\delta+1}(p_g\tau + \rho_p)\right]^{1/(\gamma+\delta+1)} \text{ and } \bar{q}^* = \left[\delta^{\gamma+1}\beta\gamma^{-\gamma}(p_g\tau + \rho_p)\right]^{1/(\gamma+\delta+1)}.$$

What this implies is that all Pareto efficient schemes are associated with a single video game advertising expenditure $\bar{a}^*$ and a single brand name investment $\bar{q}^*$. The fraction t of the platform manufacturer's contribution to the game's advertising budget is between 0 and 1.

An advertising scheme is Pareto efficient if and only if it is an optimal solution of the joint system profit maximization problem [10, p. 536]. The joint system maximization problem is given as follows:

$$\overline{\pi^*} = \operatorname*{Max}_{a,t,q} \pi = \pi_m + \pi_p \tag{25}$$

s.t.

$0 \leq t \leq 1,\ q \geq 0,\ a \geq 0.$

Since $\pi = (p_g\tau + \rho_p)(\alpha - \beta a^{-\gamma}q^{-\delta}) - a - q$ does not contain the co-op advertising sharing policy t, any value of t between 0 and 1 can be a component for any optimal solution for Eq. (25). When we take the first derivatives of π with respect to a and q, and set them to 0, we obtain

$$\bar{a}^* = \left[\delta^{-\delta}\beta\gamma^{\delta+1}(p_g\tau + \rho_p)\right]^{1/(\gamma+\delta+1)}$$

and

$$\bar{q}^* = \left[\delta^{\gamma+1}\beta\gamma^{-\gamma}(p_g\tau + \rho_p)\right]^{1/(\gamma+\delta+1)}.$$

This proves that $(\bar{a}^*, t, \bar{q}^*)$ for any t, such that $0 \leq t \leq 1$, is an optimal solution of Eq. (25). Among all possible advertising schemes, the system profit is maximized for every Pareto efficient scheme, but not for any other schemes.

Deriving from the above statements, the system profit should be higher at any Pareto efficient scheme than at both non-cooperative equilibriums calculated in the previous two sections. Lower system profits are achieved if the platform manufacturer and the game software publisher non-cooperatively optimize their profits compared to the results obtained when they act cooperatively. This implies that both players can gain more profits in comparison to what was possible in the Stackelberg and Nash equilibrium schemes.

If $1+\rho_p/p_g\tau \geq \left(p_g\tau/\rho_p\right)^{\gamma}$, then the platform manufacturer's brand name investment is higher at any Pareto efficient scheme than at both non-cooperative equilibriums; otherwise, the platform manufacturer's brand name investment q at any Pareto efficient scheme is higher than at Stackelberg equilibrium and is lower than at Nash equilibrium. On the other hand, the video game's advertising expenditure a is higher at any Pareto efficient scheme than at both non-cooperative equilibriums (see [10] for a full proof).

An important consideration is the fact that not all Pareto efficient schemes are feasible to both the platform manufacturer and the publisher. Neither party would conform to having lower profits with cooperation than without it. This leads us to the definition of feasible Pareto efficiency, which states that an advertising scheme $\bar{a}^*, t, \bar{q}^* \in Y$ is feasible Pareto efficient if

$$\Delta\pi_m(t) = \pi_m(\bar{a}^*, t, \bar{q}^*) - Max\{\pi_m^*, \pi_m^{**}\} \geq 0\,, \tag{26}$$

and

$$\Delta\pi_p(t) = \pi_p(\bar{a}^*, t, \bar{q}^*) - Max\{\pi_p^*, \pi_p^{**}\} \geq 0\,. \tag{27}$$

The only schemes that are acceptable for both players in a cooperative game are those that satisfy both of the above equations. The "*", "**" and "−*" stand for the Stackelberg, Nash and cooperative equilibriums, respectively. The Pareto efficient set of advertising schemes is denoted by

$$Z = \left\{(\bar{a}^*, t, \bar{q}^*)\colon \Delta\pi_m(t) \geq 0, \Delta\pi_p(t) \geq 0, (\bar{a}^*, t, \bar{q}^*) \in Y\right\} \tag{28}$$

From previous calculations, we know that $\pi_m^{**} \leq \pi_m^*$ and $\pi_p^{**} \leq \pi_p^*$ if $\gamma\rho_p/p_g\tau + (\rho_p/p_g\tau)^{\gamma/(\gamma+1)} < 1$; otherwise $\pi_p^{**} > \pi_p^*$. For the sake of simplicity, let us assume that $\gamma\rho_p/p_g\tau + (\rho_p/p_g\tau)^{\gamma/(\gamma+1)} < 1$. Then the feasible Pareto efficient scheme can be stated as follows:

$$\Delta\pi_m(t) = \pi_m(\bar{a}^*, t, \bar{q}^*) - \pi_m^* \geq 0 \tag{29}$$

and

$$\Delta\pi_p(t) = \pi_p(\bar{a}^*, t, \bar{q}^*) - \pi_p^* \geq 0\,. \tag{30}$$

Here, our aim is to show that there exist Pareto efficient advertising schemes such that both the platform manufacturer and the game software publisher are better off at full coordination than at non-cooperative equilibriums. To do this, let

$$k_1 = \beta\rho_m\left[(a^*)^{-\gamma}(q^*)^{-\delta} - (\bar{a}^*)^{-\gamma}(\bar{q}^*)^{-\delta}\right] + (q^* - \bar{q}^*) + a^*t^*\,, \tag{31}$$

$$k_2 = \beta\rho_p\left[(a^*)^{-\gamma}(q^*)^{-\delta} - (\bar{a}^*)^{-\gamma}(\bar{q}^*)^{-\delta}\right] + (a^* - \bar{a}^*) + a^*t^*\,, \tag{32}$$

$$t_{min} = -k_2/\bar{a}^* \tag{33}$$

$$t_{max} = k_1/\bar{a}^* . \tag{34}$$

where $k_2 < 0$. Then $\Delta\pi_m(t) = k_1 - \bar{a}^*t$ and $\Delta\pi_p(t) = k_2 - \bar{a}^*t$. Hence, Z can be simplified as follows:

$$Z = \{(\bar{a}^*, t, \bar{q}^*): t_{min} \le t \le t_{max}\} . \tag{35}$$

Since $0 \le t \le 1$, we can write $0 \le t_{min} < t_{max} < 1$. Subsequently, for any t, such that $t_{min} < t < t_{max}$, $\Delta\pi_m(t) > 0$ and $\Delta\pi_p(t) > 0$. This is the mathematical demonstration of the existence of Pareto efficient advertising schemes such that, both the platform manufacturer and the game software publisher are better off at full coordination than at non-cooperative equilibriums.

We still want to find an advertising scheme in Z which will be agreeable to both players. We define the system profit gain as the joint profit gain achieved by the platform manufacturer and the video game publisher by moving from a Stackelberg advertising strategy to a Pareto efficient advertising scheme, and it is denoted by $\Delta\pi = \Delta\pi_m(\bar{a}^*, t, \bar{q}^*) + \Delta\pi_p(\bar{a}^*, t, \bar{q}^*)$, where $\Delta\pi = \bar{\pi}^* - \pi^*$ is a positive constant. The definition of the system profit gain implies that as the platform manufacturer's share of the system profit gain increases, the publisher's share will decrease, and vice versa. Since all feasible Pareto efficient transactions occur at $(\bar{a}^*, \bar{q}^*)$, both players will agree to change total advertising expenditures for the video game from a^* to $\bar{a}^*$ and the brand name investments from q^* to $\bar{q}^*$. However, they will be bargaining over the platform manufacturer's co-op advertising sharing policy t.

The bargaining process will be settled at a level of t that produces a higher payoff for both players when compared to the non-cooperative solutions. However this does not necessarily imply that the final t value will be the profit maximizing solution for each individual player, or that they engage in bargaining in a mutually beneficial way. The primary motivation of each player to engage in bargaining is to settle at a solution that is both acceptable for the other player, and more beneficial for himself when compared to the non-cooperative equilibriums. The sales response volume is subject to some environmental uncertainty, which implies that neither player can be certain about the actual system profit gain. The only prediction we can make without adding further assumptions is that the video game software publisher would prefer a relatively high advertising budget contribution from the platform manufacturer, meaning that he would favor a value closer to t_{max}. The platform manufacturer, on the other hand, would prefer a fraction closer to t_{min}. Since the system profit gain is not known for certain by either player, the uncertainty would be modeled as a probability distribution for the system profit gain in each Pareto efficient scheme. To proceed with the bargaining analysis, it is necessary to decide whether it is safe to assume that both players would agree on these probability distributions. In order to avoid the risk of diverging from the real-life business case, we prefer not to make any further assumptions at this point and leave the bargaining analysis as a topic for future research.

7 Conclusions and Future Research

In the preceding sections, we mathematically demonstrated the importance of full cooperation and coordination between a platform manufacturer and a video game software publisher during the launch period of a platform-exclusive game. We have shown that a non-cooperative simultaneous-move game is never preferred by either player, and there exists at least one Pareto efficient solution where both players are better off cooperating than at the Stackelberg equilibrium. However, in order to reach this solution, both parties should be willing to negotiate openly over the co-op advertising sharing policy t.

Analysis of the bargaining process mentioned above is naturally the next step in future research. This will help us identify the range of t values that would make both players better off in full cooperation when compared to the non-cooperative leader-follower scenario. This bargaining scenario may be followed by the analysis of competition, where the game is not exclusive and more than one platform manufacturer and/or game software publisher exists.

A different research approach is the investigation of network effects: A platform-exclusive video game has the potential to indirectly increase console sales. How these network effects can be integrated into the model, and whether this would be reflected as a change in the platform manufacturer's co-op advertising sharing strategy is an exciting new area of research. A final untapped venue for future research is the analysis of cooperative advertising strategies among supply chain players for mobile games. By this, we refer to games developed for mobile platforms such as mobile phones and tablets. Since the supply chain and distribution network structure is different for mobile games, they have been left outside of the scope of the present analysis. However, their increasing significance in the gaming industry implies that both practitioners and academics should investigate cooperative and competitive strategies among players of the mobile gaming value chain to establish a holistic view of the industry.

Acknowledgements. This research is supported in part by Bogazici University Research Fund under grant number BAP 6525.

References

1. Dant, R.P., Berger, P.D.: Modelling Cooperative Advertising Decisions in Franchising. Journal of the Operational Research Society 47, 1120–1136 (1996)
2. Dutta, S., Bergen, M., John, G., Rao, A.: Variations in the Contractual Terms of Cooperative Advertising Contracts: An Empirical Investigation. Marketing Letters 6(1), 15–22 (1995)
3. Ferber, A.: How retailers view the co-op scene. Sales and Marketing Management 135(5), 64–68 (1985)
4. SeyedEsfahani, M.M., Biazaran, M., Gharakhani, M.: A game theoretic approach to coordinate pricing and vertical co-op advertising in manufacturer-retailer supply chains. European Journal of Operational Research 211, 263–273 (2011)

5. Vogel, M., Fiorentini, W.J.: Redefining co-op. Sales and Marketing Management 145(5), 62–65 (1993)
6. Wilcox, R.D.: Co-op Advertising: Getting Your Money's Worth. Sales and Marketing Management 143(5), 64–68 (1991)
7. Huang, Z., Li, S.X., Mahajan, V.: An Analysis of Manufacturer-Retailer Supply Chain Coordination in Cooperative Advertising. Decision Sciences 33(3), 469–494 (2002)
8. Hutchins, M.S.: Cooperative Advertising. Roland Press, New York (1953)
9. Geylani, T., Dukes, A.J., Srinivasan, K.: Strategic Manufacturer Response to a Dominant Retailer. Marketing Science 26(2), 164–178 (2007)
10. Huang, Z., Li, S.X.: Co-op Advertising in Manufacturer-Retailer Supply Chains: A Game Theory Approach. European Journal of Operational Research 135, 527–544 (2001)
11. Consalvo, M.: Console video games and global corporations: Creating a hybrid culture. New Media & Society 8(1), 117–137 (2006)
12. Johns, J.: Video games production networks: Value capture, power relations and embeddedness. Journal of Economic Geography 6, 151–180 (2006)
13. Jin, D.Y., Chee, F.: Age of New Media Empires: A Critical Interpretation of the Korean Online Game Industry. Games and Culture 3(1), 38–58 (2008)
14. Leach Waters, C.: The United States Launch of Sony Playstation2. Journal of Business Research 58, 995–998 (2005)
15. Rysman, M.: The Economics of Two-Sided Markets. Journal of Economic Perspectives 23(3), 125–143 (2009)
16. Zackariasson, P., Wilson, T.L.: Paradigm shifts in the video game industry. Competitiveness Review: An International Business Journal 20(2), 139–151 (2010)
17. Shankar, V., Bayus, B.L.: Network Effects and Competition: An Empirical Analysis of the Home Video Game Industry. Strategic Management Journal 24, 375–384 (2003)
18. Lee, R.S.: Vertical Integration and Exclusivity in Platform and Two-Sided Markets (2010), http://pages.stern.nyu.edu/~rslee/papers/VIExclusivity.pdf (date accessed March 11, 2012)
19. Stuart, K.: Assassin's Creed: Revelations – PS3 gets multiplayer beta first. The Guardian Games Blog (2011), http://www.guardian.co.uk/technology/gamesblog/2011/aug/10/assassins-creed-multiplayer-beta (date accessed March 12, 2012)
20. NPD Group: Market Research Data on Video Game Sales Figures (2012), http://vgsales.wikia.com/wiki/NPD_sales_data (date accessed March 07, 2012)
21. TS Analysis: Video Game Hype Cycle Plot (2011), http://www.tsanalysis.com/2011/05/the-video-game-hype-cycle/ (date accessed March 07, 2012)
22. Calantone, R.J., Yeniyurt, S., Townsend, J.D., Schmidt, J.B.: The Effects of Competition in Short Product Life-Cycle Markets: The Case of Motion Pictures. Journal of Product Innovation Management 27, 349–361 (2010)

A Framework for Software Ecosystem Governance

Alfred Baars[1] and Slinger Jansen[2]

[1] University of Amsterdam
alfred.baars@student.uva.nl
[2] Utrecht University
slinger@cs.uu.nl

Abstract. Many software producing organizations do not know how to measure, compare, and analyse their governance policy in software ecosystems. Without sufficient insight into governance, these organizations cannot optimally perform as keystone players. This paper outlines a framework for the analysis of software ecosystem governance for individual companies. With such a framework, software producing organizations can gain strategic advantage over other organizations, in that they can analyse and improve their software ecosystem governance in a structured way, leading to better ecosystem performance and health.

Keywords: Software ecosystems, governance, IT governance.

1 Introduction

Software Ecosystem (SECO) governance can help a company achieve its goals, make better use of available resources and can ultimately lead to an increase in revenue and lower risks. However, since it is a relatively new field, many organizations do not know how to effectively manage their SECO, or how to make their SECO explicit to begin with. Proper formalization for SECO governance is lacking and there are many challenges to overcome for software vendors in regard to SECOs [7].

This analytical research, based on two case studies, is an attempt to help formalize some of these challenges an organization has to overcome when formalizing SECOs and the governance strategy affiliated with the SECO, which is differs from traditional ways of partner management [6]. Specifically, this research attempts to formalize a number of aspects related governance structure, such as responsibility [9] and measuring effectiveness [5].

Jansen et al. define a SECO as **a set of businesses functioning as a unit and interacting with a shared market for software and services, together with the relationships among them** [7]. Bosch [1] defines a SECO as a system consisting of the set of software solutions that enable, support and automate the activities and transactions by the actors in the associated social or business ecosystem and the organizations that provide these solutions.

These definitions are very similar, except for the level of abstraction. Where Bosch defines the elements in the ecosystem as software solutions, Jansen et al. maintain

M.A. Cusumano, B. Iyer, and N. Venkatraman (Eds.): ICSOB 2012, LNBIP 114, pp. 168–180, 2012.

some abstraction by taking businesses as the atomic entity of which ecosystems are made up. For this reason, in this report the definition of Jansen et al. is used.

This paper continues in section 2 with the research approach. Section 3 goes into detail about governance, section 4 discussed the SECO Governance Analysis Framework. Section 5 describes the conducted case studies, section 6 presents a comparison between the organizations and in section 7 conclusions are drawn.

2 Research Approach

The research problem that was identified is that there is no de facto standard in terms of SECO governance modelling. In fact, the definition of "SECO governance" in itself has seen many different interpretations. With more formalization and a larger amount of case studies to base theorems on, researchers can begin to formulate ways for organizations to govern their SECO in an effective, efficient and profitable way.

In order to build the framework a literature study was done to compose a list of different governance tools, and structural components associated with governance strategy.

Subsequently, two case studies were conducted, to find out to which degree two real-life organizations currently employ governance, if this governance is formalized and made explicit, who is responsible for governing the ecosystem, et cetera.

Based on these case studies the framework was evaluated and modified. The studies were done in three steps: firstly, a description of the case was made from an observational point of view. After that, key persons at the companies were interviewed. In these interviews assumptions were validated or denied and new information was revealed. Lastly, information derived from the prior steps was summarized and conclusions were drawn.

The interviews were conducted with two managers, both of which have at least 8 years of experience within software companies. Both interviews took two hours and cases were selected because of company size and accessibility. The first segment of both interviews consisted of a set of pre-defined questions, so that assumptions based on the literature study could be verified or modified in a pragmatic way. The second segment was unstructured, in order to give the interviewees the opportunity to provide new information and elaborate on decisions and policies.

3 Governance

To be able to define SECO governance, the definition of the broader concept of governance and specifically corporate governance must first be made clear.

Merriam-Webster's dictionary defines governing as "to exercise continuous sovereign authority over; especially: to control and direct the making and administration of policy". Governance is present in every aspect of society, from governing a multi-country body such as NATO, UN or EU to the governing of one-person businesses. Any foundation, organization, body or corporation of any size that has any type of decision to make has to deal with the act of governing at some point in time.

This implication leads to a sub-definition of governance, specifically aimed at business organizations. Sir Adrian Cadbury first defined corporate governance as "the system by which companies are directed and controlled", as to not exclude all the external elements involved [2]. However, recently, more detailed and specific definitions are being used. The Organisation for Economic Co-operation and Development (OECD) endorses the following definition for corporate governance: "Procedures and processes according to which an organization is directed and controlled. The corporate governance structure specifies the distribution of rights and responsibilities among the different participants in the organization – such as the board, managers, shareholders and other stakeholders – and lays down the rules and procedures for decision-making". This definition was coined in the European Central Bank's annual report for 2004.

There are a number of keywords in the ECB's definition. First, governance implies direction and control. Both of these are executed in an on-purpose fashion. This means that governance is not something that just happens; it is something that is actively pursued and controlled. Secondly, it specifies the distribution of rights and responsibilities among different participants. This means that corporate governance is not just a definition regarding processes, rules and procedures, but it also defines who is responsible for which part of any decision that is to be made within an organization.

Some research has already been done in the attempt to formalize governance approaches specifically within software development organizations. Two notable examples are 'agile software governance' by Qumer [9] and 'software development governance' by Chulani et al [5]. While Qumer's model focuses on maximizing business value by the business alignment and application of agile software development methods, Chulani's model helps software development organizations to achieve their strategic goals by establishing the structural component and measurement component of governance [4]. However, neither of these models goes into detail about SECO governance in specific.

The definition of SECO governance I use for this research is: "Procedures and processes by which a company controls, changes or maintains its current and future position in a SECO on all different scope levels". Please note that Jansen et al. [7] discuss three scope levels in software ecosystems, from the software supply network level (a company, its customers, and its suppliers), to ecosystem (the complete ecosystem), to ecosystems (where ecosystems compete amongst each other).

This definition fits right into Qumer's 'Agile responsibility, accountability and business value governance model'. It can be seen as a small but significant part of the 'integrated agile governance' aspect of an organization. Similarly, the definition can be seen as a small, SECO-only version of Chulani et al's 'control and measure mechanisms' as brought up in their 2008 paper. This model illustrates the different relationships between governance, strategy, management structure and processes.

There is a difference between governance and governance structure. The definition for SECO governance used in this paper only refers to the processes and procedures involved. The SECO governance structure, however, refers to the distribution of rights and responsibilities among the stakeholders associated with the software vendor, and the rules and protocols that need to be followed in order to make decisions regarding the SECO.

4 The Software Ecosystems Governance Framework

In order to compare SECO governance and governance structures, a framework must be developed. The governance segment covers processes, procedures and tools used to execute governance strategy, and the governance structure segment covers responsibility, control and measurement associated with governance strategy.

In terms of SECO governance, there are a number of governance tools that an organization may use in order to maintain or change its position within an ecosystem.

For example, an organization can create a partnership network in order to expand its SECO, or to make it more explicit. There are varying degrees in which governance is involved. For example, a way of governing a partnership network would be to moderate the network, to set up rules and processes to which partners must adhere and to penalize or remove partners who fail to comply. Other governance tools associated with partnership networks are the procedures involved in acquiring new partners, the degree of division within the network itself (does it consist of layers, tiers, levels, etc?) and defining the entry requirements a potential partner must meet [8].

Contribution to other ecosystems can be manifested in several different ways. For example, there is the setting up of new suppliers, ceasing operations with current suppliers, changing the ratio by which current suppliers are used and ceasing cooperation with current customers. All of these decisions do not only affect the company's own ecosystem, but the ecosystems of the associated supplier/customer as well.

Other than these two major governance tools, there are a number of other tools that can be used. An organization can choose to create a development standard or even go as far as to enforce this development standard on its partners. It can also opt to create licenses that can be reused by other actors in the ecosystem.

In making the SECO governance of a software developing organization explicit, several questions have been defined within the framework. The framework thus consists of the following parts: explicitness of both of the ecosystem itself and of the associated governance strategy, the responsibility, measurement and degree of knowledge sharing. Please find the full framework in Table 1. This table has been annotated with the case study results for reasons of brevity.

Explicitness of the Ecosystem - These questions relate to the explicitness of the SECO in general. These are vital questions to the potential success of an ecosystem, because without making the ecosystem explicit, there cannot be an explicit governance strategy.

Explicitness of the Governance Strategy - These questions relate to the explicitness of the governance strategy. With an explicit governance strategy, organizations are able to refer to rules, procedures, protocols and formalized processes when dealing with an ecosystem, which leads to more control over the position in the ecosystem. This ultimately leads to more potential benefit gained from the ecosystem.

Responsibility - Responsibility is an important factor in ecosystem governance. Without appointed members of the organization being responsible for the ecosystem, correct execution of the governance strategy cannot always be guaranteed. Ecosystem governance could easily become "just a job on the side", being snowed under by the member's/members' main tasks.

Measurement - In order to determine the organization's benefit from its ecosystem, the ecosystem effectiveness must be measured. This can be done by applying various key performance indicators (KPIs) to specific aspects of the ecosystem. Analyzing the current state of the ecosystem and prospecting the future state can lead to higher return on investment.

Knowledge Sharing - Knowledge sharing is not necessarily a vital aspect of a successful governance strategy. For a for-profit corporation, sharing knowledge of the ecosystem is, in many cases, effectively similar to shooting oneself in the foot. For a not-for-profit organization, however, sharing knowledge may actually be an aspect of core business.

Based on the aforementioned ecosystem governance tools and the questions that arise when discussing governance structure, a framework can be used to compare SECO governance strategies.

The framework consists of an upper half that is filled in with concepts related to SECO governance, and a bottom half that is filled in with concepts related to SECO governance structure. Furthermore, the bottom half is sorted by category, in order to provide a good perspective of the current state of affairs within an organization in regard to a certain aspect of SECO governance structures.

The framework is filled in by adding empirical data to each concept. This is either in the form of yes or no, or an elaboration in natural language. For example, the concept 'Creating reusable software licence(s)' can be answered with yes if the specific company does indeed create a reusable software licence. A more specific concept, such as the degree of moderation of an active user group, requires explanation in natural language, rather than a yes or a no. This can be done by providing a short explanation together with the framework, and noting a statement in the explanation that concerns a question in the framework with (1), (2), (N). The question can then be 'answered' in the framework using the same notation.

With this framework, organizations are able to get an overview of the state of their current SECO governance strategy. Researchers can compare different companies with each other, and, based on best practice, derive which parts of strategy are viable and which ones are not [3]. Ultimately, this will lead to a better understanding of practice and thus more theoretical completeness. As for the business side, a better understanding of SECO governance will lead to better control over one's SECO, thus eliminating risks and increasing profitability.

5 Case Studies

In this part of the report the case studies performed on UNIT4 and the Eclipse Foundation are described. These case studies were conducted in the form of unstructured interviews.

UNIT4 N.V.[1] is a Dutch software company that mainly provides enterprise software and related professional services. Its headquarters are located in Sliedrecht,

---

[1] UNIT4 NV, `www.unit4.nl`

The Netherlands. In 2010 the company employed 4,200 FTE and its total revenue was just over €420 million. The company's best-known products are Agresso Business World ERP Suite and Coda Financials.

Several significant acquisitions have taken place in recent history. The first one of these took place in 1998, when UNIT4 took over three companies with significant market share in the health care and wholesale sectors. In the beginning of the new millennium UNIT4 took over Agresso, a Norwegian software company, which was the company's first major step towards internationalization. In 2006 Spain was added to the list by a number of local takeovers, and in 2008 the biggest takeover in UNIT4's history was realized when CODA became a part of the company.

UNIT4 does not have any formalization regarding expanding the company. The ultimate goal when planning an acquisition is always to increase the company's scale of operations and to become or remain a top 3 player in a specific sector. However, this is usually realized by taking relatively small steps. The ultimate responsibility for acquisitions lies with the Board of Directors of UNIT4 international.

The significant acquisitions from the past can be divided into two different categories: takeovers of companies with knowledge of sectors in which UNIT4 is not present (enough), and takeovers of companies in countries where UNIT4 is not operating (significantly).

An example of acquiring a company from a new sector is the takeover of Acoso, which allowed UNIT4 to expand its business into the accountancy and health care sectors. The greater idea behind acquiring a company, rather than setting up UNIT4 in a new sector, is that the added benefit of (potential) customers being familiar with the already active company is of great importance. The decision to actually acquire another company is based on the market share this company has, the return on investment (ROI) involved, and the technology that the company possesses.

On an international level, UNIT4 depends on several suppliers. These include major enterprises such as Microsoft and Oracle, but also smaller companies such as the hosting companies that run the Software-as-a-Service (SaaS) solutions UNIT4 provides.

UNIT4 recognizes that it is important for a company of its size not to be dependent on only one supplier, to prevent any supplier from being 'too influential'. However, again, this is not formalized in any documentation or rule set.

The organization has created user groups, in order to provide opportunities for UNIT4 software users to share experiences and ideas to improve their understanding and use of the UNIT4 solutions. The groups organise workshops, meetings and social events around shared interests.

To sell its products to medium and small businesses in The Netherlands, UNIT4 has contracts with several local resellers who are each assigned to a specific region within the country. This is the only partnership model UNIT4 currently uses.

Reseller contracts are renewed yearly and, based on market analysis performed by UNIT4, have formal goals in terms of new customers, licenses sold and total revenue generated. If these goals are met, the reseller gets a higher discount on UNIT4 products in the next year (thus increasing its own margin and therefore profit).

In 2009 most of these targets were not met due to the global financial crisis, and many resellers lost a percentage of their margins when the 2010 contracts were signed. New resellers are acquired based on the market share and the amount of potential customers in certain areas of the country.

One can conclude that UNIT4 is not yet in a mature phase when it comes to SECOs and SECO governance. Currently, governance takes place at the very top level of the organization when it comes to decisions that are going to affect the company's core business internationally, and at the highest level of a national branch of the organization when a decision is only going to affect the activities in that specific country. However, none of this is actually formalized. The SECO is not explicit and there is no formal documentation describing policies or protocols. Inherently, there is no formalized documentation about SECO governance, either.

The company does use one of the listed governance tools: the creation of a partnership network. As discussed in an earlier paragraph, UNIT4 has contracts with several Dutch resellers who are each assigned to a specific region within the Netherlands. However, there is very little formalization when it comes to partnerships, other than the reseller contracts that are being renewed each year. There is a very low degree of moderation. If a reseller does not manage to sell the target amount of products, this is essentially 'their problem' and UNIT4 will renegotiate the contract or even terminate it, but there are no moderation tools being used while a contract is still running (1).

UNIT4's partnership system does not have a division in tiers or levels. Every reseller is the same, except for the contracts that are being signed. Goals are defined based on "what seems realistic", based on analyzing previous results and doing extensive market research (11). These goals are also used as a measurement tool, to see if the reseller manages to sell the target amount of products (9)(10).

Acquiring new partners is a vital aspect of UNIT4's partnership strategy (2). However, the acquisition of a new reseller is done by 'gut feeling'. If market share is lacking or dropping in a specific area of the Netherlands, potential candidates are being selected based on having affinity with IT reselling, and interviews are conducted. Based on those interviews, a winner is selected. There is no protocol or documentation for this procedure.

The effectiveness of the ecosystem in itself is not measured, other than the effectiveness of the partnership system, and contributions to other ecosystems are not coordinated. The sub-attributes of contribution coordination (new suppliers, ratio, ceasing cooperation) are in fact used, but again without any formalization (3)(4)(5). Also, there is no form of a reusable software license created by UNIT4. However, the organization does host User Groups in which users are invited to share experiences, join workshops and increase their understanding of UNIT4 business software. These user groups are moderated extensively, with UNIT4 answering questions in a knowledge base, organizing meetings and workshops, and handling questions and feedback (6).

Lastly, knowledge on any of the aforementioned attributes is not shared with other companies within the ecosystem.

The Eclipse Foundation[2] is a not-for-profit organization whose projects are focused on building an open development platform comprised of extensible frameworks, tools and runtimes for building, deploying and managing software. Originally founded by a consortium of IT companies in 2001, Eclipse now is a stand-alone corporation with 40 staff employees around 950 dedicated developers.

All of Eclipse's products are free to use under the Eclipse Public License, which is approved by the Open Source Initiative. Many of the member companies have dedicated programmers working with Eclipse code. Out of the roughly 950 dedicated developers, 800 are not actually employed by the Foundation but by member companies. This results in a highly knowledgeable community of developers with varying personal and corporate interests, allowing the Eclipse platform to be expanded in many different directions.

Currently Eclipse has a variety of products available, for example an integrated development environment (IDE) for Java developers, a PHP development environment and a collection of modelling tools.

The Eclipse ecosystem is explicit. This can be seen through various instances, like the Eclipse Plug-in Central (EPIC), Eclipse Live, the Eclipse Membership model and EclipseCon.

There is a very distinct difference between companies with a membership model such as Eclipse, and companies with a partnership model such as UNIT4 or Microsoft. The latter implies that there is a keystone company and a dominator company, where one company has a lot of influence over the other. This is not the case with Eclipse, where a membership model is used to 'help members help themselves'. The members themselves are the ones who set up the rules, as opposed to a traditional partnership model where the company with the model decides everything. Reselling and whitelabeling are allowed, but a partnership model for this is not needed because the Foundation is not-for-profit.

The Foundation has a five-tier membership model with a very large member base, consisting of many different IT companies like Motorola, IBM, Oracle and Nokia. Each membership type has different privileges and different obligations. Since many of these companies provide the developers that develop Eclipse projects, one could say that the Foundation uses its members as suppliers. However, the members are also customers, because they use the Foundation's benefits to strengthen their own products or services.

The plug-in central is a marketplace-like platform where everyone can contribute with any kind of plug-in or add-on for Eclipse. This can be seen as an ecosystem in itself: the suppliers are the people who write extensions for the platform, and the clients are the people who then download and use the products.

The Eclipse Foundation also facilitates so-called Industry Working Groups or IWGs. These are established to facilitate the collaboration between their members. The collaboration should be intended to focus, promote and augment Eclipse technologies to meet the needs of specific industries. This can be done in the form of developing materials for a specific community or joint marketing programs to

---

[2] Eclipse Foundation, `www.eclipse.org`

promote Eclipse in a specific industry. Unlike Eclipse's open source projects, participation in an IWG is only open to Eclipse members. There is some governance involved; for example, all code content must be developed as part of an open source project, and any third party content used by an IWG must be submitted to Eclipse under the Eclipse terms of use.

The Eclipse Foundation feels that all of the separate Eclipse projects should be governed by the people who are working on them. Because Eclipse is an open source, not-for-profit platform, there is no profit goal to which the ecosystem should be directed. There is no coordination from inside the Foundation, there is no council of directors telling the individual project leaders what to do and how to do it. The membership system is largely governed by itself. In fact, the Eclipse ecosystem has produced innovation in areas where the Foundation did not expect it.

The other community services Eclipse provides, such as Eclipse Live and the Eclipse Plug-In Central require very little governance as well. For example, the only requirement for plug-ins to be added to the Plug-In Central is "it has to work with Eclipse".

The Foundation measures its effectiveness through a number of key performance indicators (KPIs). These are, for example, measuring the growth of membership to see if the ecosystem is developing in the way the organization had in mind. Because of the organization's not-for-profit profile, there is no way of measuring effectiveness by conventional KPIs such as return on investment (ROI).

The first obvious conclusion that can be derived from the case study is that the Eclipse Foundation is in an advanced stage of ecosystem maturity. The organization has a very explicit ecosystem with four people who are responsible for managing the ecosystem and applying its governance. These are situated directly under the Board, with one of the Ecosystem Directors working with the Foundation full-time (8)(9).

Furthermore, the ecosystem is fully documented and formalized, and there are a number of protocols for many situations, such as application procedures for new members, roadmaps for future development, etc. To a degree, there is a formalized way of translating Eclipse's business strategy to a SECO strategy. The idea behind the Foundation is that it serves as a not-for-profit platform to 'help members help themselves', and the SECO is designed with this philosophy in mind (5).

An important factor about the Eclipse ecosystem is that its effectiveness is measured in an objective way. The Ecosystem Directors for the different regions have a number of KPIs by which they can see how well the ecosystem is performing. Some of these KPIs include amount of new members joined, amount of members who do not renew their annual membership and amount of downloads from the Eclipse Plug-In Central (10)(11). Goals are defined based on the results achieved in previous years and continuous market analysis (12). Furthermore, the acquisition of new members is governed in a very light sense. Only organizations where ethical questions might pose a problem are screened, but other than that, every organization is welcome as long as it follows the rules the Foundation has set up (2).

There is not a very high degree of governance within the membership system (1)(5). Most of the tiers that are active now were set up when the membership system itself was set up. Over time, two extra tiers have been added. These tiers each have separate entry requirements (3), but other than that, the system pretty much governs itself. This is mainly because Eclipse is not-for-profit and there is no 'greater goal' for the Foundation other than to serve its members. Within reason, there is no real reason not to let members do as they please to help each other and themselves.

Another important governance tool is the creation of a reusable software license. Eclipse uses the Eclipse Public License (EPL) for its software. This is an Open Source Initiative-approved free software license.

Finally, since the Foundation is completely open source, any knowledge shared by a member within the ecosystem can and will be shared with the other members (4). For knowledge sharing, Industry Working Groups are a very effective tool. These groups can also be seen as active user groups, but with a goal greater than just 'delivering feedback'. Once again, there is no real reason for a lot of governance or moderation within these groups, because members are supposed to help each other help themselves (6).

6 Comparing the Organizations

In analyzing the two organizations, the following observations can be made. First of all, it is not a big surprise that the closed source, for-profit software vendor does not share any knowledge about the ecosystem, and that the open source, not-for-profit organization does. It is worth mentioning that the two organizations can be seen as Raymond's cathedral and bazaar [9], albeit a closed-source cathedral. Within Eclipse, all of the processes are publicly available, all the documentation can be viewed by everyone and software can be resold by anyone, much like Raymond's bazaar where code is developed in a bottom-up way. On the other hand, code is developed from a top-down perspective within UNIT4, where the majority of revenue is generated through maintenance and support. This is much like a closed source version of Raymond's cathedral. Software vendors traditionally employ a top-down oriented approach, in order to have full control over every aspect of the organization. Because of this, it is strange to see that a potentially profitable area such as SECO governance has been left untouched so far.

A similarity can be found in the creation of a partnership network (or membership network in the case of Eclipse). Both vendors seek to bind other organizations to them, in order to achieve their own business goals. In the case of UNIT4 the goal is simple: more profit. Resellers are contracted in order to increase revenue generated through licenses. In the case of the Eclipse Foundation, the goal is to serve as a platform where members can help each other and themselves.

The degree of how vital the network is to the organization is very different, though. Without UNIT4's partnership network, the amount of revenue generated would decrease, but not by a very significant amount. The company would still be able to perform its core business in an effective and profitable way. However, as for the Eclipse Foundation, without the membership network a very important aspect of the organization would cease to exist. Facilitating an ecosystem is part of the company's core business, rather than 'just something to get a little more revenue'.

7 SECO Governance Analysis Framework

Table 1. SECO Governance Analysis Framework

	Category	SECO Governance concept	U4	Ecl
Framework for SECO governance strategy	**Partnerships**	Creating a partnership network	Yes	Yes
		Degree of moderation	(1)	(1)
		Degree of division in tiers, levels, etc	No	Yes
		Acquiring new partners	(2)	(2)
		Formalization of entry requirements	No	(3)
	Supplier and customer governance	Coordination of contribution to other ecosystems	Yes	(4)
		Setting up new suppliers	(3)	No
		Changing the ratio of current suppliers	(4)	No
		Ceasing cooperation with suppliers or customers	(5)	No
		Using intermediaries	Yes	No
	Development	Creating a development standard	No	Yes
		Enforcing a development standard	N/A	Yes
	Partner directory	Creating a partner directory	No	Yes
		Degree of moderation	N/A	(5)
	Customer directory	Creating a customer directory	No	No
		Degree of moderation	N/A	N/A
	User groups	Creating active user groups	Yes	Yes
		Degree of moderation	(6)	(6)
	License(s)	Creating reusable software license(s)	No	Yes
	Category	**SECO governance structure concept**	**U4**	**Ecl**
	Ecosystem explicitness	Is the SECO explicit?	No	Yes
		Is there documentation describing its current state?	No	Yes
	Governance explicitness	Is the SECO governance strategy explicit?	No	Yes
		Are processes and procedures formalized?	No	Yes
		Are there formalized and documented rules?	No	Yes
		How is business strategy formalized to governance strategy?	N/A	(7)
	Responsibility	Where in the organization does SECO governance take place?	(7)	(8)
		Who does the decision making unit consist of?	(8)	(9)
		Is this decision making unit made explicit?	No	Yes
		Does the decision making unit report to the Board?	Yes	Yes
	Measurement	Is the effectiveness of the SECO measured?	Yes	Yes
		Which parts of it are measured?	(9)	(10)
		Which KPIs are used?	(10)	(11)
		How are goals defined?	(11)	(12)
	Knowledge sharing	Does the organization share its knowledge with other companies?	No	Yes

8 Conclusions

This research has provided a basic framework by which SECO governance and SECO governance structure can be analyzed. In order to extract all the data required to fill in the framework, in-depth interviews with companies must be held.

It is too soon to consider this framework as a 'set in stone' basis for everything SECO governance-related.

It is important to realise that the framework can be used to describe, analyze and compare SECO governance policies, but it does not in fact dictate the importance of individual factors. For example, knowledge sharing may not always be desired, and an organization can have a very mature SECO governance policy while deliberately not sharing any knowledge within its SECO.

The first and foremost limitation of this research is the lack of expert reviews to validate the framework presented. Expert reviews are needed to verify the accuracy of the model, and, in order to adopt this model for future research, four to six experts who work with software ecosystems on a daily basis need to edit and eventually approve this framework.

Another one of the limitations for this research is the quantity of case studies. Two case studies are not enough to allow for any deduction of theorems. While the current framework is a solid basis upon which further research can be carried out, more case studies are needed to confirm or deny the differences and similarities that this research points out.

9 Future Research

As stated in the previous segment, more case studies are required to allow for formalization of software ecosystem governance. The basis for this research is relatively thin and with more researches similar to this one, theorems could be derived, tested and approved. This would transform the field of SECO governance from analytical, where researches study 'best practices', to a situation where organizations take established theorems into account when developing a SECO governance strategy.

In general, however, the field of SECO is a relatively new one and more research on for example SECO modelling, business strategies versus SECO strategies, the architectural and social implications of SECOs, and SECO optimization is required. With the development of the International Workshop on Software Ecosystems (IWSECO) and its association with the International Conference on Software Business (ICSOB), a solid platform for future research is established.

References

[1] Bosch, J.: From Software Product Lines to SECOs. In: Proceedings of the 13th International Software Product Line Conference, SPLC 2009 (2009)

[2] Cadbury, A.: Financial Aspects of Corporate Governance. European Corporate Governance Institute (1992), http://www.ecgi.org/codes/documents/cadbury.pdf

[3] Chaffey, D.: E-Business and E-Commerce Management: Strategy, Implementation and Practice. Prentice Hall (2009)
[4] Cheng, T.H., Jansen, S., Remmers, M.: Controlling and Monitoring Agile Software Development in Three Dutch Product Software Companies. In: Proceedings of the 2nd Workshop on Software Development Governance (2008)
[5] Chulani, S., Williams, C., Yaeli, A.: Software development governance and its concerns. In: Proceedings of the 1st International Workshop on Software Development Governance (2008)
[6] Den Hartigh, E., Tol, M., Visscher, W.: The Health Measurement of a Business Ecosystem. In: ECCON 2006 Annual Meeting (2006)
[7] Jansen, S., Finkelstein, A., Brinkkemper, S.: A Sense of Community: A Research Agenda for SECOs. In: 31st International Conference on Software Engineering, New and Emerging Research Track (2009)
[8] Jansen, S., Brinkkemper, S., Luinenburg, L.: Shades of Gray: Opening up a Software Producing Organization with the Open Software Enterprise Model. Journal of Systems and Software, accepted for publication in the special issue on Software Ecosystems (2012)
[9] Qumer, A.: Defining an Integrated Agile Governance for Large Agile Software Development Environments. In: Concas, G., Damiani, E., Scotto, M., Succi, G. (eds.) XP 2007. LNCS, vol. 4536, pp. 157–160. Springer, Heidelberg (2007)
[10] Raymond, E.S.: The Cathedral and the Bazaar. O'Reilly (2005)
[11] van Angeren, J., Blijleven, V., Jansen, S.: Relationship Intimacy in Software Ecosystems: A Survey of the Dutch Software Industry. In: Proceedings of the Conference on Management of Emergent Digital Ecosystems, MEDES 2011 (2011)

Current Software-as-a-Service Business Models: Evidence from Finland

Eetu Luoma[1], Mikko Rönkkö[2], and Pasi Tyrväinen[1]

[1] University of Jyväskylä, Department of Computer Science and Information Systems
P.O. Box 35(Agora), FI-40014 University of Jyväskylä, Finland
{eetu.luoma,pasi.tyrvainen}@jyu.fi
[2] Aalto University School of Science
P.O. Box 15500, FI-00076 Aalto, Finland
mikko.ronkko@aalto.fi

Abstract. This paper characterizes the business models of Software-as-a-Service (SaaS) firms based on their value proposition, customer segments, revenue streams, and customer relationship, and analyzes interconnections of these business model elements. The target set of 163 Finnish SaaS and ASP firms was first compared to other software firms and then clustered into four clusters based on indicator data of their business model elements. The comparison reveals that the SaaS and ASP firms have smaller customer and transaction sizes than software firms in general. The resulting classification reveals two different configurations, a pure-play SaaS model and an enterprise SaaS model, and the typical factors of these business models.

Keywords: Software-as-a-Service, Business model, Classification, Cluster analysis, Software Industry.

1 Introduction

The concept of *Cloud Computing* includes three types of services, in which the key component is either an application provided to the end-users, platform and development tools provided to the application developers, or processing and storage capacity shared among multiple applications using virtualization techniques [1]. In *Software-as-a-Service (SaaS)*, a software company provides a single version and instance of an application to several end-users, on top of a multi-tenant infrastructure and over the Internet [2].

The current academic and trade literature contain a rich variety of architectural descriptions, which define technical characteristics and details of different SaaS offerings, and numerous articles focus on the benefits and problems of adopting such SaaS offerings. However, to date relatively few papers have been published about the business model aspects of SaaS. We find this shortage engaging since technology *per se* has no essential value [3], and as a business model SaaS exhibits some major changes, compared to traditional software business models like professional services, software product business, and application hosting.

M.A. Cusumano, B. Iyer, and N. Venkatraman (Eds.): ICSOB 2012, LNBIP 114, pp. 181–194, 2012.

We also found that the recent studies on perceptions of SaaS among customers [4] and on suitable governance structures [5] consider SaaS as a uniform offering. The recent studies consider product innovation as part of the offering insignificant. Also, the variety of software companies' means to operate and conduct marketing and sales has not been considered, while these may have a considerable effect on the adoption.

In addition to technological innovations, SaaS companies have also introduced various business models innovations. A *business model* generally refers to a conceptual description of how a company creates and captures value [6]. Business model concept has been used to design frameworks or classifications of companies and to describe business logics of individual companies [7] and, although a clear and commonly accepted definition of the concept does not yet exist, business model is becoming a relevant unit of analysis [6]. Either as a classification or an actualization of firms execution [8], business model implies holistic thinking on how a firm operates, communicates with its surroundings, and how it makes money. We therefore adopt the view that business model is a configuration of several different factors that jointly describe how the firm does business.

We chose the business model framework suggested by Osterwalder, et al. [7] as a basis for our study. This framework is a synthesis of a large number of prior business model studies considering individual elements and their connections. Therefore, this model compatible with our conceptualization of business model as a configuration of elements. It is also perhaps the most popular one when analyzing firms in the IT industry. The framework includes nine elements and their relationships: value proposition, customer segments, customer relationships, channels, revenue streams, activities, resources, partners, and cost structure.

While business models of software firms have been studied in numerous papers, studies attempting to classify and characterize SaaS companies are virtually non-existent. To fill this gap, we analyze SaaS companies from the business model perspective. The analysis uses survey data from the Finnish software industry and produces a new classification of these firms, enabling identification of factors and configurations that are typical for SaaS companies' business model, and highlighting the differences among these firms.

2 SaaS Business Model in the Previous Research

In this section, we present and discuss the relevant literature examining Software-as-a-Service from the business model perspective. The focus is on business models as configurations of many elements and on previous classifications thereof. After collecting applicable literature from research article databases, and screening them based on their abstracts, a total of twelve articles were chosen for closer examination[1].

[1] The digital libraries of IEEE and ACM, Springerlink, Ebscohost Academic Search Elite and Google Scholar were used. The examined publications include Armbrust, et al. [9], Benefield [10], Choudhary [11], Desai, et al. [12], Cusumano [13], Durkee [14], Jacobs [15], Liao [16], Dubey and Wagle [17], Sääksjärvi, et al. [18], SIIA [19] and Tyrväinen and Selin [20].

Value propositions of SaaS, denoting a description of SaaS firm's offering and its relative advantage, are well represented and recognized in all of the analyzed articles. In brief, the key property of SaaS seems to be a highly standardized offering with minimal value adding services, enabling low costs and prompt deployment. Accordingly, it has been suggested that SaaS firms should be "productizing" their services so these can be provided them more efficiently [13].

The offering includes either a traditional enterprise application delivered over the Internet, a web-native application, or a web service component [19]. Liao [16] moreover points out that there may be applications intended for individual consumers and for enterprise users. In addition to outsourced application development, SaaS business model also includes providing the IT infrastructure required for the online service [11][17][18]. Therefore, after attaining low-cost offering, SaaS vendors compete on functionalities, reliability and service availability [10].

Another business model element elaborated in many of the examined articles is the SaaS revenue streams, which is often considered together with the cost structure element. In this regards, the previous studies have compared SaaS to more traditional packaged software product business. Similarities of software product business and SaaS business have been found in high number of customers, small revenue per customer, higher up-front investments on software development and in high customer acquisition costs [18][19][20]. In addition to the low delivery cost of online provisioning, the main difference seems to be found in the on-demand licensing and pricing; in traditional product business model users buy a perpetual-use license, in contrast to paying a monthly or a usage-based subscription fee SaaS [11]. In general, SaaS business model economics are linked to one-to-many delivery model. By aggregating many users together, SaaS vendors may leverage economies of scale [15].

On this value capture side, SaaS business model has also been also characterized as a movement from "high-touch, high-margin, high-commitment" provisioning of professional software services to "low-touch, low-margin, low-commitment" self-service [9]. This means that the customer relationship, channels and customer segment elements of the SaaS business models are all about efficient marketing and sales model and about automated delivery of services in large volumes [19], enabling efficiently serving even small and medium-sized (SME) customers. Consequently, SaaS offering may appeal more to the SME customers, and SMEs and enterprise customers are likely to adopt applications at different rates [17].

On the value creation side, SaaS vendors are trying to minimize the cost per customer and therefore seek for new ways to produce services of high quality more efficiently than before [10]. This may be achieved through automated processes [14] and scalable IT resources, likely obtained from service provider with economies of scale in producing computing capacity [9].

Overall, we found that the majority of the current literature still remains at a conceptual level. While case studies have also been employed, we find room for further empirical examination of different business models. Also, the articles tend to concentrate on value propositions of SaaS offerings and value capture through alternative revenue logics. In addition to industry reports, only a few articles considered SaaS business model as configuration of elements.

Among the few, Cusumano [13] looked at business model as combinations of different customer segments, revenue models and delivery models. Tyrväinen and

Selin [20] focused on marketing and sales of SaaS and analyzed a combination of different aspects of customer segments (through customer lifecycle value, customer size, and buyer role), customer relationship and channels elements (including service model, sales channel, and marketing channel), and revenue logic through entry transaction size. We argue that more of this holistic business model thinking is needed to advance the literature on SaaS. Identifying feasible configuration for the business model would help software companies in aligning and balancing otherwise separate elements in order to perform and run successful business.

The examined articles analyze both SaaS and preceding application service provisioning (ASP) business models. The existing SaaS literature, examined through the business model framework and its elements, helped in identifying the primary characteristics of SaaS models, and also distinguishing the SaaS models from the ASP models. While the delivery model of ASP and SaaS over the Internet are similar, the business models for ASP and SaaS firms are fundamentally different. In the ASP model, a service provider hosts a customer-specific and integrated pieces of software. Since customization, integration and hosting services add value and distinctiveness through customer intimacy [13], they may be more profitable also with smaller volumes. In contrast, *scalability* of the entire business model aiming at ease of adoption on the client side seems to be the most important premise for the SaaS vendors [9], requiring efficiency in producing and delivering the services and in handling customer relationships.

To summarize the existing literature, we submit a definition of a SaaS business model as configuration of business model elements (using the elements suggested in [7]). Software-as-a-Service business model is essentially about:

- Standardized and simple offering with minimal services enabling low costs and prompt deployment over the Internet (value propositions),
- Automated processes and scalable IT resources, to achieve economies of scale (activities, resources, and partners),
- Efficient mode of sales that can be efficiently used to target small and medium-sized customers and buyers at all levels of an end-user organization (customer relationships, channels, and customer segments),
- Increased focus on customer acquisition and retention, but also automated delivery of the offering and support (activities, customer relationship),
- Usage-based pricing with small transactions and minimal costs per customer, but higher up-front investments on software development and customer acquisition (revenue streams and cost structure).

The analyzed literature also suggests some ASP and SaaS business model classifications, based on types of the offering and customer segmentation [12][19]. For both ASP and SaaS, the first wave of offering seem to include the characteristics of traditional software project business aimed at enterprise customers with complex software product elements and service elements for integration and training. Only afterwards, pure-play firms enter with more focused and scalable business models targeted to broader customer market. In the following analysis, our classification is based on combination of business model elements and on thinking where a continuum of different business models is in between ideally scalable SaaS model and customer-specific ASP model. Accordingly, we position the derived definition of SaaS business model at the other extreme of the continuum and anticipate that the market consists of these pure-play SaaS firms and enterprise SaaS firms.

3 Data and Analysis Method

The empirical part of our study aimed at classifying SaaS companies and examining their business model configurations. We used data from the annual Finnish Software Industry Survey targeting all software companies in Finland. The definition of software company and thus the framing of the study followed the tradition of the Software Industry Survey [21], focusing on firms whose main activities are providing software as either products or services to their customers. The details of the survey can be found in the final report available online [21], so we will provide only a short overview of the sample and survey procedures. The mailing list of the survey contained 5469 companies. However, this number contains many non-software firms because the industry code to which most of the software companies fall into contains also a substantial amount of companies that provide IT related services but that are not software companies. The data collection started in April and ended in May 2011 resulting in 506 complete and 168 partial responses.

The survey form contained question that asked the informants to indicate how their revenue was divided between ten different sources. Asking for SaaS revenue directly is problematic because some ASP and software product companies market their offering as SaaS and would be likely to give erroneous responses. Instead, we used the item "Providing an application as a service used over the Internet" as a qualifier for identifying companies that might be using a SaaS business model. While this is a necessary condition for a company being a SaaS firm, it is not a sufficient condition because this item also captures ASP companies.

To describe and classify SaaS firms, we decided to focus on the characteristics of the product and the transactions with the customers since they were central in the chosen business model framework. In particular, we developed measures for the value capture side of the business model framework [7]:

- Customer segments; customer size and buyer role
- Value proposition; online delivery, customer specificity and complexity
- Revenue streams; sales case size, usage-based pricing
- Channels and customer relationship; on-demand model, self-service purchasing

The survey questions that were used to measure the business model components are included as an appendix. The two multiple choice questions (customer size and transaction size) were converted to single measures by giving the options scores from one to five and using the largest chosen item as the measure.

We used cluster analysis to develop a classification for the firms. Cluster analysis is a family of methods that group cases based on their similarity [22]. Because the items were measured with different scales and have different distributional characteristics, correlation rather than the most commonly used Euclidean distance as the similarity measure. The mean and maximum similarity between each case and the rest were used to remove several firms that were far different from the rest as to be considered outliers leaving 163 firms for the final analysis.

The final analysis started with hierarchical average linkage clustering to determine the number of clusters that best describe the data. We analyzed the results by inspecting the resulting dendrogram, which suggested that four clusters were sufficient to describe the data. To arrive to the final results, we used these four clusters as seeds for confirmatory k-means cluster analysis. After the cluster memberships were established, we profiled the clusters by inspecting descriptive statistics of each cluster.

Although cluster analysis has been used in previous business model studies [23], the method has a key weakness that it will always provide a solution even if no structure existed in the data and does not have a test statistic that can be used to assess statistical significance [24]. Thus the goodness of the results rely solely on researcher judgment, which is the most significant weakness of our study.

4 Results

4.1 Comparing SaaS and ASP Firms and Other Software Firms

In the examined literature, authors [9][18][20] hypothesize that SaaS business model is distinguished by aiming at serving large segment of smaller customers and adjusting the revenue logic to match the segment's needs. Results of our empirical analysis are shown in Figure 1. They illustrate the customer segmentation and the revenue logic of the operating SaaS firms by showing correlation of increasing SaaS revenue with marketing and sales indicators. The analysis should be interpreted as follows.

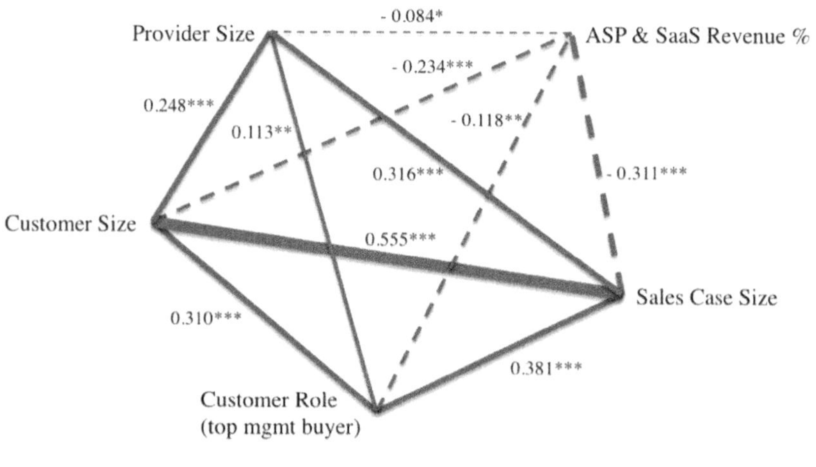

$* p < 0.05$, $** p < 0.01$, $*** p < 0.001$

Fig. 1. Correlations of increasing ASP and SaaS revenue percentage and sales indicators among software firms. Dotted lines represent negative correlations, solid lines positive correlations. The strength of the line designate stronger association between indicators.

The solid lines represent positive correlation of the sales indicators. We find that as the customer size increases, also the value of sales case (transaction) increases. Accordingly, the large software vendors tend to sell to large customers, and the transaction size is higher when a large customer is acquiring or when a large software vendor is selling. In large organizations and large sales cases the decision maker is more often a top manager while end users and middle managers buy software in smaller transactions and in smaller firms.

The dotted lines indicate negative correlation. Accordingly, firms with higher share of revenue from ASP and SaaS are somewhat smaller than other software companies. The analysis indicates that these firms sell to smaller customers than other software companies. Also, their sales cases are typically smaller and their buyer is more often an end user or middle manager than the buyer of other software. The smaller transaction size is likely to be related to recurring revenue logic.

The relation of growing ASP and SaaS revenue with smaller customer size and smaller sales case size is not only due to smaller average size of the analyzed firms. This was verified with two regression analyses (see Table 1). In the first regression, low ASP and SaaS revenue share and high software provider size together explained large customer size. In the second, they explained large sales case size.

Table 1. Regression tests to verify the associations between ASP and SaaS revenue percentage and sales indicators; provider size, customer size and transaction size

	Customer size	Sales case (transaction) size
	(1)	(2)
ASP and SaaS	-0.773***	-1.090***
Provider size (personnel class)	0.250***	0.351***
Intercept	3.123***	3.227***
Observations	474	468
R^2	0.110	0.185
Adjusted R^2	0.106	0.182
F	29.119	52.846
p	0.000	0.000

$^{+}$ $p < 0.1$, * $p < 0.05$, ** $p < 0.01$, *** $p < 0.001$
Linear regression

Thus, these results communicate that when comparing two software companies of the same size, the customers and transactions sizes of ASP and SaaS companies are smaller. The important implication in context of this study is that, for SaaS business model, a different mode of sales and sales channel is required than e.g. in selling larger software system deliveries.

These results are also in line with the SaaS business model characteristics reported in other sources [25]. That is, SaaS firms spend close to half of their budget to marketing and sales to gradually acquire a high number of customers, each of which is spending relatively small monthly or annual fees on the services. These add up to an increasing customer base, which generate growing recurring revenue ensuring predictability for business development and success of the SaaS firm.

4.2 Classification of SaaS and ASP Firms

We employed cluster analysis to find suitable classification of operating ASP and SaaS companies and to describe the properties of their business models. Table 2 shows the cluster profiles for the four identified clusters. We interpret the findings as follows.

In the first and second clusters we find companies with browser-based products, but with high customer specificity indicated by high marks in "Customer specific product" and "Product needs integration". Thus, we regard these clearly more ASP than SaaS companies. These two clusters are distinguished by their revenue logic ("Product sold with on-demand model" and "Product pricing is based on actual user") and by customer size. The companies in the second cluster are targeting smaller firms, include less professional services and have more on-demand elements in their business model. We chose to label these two clusters as "Enterprise ASP" and "Pure-play ASP".

The software companies appearing in clusters three and four do not evidently customize their products and services for each customer indicated by low medians in customer-specificity, need for integration and need for training. For this reason, we account them much closer to using a SaaS business model than the companies in clusters one and two.

The latter two clusters are differentiated by the sales model and customer size ("Product sold with on-demand model" and "Customer size"). Companies in the third cluster are not involved as much in online sales and focus on larger corporations, with some service elements included in their offering. The fourth cluster relies heavily on on-demand and online sales and focuses on smaller customers. We label these two SaaS clusters as "Enterprise SaaS" and "Pure-play SaaS" respectively.

Table 2. Cluster profiles revealing two types of ASP and two types of SaaS companies

	SaaS business model							
	Enterprise ASP		Pure-play ASP		Enterprise SaaS		Pure-play SaaS	
	Mean	Med	Mean	Med	Mean	Med	Mean	Med
Browser based product	4.4	5.0	4.6	5.0	4.7	5.0	4.4	5.0
Customer specific product	3.5***	4.0*	4.0***	4.0***	2.7*	2.0	2.1***	2.0***
Product needs integration	4.1***	4.0***	3.3	4.0	2.5***	3.0***	2.0***	2.0***
Product sold with on-demand model	1.9***	2.0***	4.0***	4.0***	2.4**	2.0**	4.0***	4.0***
Product purchased online	1.8***	2.0***	2.1	2.0	2.1*	2.0	4.2***	4.0***
Product requires training	4.1***	4.0***	3.8*	4.0	2.8**	3.0**	2.2***	2.0***
Product pricing is based on use	2.4***	2.0***	3.5	4.0	3.9***	4.0***	3.7**	4.0*
Sales case (transaction) size	3.6***	4.0**	2.9	3.0	3.6**	4.0*	2.4***	2.0***
Customer size	3.3*	4.0	2.6**	2.0**	3.7***	4.0***	2.3***	2.0***
N		56		25		41		41

Mann-Whitney U tests between one group and the rest. * $p < 0.05$, ** $p < 0.01$, *** $p < 0.001$

The interrelations of business model elements in the found clusters makes possible to discover the following SaaS business model configurations. The "Pure-play SaaS" model reveals a combination, where simple and non-customized software may be delivered without the need to instruct the users or integrate it and, thus, provide the software as-a-service with lower fees that appeal to SME customer segment (low values in "Sales case size" and "Customer Size"). The "Pure-play SaaS" model is also associated with online channels for marketing, sales and delivery ("Product purchased online") that, in turn, entail high level of automation to these activities. Such low-touch customer relationship can be established either through push-oriented high-pressure sales or as pull-oriented self-service. In both cases, the production and channel costs per customer needs to be minimized to enable attractive pricing.

The "Enterprise SaaS" cluster indicates a combination where software is more complex, although standardized for all customers, or perhaps supports more comprehensive process and therefore requires supporting service like training and integration to existing systems. This increases the deployment costs and demands for more effort in nurturing customer relationship (low value in "Product purchased online"). Thus marketing and sales is based on personal business relations and delivery includes customer-specific, even on-site work. For this reason, the pricing for "Enterprise SaaS" may be higher compared to "Pure-play SaaS".

Table 3 shows three sets of descriptive statistics for the firms. The first basic statistics show that the "Pure-play SaaS" companies are both younger and smaller than the other companies. This would be in line with the analyzed literature with regards to evolution of ASP and SaaS business models, in which "Pure-play SaaS" firms emerge after "Enterprise SaaS" firms closer to traditional software business models. The first set of statistics further indicates that "Pure-play SaaS" firms are less profitable. This could be explained by their revenue logic where the software vendor needs to invest on product, service and customer base development up-front and recurring revenue logic delays the return to these investments.

The second set of descriptive statistics describes how these companies accumulate their revenues. These statistics show clear differences between the clusters. First, the SaaS clusters create approximately twice as large share of their revenue from sales of software as a service over the Internet than the ASP firms. This highlights the fact that whereas a firm can be classified as an ASP firm just based on the delivery model, certain elements need to be changed in the business model level as well for a firm to be considered as a SaaS firm.

The third set of descriptive statistics shows how the firms view themselves on a multiple choice question asking which of the given five firm types describes them best. The software product firm and software project contractor were the most commonly chosen options and the SaaS firm viewed themselves more often as product firms than the ASP firms.

Table 3. Descriptive statistics for clusters of ASP and SaaS firms

	SaaS business model							
	Enterprise ASP		Pure-play ASP		Enterprise SaaS		Pure-play SaaS	
	Mean	Med	Mean	Med	Mean	Med	Mean	Med
Basic statistics								
Age	10	8	8	6	10	10	6**	3*
Revenue (M€)	1.50**	0.57	4.32	0.25	0.87	0.42	0.61**	0.13**
Total personnel	17*	8	40	4	11	6	5*	3*
Profitability	0.09**	0.09**	0.02	0.02	0.00	0.04	-0.03	0.00*
Productivity (k€)	85.4	74.8	106.8	60.0	81.9	76.3	73.7*	40.0
Sources of revenue								
3rd party sw. licenses	3.7**	0.0**	1.7	0.0	1.7	0.0	1.6*	0.0*
ASP and SaaS	24.6***	10.0**	27.3	15.0	40.6	30.0	52.2**	50.0**
Content and ads	0.8	0.0	0.8	0.0	0.7	0.0	6.4	0.0
Deployment project	11.0***	7.5***	6.2	0.0	6.1	3.0	4.6***	0.0***
Development project	21.9	10.0	32.9*	25.0	12.6	5.0	16.0*	0.0*
Hardware	1.4	0.0	1.6	0.0	3.2	0.0	0.1	0.0
Maintenance	11.8**	5.0**	10.0	0.0	10.4	0.0	1.6***	0.0***
Not software related	9.9	0.0	4.6	0.0	7.9	0.0	3.2*	0.0*
Other software related	3.9	0.0	9.5	0.0	5.6	0.0	3.2	0.0
Own software licenses	11.1*	5.0**	5.4	0.0	11.1	0.0	11.1	0.0*
Firm type								
Software product firm	.446*	0	.48	0	.634	1	.732*	1
Device manufacturer	0	0	.04	0	.024	0	0	0
Software project contractor	.375	0	.36	0	.22	0	.171	0
Consulting firm	.161	0	.12	0	.122	0	.098	0
Reseller	.018	0	0	0	0	0	0	0
N		56		25		41		41

Mann-Whitney U tests between one group and the rest. * $p < 0.05$, ** $p < 0.01$, *** $p < 0.001$

5 Discussion and Conclusions

In this article, the characteristics of the Finnish software companies delivering Software-as-a-Service were examined. Compared to the current literature on SaaS business models, we were interested in gaining a holistic view of how these companies operate to create and appropriate value. We chose to describe the properties of SaaS business model against a widely adopted and comprehensive framework. We envision that there shall be a multitude of innovative SaaS offerings and business models and, therefore, also the future scientific studies would benefit from examining SaaS adoption through different types of business models and offerings. This study was therefore conducted to identify factors archetypal in this type of business model and to produce classification of the current SaaS business models.

Current literature on Software-as-a-Service is mostly written from software engineering viewpoint. By reviewing articles on the SaaS business model, we learned that classifications of operating SaaS companies did not yet exist, and that essential facet of the SaaS business model seems to be scalability of the entire business model. We find that this scalability of the business model is attributed to standardized application, which is easily sold and delivered to large volumes of customers, while maintaining low marginal costs. In other words, scalability of the SaaS business model is based on avoiding customer specificity. Scalability is also the factor separating SaaS and ASP business models. ASP in our analysis is considered as hosting of customer-specific software.

In this paper, the properties operating SaaS firms were analyzed and described in various perspectives. The firms were found to target smaller customers as software firms on average and direct their marketing and sales also at end-user. This observation verifies some of the assumptions made in the previous studies [20] on SaaS firms' marketing and sales. Further, our cluster analysis enabled forming a classification of the operating SaaS firms. Two different types of SaaS business models were discovered: “Pure-Play SaaS” and “Enterprise-SaaS”.

Properties of “Pure-Play SaaS” business models have not been previously presented as configuration of multiple elements. To summarize and elaborate the business model according to the selected business model framework, we put forward a definition of representative “Pure-Play SaaS” business model:

- Value proposition includes a horizontal, standardized web-native application.
- Revenue streams are obtained through a small entry fee and a recurring fee.
- SaaS firms mainly target SMEs and sell to middle management and end-users.
- Sales channel is push-oriented and SaaS firms engage in inbound high-pressure sales. Less human contact in deployment in required than traditionally, owing to more simple applications.
- SaaS firms are required to have both domain expertise, to include the best practices to the application, and application development capabilities. They partner with IT-service providers for infrastructure and support services.
- Initial development costs may be high, but firms aim for minimal marginal costs.

The “Pure-Play SaaS” business model brings accessible new smaller underserved customer segment, where small software companies are more credible than in traditional software business. Finally, SaaS represents an attractive model for investors; SaaS requires relatively low initial investment with opportunity to deploy more capital over life, and rapid development cycle allow determining quickly whether the business model works in the markets.

Majority of the analyzed companies, despite delivering software over the Internet, do not employ the scalable SaaS business model. It means that SaaS may turn out infeasible for certain types of applications or customer segments. Our classification reveals the "Enterprise SaaS" model that can be seen as possibility to those software firms who do not want the radically change their business model or wish to focus on larger customers. We suggest “Enterprise SaaS” business model to include:

- A mass-customized, but complex application requiring also support services.
- Vendors charge an entry fee, recurring fee and service fees.
- Target at larger enterprises and their IT-managers and top executives.
- Aim at high-touch, trust-enhancing customer relationships with tailored contracts.
- Perform personal sales to do consultative sales, and employ channel partners.
- Possess domain expertise and utilize an ecosystem of companies as a resource.

- Use partners to deliver value-adding applications and services.
- Have varying marginal costs, owing to the long sales cycles and required support.

These software companies, take Salesforce as an example, may benefit from more standardized offering and scale economics, but maintain the customer-specific features as part of their offering due to customer demand and additional revenues.

We are also aware of another alternative business model referred as "Self-Service SaaS", which exhibits software offering simplified and standardized to the extent that customers can themselves find, evaluate and deploy the software, i.e. the channel is pull-oriented. We propose characteristics of "Self-Service SaaS" to include:

- A very simple application, which is easy to adopt. Consider Dropbox.
- Use of freemium model, ad-based revenues or small recurring fees.
- Adopted first by end-users and individual consumers, then SMEs.
- Fully automated self-service, as little interaction between customer as possible.
- Outbound and viral marketing used to attract customers to vendors home page. Landing page critical in turning prospects into customers.
- Close to zero marginal costs.

The software firm's business model includes several factors, which may promote or hinder the adoption of SaaS offering in customer organizations. The results of the present study can therefore be utilized in future research to produce more accurate information on adoption of SaaS model. For instance, the perception of compatibility with existing practices in large customer organization may differ notably when faced with "Pure-Play SaaS" or "Enterprise-SaaS" offerings. The results also have practical significance. We argue that identifying feasible configurations is particularly relevant as software companies need to align and balance otherwise separate elements in order to perform and run successful business. The identified "Pure-Play SaaS" and "Enterprise-SaaS" models offer executives and software product manager a starting point for creating and assessing new ways to operate and make money.

The acknowledged weaknesses of our study mainly relate to the limitations of cluster analysis as the analysis method [24]. A cluster analysis will always produce a classification regardless of the existence of any structure in the data. Thus, the categories are always to some extent artificial and can present an oversimplification of the reality. While the same risk of our classification remains, we believe that this risk is small considering the feasibility of our classification. In further studies, we also need to consider that the measures for the examination of SaaS model did not include all the elements suggested by the business model framework. For instance, the alignment of value creation and value capture sides of SaaS business model is interesting topic for further research.

Acknowledgements. The research reported in this paper was carried out within the framework of the Cloud Software Program which was governed by TIVIT Oy nominated to organize and manage the programs of the Strategic Center for Science, Technology and Innovation in the field of ICT funded by the Finnish Funding Agency for Technology and Innovation (TEKES).

References

1. Vaquero, L., Rodero-Merino, L., Caceres, J., Lindner, M.: A break in the clouds: towards a cloud definition. ACM SIGCOMM Computer Communication Review 39, 50–55 (2008)
2. Mell, P., Grance, T.: NIST Working Definition of Cloud Computing. National Institute of Standards and Technology, Information Technology Laboratory (2009)
3. Chesbrough, H.: Business model innovation: It's not just about technology anymore. Strategy and Leadership 35, 12–17 (2007)
4. Benlian, A., Hess, T.: Opportunities and risks of software-as-a-service: Findings from a survey of it executives. Decision Support Systems 52, 232–246 (2011)
5. Susarla, A., Barua, A., Whinston, A.: A Transaction Cost Perspective of the "Software as a Service" Business Model. Journal of Management Information Systems 26, 205–240 (2009)
6. Zott, C., Amit, R., Massa, L.: The Business Model:Theoretical Roots. Recent Developments, and Future Research (2010)
7. Osterwalder, A., Pigneur, Y., Tucci, C.L.: Clarifying Business Models: Origins, Present, and Future of the Concept. Communications of the Association for Information Systems 16, 1–25 (2005)
8. Magretta, J.: Why business models matter. Harvard Business Review 80, 3–8
9. Armbrust, M., Fox, A., Griffith, R., Joseph, A., Katz, R., Konswinski, A., Lee, G., Patterson, D., Rabkin, A., Stoica, I., Zaharia, M.: A View of Cloud Computing. Communications of the ACM 53, 50–58 (2010)
10. Benefield, R.: Agile Deployment: Lean Service Management and Deployment Strategis for the SaaS Enterprise. Presented at the 42nd Hawaii International Conference on System Sciences (2009)
11. Choudhary, V.: Software as a Service: Implications for Investment in Software Development. Presented at the 40th Hawaii International Conference on System Sciences (2007)
12. Desai, B., Weerakkody, V., Currie, W., Tebboune, S.D., Khan, N.: Market Entry Strategies of Application Service Providers: Identifying Strategic Differentiation. Presented at the 36th Hawaii International Conference on System Sciences (2003)
13. Cusumano, M.: The Changing Software Business: Moving from Products to Services. IEEE Computer, 20–27 (January 2008)
14. Durkee, D.: Why Cloud Computing Will Never Be Free. Communications of the ACM 53, 62–69 (2010)
15. Jacobs, D.: Enterprise Software As Service: Online Services are Changing the Nature of Software. ACM Queue, 36–42 (July/August 2005)
16. Liao, H.: SaaS business model for software enterprise. Presented at the Information Management and Engineering, Chengdu, China (2010)
17. Dubey, A., Wagle, D.: Delivering Software as a Service (2007)
18. Sääksjärvi, M., Lassila, A., Nordström, H.: Evaluating the Software as a Service Business Model: From CPU Time-Sharing to Online Innovation Sharing. Presented at the IADIS International Conference e-Society, Qawra, Malta (2005)
19. Software & Information Industry Association: Software as a Service: Changing the Paradigm in the Software Industry. SIIA and TripleTree Industry Analysis Series (2004)
20. Tyrväinen, P., Selin, J.: How to Sell SaaS: A Model for Main Factors of Marketing and Selling Software-as-a-Service. In: Regnell, B., van de Weerd, I., De Troyer, O. (eds.) ICSOB 2011. LNBIP, vol. 80, pp. 2–16. Springer, Heidelberg (2011)

21. Rönkkö, M., Peltonen, J., Pärnänen, D.: Software Indusry Survey (2011), http://www.softwareindustrysurvey.fi/ReportFinland2011.pdf
22. Hair, J.F., Anderson, R., Tatham, R.L., Black, W.C.: Multivariate Data Analysis. Prentice Hall, Upper Saddle River (2006)
23. Bigliardi, B., Nosella, A., Verbano, C.: Business models in Italian biotechnology industry: a quantitative analysis. Technovation 22, 1299–1306 (2005)
24. Ketchen, D.J., Shook, C.L.: The Application of Cluster Analysis in Strategic Management Research: An Analysis and Critique. Strategic Manage. J. 17, 441–458 (1996)
25. Radizeski, P.: Top 3 Reasons its Hard to Sell SaaS (2009), http://blog.tmcnet.com/on-rads-radar/2009/03/top-3-reasons-its-hard-to-sell-saas.html

Appendix: Survey Questions

How well do the following statements describe your firm's main product or service?	Strongly disagree	Disagree	Do not agree or disagree	Agree	Strongly agree
Our product or service is used through a web browser	1	2	3	4	5
Our product or service is tailor-made for each customer	1	2	3	4	5
The pricing of our product or service is based on its actual usage	1	2	3	4	5
Our product or service requires customer-specific integration or installation work	1	2	3	4	5
Our product or service requires customer-specific user training	1	2	3	4	5
Our product or is purchased online through an automated system	1	2	3	4	5
We sell our product with on-demand model without the need for longer commitment by the customer	1	2	3	4	5

Please estimate the following about your typical customer and sales case.	Under 10€	10-1,000€	1,000€-10,000€	10,000€-100,000€	Over 100,000€
The typical total value of one sales case:	☐	☐	☐	☐	☐
	Private persons	Firms, under 50 employees	Firms, 51-250 employees	Firms, Over 250 employees	Public sector
The typical customers:	☐	☐	☐	☐	☐
	End user	Technical personnel	Business management	Top management	Reseller
Typical buyer of our product or service:	☐	☐	☐	☐	☐

Advantages of Public Cloud Infrastructure in Different Technology Adoption Lifecycle Stages

Oleksiy Mazhelis, Eetu Luoma, and Arto Ojala

Department of Computer Science and Information Systems
Agora, P.O. Box 35, FI-40014, University of Jyväskylä, Finland
firstname.lastname@jyu.fi

Abstract. Independent software vendors (ISV) utilize cloud infrastructure for different reasons. We hypothesize that the motivation to adopt cloud infrastructure-as-a-service (IaaS) changes as the ISV's product is getting adopted by the market. In this paper we consider how the infrastructure needs of ISVs change along the stages of ISV product's adoption lifecycle, and analyze the potential benefits of utilizing IaaS in different stages. The analysis is illustrated with the cases of ISV firms with documented use of IaaS. These cases support the hypothesis that different benefits of IaaS are gaining importance along the adoption lifecycle.

Keywords: Cloud computing, infrastructure as a service (IaaS), technology adoption lifecycle.

1 Introduction

Infrastructure-as-a-Service (IaaS) is a cloud computing service model that offers the consumers remotely managed, on-demand provisioned, and rapidly scalable processing, storage, networks, and other computing resources, on top of which the consumers deploy the software of their choice [1]. IaaS promises the independent software vendors (ISV) wishing to deploy their own offerings a number of potential benefits, notably improved scalability [2], as well as savings in start-up and/or operations costs [3,4]. Owing to these and other promises, the IaaS services are adopted rapidly: according to Gartner, the market for cloud infrastructure services exceeded \$5.6 billion in 2011 and will reach \$22 billion by 2015 [5].

ISVs may adopt IaaS for different reasons. For some, the low start-up cost is of utmost importance, whereas some other ISVs may use IaaS due to the possibility of scaling the infrastructure resources rapidly and cost-efficiently. While the needs of ISVs differ, the IaaS providers still exhibit the "one size fits all" approach, which may limit the adoption of their services due to a mismatch between the differentiated needs of a particular ISV category and the properties of the service offering [5].

The paper aims at increasing the IaaS providers' understanding of how their services are adopted by the software firms, so that they could adjust and tailor their offerings according to the potential customer needs. In particular, in line

M.A. Cusumano, B. Iyer, and N. Venkatraman (Eds.): ICSOB 2012, LNBIP 114, pp. 195–208, 2012.

with technology adoption models, we hypothesize that the infrastructure needs of ISVs change as the ISVs' market matures. On this premise, the paper considers *how* the ISV's infrastructure needs evolve along the development of ISV's market, and *how* the IaaS offerings could match these needs. The research question addressed in the paper can thus be formulated as *whether a difference exists in the value IaaS offers to ISVs at different stages of the technology adoption lifecycle.*

In this paper, we shall use Rogers' diffusion of innovations (DOI) theory [6,7] together with Moore's work [8] on technology adoption lifecycle (TAL) as a theoretical background of this study. In our empirical part, we shall use illustrative cases to demonstrate the value of IaaS to IVS in the different stages of the technology adoption lifecycle.

The remainder of the paper is organized as follows. In the next section, the advantages offered by cloud infrastructure to the ISVs are considered. The stages of the technology adoption lifecycle are overviewed in section 3. In section 4, we analyze how the importance of IaaS changes as the ISV product is evolving along the stages of the TAL; the analysis is based on the reported cases of using Amazon's IaaS offerings by the ISVs. Finally, section 5 discusses the results of the analysis, considers the implications of the findings, and outlines the areas for further research.

2 Cloud Computing and Its Benefits

Cloud computing generally refers to the provision of computing capacity, storage capacity, and applications as a service across the Internet. Architecturally, cloud computing is usually seen as consisting of three service layers: (i) Infrastructure as a Service (IaaS), which provides computation and storage capacity, (ii) Platform as a Service (PaaS), which provides software development tools plus an application execution environment, and (iii) Software-as-a-Service (SaaS), which provides applications on top of PaaS and IaaS [9,10]. Cloud computing is also seen as a set of "consumer and business products, services and solutions delivered and consumed in real-time over the Internet" [11], implying that especially SaaS offerings may appear in a variety of different forms. In our analysis, the focus is both on the applications provided as-a-service by an ISV to its customers, on the development of market for such SaaS offerings, and on simultaneously changing needs for infrastructure services provided to the ISV.

The data center hardware and software forming a cloud infrastructure can be deployed in a form of a public cloud, a private cloud, or a hybrid cloud infrastructure [1]. In case of a public cloud, a software vendor uses a third party's cloud infrastructure (data center) to offer SaaS for customers on demand. A private cloud is deployed in the customer's internal data center, with the software being installed and used in a centralized manner [9,12]. In the case of a hybrid cloud, a firm using a private cloud may, for example, offload a part of the workload onto a public cloud, and in that way acquire more computing capacity [13,12].

The adoption of cloud computing in general and SaaS in particular offers a number of benefits to its customers. Building on study by Lacity et al. [14],

Benlian and Hess [15] grouped the SaaS benefits under the categories of cost advantages, strategic flexibility, focus on core competences, access on specialized resources, and quality improvements. Based on a survey conducted among 2000 randomly selected German companies, the authors identified cost advantages, strategic flexibility (in switching providers as well as in scalability), and quality improvements as empirically supported opportunities behind SaaS adoption.

In the study by Benlian and Hess [15], these benefits are mainly attributed to IT outsourcing, multi-tenant architecture and shared infrastructure controlled by the ISV, whereas other properties of the ISV's SaaS offering are not explicitly considered as the sources of relative advantage. This leaves the room to consider the adoption of different types of applications as-a-service, varying for instance in the degree of innovation and complexity, and consider the impact of IaaS on the value creation of the ISVs providing SaaS offering.

The advantages of IaaS to ISVs include, among others, on-demand provisioning, client platform independence, rapid elasticity, charging based on the actual usage, possibilities for lowering the costs, ease of use, reliability, and streamlined maintenance and upgrade [16]. We find it safe to assume that some of the benefits of SaaS, which an ISV passes on to its customers, are in fact associated with the advantages of IaaS:

- *Cost advantages.* Due to the effect of both economies of scale and scope, IaaS firms may provide the infrastructure services at a price lower than the cost of internally provisioning the same services. This in turn is due to the IaaS provider's ability to fully control the infrastructure, standardize it and share among multiple users via a multi-tenant environment. IaaS customers also benefit from lower up-front investments, as IaaS providers usually charge a subscription fee without a need to make (large-scale) initial payments.
- *Strategic flexibility.* When using IaaS, ISVs are more flexible in switching providers, thus reducing the switching costs of replacing one infrastructure solution with another. Additionally, the ISVs' ability to scale improves: using IaaS, they are able to rapidly provision (and de-provision) the resources in response to the workload. Finally, the use of IaaS enables quicker implementation of applications and thus shortens the time-to-value for the ISVs.
- *Quality improvements.* Owing to the IaaS providers' ability to concentrate on operational excellence, they are able to attain a high level of service quality. The quality of IaaS provider's service is usually expressed in measurable quantities (including uptime, response time, etc., as well as related fines and penalties), and the IaaS provider is motivated to maintain a high service level as the customers may otherwise switch to another IaaS provider.

These benefits are likely to appeal differently to an ISV depending on the products and services, which the ISV deploys on top of the IaaS, as well as on how far these products and services are in their lifecycle. The latter is considered by the technology adoption lifecycle models which are summarized in the next section.

3 Technology Adoption Lifecycle

According to Rogers' Diffusion of Innovations (DOI) theory [6,7], perceived attributes of innovations include five characteristics that impact on the rate of adoption. These include relative advantage such as an economical or practical benefit, compatibility with existing values and experiences, complexity of the innovation, trialability and observability of the innovation. Rogers describes how an innovation is adopted by a social system that consists of individuals, informal groups, organizations, and/or subsystems with a shared problem-solving goal. The theory presents five ideal types of adopter categories [7]. These categories include: (i) Innovators, (ii) Early adopters, (iii) Early majority, (iv) Late majority, and (v) Laggards.

Moore [8] used the DOI theory as a starting point for identifying and explaining the technology adoption patterns in high-tech industries (including software industry), and introduced the Technology Adoption Lifecycle (TAL) model. In the context of IT innovation adoption, this lifecycle suggests that a high-tech market evolves through the set of stages, from the early market through the so-called 'chasm' and 'bowling alley' to the 'tornado' market and then eventually to the 'main street' stage.

The early market starts with the emergence of a discontinuous innovation. This innovation is employed by the firms to produce specific solutions to accommodate the needs of visionaries in customer organizations [8]. In terms of the Rogers' work [7], the adoption in this stage relies on Innovators and Early adopters. Innovators are the persons able to understand and apply more technical products than average population. Early adopters represent opinion leaders that have a central position in their networks. They both decrease the uncertainty associated with the adoption of a new idea and give a justification whether the innovation is good or not for the adopters in the next stage.

When crossing the chasm and in the bowling alley, products sharing a significantly similar core are gaining the leading positions in adjacent market niches. Firms with such offering target new niches, trying to occupy them as well. Within a niche, the product is standardized, but changes are needed when bringing the product to a new niche [8]. If the product is successful in several adjucent niches, it may enter the tornado stage, implying that the product becomes a de-facto standard, both establishing the market and taking the leading role in it. Customizations are no longer provided, and the configuration and support are likewise scarce or absent. In these phases, the innovation is adopted by the pragmatist firms or individuals, referred to as Early majority in the Roger's theory [7]. These customers decide to adopt the innovation only when the technology matures, and when a market-leading vendor emerges [8]. Accordingly, the period to adopt is relatively long compared to the early market.

Main street represents a market after the tornado, when the product's value to specific customer can be increased by adding extra (easy to make) features, thus, justifying greater margins for otherwise the same product [8]. In the DOI theory [7], this stage is related to the large group of Late majority that amounts to circa 34% of all adopters. Late adopters embrace new ideas mainly based on economic necessity or increasing peer pressures. They are more skeptical and cautious toward innovations and do not adopt the innovation until their peers have done so. Thus, the most of the uncertainty must be eliminated before Late majority adopt the innovation. After Main street markets, products come to the end of their life cycle [8]. In this stage, only Laggards adopt the innovation as they have very traditional values and are suspicious toward new ideas. According to Rogers [7], this might be also related to precarious economic position that forces Laggards to be cautious toward innovations.

Moore [8] analyses how the firms' strategies, competitive advantage, positioning, and organizational leadership change as the firm progresses through the technology adoption lifecycle. In particular, the key competitive values of the firm – *product leadership, operational excellence, and customer intimacy* – are gaining different priorities at different stages. Whereas in the early market, product leadership alone is the key, in the chasm and in the bowling alley the customer intimacy plays a critical role along with the product leadership in meeting the expectations of a particular niche. During the tornado, in addition to product leadership, the firms focus on operational excellence to meet the rapidly scaling demand, and to benefit from the resulting economies of scale. Finally, on the main street stage, along with the operational excellence, the customer intimacy is important again, to combat diminishing margins with low-cost customization offerings. In the next section, we shall consider how the characteristics of IaaS match the ISV's key competitive values at different stages in the TAL.

4 Benefit of IaaS in Different Stages of TAL

In this section, for each stage of TAL, we shall consider the benefits of utilizing IaaS. We shall also consider the examples of case firms having products in that TAL stage, and their justification for using the IaaS. The cases are based on the secondary data gathered from the Amazon.com case study database and the executive interviews of companies utilizing Amazon's IaaS offering. As advised in the study of Eisenhardt [17], the cases were selected for particular theoretical reasons rather than on the basis of random sampling. Thus, the aim is to increase the theoretical understanding of the phenomenon under the study instead of statistical generalization [18]. In the data analysis, guidelines suggested by Eisenhardt [17] and Yin [18] were followed. First, the case firms were identified from the database based on characteristics of their software product and services. In particular, we searched for clear examples of product or services requiring focus either on product leadership, customer intimacy or operational excellence. Thereafter, the unique patterns of each case were identified and similar patterns were categorized under each stage of TAL. Table 1 provides an overview of the analyzed companies and their type of software offering.

4.1 Early Market

The firms in the early market are serving the needs of visionaries through customer-specific offerings. In this stage, *product leadership* is the key [8]. Often

Table 1. Overview of the case companies

Case company	Product / Service	Ref
Peixe Urbano	A deal-a-day website	[19]
BigDoor Media	Game mechanics for online apps	[20]
Ci&T	Customer-specific social networking	[21]
Ooyala	Video encoding and delivery	[22]
SundaySky	Video encoding and delivery	[23]
Razorfish	Data mining for marketing industry	[24]
Assay Depot	Portal for pharmaceutical industry	[25]
MarketSimplified	SaaS app for online brokerage	[26]
Zynga	Social network games	[27]
Dropbox	Online file hosting service	[28]
Altexa	Online file hosting service	[29]
SmugMug	Online photo sharing service	[30]
photoWall	Online photo sharing applications	[31]
Salesforce.com	SaaS platform for CRM	[32]

such products are made by SMEs or start-ups built around the innovative idea and, for such companies with limited resources, reducing upfront investments and launching the product or service fast to attain visionaries feedback are both critical. Let us consider Peixe Urbano and BigDoor Media as examples of the companies in the early market.

Peixe Urbano is a Brazilian startup company that runs a deal-a-day website offering discounts in Brazil, Argentina, Mexico, and Chile. Having chosen the bootstrapping approach, the firm faced the challenge of developing and rolling out their offering with minimal investments. The management had decided to use Amazon Web Services (AWS) IaaS to minimize the upfront infrastructure investments, while still having an opportunity to scale rapidly in case the offering succeeds: "we needed a solution that was both very small on capital expenditure, as well as highly scalable. Amazon Elastic Compute Cloud (Amazon EC2) was the most mature of the available options that met both requirements" [19]. By adopting Amazon IaaS, the firm was able to *cut the expenses of investing in physical hardware*, and, within a short time, it had grown to become the largest group-based deal site in Brazil.

Another ISV announcing benefits from IaaS in the early market is BigDoor Media [20] that develops a software platform to assemble game mechanics for websites and mobile applications. The company currently utilizes a variety of different IaaS components from Amazon's repertoire. Similarly to many start-ups, the company changed its initial product to totally different one. The case study reports that without AWS the new product would have taken longer to get to the market. Delay in launching the new product would have caused serious financial problems.

We find that IaaS allows the startups in the early market to *save on the up-front investments*, thus giving the opportunity to invest their scarce resources in core product development (*cost advantages*). IaaS also brings the opportunity to *shorten the development cycle* (*strategic flexibility advantage*). In our view, the need to minimize the up-front investments (i.e. cost advantage) was a driving force behind both Peixe Urbano's decisions to adopt IaaS. In another similar case with an IT services company Ci&T [21], AWS was chosen due to "its ability to create infrastructure with no up-front costs; performance, price, reliability, and API maturity; on-demand scaling; and its pay-as-you go philosophy". In case of BigDoor Media, the use of public IaaS was justified, in addition to low up-front investments, by the shorter time to market (i.e. strategic flexibility). Similar representative cases include companies like Ooyala [22] and SundaySky [23].

4.2 Chasm and Bowling Alley

When in the chasm and the bowling alley, the software vendors are focusing on the previously unserved needs of individual niches. Within a niche, the offering is usually harmonized; however, modifications and customizations are usually required when entering a new niche. In order to get a better position in the expected tornado stage, the firm strives to gain the leadership in multiple niches. To secure such position, a short time-to-market is critical as well as delivering the promised whole product to get the leadership within the niches. Achieving the whole product further requires both the *customer intimacy* to identify the customer's unserved needs and *product leadership* to meet these needs. It is therefore of utmost importance for the firm to have both the reliable infrastructure, as well as to preserve the flexibility of modifying the offering, including the infrastructure, upon the need. This can be illustrated with the examples of Razorfish, Assay Depot, MarketSimplified and Zynga.

Razorfish [24] applies data mining methods on data from browsing sessions to identify usage patterns and segment Internet users and customers. The mining algorithms are customized on a client-by-client basis, but the overall solution is applicable across multiple industries. The company opted for IaaS to handle increasingly large datasets. Compared to traditional hosting environment, Razorfish's benefits included cost savings and reduced procurement time frame. Technical advantages stem from IaaS *strategic flexibility* and include efficiency and scalability, ease of integration, flexibility and adaptablility in implementation, which all contribute to reduced time-to-market in expanding business.

Assay Depot [25] provides pharmaceutical companies with tools for managing outsourcing and internal services. The firm creates custom versions of its Storefront and Backoffice applications for different customers, and is running different versions of the code on different Amazon AWS servers. In addition to the domain-specific requirement for security guarantees, the reported reasons for using AWS was the gain in *flexibility* and *quality*, that is, the possibility to deploy changes quickly, reliably, in a manageable and efficient manner.

The case study of MarketSimplified [26] exhibits the need to achieve product leadership. The company offers real-time online brokerages in SaaS mode of delivery, with high requirements for reliability, security and availability. Brokerage clients access account details, real-time quotes, market data, news and technical analysis tools using mobile devices. Using IaaS enabled lowering costs, but more importantly allowed for the *service quality* matching the customers needs and the *flexibility* of increasing the capacity when needed.

Zynga specializes in developing online games that are offered e.g. to the Facebook users. Having realized that it is practically impossible to predict which of the games would gain popularity and consequently result in a rapidly growing customer demand, and hence realizing that accurately planning for infrastructure needs is challenging at best, the firm decided to launch new games on Amazon EC2 infrastructure. Despite the EC2 services being more expensive as compared with the in-house or leased datacenters, the use of EC2 gives the needed *flexibility*, namely, the possibility to scale up rapidly in case the game is successful. Only when the game uptake is well underway and predicting future demand becomes possible, the company shifts the game into the in-house infrastructure [27].

The case examples suggest that the use of IaaS gives the firms in this stage both the *quality advantage* of the mature infrastructure services, and the *flexibility* to add new infrastructure resources when the business is expanding. As the examples of Razorfish, Assay Depot, Zynga and MarketSimplified show, the flexibility and quality of public IaaS help in rapidly developing, modifying, and scaling an appealing whole product, and hence justify its use by the ISVs aiming at a leadership position in a specific niche.

4.3 Tornado

During the tornado market, the adoption of technological product increases rapidly. The product itself is becoming standardized and commoditized. Due to a significant customer base, customization and tailoring may not be financially rewarding. Instead, the firms focus on delivering the product at a large scale. Consequently, *operational efficiency* along with *product leadership* are important factors [8]. The needs in the tornado market can be illustrated with the examples of applications for online storage and backup and online photo sharing, both embodying market for relatively standardized offering.

Dropbox, a provider of an online backup service, is apparently experiencing a tornado-like adoption of its service. Established in 2007, the startup has recently reached 45 million customer base, increasing from 25 million customer base within seven months period. The company keeps the data of its customers on Amazon Simple Storage Service (S3) buckets. According to the interview with the founder and CEO of the company, Drew Houston, one of the primary reasons for using Amazon IaaS is the Amazon's capability of reliably handling large volumes of data (i.e. its *operational efficiency* and *mature quality*), along with the offered built-in redundancy allowing the Dropbox team to focus on client software and the layer above [28].

In the tornado, the growing market is typically shared by several providers. A rival to market leaders in the online storage market, Altexa, provides a simple solution for offsite backup. Their case study [29] reveals the competitive pressures in terms of both product leadership and operational efficiency. In the case description a company executive describes that Altexa "knew its solution had to be reliable and competitively priced". Using Amazon's IaaS offering, the company could rely on mature infrastructure to increase the product *quality*, offer storage with *competitive pricing*, while focusing on developing their product offering further.

We shall also consider the examples of SmugMug and photoWall, both online photo sharing companies that process, store and enable sharing of masses of digital photos. The case study for SmugMug for instance sets out that the company adds approximately ten terabytes of new images each month. In addition to high volumes, both solutions seem to demonstrate relatively uniform overall offering, typical to the tornado stage. In this market, SmugMug reportedly justifies the use of Amazon IaaS, in addition to *reliability*, by its *cost-effectiveness* and ability to scale (*i.e. flexibility*) as SmugMug grows [30]. Likewise, photoWall case study [31] indicates the selection of IaaS based on the low cost and ability to increase capacity on-demand.

As the cases of storage applications and online photo sharing suggest, the mature quality, scalability, and cost-efficiency of IaaS provider's offering were important factors in favor of adopting IaaS by the companies in the tornado stage. Accordingly, the public IaaS supports the companies in the tornado market with the required *flexibility*, *quality*, and *cost-efficiency*, i.e. with the ability to scale rapidly in a cost-efficient manner while maintaining the required reliability.

4.4 Main Street

When in the main street stage, the ISVs are serving their existing customer base, by providing value-adding customization to specific customer groups at nearly zero cost to the vendor. This is referred to as the so-called "+1 offerings" representing simple customizations appealing to a specific niche and allowing the firm to differentiate the product. Meanwhile, the core product becomes commoditized in this stage, reflected in a multitude of mimicking copies of the core product competing in the market, and margins decline accordingly. Thus, the combination of *cost-efficiency* to earn the margins despite commoditization and *customer intimacy* to be able to target specific customer groups is needed in this stage [8].

The use of cloud computing infrastructure in post-tornado market can be exemplified with Zynga (considered above in section 4.2): When the adoption of individual game saturates, the company shifts the game into the in-house infrastructure to save costs [27].

The in-house infrastructure is also the choice of Salesforce.com, a market leader in SME-oriented customer relationship management (CRM) software as a service, and apparently the largest SaaS company on the market (its market capitalization is larger than the next 12 SaaS companies combined including its competitor, NetSuite) [33]. The company operates in a rather saturated main street market, where it offers to its customers multiple version of its applications having various combinations of modules and different pricing schemes [32].

Salesforce.com applications run on top of its proprietary Force.com platform (PaaS), which in turn relies on the in-house infrastructure consisting of three geographically distributed data centers [34]. Similarly to Zynga, the Salesforce.com's choice of the infrastructure was driven by the aim to cut the costs [35], and the offerings of public IaaS providers are likely to be more expensive as compared with the in-house infrastructure [36].

In this stage, the use of public IaaS in combination with private IaaS can bring the ISV cost advantages in case the ISV's demand for infrastructure resources exhibits significant fluctuations [37]. However, in case of predictable demand with little or no sharp peaks, the use of public IaaS may bring little benefit to the ISV. Indeed, if rapid scalability is not needed any more, the cost-per-unit of infrastructure services may be significantly lower in own datacenters [38]. Still, the company may prefer to focus its limited resources on the value-adding layers while minimizing the efforts on managing the infrastructure; in this case, the company may decide to continue using public IaaS despite its lower cost-efficiency.

5 Discussion and Concluding Remarks

The competitive values and needs of an ISV are changing as the ISV's product is adopted by the market. Intuitively, one would presume the value of IaaS offering to be highest in the early phases of product development or at the time when the ISV's business is accelerating. However, by aligning the value of IaaS with the existing lifecycle models, we found that different facets of IaaS offerings seem to appeal to the ISVs depending on the current lifecycle phase of their products. Namely, product leadership, customer intimacy and operational efficiency are emphasized to varying degree in different lifecycle phases, and the ISVs adopt IaaS to achieve the advantages matching the needs of the current phase. In the previous section, we have considered how these needs of ISVs are supported with the infrastructure services of IaaS providers. The results of the analysis are summarized in Table 2.

In the *early market*, where low start-up costs and short time-to-market are critical for achieving the required product leadership, IaaS supports these needs with the cost advantages (low or absent start-up costs) and required strategic flexibility (ability to shorten the development cycle).

The customer intimacy along with product leadership, that are important in the *chasm* and the *bowling alley* stage, imply that the ISV should deliver the functionality expected by targeted niches, with reasonable quality, and ahead of competitors. IaaS supports these requirements by providing highly reliable and flexibly changeable infrastructure resources.

During the *tornado* stage, the product leadership needs to be combined with operational efficiency. This necessitates the high product quality and short development cycles to stay ahead of competitors, as well as the ability to cost-efficiently cope with the rapidly increasing demand for the product. Therefore, the cost advantage and strategic flexibility offered by the IaaS facilitates the

Table 2. Competitive values of ISVs vs. IaaS benefits at different stages of adoption

Market stage	Adopter type	ISV competitive values	Relevant IaaS benefits
Early market	Innovators & early adopters (technology enthusiasts & visionaries)	Product leadership	Cost advantages, Strategic flexibility
Chasm & bowling alley	Early majority (pragmatists)	Product leadership & Customer intimacy	Strategic flexibility, Quality improvements
Tornado	Early majority (pragmatists)	Product leadership & Operational efficiency	Strategic flexibility, Cost advantages, Quality improvements
Main street	Late majority (conservatives)	Operational efficiency & Customer intimacy	Cost advantages (tolerating demand peaks)

ISV in serving the quickly growing customer base cost-efficiently, while the IaaS-supported quality helps the ISV in maintaining the product quality high.

Finally, in the main street stage demanding operational efficiency coupled with customer intimacy, IaaS offers the strategic flexibility and operational efficiency to those ISVs who experience peaks in the demand.

Thus, the advantages of IaaS change along the adoption lifecycle: from cost advantages and strategic flexibility (in the early market) through strategic flexibility and quality improvement (in the chasm and bowling alley) to strategic flexibility, quality improvement, and cost advantage (in the tornado) to cost advantage (in the main street). As could be seen, the strategic flexibility is important throughout the adoption lifecycle. Meanwhile, the quality improvement is important in the chasm & bowling alley as well as in the tornado stage, whereas the importance of the cost advantage in the chasm & bowling alley stage appears to be less critical.

The above findings have some implications both for the users (ISVs) and providers of IaaS. For the ISVs, the knowledge of how the IaaS benefits match their needs in different stages gives the possibility to plan ahead their use of public IaaS. For instance, an IaaS with proven reliability and scalability can be selected in the chasm & bowling alley, to be replaced with a less expensive alternative in the tornado and/or main street stage. For the IaaS providers, this knowledge gives the possibility to adjust their offerings and pricing strategies to the ISV segments depending on the stage of lifecycle in which the ISVs' own products are. For example, a low up-front fee can be imposed on the ISVs in the early market to help them minimize the up-front investments, while a subscription fee with notable quantity discount may be offered to the ISVs with rapidly increasing demand in the tornado stage.

The analysis presented in this paper is grounded on the theoretical works of Rogers [6,7] and Moore [8]. Our research method relies on secondary data and we were not able to validate the collected data. In future work, the results of this theoretical analysis shall be empirically confirmed. For instance, a large survey would likely reveal more details on ISVs needs and manifest how ISVs perceive other IaaS providers' offerings. It should be also noted that the analysis in the paper has focused on the three cloud computing benefits that were empirically supported by the study of Benlian and Hess [15]. However, besides these three benefits considered in this paper, other benefits, such as the focus on core competences or the access to specialized resources may be essential for the ISVs. Whether the other factors are prevalent, and whether their importance changes with the stages of adoption lifecycle shall be studied as a part of future work.

Acknowledgments. The research reported in this paper was carried out within the framework of the Cloud Software Program which is governed by TIVIT Oy nominated to organize and manage the programs of the Strategic Center for Science, Technology and Innovation in the field of ICT funded by the Finnish Funding Agency for Technology and Innovation (TEKES).

References

1. Mell, P., Grance, T.: The nist definition of cloud computing. Special publication 800-145, National Institute of Standards and Technology (September 2011), `http://www.csrc.nist.gov/groups/SNS/cloud-computing/`
2. Youseff, L., Butrico, M., Da Silva, D.: Toward a unified ontology of cloud computing. In: 2008 Grid Computing Environments Workshop (GCE 2008), pp. 1–10. IEEE (2008)
3. Weinman, J.: Mathematical proof of the inevitability of cloud computing. Working paper (January 8 2011), `http://www.joeweinman.com/Resources/Joe_Weinman_Inevitability_Of_Cloud.pdf` (last retrieved on March 10, 2011)
4. Lee, C.A.: A perspective on scientific cloud computing. In: Proceedings of the 19th ACM International Symposium on High Performance Distributed Computing, HPDC 2010, pp. 451–459. ACM, New York (2010)
5. Leong, L., Chamberlin, T.: Magic quadrant for public cloud infrastructure as a service. Technical report, Gartner (December 2011)
6. Rogers, E.: Diffusion of Innovations. The Free Press, New York (1962)
7. Rogers, E.: Diffusion of Innovations, 4th edn. The Free Press, New York (2003)
8. Moore, G.A.: Inside the Tornado : Marketing Strategies from Silicon Valley's Cutting Edge. HarperBusiness (July 1999)
9. Armbrust, M., Fox, A., Griffith, R., Joseph, A.D., Katz, R., Konwinski, A., Lee, G., Patterson, D., Rabkin, A., Stoica, I., Zaharia, M.: A view of cloud computing. Commun. ACM 53, 50–58 (2010)
10. Hugos, M., Hulitzky, D.: Business in the Cloud: What Every Business Needs to Know About Cloud Computing. John Wiley & Sons, Inc. (2011)
11. Gens, F.: Defining "cloud services" -an IDC update (2009) IDC exhanges, `blogs.idc.com/ie/?p=422` (retrived on January 15, 2012)
12. Louridas, P.: Up in the air: Moving your applications to the cloud. IEEE Software 27(4), 6–11 (2010)
13. Sotomayor, B., Montero, R., Llorente, I.: Virtual infrastructure management in private and hybrid clouds. IEEE Internet Computing 13(5), 14–22 (2009)

14. Lacity, M., Khan, S., Willcocks, L.: A review of the it outsourcing literature: insights for practice. The Journal of Strategic Information Systems 18(3), 130–146 (2009)
15. Benlian, A., Hess, T.: Opportunities and risks of software-as-a-service: Findings from a survey of it executives. Decision Support Systems 52(1), 232–246 (2011)
16. Sosinsky, B.: Cloud Computing Bible. Wiley Publishing, Inc., Indianapolis (2010)
17. Eisenhardt, K.: Building theories from case study research. Academy of Management Review 14(4), 532–550 (1989)
18. Yin, R.: Case study research: Design and methods. SAGE Publications, CA (2009)
19. Amazon Web Services: AWS Case Study: Peixe Urbano (2011), http://aws.amazon.com/solutions/case-studies/peixe-urbano/ (retrived on January 23, 2012)
20. Amazon Web Services: AWS Case Study: BigDoor Media Opens the Door to Success with AWS (2011), http://aws.amazon.com/solutions/case-studies/bigdoor-media/ (retrived on January 23, 2012)
21. Amazon Web Services: AWS Case Study: Ci&T (2011), http://aws.amazon.com/solutions/case-studies/ciandt/ (retrived on January 23, 2012)
22. Amazon Web Services: AWS Case Study: Ooyala (2011), http://aws.amazon.com/solutions/case-studies/ooyala/ (retrived on January 23, 2012)
23. Amazon Web Services: AWS Case Study: SundaySky Scales the Cloud with AWS (2011), http://aws.amazon.com/solutions/case-studies/sundaysky/ (retrived on January 23, 2012)
24. Amazon Web Services: AWS Case Study: Razorfish (2010), http://aws.amazon.com/solutions/case-studies/razorfish/ (retrived on January 23, 2012)
25. Amazon Web Services: AWS Case Study: Assay Depot (2011), http://aws.amazon.com/solutions/case-studies/assay-depot/ (retrived on January 23, 2012)
26. Amazon Web Services: AWS Case Study: MarketSimplified (2011), http://aws.amazon.com/solutions/case-studies/marketsimplified/ (retrived on January 23, 2012)
27. Babcock, C.: Lessons from FarmVille: How Zynga uses the cloud. Technical report, InformationWeek (May 2011), http://www.informationweek.com/news/global-cio/interviews/229402805 (retrived on January 23, 2012)
28. Drager, D.: DropBox: Review, invites, and 7 questions with the founder. Technical report, MakeUseOf (March 2008), http://www.makeuseof.com/tag/dropbox-review-invites-and-7-questions-with-the-founder/ (retrived on January 23, 2012)
29. Amazon Web Services: AWS Case Study: Altexa (2011), http://aws.amazon.com/solutions/case-studies/altexa/ (retrived on January 23, 2012)
30. Amazon Web Services: AWS Case Study: SmugMug (2006), http://aws.amazon.com/solutions/case-studies/smugmug/ (retrived on January 23, 2012)
31. Amazon Web Services: AWS Case Study: photoWALL (2009), http://aws.amazon.com/solutions/case-studies/photowall/ (retrived on January 23, 2012)

32. Schwartz, E.: Calculating the cost of SaaS: Pay-as-you-go pricing might just mean forgoing software as a service altogether. Technical report, InfoWorld (March 2007), http://www.saas-capital.com/advisory-resources/ (retrived on January 23, 2012)
33. Capital, S.: OPEXengine: Leaders & laggards: SaaS growth and the cost of capital. White paper, SaaS Capital (March 2011), http://www.saas-capital.com/advisory-resources/ (retrived on January 23, 2012)
34. Salesforce.com: Force.com: A comprehensive look at the world's premier cloud-computing platform. White paper, Salesforce.com (March 2009), http://www.developerforce.com/media/Forcedotcom_Whitepaper/WP_Forcedotcom-InDepth_040709_WEB.pdf/ (retrived on January 23, 2012)
35. Dell: Building a scalable cloud. Case studies, Dell (March 2009), http://i.dell.com/sites/content/corporate/case-studies/en/Documents/2010-sfdc-10008118.pdf (retrived on January 23, 2012)
36. Khajeh-Hosseini, A., Greenwood, D., Smith, J.W., Sommerville, I.: The cloud adoption toolkit: supporting cloud adoption decisions in the enterprise. Software: Practice and Experience - Special Issue on Software Architectures and Application Development Environments for Cloud Computing (2011)
37. Mazhelis, O., Tyrväinen, P.: Economic aspects of hybrid cloud infrastructure: User organization perspective. Information Systems Frontiers, 1–25 (2011), doi:10.1007/s10796-011-9326-9
38. Harris, D.: Backblaze open sources 135TB storage architecture. Technical report, GigaOm (July 2011), http://gigaom.com/cloud/backblaze-open-sources-135tb-storage-architecture/ (retrived on January 23, 2012)

Revenue Models of Application Developers in Android Market Ecosystem

Sami Hyrynsalmi[1,2], Arho Suominen[3], Tuomas Mäkilä[2,1], Antero Järvi[3], and Timo Knuutila[2]

[1] Turku Centre for Computer Science TUCS, Turku, Finland
[2] University of Turku, Business and Innovation Development BID, Turku, Finland
{sthyry,tuomas.makila,knuutila}@utu.fi
[3] University of Turku, Department of Information Technology, Turku, Finland
{arho.suominen,antero.jarvi}@utu.fi

Abstract. Mobile application ecosystems have growth rapidly in the past few years. Increasing number of startups and established developers are alike offering their products in different marketplaces such as Android Market and Apple App Store. In this paper, we are studying revenue models used in Android Market. For analysis, we gathered the data of 351,601 applications from their public pages at the marketplace. From these, a random sample of 100 applications was used in a qualitative study of revenue streams. The results indicate that a part of the marketplace can be explained with traditional models but free applications use complex revenue models. Basing on the qualitative analysis, we identified four general business strategy categories for further studies.

Keywords: Mobile ecosystem, Android Market, revenue model, business model.

1 Introduction

During the past few years, the mobile device industry has been more driven by software development than hardware. The creation of new mobile ecosystems is providing end-users the abundance of possibilities to consume content, adopt new ways to interact and emerge as, not mere consumers, but content providers and developers. This has made the complexities of revenue streams and ecosystems related to mobile devices even more difficulty to be clearly understood, but simultaneously interesting to study. Subsequently, we have seen researches on the different ecosystems relating to mobile devices [1,2]. It has, however, been argued that the software marketplaces would have a significant effect on the overall health of a larger mobile device ecosystem [3].

Motivated by the complexities, the authors study the argued root cause of how to create a revenue stream within a mobile marketplace. Arguing that, we should be able to identify clear revenue streams or models used by developers. Even if we accept that a significant portion, in a practically open marketplace, would be created without any practical revenue model in mind, the portion

M.A. Cusumano, B. Iyer, and N. Venkatraman (Eds.): ICSOB 2012, LNBIP 114, pp. 209–222, 2012.

of developers actively publishing products should have a practical approach to holding the efforts profitable. Thus, the paper focuses on the revenue streams, the ways of getting compensation from the services and products offered, of mobile ecosystem applications.

To approach the problem, Google Android Market is selected as a case study. Although not claiming that the results of this study would clearly explain the interactions within other device ecosystems, we have selected Android due to its relatively low entrance cost, high perceived adoption rate, and as a practical point, the information provided for researchers.

The study was conducted by gathering data on applications published in the Android Market. This resulted in a database of 351,601 separate applications, that are available in the Android Market, being used for the analysis. Approaching the data first from a quantitative perspective we tried to make distinctions on the overall content provided. Second, we relied on a qualitative approach to further identify practical revenue streams. For the qualitative study, a random sample of 100 applications was created. In the following, we are studying the revenue streams of applications based on the models discussed by Coursaris & Hassanein [4]. Furthermore, we will discuss general business strategy categories found in the random sample.

The study revealed that a significant portion of the marketplace will remain uncategorized if we are purely looking at revenue streams. There is a strong democracy effect in the marketplace, where the low entry cost gives developers an opportunity to create practical software solutions with very different expectations on income. In addition, the notion that mobile ecosystem health would directly correlate with its size remains without evidence. The number of software without any practical use is significant. This phenomenon is seen also with the applications that have been installed thousands of times. However, how the application developers get compensated is interesting. In this study, we do not take to consideration a small portion of the top developers, such as Rovio and Electronic Arts.

Our paper is structured as follows. The next section focuses on the background of business, mobile and software ecosystems. This is followed by our data and descriptive analysis of the data gathered. Section 4 introduces the results of a random sample's qualitative analysis and identified general business strategy categories. Section 5 discusses on the results, limitations and notices made during the study with suggestions for future works. The paper is concluded in the last section.

2 Business, Mobile and Software Ecosystems

A Business Ecosystem (BECO) is defined by Moore [5] as *"an economic community supported by a foundation of interacting organizations and individuals the organisms of the business world"*. Looking at the more well-known biological definition of an ecosystem, defined as *"a biological community of interacting organisms and their physical environment"*, the conceptualization of a business ecosystem is easy to understand. We use the term 'ecosystem' to define an interacting community of organism, and by directing our focus to different aspects of social interaction, we have adopted different ecosystem entities such as Mobile Ecosystem (MECO) and Software Ecosystem (SECO).

Focusing on the Mobile Ecosystem, scholars have endeavored to define the interactions of an MECO. Developed through the growth of mobile communication, the MECO has changed the landscape of telecommunication significantly. In the landline based ecosystem the complexity of the systems was significantly simpler, but with the current multiple service, device, and service provider ecosystems, the complexity is self-evident. Looking at the structure of the ecosystem, Xia *et al.* [2] define the MECO as having three stakeholders: mobile network operators, handset manufacturers and mobile operating systems. Suggesting a narrow view on the ecosystem, Xia *et al.* studied the business models in the MECO arguing that the complexities of business models forced the different stakeholders to interact and create a more interconnected ecosystem. To some extent, we could argue the definition by Xia *et al.* to be an oversimplification. Basole [6] has reviewed the work of several authors in defining a broader view of a MECO. Basole argues that an ecosystem consists of 6 emerging, such as gaming providers, and 9 existing segments, such as mobile network operators.

The structure of a MECO is however unclear [7]. The ICT sector as a whole is a highly dynamic interdependent market [8]. In this interdependent market, actors are looking for dominance and stability through the adoption of standards, resulting in a development where competitors have collaborative arrangements while competing in the same market [9]. In addition, while business communities are often structured around a leader, in the case of a mobile handset provider, the structure is more complex with several dominant organizations [7]. Using a similar strategy, these dominant organizations have established marketplaces, which would entice a large number of actors to join the ecosystem. The marketplace leverages a large developer base that would ultimately establish a dominant position in the market [3]. The health of this marketplace is arguably a key success factor for the successfulness of the ecosystem.

To some extent, traditional models of supply chain value creation lack in ability to model the complexities of the MECO. Dedrick *et al.* [1] approached the value creation of a MECO through a traditional supply chain approach. This approach, however, is limited by the rise of significance of the content. Content creation has risen to be a something other than a piece of the value chain, resulting in added complexity when trying to understand the mobile domain.

Focusing on the SECO, the concept was first presented by Messerschmitt and Szyperski [10]. Jansen *et al.* [11] defined a SECO as *"a set of businesses functioning as a unit and interacting with a shared market for software and services, together with the relationships among them"*. We would argue that there is a clear separation in the definitions of MECO and SECO, although sometimes left ambiguous [12]. With SECO, we would understand an ecosystem of software products or services, enabled by a core service. In the case of the MECO, we would see a SECO working within the MECO, where the operating system is the enabling core service. This results in two clear distinctions. First, in the case of current MECOs, we have seen that the health of a SECO working within the MECO is seen as being significant [3]. Second, SECOs are not limited to existing within a MECO. However, the discussion on different ecosystems are to some extent trivial. The significant notion made through the definitions is the overall complexity of business in the mobile domain.

Business models of the new emerging markets have discussed recently [2,13,14]. However, in this study we are focusing on the *revenue streams* instead of full-scale business models. For Osterwalder & Pigneur [15], the revenue model, which consists of one or more revenue streams, is only one building block of a business model. A revenue stream defines the way of getting compensation from a good or service provided [16].

Coursaris & Hassanein [4] listed eight revenue models seen in mobile commerce. In the following, each of these revenue models is shortly presented: *Access* is the enabling revenue model on which all other revenue models rely on. Access revenue model is based on providing the end-user with access to the network. In the *Subscription* model, the application provider get compensation from users subscriptions, for example by monthly fees.

Pay-per-Use model is an alternative to the previous model, where the customer can buy a single portion instead of whole offering. The marketplaces offer integrated tools for micropayments when a customer can, *e.g.*, buy additional levels for games for a small price. In the *Advertising* model, a content provider earn revenue through placing advertisements in its product. Although the pricing models and compensations in mobile advertising vary, for example TapJoy[1] estimates the usual income from banner advertisements in games is $ 0.35–0.90 and for a top application even $ 2.00 per thousand view.

A *Transaction* based revenue model is most often based on an enabling service created by an intermediary organization. For example, in the case of Android Market, Google is providing the infrastructure to make software offering to end-users and charges a transactional fee for both access and sales. Moving forward to the *Payment Clearing* revenue model is distinct as the distributor role is not relevant to this. Payment Clearing is defined only as a third party merchant collecting a percentage based on processing fees. In the case of an intangible object the distinction on Transaction and Payment Clearing is hard to make.

In the *Hosting* model the content provider uses a third party to host their content. This is due to lack of technology and/or expertise. Finally, the revenue model of *Point-to-Traffic* operates on the assumption that created content will yield larger volumes of traffic to a third party website, thus supporting the revenue model of the third party website. For this, the third party compensates the content provider with a fee.

For the revenue models listed by Coursaris & Hassanein [4], Access, Transaction, and Payment Clearing are present in the mobile ecosystems, but they are not used by application providers. Therefore, they are not relevant for this study.

---

[1] *5 Ways to Improve your Android Apps* by Rob Caroll, Tapjoy – Available at `http://knowledge.tapjoy.com/best-practices`

In addition to the listed revenue models, it should be noted that an application might not form a revenue stream of own — it, however, might strengthen the revenue stream of the main products or services. Furthermore, the ecosystem contains other possibilities for the monetization of an application. For example, a device manufacturer might pay for the right to add an application on their devices.

3 Methodology, Data and Descriptive Statistics

In this study, we utilize both quantitative and qualitative research methods. First, we collected a set of data from the marketplace and analyzed it with quantitative approach. From the collected set of applications we selected a random sample which was then studied with qualitative approach in which we utilize grounded theory approach [17]. The research methodology used is described in the following in more details. Furthermore, the descriptive statistics of the Android Market is given.

In the beginning of the December 2011, we gathered a list of package names — the unique identifiers of the applications — from AndroidPIT[2] due to the reason that Google Android Market does not provide an easily readable list of all applications. AndroidPIT is a third party's listing services of marketplace's applications. The list was then used to parse information on applications from its public page at Android Market. The data gathering process is presented in [18] with more details.

The data gathering was reproduced in January 2012 resulting in the data of 351,601 applications. Compared with the dataset of December 2011, the number of applications in the marketplace is increased by 11,740. Furthermore, 7,097 applications that were present at December are no more accessible through the market. The high number of removed applications might be the consequence of the change of the year because some applications are meant only for a specific event or time period. However, during a time period of a month almost 19,000 new applications were introduced at the marketplace.

In the reproduced dataset, 69 % of applications are free to install and 31 % are subject to a charge in the marketplace. Only 2.7 % of all directly paid applications have more than 1,000 installs. Only one paid application has been installed from 1 million to 5 million times. As discussed in [18], the direct sale through the marketplace seems rather low.

The quantitative research methods alone do not seem to sufficient tools for analyzing the revenue models of gathered applications because, *e.g.*, in the question "does the application use advertisements" can only be answered if the public description contains information about the advertisements. Therefore in this study we used a more qualitative approach to study revenue models and streams of MECO applications. For this study, we selected a random sample of 100 applications from the set of all applications that have been installed over 1,000 times, which totals 121,197 (34.5 % of all) applications. In order to ignore applications

[2] AndroidPIT – `http://www.androidpit.com`

that are either so new that they have been installed by a few or are not meant to be real business, we focus only on the most downloaded one third of the marketplace.

For every applications that have been installed over 1,000 times, a random number from a closed interval was generated using Microsoft Excel 2010. The applications were then ordered with the random number and the top one hundred applications, based on the generated random number, were then chosen into the sample. Three authors of the study evaluated each a set of 30–40 applications manually by analyzing at the public page of an application at the marketplace, other applications published by the same developer and the developer's homepage. If the language used in the descriptive text or in the homepage was not familiar for the author, Google Translate was used to roughly gain an understanding of the application.

The authors answered beforehand prepared questions concerning the application, its revenue streams and its developer. Each application was studied only by one researcher. In the following phase, the gathered data was reviewed application by application in the meeting of all authors and incoherent answers were revised after thorough discussion.

In the final phase, applications were installed and tested with an Android device to verify findings. In the study, we used several devices — three tablet computers and three smart phones with different Android OS versions and equipments — for ensuring that the applications would work. However, four applications were found to be unfit for all devices used in the study. Furthermore, three applications were removed from the marketplace during the study. Thus, the data gathered is partial for seven applications. In the following analysis, it will be mentioned if these applications are included into the discussion in question.

4 Qualitative Analysis of the Random Sample

4.1 Conventional Revenue Streams

In the following, we are categorizing applications into different revenue models based on the list given by Coursaris & Hassanein [4]. It should be noted that one application can utilize more than one model. From the revenue models discussed, we could not find Point-of-Traffic — although applications that only works as a web page viewer could have be counted here, they were analyzed case-specific — from Android applications evaluated.

Paid Downloads model was not included in the list given by Coursaris & Hassanein [4] but it might be the most traditional revenue model in the mobile application business. The model was utilized by only four applications of our 100 applications random sample. As discussed in [18], the direct sale seems to be useful only for a handful of developers.

Free to try -publishing is a kind of subcategory of directly paid downloads where a version of the application is free — it might contain advertisements, be time or feature limited — but a premium version is available with a price. The model was studied in our previous paper [18] by using a fuzzy algorithm to match two applications of the same developer when other one is free and other one is paid and the names of two applications are similar enough. With the algorithm, we found 11,536 pairs of free and paid applications. Of all paid applications, 10 % was published using this kind of Freemium -model. Furthermore, an average income of this kind of publishing was almost three times higher than the average of the marketplace [18]. This indicated that the Freemium models might be useful when monetizing Android application.

In the random sample of this study, 18 applications from 98 studied — two applications that were removed from the market are not included — is a part of Free to try -application pair. From these, 3 are paid and 15 are free. Free to try -publishing model has a clear share in the dataset.

Advertising seems to be a rather common revenue stream in Android Market. From our sample set, 37 contain advertisements and 56 applications do not. Four applications, that could not be installed, and three removed applications are excluded from the evaluation.

Based on our material, it is impossible to estimate the earned revenue of an application that contains advertisements. However, basing on the subjective analysis majority of applications utilizing advertising revenue stream in this random sample were 'single-use' products *i.e.* they are most likely used few minutes every now and then. Therefore, the total number of impressions might be rather low, furthermore noticing the low installation counts of the random sample, which will cause the revenue earned from advertising will also be small.

The random sample contains one developer, who have published over one hundred games utilizing most of the time the same game mechanic and only changing a theme of the game. Although the games do not offer more than fun for a few minutes and most of the reviews are negative, the games have been installed over 1.82 million times in total. The compensation generated from the advertisements of all applications might altogether be reasonable for this developer.

Subscription revenue model is found on 10 out of 98 applications when the application usually works as a front-end for a service outside of the ecosystem. One of the removed applications and the applications that could not be installed were evaluated based on the web page. The other removed applications were excluded.

Pay-Per-Use model, in this context is understood as *In-application Purchase* model where the customer can buy premium content in the application. In-application purchase was utilized only by one application in the dataset of this study. However, the result was expected because the feature was introduced in 2011 by Google although a few third party's implementation existed earlier. For example, *AppBrain*[3], an Android application directory, estimates that only 6,000 applications utilize in-application payment. However, the number is increasing rapidly.

Hosting model was clearly identified in 5 cases out of 98 evaluated. In these, application developers offer services to specific segments such as a platform for radio stations for mobile radio applications or a map application for travelers in a national park.

A summary of found revenue models is presented in Table 1. It should be noted that in our dataset, 47 applications out of 93 — removed and those that cannot be installed to our devices were excluded — are not using nor are part of any conventional revenue streams. In addition, 14 applications, from the set of applications without clear revenue streams, can be classified as front-ends for the major service and two applications promote the service of application subscribers. These ones clearly strengthen the revenue stream of main products or services without the revenue stream of their own.

Table 1. The frequencies of the revenue models studied applications. One application can utilize multiple revenue streams.

Revenue model	#
Paid download	4
Free Trial	18
Advertising	37
Subscription	10
Pay-per-use	1
Hosting	5
Point-of-Traffic	0
No evident revenue stream	47

4.2 Categorization of the Business Strategies

After the revenue stream analysis, 31 applications were still without any conventional monetization plan. Therefore the authors evaluated also the business models used by the application developers. To objectively analyze the business, the nature of each application was briefly summarized and an opinion whether the application was a part of a sustainable business was formed. The criterion for the sustainable business was deliberately set low, *i.e.* the following question was asked for each application: *"Is this application a part of a business that can in the best case scenario support at least one person?"* Except analyzing the download amounts, the authors did not take a stance on whether the business was actually successful or not.

[3] *Top Androids applications with in-app billing* by AppBrain. Available at `http://www.appbrain.com/stats/in-app-billing-android-applications`

Based on the analysis we form the following categories which help to divide the developers by their business strategies[4]. Common characteristics for categories are the revenue models used and the overall impression of the 'seriousness' of the business. These categories represent developer groups, who utilize clearly different way of business, in the Android Market. The categories should be useful in the future studies of ecosystems. The categorization is based on the grounded theory approach [17], where we are trying to characterize and to build a model which would explain the gathered data. The categories are presented in Figure 1 below the related revenue streams.

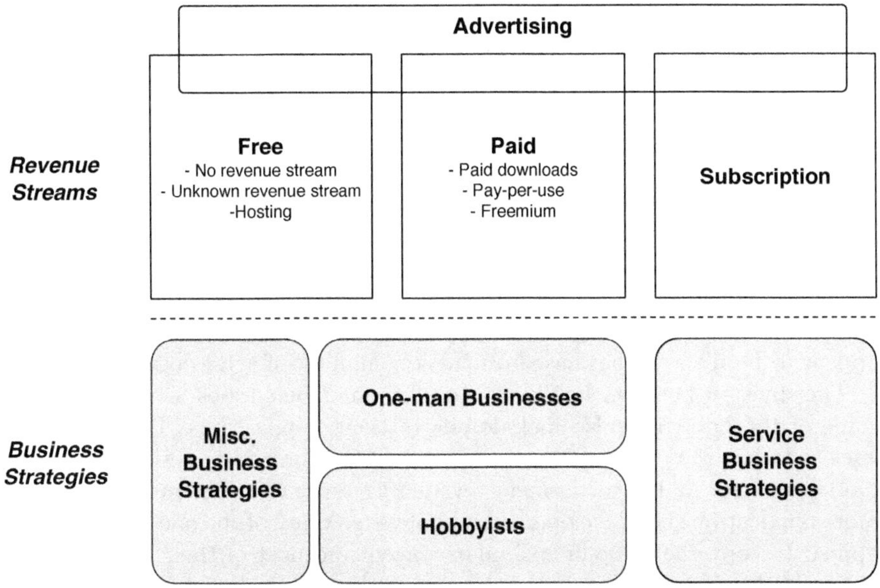

Fig. 1. Revenue streams and business strategy categories and their relationships

Miscellaneous Business. Applications in this category clearly have some kind of business idea behind them, but the business model is too complex or vague to map to the revenue streams. In addition, there are no clear similarities between the business models utilized by the applications in the category. For example, amongst the sample there is an application made with a popular do-it-yourself application machine[5], which do not have an evident revenue stream, and an Internet radio application which was built by third party developer[6] specialized in Internet radio applications. Most of the applications in this category are completely free for the end-users.

[4] The term 'strategy' is used loosely to describe a plan of action designed to achieve a vision.

[5] Appsbar Ltd.: `http://www.appsbar.com/`

[6] Airkast Ltd.: `http://airkast.com/`

The high number of applications and diversity of business models in this category might indicate that it will be hard to comprehensively analyze the Android Market based solely on the business models utilized in the applications.

Hobbyists. Since the Android and the Android Market are quite open platforms, it is evident that they nourish some kind of hacker culture. In our sample there is several applications which seem to be done solely as hobby projects. Characteristically, the developers in this category have only a few applications in the Android Market and the applications are usually small utility programs, which solve very specific problems. The hobbyist category might explain at least a portion of 31 applications without any conventional monetization plan.

It should be noted that some of the developers in the hobbyist category have advertisements in their applications, but it appears that the purpose of the ads is not to build a sustainable business but rather to get a little extra income. This conclusion is based on the small number of applications each hobbyist have in the sample and the relatively low download amounts of these applications.

One-Man Businesses. One of the most interesting findings in the sample is the large number of 'one-man businesses'. These developers utilize traditional revenue streams to collect some income, but do not have clear ambition to grow into larger businesses. The developers in this category seem to be highly productive in terms of the number of applications, but the revenues they generate appear to be rather small based on the low number of total downloads.

The division between hobbyists and one-man businesses is not clear, since some of the hobbyists also include ads in their applications. The main difference between these two categories seems to be that one-man businesses mix paid downloads and advertisement revenue streams, and they publish on average more applications per developer than hobbyists. Many of the one-man businesses appear to copy the same or a similar concept on most of their applications by *e.g.* publishing essentially the same game with quickly changed graphics.

Service Business Models. The last category includes Android front-ends of more complex web-based services which utilize traditional Software as a Service (SaaS) business models. Some of the services in the sample use subscription revenue streams, where the end-users pay monthly subscriptions, while others monetize user-base *e.g.* by billing the shop keepers which contact the end-users through the service[7].

It should be noted that there is no category for large companies who are utilizing paid downloads as their main revenue source and are usually selling the product for multiple platforms, *e.g.* Electronic Arts. However, in our sample, there was only one developer utilizing this kind of business model. Their only product in the marketplace was bought only a few thousands of times which indicates, based on the authors evaluation, that the application have not reached the break-even point. Therefore, this kind of companies are included into the miscellaneous business strategy category.

---

[7] DuckDuck Deal: `http://www.duckduckdeal.com/`

As a remark, there are also developers who generate considerable revenue by selling applications in the Android Market. However, none were present in the sample, which might indicate that these developers are small minority. Findings in [18] support this claim.

When the business strategy categories are compared with the revenue streams presented in the previous section, it can be said that these two analysis overlap. This is presented in Figure 1. Applications which utilize miscellaneous business models are usually distributed free in the Android Market. Therefore, the monetization mechanisms are more complex and cannot directly be analyzed based on the information gathered from the Android Market. Hobbyist and one-man businesses distribute the applications either free or paid. Most of the applications developed by hobbyists and one-man businesses include advertisements. It should be noted, that the advertising cannot be seen as an independent revenue stream category, since it is commonly mixed with other revenue streams. The applications using the service business models map almost directly to the subscription revenue stream. However, the service front-ends were actively searched during the qualitative analysis as an indication of SaaS services. Therefore this might explain the direct mapping.

Figure 2 presents summary of the business strategy categories, identified from the random sample, and the number of developers of the studied set in each categories. The diagram visualizes how the one-man business category overlaps with the hobbyist category. For certain developers it is very hard to say whether they are developing a professional application or just doing a hobby project. Similarly the miscellaneous and service business strategy categories overlap with each other. The both categories contain almost purely professional applications. Some of these resembles SaaS solutions although they use unorthodox or vague service business models.

The business strategy categories presented above provide one viewpoint to the qualitative data used in the study. The relevance of the categories should be verified further studies with a larger set of applications. However, the categories help us to understand the Android Market ecosystem better and act as a framework for further analysis of the developers and the business models of the ecosystem.

5 Discussion

The Android application ecosystem has four characteristics that together explain a lot of what we see in the application data: 1) The ecosystem has no constrains for who can publish applications, nor any acceptance procedure for the applications. 2) The entry barrier to the application market is very low; applications can be created with a very low or zero investments and small amount of work. Most applications have clearly been created with less than a few man months of work, and there are applications that seem to be created by a single developer in a few days. 3) The ecosystem offers a distribution channel potentially to a huge number of users. 4) The applications generally have very low

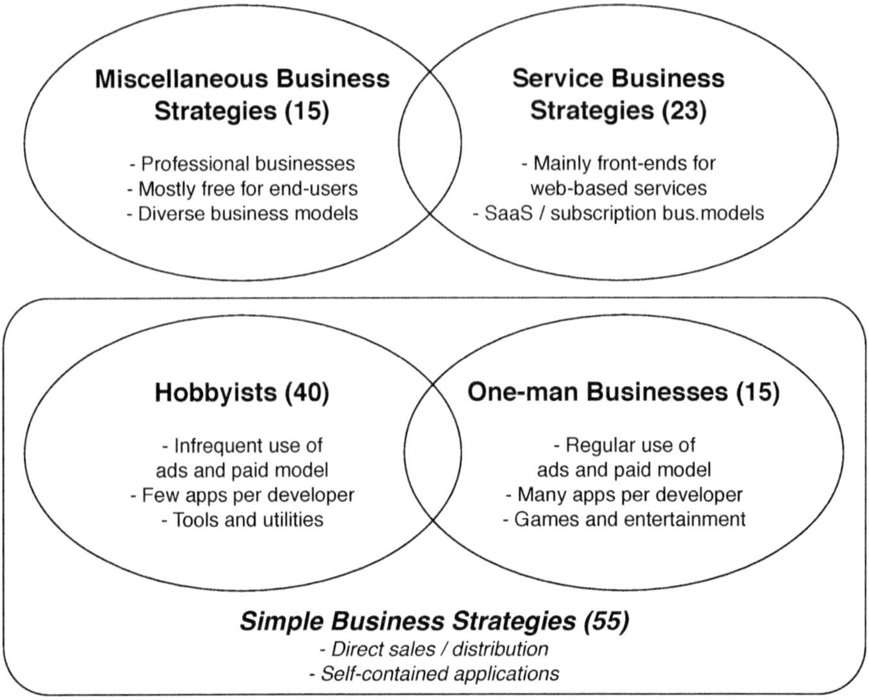

Fig. 2. A Venn diagram of business strategies and the distribution of the the developers from the random sample

customer value, mostly solving small problems or providing casual entertainment. Reflecting these characteristics on the globalized world we can see reasons why the Android ecosystem grows very fast in volume, supports poorly serious businesses, and contains so much applications that have very simple or vague business- or revenue models.

We clearly see from the application data that the most common revenue streams within the Android ecosystem generally fail to sustain serious businesses, *i.e.* it is very difficult to monetize the application using any of the existing revenue mechanisms in the ecosystem. When using straightforward paid downloads revenue models, low customer value combined with very low entry barriers make application price an important competition factor, which leads to 'race to the bottom' type competition models. In fact, this has created a culture for Android users where it is assumed that applications are free or very cheap. In this pricing landscape, only those businesses that reach very high volumes, or that originate from areas where labor and other costs are extremely low can survive. For some developers, a thin revenue stream of only a few hundred dollars in a month is enough. Furthermore, the low entry barrier together with possibility to reach a large number of users gives rise to other motivations than business. Examples are meritocracy, fame, improving the CV, or just a hobby.

As a result of the study, it appears that especially free applications contain interesting, complex business models that seems to be connected with sustainable, growing businesses. Analyzing these models is more difficult and therefore requires more study.

However, the generalization of the results is limited by restricting on Android Market. The marketplace has its unique characteristics, in addition to the previous discussion *e.g.* a large number of free applications and the lack of prescreening in publishing, when compared with the others. These characteristics have significant effects on the revenue and business models utilized in the ecosystem. For example, the use of paid download model might be more profitable in other ecosystems. Although the results could help to characterize the application business, the other marketplaces should be also further studied.

6 Conclusion

In this paper, we used both quantitatively and qualitatively approach to analyze Google Android Market. A random sample of 100 Android Market applications were selected and analyzed. The aim was categorize the high-level business strategies of application developers. We started by studying the revenue streams used by applications in the ecosystem. Conventional revenue models were found, but not all applications could be explained with these. Particularly, the monetization of the free applications should be further studied. Based on the streams, we identified four general business strategy categories: hobbyists, one-man businesses, service business and miscellaneous business strategies. Although these present only one viewpoint to the market, they help us to perceive the marketplace. Future work is needed on this topic, specially for understanding which business models are viable for startups. In addition, the current ecosystem models do not directly seem to explain an application ecosystem build on the top of a mobile ecosystem.

Acknowledgments. Hyrynsalmi is grateful for the financial support of Nokia Foundation.

References

1. Dedrick, J., Kraemer, K.L., Linden, G.: The distribution of value in the mobile phone supply chain. Telecommunications Policy 35, 505–521 (2011)
2. Xia, R., Rost, M., Holmquist, L.: Business models in the mobile ecosystem. In: Ninth International Conference on Mobile Business and 2010 Ninth Global Mobility Roundtable, ICMB-GMR, pp. 1–8 (2010)
3. Evans, D., Hagiu, A., Schmalensee, R.: Invisible engines: how software platforms drive innovation and transform industries. The MIT Press (2006)

4. Coursaris, C., Hassanein, K.: Understanding m-commerce: A consumer-centric model. Quarterly Journal of Electronic Commerce 3(3), 247–271 (2002)
5. Moore, J.F.: The Death of Competition: Leadership and Strategy in the Age of Business Ecosystems. HarperCollins, Australia (1996)
6. Basole, R.: Visualization of interfirm relations in a converging mobile ecosystem. Journal of Information Technology 24(2), 144–159 (2009)
7. Gueguen, G., Isckia, T.: The borders of mobile handset ecosystems: Is coopetition inevitable? Telematics and Informatics 28, 5–11 (2011)
8. Eisenhardt, K., Brown, S.: Patching. restitching business portfolios in dynamic markets. Harvard Business Review 77, 72–82 (1999)
9. Luo, Y.: Coopetition in International Business. Copenhagen Business School Pr. (2004)
10. Messerschmitt, D., Szyperski, C.: Software ecosystem: understanding an indispensable technology and industry. The MIT Press (2003)
11. Jansen, S., Finkelstein, A., Brinkkemper, S.: A sense of community: A research agenda for software ecosystems. In: 31st International Conference on Software Engineering - Companion Volume, ICSE-Companion 2009, pp. 187–190. IEEE (2009)
12. Kabbedijk, J., Jansen, S.: Steering Insight: An Exploration of the Ruby Software Ecosystem. In: Regnell, B., van de Weerd, I., De Troyer, O. (eds.) ICSOB 2011. LNBIP, vol. 80, pp. 44–55. Springer, Heidelberg (2011)
13. Bernardos, A.M., Casar, J.R.: Analyzing business models for mobile augmented reality. In: 15th International Conference on Intelligence in Next Generation Networks (ICIN), pp. 97–102 (October 2011)
14. Komulainen, H., Mainela, T., Sinisalo, J., Tähtinen, J., Ulkuniemi, P.: Business models in the emerging context of mobile advertising. In: Seppä, M., Hannula, M., Järvelin, A.M., Kujala, J., Ruohonen, M., Tiainen, T. (eds.) Frontiers of e-Business Research (FeBR 2004), pp. 590–605. Tampere University of Technology and University of Tampere, Tampere (2004)
15. Osterwalder, A., Pigneur, Y.: Business Model Generation: A Handbook for Visionaries, Game Changers, and Challengers, 1st edn. Wiley, West Sussex (2009)
16. Popp, K., Meyer, R.: Profit from Software Ecosystems: Business Models, Ecosystems and Partnerships in the Software Industry. Books on Demand GmbH (2010)
17. Glaser, B.G., Strauss, A.L.: The Discovery of Grounded Theory: Strategies for Qualitative Research. 8th printing edn. Aldine Transaction (1967)
18. Hyrynsalmi, S., Suominen, A., Mäkilä, T., Knuutila, T.: The emerging mobile ecosystems: An introductory analysis of Android Market. In: The 21st International Conference on Management of Technology (IAMOT 2012), International Association for Management of Technology (March 2012)

The Effects of Software and Service Orientations on Sales Productivity in Canadian Software Companies from 1993 to 2011

David Maslach[1], Rakinder Sembhi[2], and Rod McNaughton[1]

[1] Conrad Business, Entrepreneurship and Technology Centre, The University of Waterloo
295 Hagey Boulevard, Suite 240, Waterloo, Ontario, Canada, N2L 6R5
[2] Financial Services, Deloitte Consulting LLP
djmaslach@gmail.com, rakinder@alumni.uwaterloo.ca,
rmcnaughton@uwaterloo.ca

Abstract. Software development can be viewed as manufacturing a knowledge-intensive tool. Managers of software companies can either specialize in developing underlying software technologies or specialize in developing services that support software technologies. We explore the revenue generated by product and service orientations in public and private Canadian software firms from 1993-2011. Our analysis finds that service orientation contributes significantly more to service sales productivity than product orientation contributes to software sales productivity. The analysis implies that software firms should strengthen service-oriented capabilities, however we discuss that managers may find specialization in services difficult to do.

Keywords: Canadian Software Companies, Service-Orientation, Product-Orientation, Business of Software.

1 Introduction

In the software industry, it seems obvious that many firms orient towards developing software products (ie. programming and distributing code for core products). However, software is a knowledge-intensive tool. Users often require a significant learning investment. Software often requires customization. Consequently, not so obvious are all of the services that are required to make software useful. Many software firms focus on providing services to support their software development. Further, a large number of firms do not even develop core products, but rather focus on providing far-reaching services; including consulting, maintenance support, customizing pre-packaged software, and training.

In this paper, we explore the sales revenue of firms with product and service orientations in the software industry. A move towards service orientation in firms and its consequences has received both academic and practitioner attention [1-4]. It is interesting to note that studies have not yet explored product and service revenues generated from product and service orientations. There is little evidence if managers should focus on improving services, the underlying technology, or both. Consider

M.A. Cusumano, B. Iyer, and N. Venkatraman (Eds.): ICSOB 2012, LNBIP 114, pp. 223–234, 2012.

IBM's turnaround from a product-oriented company to a service-oriented company [5]. During this turnaround, the former Chairman of the Board, Lou Gerstner, notes that IBM had to develop different contracts for outsourcing product development, hire service-oriented personnel, and change human resources practices to leverage the new service-oriented labor. The IBM turnaround is generally thought be a clear success in the industry, but choosing between a service orientation or a product orientation is not always clear. It is important to study the sales revenue of product and service orientations to provide guidance to managers of software companies and software entrepreneurs.

The specific questions we ask are (1) whether a service-orientation generates more revenue per employee than a product-orientation, (2) if a service orientation would be advisable for software companies, and (3) which firm factors contribute to service revenue and which factors contribute to product revenue. We investigate these three questions using 2,990 firm-year observations of the top 300 Canadian software companies from 1993 to 2011. We think our study is interesting for three reasons. First, we are able to capture the sales productivity of both private and public firms. The sample of private firms is unique because most studies on strategic orientations focus on larger publically owned firms [1, 3], which could create selection bias. Second, our study suggests that stable strategic orientations can persist in a dynamic industry [6]. Third, our analysis shows how software sales per employee and service sales per employee dynamically evolve because of product and service orientations.

We expect that our paper will contribute to the literature on strategic orientations by showing that product or service specialization is often required to improve sales productivity. We also hope that the study provides a basis for further investigation into the business of software [3, 6, 7].

1.1 Product versus Service Orientation

The business activities of product-oriented firms are primarily focused on the development and marketing of core products. Product-oriented firms typically excel at product development, and as a result, the majority of their revenue comes from product sales [8]. This definition is congruent with the Prahalad and Hamel [9] view of strategic orientations, which proposes that a strategic orientation serves as its organizational compass, guiding the firm's strategy, decision-making and operational activities.

In the software industry that we study, software firms that produce packaged software and earn the majority of their revenue from products are primarily product-oriented. Of course, product-oriented firms may also supplement these activities with value-added services. However, product-oriented software firms require focus on the product because there is usually a large investment required to build a product (write the software), and, the marginal cost of producing an additional unit is negligible (making a copy of a CD, or making software available for download to an additional user). The resources required to develop the product is primarily is driven by knowledge embedded within its personnel, routines, and technological infrastructure.

Firms in the software industry sometimes leverage the knowledge assets that they possess to provide services such as custom software development and software outsourcing solutions. In this paper, we follow Lynn's et al. [10] definition of a service-oriented firm as one whose organizational policies, practices and procedures support services. Studies argue that service-orientations are linked to customer loyalty and pricing power because firms are better able to exchange information with customers [1]. We expect to see that service-oriented firms would have the majority of their revenue derived from services.

Of course, this dichotomy is idealistic. One would expect to see some firms having a hybrid form, some combination of product orientation and service orientation, or even some firms of one type of orientation deriving profits from the other type. Even still, there is the possibility of firms transitioning from one-type to another. For example, Cusumano [3] examines cases of software firms struggling to develop and maintain product orientations. In attempts to grow and fund research and development activities, software firms often engage in service related activities. Unfortunately, as Cusumano highlights, these firms often begin to focus on services and fail to succeed with their own product development.

While such complications will arise, we expect that specialization into either product or service orientations will occur in the software industry for two reasons. First, software development requires a significant initial investment. Services, such as custom software and consulting, require a significant ongoing investment. Typically, firms will not have enough resources to do both. Second, firms focusing on service orientation are geographically bound. Product-oriented firms can export its products in a global (larger) market without worrying about service-deployment; a much more challenging task with higher marginal costs than exporting products.

2 Sample and Methods

We focus on the Canadian software industry. A software product is defined "as a packaged configuration of software components or a software-based service, with auxiliary materials, which is released for and traded in a specific market [11, Pg. 4]." The decision to either focus on the product or services matter for Canadian software companies because many of customers they serve are outside the country. Empirical evidence on the Canadian information technology industry suggests that software producers are more likely to export products. If software firms sell services (ie. consulting), they are likely to travel extensively because services require face-to-face information exchange of tacit knowledge [12, 13]. As a result, the decision to orientate towards services requires some thought into whether the significant expenditure in consultant travel is warranted.

We investigate the Branham 300 survey to provide insight to the Canadian software industry. The Branham Group is a leading consulting group that focuses on strategy and innovation in the Canadian technology sector. In particular, the consultancy specializes in software, hardware and service companies in Canada, so it is well aware of up-to-date industry patterns. Since 1993, the Branham Group publishes an annual survey listing the top 300 information technology companies operating in Canada. The ranking is based on sales revenues. Within Canada, the Branham 300 has become a well-recognized gage of the Canadian software industry.

We purchased the Branham data and analyzed it for patterns between 1993 to 2011. Our analysis is unique as it contains both repeated observations of the same firm, and new start-up companies that quickly appear and die within this 19 year period. In addition, our sample minimizes sample selection concerns because it includes a broader sample of firms than would be accessible if one only analyzed firms that are listed on public stock exchanges.

In the population of the Branham Top 300 information technology firms in Canada, we had 5,907 firm-year observations and 1,554 firms. The total revenue generated from Canadian information technology firms grew by 10.7% year-over-year from 1993 to 2011. Adjusting for inflation, the total accumulated revenues over the period was $1,154 billion, which is a substantial contribution to the Canadian economy.

The level of analysis is at the firm-level, and we use a matched sample technique to control for heterogeneity in our data. We match service-oriented firms with product-oriented firms, and thereby exclude mobile telecommunications service providers (ie. Shaw, MTS Communications), internet service providers (ie. Telus, Rogers Communications), and hardware infrastructure companies (ie. Nortel, Com Dev).

Our analysis classified service-orientation and product-orientation based on where the firm was placed in an industry categories designated by the Branham Group. Our methodology is similar to category classification work using Software Magazine's Top 500 companies [14], as the methodology leverages the knowledge of industry insiders. Further, we choose to exploit the Branham Groups classification scheme because the consulting firm has substantial tacit knowledge of how each firm is structured and the probable orientation that the firm is seeking. Notice that our approach is similar to Fang et al. [1], who classify service orientation based on a firm's SIC industry classification code. An alternative approach is to classify product and service orientations by using the percent of revenues derived from software and services. This approach may be tautological in cases where firms intend to be product-oriented and only obtain service revenues (or vice versa). Further, it allows us to explore how service and product revenue is generated by each type of orientation.

We classified service-oriented firms as those named by the Branham Group[1] as:

- Service Companies
- Top 25 Canadian IT Service Companies
- Top 25 Canadian IT Professional Services Companies
- Top 10 Canadian IT Security and Related Consulting Companies
- 50 Top Canadian Professional Services Companies
- 100 Top Canadian Professional Services Organizations
- Top 25 Canadian ICT Professional Services Companies
- Top 10 Canadian ICT Staffing Companies
- Top 5 Canadian Software as a Service Companies

[1] These classifications changed from year to year, so we included all firms in relevant categories.

We classified product-oriented firms as those named by the Branham Group as:

- Software Companies
- 100 Top Independent Canadian Software Companies
- 20 Top Canadian Wireless Software Developers
- Top 10 Canadian Wireless Solutions Companies
- Top 10 Canadian Healthcare Solution Companies
- Top 25 Canadian Software Companies
- The Next 50 Canadian Technology Companies
- Top 5 Pure-play Healthcare ICT Companies
- Top 5 Mixed-play Healthcare ICT Companies
- Top 5 Canadian Mobile Technology Companies

Our final matched sample contained 2,938 firm-year observations of 747 firms in the software industry. Within this sample, 1,365 firm-year observations (510 firms) were for product-oriented firms and 731 firm-year observations (286 firms) were for service-oriented firms.

2.1 Variables of Interest

Dependent Variables. We have two dependent variables. The first dependent variable is the natural logarithm of service revenues per employee for a given firm-year. The second dependent variable is the natural logarithm of software revenues per employee for a given firm-year. We use revenues per employee as a measure of sales productivity. Revenues are inflation adjusted using consumer price indexes to 1980. Note that this data is unique as firms are not required to publically disclose sales in different revenue segments [1]. Our choice of dependent variables is based on Cusumano's [3] recommendation. He discusses that in the software industry, profits tend to be skewed as many software firms have substantial R&D costs early on and higher than average marketing expenses in general. Skewness can also occur if a single software product becomes 'viral' from network externalities. Further, we choose to use two dependent variables because we can see the interdependent effects of service and product orientation on both service sales productivity and software sales productivity.

Independent Variables. We use two independent variables. Our first independent variable is whether a firm is service-oriented in the previous year *(t-1)*. The variable is coded as 1 if the Branham Group categorizes the firm as having a service orientation and 0 otherwise. Our second independent variable is whether a firm is product-oriented in the previous year *(t-1)*. Similar to service orientation, product orientation is binary coded (1 if product-oriented, 0 if not).

Controls Variables. We control for firm size with the log of total sales and log of total number of employees. Including sales and number of employees as lagged variables also controls for autocorrelation in the dependent variables. We control for firm age and whether the firm is privately owned. We include year dummies to control for time effects. Note that all of the controls are lagged one year to address simultaneity concerns.

2.2 Methods

We use a seemingly unrelated regression (SUR) with pooled ordinary least squares regression for each equation. We choose the SUR methodology because it assumes that the error terms in both the software sales productivity and the service sales productivity equations are correlated. This assumes that services and software sales are subject to similar shocks and growth patterns. For example, if software sales increase (decrease) we expect service sales will increase (decrease) because of the overall performance of the company. Our analysis was performed in Stata 11. To gain efficiency and to control for heteroscedasticity in our estimates, we included firm-level clustered variances. In addition, to protect against biased estimates we included year dummy variables.

3 Results

Figure 1 shows that revenues per employee are steadily increasing for all revenue sources, suggesting that the Canadian software industry is growing. The circle marker represents service revenue by service-oriented firms, the square marker represents software revenue by service-oriented firms, the diamond marker represents software revenue by product-oriented firms, and the triangle marker represents service revenue by product-oriented firms. We scaled by number of employees to account for firm size and the different effects of labor in service and product-oriented firms. There are three notable points to be made with Figure 1. First, service revenue per employee for service-oriented firms generates substantially more revenue than product revenue with product orientation.

Second, service revenue has become equally as important as software revenue to product-oriented firms. The convergence pattern implies that firms are relying more on service revenues.

Third, service orientation appears to require much more specialization than product orientation. Figure 1 shows that service orientation requires more specialization as product revenue contributes to a much smaller portion of total revenue of service-oriented firms than service revenue does for product-oriented firms. Across all years, service-oriented firms generate 1.89 times more revenue from services than from software, and product-oriented firms generate 1.19 times more revenue from software than from service. These three points are in line with the view that we are moving towards a service-oriented knowledge-based economy, however such service orientation requires substantially more specialization and resources.

In Table 1, we present descriptive statistics for software firms in our sample. Two key points are observed. Firstly, the majority of the firms (>70%) are privately owned in the sample, and our results generalize to firms that receive little attention in the literature. Secondly, the top 10 service-oriented and product-oriented differ in the significantly. The product-oriented firms develop a core product, such as Merak Projects and Peloton which both develop oil and gas software. These firms may provide services that support the core product. However, the service-oriented firms provide an array of IT solutions and consulting services.

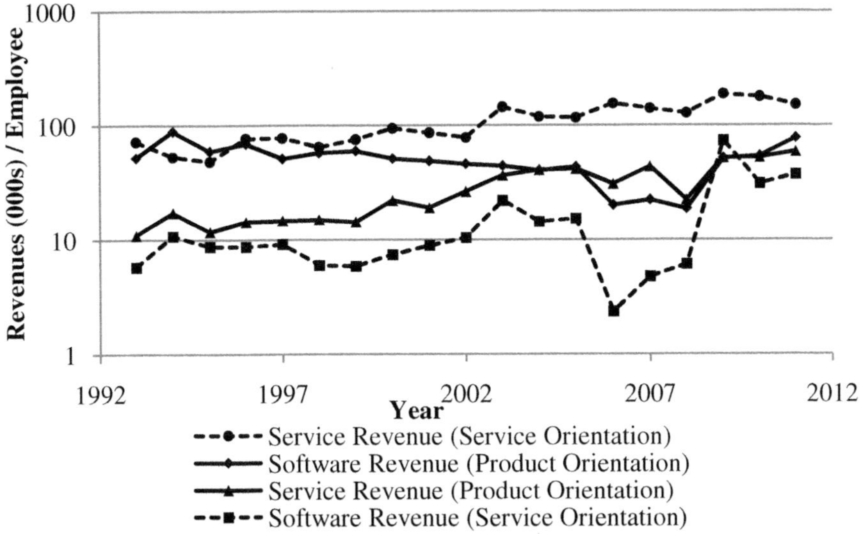

Fig. 1. Revenues (000s) per employee for the Top 300 software and software service firms in Canada from 1993 to 2011

Table 1. Descriptive statistics for product-oriented and service-oriented software firms in Canada from 1993 to 2011

Product-oriented (N=510)		Service-oriented (N=286)	
Mean total revenues (000s)	19,519	Mean total revenues (000s)	38,798
Mean total employees	166	Mean total employees	439
Mean age (years)	12	Mean age (years)	13.2
No. privately owned	290 (77%)	No. privately owned	191 (70%)
No. large firms (>250 emp.)	61 (16%)	No. large firms (>250 emp.)	81 (30%)
No. small and medium-sized firms (< 250 emp.)	318 (84%)	No. small and medium-sized firms (< 250 emp.)	193 (70%)

Top 10 product-oriented firms	Software rev. (000s) / employee	Top 10 service-oriented firms	Service rev. (000s) / employee
Software Spectrum *	593	Object Systems Group	540
Footprint Software *	313	Sirius Consulting Group *	460
Merak Projects	279	SI Systems	415
Dreamcatcher Interactive *	279	Veritaaq	400
Peloton	258	Computer Horizons *	388
Klein Systems Group	241	M3K Solutions *	362
PC Docs *	232	Arqana Technologies *	362
ParetoLogic	203	Procom Consultants Group	341
DIL Multimedia *	194	CNC Global *	315
Connect Tech.	167	Ward Associates *	312

* Acquired during 1993 to 2011.

In Table 2, we present our seemingly unrelated regression results of sales productivity. Model 1 presents the control model. Model 2 presents the estimates for software and service sales productivity. The significant model explains 12% of the variance in software sales productivity and 7% of the variance in service sales productivity, over the effect of the control variables. Service-orientation generates significantly more service revenues per employee (p-value < 0.001) and product orientation generates significantly more software revenues per employee (p-value < 0.001), all else equal.

It is interesting to see that service orientation does require specialization as the coefficient for service orientation in the software sales productivity is significantly negative (p-value<0.001). The negative coefficient indicates that firms with a service orientation will drive down software sales productivity. The specialization effects are the same for firms with a product orientation. A product orientation has a significant negative effect on service sales productivity.

In a post-hoc test, we observe that there is a significant difference between the constants in the model 2 (p-value < 0.001), indicating that the mean of software sales productivity is higher than service sales productivity. Further, service orientation contributes significantly more to service sales productivity than product orientation contributes to software sales productivity (p-value < 0.001). This differing effect means that product-oriented firms often complement product revenue with services and service-oriented firms are less likely to develop products. Firms are more likely to complement software sales with services. Further, services may be used to smooth revenues when times are tough.

The controls themselves deserve some thought. Unexpectedly, older software firms have significantly higher service revenues per employee than younger firms. This finding fails to support Cusumano's [3] claim that software firms often start with a service-orientation and gradually move towards a product-orientation when the firm establishes a product market. Larger software firms (in terms of sales) have more service revenues per employee than smaller firms, consistent with the idea that larger software firms often combine value-added services (eg. consulting) to their products.

Interestingly, privately-owned firms seem to be more efficient with service sales and less efficient with software sales than publically-owned firms. This is perhaps either because 1) privately-held software companies that are doing well are often acquired by larger public companies, or 2) public companies require minimum size thresholds to list on stock exchanges.

We present the year dummies to show that service revenue compensates for product revenue during bad economic times. The coefficients for software sales productivity are significantly negative and the coefficients for service sales productivity are significantly positive during the dot.com bust (1999 thru 2002) and the financial crisis (2009 thru 2010). This confirms Cusamano [3] proposition that when times are bad, software companies turn to service revenues. The negative dummies for product sales and positive service sales in subsequent years show that the transition to service revenues may have resulted in a capability trap. Firms had to switch to service orientations to maintain total revenues but they began to specialize and never reverted back to software sales. Finally, these negative values suggest that firms are becoming more service-oriented with time. The pattern supports the notion that better information technology infrastructure will likely lead to a greater diffusion of services because the costs of communicating the tacit knowledge contained in services is decreasing [4, 12].

Table 2. Regression results for logged revenue (000s) per employee for the top 300 software and software service firms in Canada from 1993 to 2011. Significance at p-values less than 0.1, 0.05, 0.01, and 0.001 are denoted +, *, **, and ***.

	(1)		(2)	
Sales Productivity:	Software	Service	Software	Service
Independent Variables				
Product Orientation (t-1)			0.67***	-0.52***
Service Orientation (t-1)			-1.47***	1.00***
Controls				
Log Sales (t-1)	0.16+	0.52***	0.22**	0.47***
Log Employees (t-1)	-0.29**	-0.44***	-0.24**	-0.47***
Age (t-1)	0.01**	0.00	0.01**	0.00
Private (t-1)	-0.59***	0.37**	-0.32***	0.18+
1995	-0.37**	0.10	-0.07	-0.11
1996	-0.50**	0.53**	-0.19	0.31+
1997	-0.50**	0.45*	-0.26+	0.28+
1998	-0.70***	0.11	-0.57***	0.00
1999	-0.61**	0.35+	-0.44**	0.56**
2000	-0.59**	0.72***	-0.36**	0.55***
2001	-0.88***	0.79***	-0.65***	0.61***
2002	-0.71***	1.03***	-0.78***	1.06***
2003	-1.09***	0.84***	-0.33+	0.27
2004	-1.33***	0.63**	-0.94***	0.31
2005	-1.35***	0.67**	-1.00***	0.38+
2006	-2.64***	-0.62**	-2.27***	-0.90***
2007	-2.39***	-0.30	-2.10***	-0.54*
2008	-1.97***	-0.14	-1.72***	-0.35+
2009	-1.12***	0.58**	-0.92***	0.40*
2010	-1.23***	0.57**	-1.05***	0.42*
2011	-1.41***	0.34	-1.22***	0.17
Constant	3.81***	-0.41	2.62***	0.47
Variance	1.20***	1.12***	1.04***	1.04***
R-Squared	0.13	0.10	0.25	0.17
F-Stat	20.6	16.0	42.02	16.0
F-test			232.8***	117.0***
Δ R-Squared			0.12	0.07

4 Discussion and Conclusion

We reveal patterns of revenue generation by Canadian software firms with product and service orientations. In our analysis of the Top 300 software and software service companies in Canada from 1993 to 2011, we show that service-oriented firms produce substantially more service revenues per employee than product-oriented firms produce product-based revenues per employee. We also find that service-oriented software firms require substantially more specialization than product-oriented software firms. This adds to past work [3] by suggesting that service-oriented software firms are less likely to develop hybrid strategies than product-oriented firms.

We make two subtle but important contributions to the literature on the business of software. First, software development requires substantial focus in their capabilities development. It appears that specialization is generally required for both service and product orientation, however firms with a product orientation can complement products with services. The result of specialization is shown in manufacturing industries [1], but not specifically within software firms. That is, the most revenue per employee is generated by firms with a service orientation selling services, and secondly by product-oriented firms selling software. Such firms should develop capabilities in a specific strategic orientation early on and resist from deviating from the orientation.

The reason why specialization is important for service-oriented software firms is evident in the example of two Canadian software firms contained in our sample. OpenText, a provider of Enterprise Content Management (ECM) software, is arguably Canada's most successful software company over the past decade and has a product orientation. CGI is Canada's largest IT services firm by revenue and has a service orientation. While both OpenText and CGI are both successful in the software industry, they conduct business in fundamentally different ways and offer different types of outputs to their clients. It is relatively easier for OpenText to maintain focus because OpenText uses a reseller/distributor channel to sell its packaged products. While the company has a direct channel, 25% of its total sales come from resellers and distributors. On the other hand, CGI has a less structured process for selling their services. A service-oriented firm can offer a very diverse set of services. Because CGI consults to a number of companies, specialization in service orientation allows the firm to reduce an already heterogeneous set of resources and consulting projects. Specialization for service firms is required to maintain adequate revenue generation and to avoid cost overruns related to resource heterogeneity. Service-oriented firms should continue to focus on services over products.

Second, our data suggests that a service orientation contributes more to service sales productivity than a product orientation contributes to software sales productivity. These results go against current anecdotal understanding that product-orientation rather than a service-orientation generates more revenue in the long run because of its lower long-run marginal costs. Further, our results show that hybrid strategies with both product and service orientations significantly reduce software and service sales productivity. This builds on previous work [3] by showing that hybrid companies should have a primary strategic orientation.

We also make a contextual contribution to the literature on service and product orientations. Beyond the initial definition of the product and service orientation constructs, research in these two areas is in its infancy. Much of the work in the area of service orientations focuses on the food service and hospitality industries [15]. This research is the first to examine the concepts of product and service orientations in the context of software firms (see Cusumano [3] for anecdotal evidence). Further, we present a novel dataset on the Top 300 software companies in Canada over a 19 year period. We feel that this data may provide a foundation for further research in Canadian software companies.

Like most studies, there are limitations to this study. First, we focus on revenue data without accounting for costs. It would be prudent to understand the profitability (revenues – costs) of product and service orientation. Access to cost data would benefit our study for many reasons. Service-oriented firms are likely to have more costly labor-related resources than product-oriented firms. The software industry is witnessing a general trend towards lower labor costs through outsourcing (ie. contract manufacturing in India). However, we do not have access to such data given that we have both private and public firms in our sample. To that end, while we control for industry pricing trends using year dummies and firm clustered variances, our 19 year study of a dynamic industry inevitably ignores many pricing trends, including the effects of software fads and fashions. For example, free open source software and software bundling may have placed downward pressure on software revenues. Future research using fine-grained data or firm-specific case-studies on how service or product prices are negotiated from costumer to costumer [e.g. 16, 17] in the software industry is warranted.

Second, our study focuses on the top software companies in Canada, which may bias the revenue estimates upward. Further, there may be a bias in the differences between service and product-oriented firms as top performing Canadian software developers may select to start companies in a region with larger agglomeration economies, such Silicon Valley, California. A selection bias could be the case, as there appears to be a significant size difference between product-oriented and service-oriented firms (See Table 1).

Third, we define 'orientation' on the basis of Branham Group's classification. The view of orientation may be broader than viewing orientation based on revenue sources as done in previous studies [10]. However, the definition of the Branham Group's classification scheme is somewhat vague as we have little information about how the company classifies companies. In general, we think our methodology holds, but it does raise questions about classification ambiguities. For example, Pontikes' [14, 18] work on categorization in software companies show that these firms often have ambiguous labels and could belong to many categories. Building closely Pontikes' [14] work, it would be interesting to investigate the software firms that are newly classified with a product or service orientation. Further, one could explore whether companies using state-of-art technology are classified and then re-classified as knowledge about the technology emerges in the industry.

We believe that these limitations provide an excellent basis for future work. Questions arise about the capabilities that drive product and service orientation in software companies. Are the underlying routines and knowledge structures that drive a product orientation the same as a service orientation? Can they be developed? Questions also arise about new forms of revenue models that are becoming increasingly popular in the software industry. Are there fundamentally different patterns with software as a service (SaaS), or other forms of on-demand software?

We would like to conclude by stating that our paper should not be the definitive research article on product-orientation and service-orientation in software firms. Nor should anecdotal evidence be considered conclusive, such as Lou Gerstner's famous IBM turnaround from a product-oriented to a service-oriented firm [5]. Rather, we point out the many choices made to orient a software firm towards its products or its services are complex. Further research into these strategic choices will undeniably improve our understanding of the business of software.

References

1. Fang, E., Palmatier, R.W., Steenkamp, J.-B.E.M.: Effect of service transition strategies on firm value. Journal of Marketing 72, 1–14 (2008)
2. Barley, S.R., Kunda, G.: Gurus, Hired Guns, and Warm Bodies. Princeton University Press, Princeton (2004)
3. Cusumano, M.A.: The business of software: What every manager, programmer and entrepreneur must know to thrive and survive in good times and bad. The Free Press, Cambridge (2004)
4. Cusumano, M.A.: The changing software business: Moving from products to services. Computer, 20–27 (2008)
5. Gerstner, L.V.: Who says elephants can't dance? HarperCollins Publishers, New York (2002)
6. Lee, C.-H., Venkataraman, N., Tranriverdi, H., Iyer, B.: Complementarity-based hypercompetition in the software industry: Theory and empirical test, 1990-2002. Strategic Management Journal 31, 1431–1456 (2010)
7. Cottrell, T., Nault, B.R.: Product variety and firm survival in the microcomputer software industry. Strategic Management Journal 25, 1005–1025 (2004)
8. Voss, G.B., Voss, Z.G.: Strategic orientation and firm performance in an artistic environment. Journal of Marketing 64, 67–83 (2000)
9. Prahalad, C.K., Hamel, G.: The core competence of the corporation. Harvard Business Review 68, 79–91 (1990)
10. Lynn, M.L., Lytle, R.S., Bobek, S.: Service orientation in transitional markets: Does it matter? European Journal of Marketing 34, 279–298 (2000)
11. Xu, L., Brinkkemper, S.: Concepts of product software: Paving the road for urgently needed research. European Journal of Information Systems 16, 531–541 (2010)
12. Cornish, S.L.: Marketing software products: The importance of 'being there' and the implications for business service exports. Environment and Planning A 28, 1661–1682 (1996)
13. Hitt, M., Bierman, L., Uhlenbruck, K., Shimizu, K.: The Importance of Resources in the Internationalization of Professional Service Firms: The Good, the Bad and the Ugly. Academy of Management Journal 49, 1137–1157 (2006)
14. Pontikes, E.G.: Two sides of the same coin: How category leniency affects multiple audience evaluations (Working paper)
15. Kelley, S.W.: Developing customer orientation among service employees. Journal of the Academy of Marketing Science 20, 27–36 (1992)
16. Zbaracki, M.J., Bergen, M.: When truce collapse: A longitudinal study of price-adjustment routines. Organization Science 21, 955–972 (2010)
17. Zbaracki, M.J., Ritson, M., Levy, D., Dutta, S., Bergen, M.: Managerial and customer costs of price adjustment: Direct evidence from industrial markets. The Review of Economics and Statistics 86, 514–533 (2004)
18. Pontikes, E.G.: Fitting in or starting new? An analysis of invention, constraint, and the emergence of new categories in the software industry (Working paper)

Value Creation and Firm Integration: First Empirical Insights for the Software Industry

Anton Pussep, Stefan Harnisch, and Peter Buxmann

Technische Universität Darmstadt, Chair of Information Systems,
Hochschulstraße 1, 62849 Darmstadt, Germany
{pussep,harnisch,buxmann}@is.tu-darmstadt.de

Abstract. The value added created by a firm is a widely used figure. Major elements of a firm's strategy and business model deal with how the firm creates value and brings it to the customer. This paper focuses on a particular measure which has been broadly applied to measure the degree of vertical integration: value added to sales (VA/S). To our best knowledge, this measure hasn't been applied in software business research. We hence outline its application in other fields by conducting a broad and structured literature review. First empirical insights are gained by analyzing the VA/S development for 44,171 software firms in the period 2002-2009. These results indicate an increasing degree of vertical integration in the software industry. While practitioners can use the results as a benchmark for their own firms, researchers are provided with a comprehensive literature review, first empirical results on a large sample and avenues for research.

Keywords: Software industry, vertical integration, value added to sales, degree of vertical integration.

1 Introduction

It is inherent to the understanding of a firm that it creates and adds value to the products and services it sells. In macroeconomics, the sum of value added in a country (Gross Domestic Product, GDP) is a main measure of a country's wealth and growth [1]. On an industry or firm-level view, a firm's value chain defines the activities that add value to its products and services. The firm's value chain configuration is aimed at maximizing the value delivered to the customer [2]. Furthermore, many authors agree that business models define how value is created and brought to the customer [3]. The scope of the firm is an important aspect of business models and especially relevant for a platform leadership strategy. Every software vendor has to decide (in addition to typical make-or-buy-decisions) what complements to a specific product or service to make itself versus what to encourage partners to make or leave to others [4]. In some high technology industries vertical integration seems to make a comeback. There are advantages in being able to control a complete value chain – the most prominent example being Apple [5].

M.A. Cusumano, B. Iyer, and N. Venkatraman (Eds.): ICSOB 2012, LNBIP 114, pp. 235–247, 2012.

In empirical research, the percentage of a firm's value added to sales (VA/S) became the most popular measure of vertical integration [6]. Despite serious weaknesses, the application of the VA/S method yielded results consistent with major theories such as the Transaction Cost Theory. However, it has been mostly applied to the manufacturing sector. In particular, we are not aware of any results specific to the software industry. Arguably, different economics come into play when creating software [7]. For instance, vertical integration is argued to be particularly favorable in presence of network effects [8].

In this paper, we outline the potential of the VA/S method for the software industry and provide first empirical insights: First, we conduct a broad and structured literature review of previous work defining and applying the VA/S measure. The review results indicate avenues for research which are applicable to the software industry. Second, we measure VA/S for 44,171 software firms for the period of 2002-2009. Our results provide first empirical insights on the degree of vertical integration in the software industry. Researchers will find our results useful to test theories related to a firm's vertical integration, especially where VA/S is used as a dependent or independent variable in regressions. Practitioners are provided with a benchmark for their own firms and can use it as a tool for strategy and business model definition.

The remaining paper is structured as follows. Section 2 provides a structured literature review on the application of the VA/S method in research. In section 3, we describe the method and data sample used in this paper. Section 4 shows the results obtained for the sample software firms. Next, section 5 proceeds with a discussion of the results and compares those briefly to the results obtained from the literature review. Finally, section 6 concludes the paper and outlines avenues for further research.

2 Literature Review

Within this section, we conduct a structured literature review on the usage of VA/S for vertical integration measurement. The various usages show the potential of the measure for software business research, where VA/S hasn't been applied so far. The following sub-section outlines the method that we used to find, evaluate and classify relevant sources. We then summarize the literature according to the five groups of usages that we identify from our literature classification.

2.1 Method

In this paper, we provide a current, holistic and structured review on the application of the VA/S method. Our approach is motivated by the method suggested by vom Brocke et al. [9] and can be outlined in seven phases: (1) initial search of literature on the VA/S measure and identification of relevant keywords; (2) broad search for sources containing the relevant keywords; (3) selection of sources based on their titles and given keywords; (4) selection of sources based on their abstracts; (5) selection of sources based on their full texts; (6) backward and forward search for other relevant sources; (7) reading and classifying all relevant sources. A summary of the phases and the respective source numbers are shown in Table 1.

Within the first step, an initial unstructured literature review was performed in order to familiarize ourselves with the field and identify relevant keywords. For that, we reviewed 23 sources, most of which made it to the final selection in phase 6. Within the second step, we retrieved a broad set of potentially relevant sources. For that, we searched Ebsco's Business Source Premier database for previously identified keywords (see for similar usages [10]). The search was executed on the full text of the sources and was limited to peer-reviewed publications. This left us with 610 potentially relevant sources for further processing.

Table 1. Overview of relevant source numbers after each phase

	Phase	Relevant sources
1	Initial search for keyword identification	23
2	Holistic search with specific keywords	610
3	Selection based on the title and provided keywords	193
4	Selection based on the abstract	96
5	Selection based on the full text	28
6	Backward and forward search	34
7	Evaluation and classification	34

The next steps aimed at identifying the relevant sources. For that, we reviewed the titles, keywords, abstracts and finally, the full texts of the articles. Our criterion for selection was that the source must have applied the VA/S method for empirical calculations in order to be included in our set of relevant sources. This left us with 28 sources. Using backward and forward search, our final sample contained 34 sources. A distribution of the relevant sources according to the years of publication is shown in Figure 1.

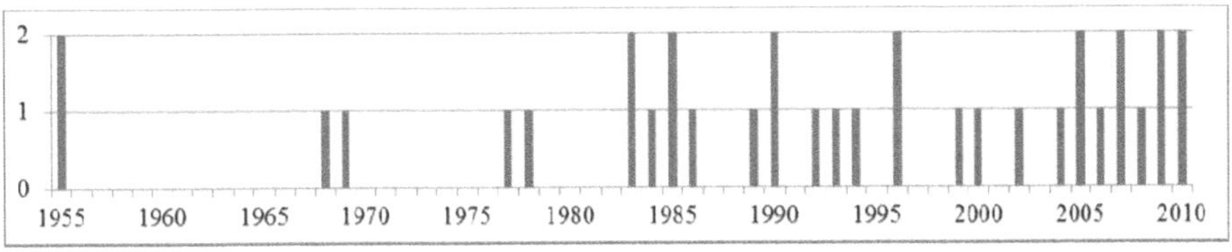

Fig. 1. Distribution of the relevant literature over time

Finally, we reviewed all sources in detail and classified those as illustrated in Table 2. We classify the sources in five dimensions: (1) development of the VA/S measure; (2) comparison of various VA/S calculations and other methods for vertical integration measurement; (3) descriptive empirical results using VA/S; (4) usage of the VA/S measure as an independent variable in regression analyzes; (5) usage of the VA/S measure as a dependent variable in regression analyzes.

Table 2. Classification of the relevant VA/S literature. DEV: method development; CMP: method comparison; DSC: descriptive statistics; IND: independent variable in regression analysis; DEP: dependent variable in regression analysis.

Source				Usage of the VA/S measure				
#	Author	Year	Ref.	DEV	CMP	DSC	IND	DEP
1	Adelman	1955	[11]	X		X		
2	Barnes	1955	[12]	X				
3	Crandall	1968	[13]			X		
4	Laffer	1969	[14]			X		
5	Tucker & Wilder	1977	[15]	X		X	X	X
6	Bowman	1978	[16]					X
7	Greene	1983	[17]			X		
8	Buzzell	1983	[18]	X				
9	Levy	1984	[19]					X
10	Madiggan & Zaima	1985	[20]		X			
11	Levy	1985	[21]				X	X
12	Balakrishnan & Wernerfelt	1986	[22]					X
13	Bryant	1989	[1]			X		
14	Cho	1990	[23]				X	
15	Van Ark	1990	[24]			X		
16	Barney et al.	1992	[25]				X	
17	Lindstrom & Rozell	1993	[26]		X			
18	Balakrishnan	1994	[27]				X	X
19	Brush & Karnani	1996	[28]				X	
20	Dean & Meyer	1996	[29]				X	
21	Holmes	1999	[30]					X
22	Lipovatz et al.	2000	[31]				X	
23	Sumner & Wolf	2002	[32]				X	
24	King & Hamman	2004	[33]			X		
25	Nakamura & Odagiri	2005	[34]				X	
26	Van Aswegen et al.	2005	[35]			X		
27	Nor et al.	2006	[36]					X
28	Thesmar & Thoenig	2007	[37]				X	
29	Waldenberger	2007	[38]				X	
30	Macchiavello	2008	[39]					X
31	Hutzschenreuter & Gröne	2009	[6]		X			X
32	Bamiro & Shittu	2009	[40]				X	
33	Yao et al.	2010	[41]				X	
34	Li & Tang	2010	[42]				X	

2.2 Results

As Figure 1 indicates, the VA/S method received continuous interest during the past 65 years. In particular, it appears to become increasingly popular, as one third of the papers were published in the last ten years. We further review the main results from the literature review based on the classification of the contents as shown in Table 2.

The VA/S measure was first suggested and used by Adelman [11], who calculated it as the ratio of income to sales. In order to account for serious weaknesses, there have been two major attempts to adjust the calculation formula: Tucker & Wilder adjust for profitability [15]. Buzzell additionally adjusts for 20% of investments [18]. He aims to account for the negative impact of investments on profitability (using the Profit Impact of Market Strategies database), which arguably should not impact the degree of vertical integration. It becomes apparent that while VA/S is becoming more popular in research, the last major modification dates back to 1983.

Notably, different approaches exist to calculate the value added itself. They vary in the components that are included in the figure [1]. Broadly speaking, all approaches can be classified in additive (summing up components) and subtractive (subtracting components from sales) approaches [17].

Interestingly, while many approaches to calculate the VA/S measure exist, there seems to be a high correlation between them [6]. Whereas the particular VA/S calculation method seems to be less important, there are other measures of vertical integration that yield results contradicting the VA/S measure [20], sometimes even showing negative correlations between the measures [26]. As pointed out by Li & Tang, "a strategy of vertical integration is a multi-dimensional concept; thus, different measures of vertical integration, each of which assesses a specific dimension, can yield complementary insights into an extremely complex phenomenon" [42]. We should therefore regard VA/S as an important, but not the only measure of the vertical integration concept.

First sources providing empirical results used the VA/S measure for descriptive purposes as a measure of vertical integration (see [11], [13], and [14]). However, since vertical integration is a multi-dimensional concept, those attempts to express vertical integration turned out to be less fruitful. Later works using detailed descriptive statistics mainly analyzed value added (see [1], [24], [33], and [35]). Nearly all relevant sources focus on the manufacturing and industrial sector. While most descriptive sources find no perceptible change over time, the absolute values range from 0.30 to 0.50 (see [11], [14], [24], and [15]).

Most sources use VA/S to operationalize vertical integration as a dependent or independent variable. Due to the broad range of results, we present only selected results here. The usage of VA/S as an independent variable allows for empirical analyzes of the impact of vertical integration. For instance, Yao et al. find that firms with higher VA/S realize higher IT business value [41]. Unfortunately, this is the only study we are aware of that analyzes a sector relevant to the software industry. Lipovatz et al. suggest that higher VA/S has a positive impact on productivity [31]. Li & Tang find that too high and too low levels of VA/S hinder the innovativeness of the firm [42]. As opposed to those rather positive effects of the VA/S level, Thesmar & Thoenig find that higher levels of VA/S are associated with higher business risks [37], similar results are obtained by Levy [21]. Other rather neutral results suggest that firms with higher VA/S also seem to engage more in R&D activities and perform those with external partners [34]. Also, higher levels of VA/S in an industry are associated with more venture formations [29].

The usage of VA/S as a dependent variable allows for empirical analyzes of the determinants of vertical integration. For instance, results show that the degree of vertical integration depends on the life-cycle of the firms [15]. This is consistent with Stigler's hypothesis, which claims that the degree of vertical integration is high for young firms, as well as for firms operating in mature industries [43]. Holmes finds that VA/S is higher where local industry concentration is low [30]. Hutzschenreuter & Gröne find that firms de-integrate where foreign competition increases [6].

3 Data and Method

We use the Bureau van Dijk Orbis database to retrieve the data on value added and sales of the firms in our sample. It contains data for the period 2002-2010. No data was available for 2011, as the data collection took place in December 2011. In order to define the scope of the software industry we use the industry classification NACE Rev. 2. While SIC is the predominant industry classification, it dates back to 1987 and hardly contains codes which can be associated with software activities. From NACE, we used the primary divisions 62 ("Computer programming, consultancy and related activities") and 63 ("Information service activities"), which cover software product and service activities. We further narrowed down the selection to firms from OECD countries, assuming that figures reported by non-OECD countries could be less reliable. Only firms were selected where at least one value was available in each figure. This left us with a selection of 64,824 firms.

Some additional data cleansing had to be done in order to ensure consistent and valid results. We removed all data points where one of the two needed values was not available or one of the two values was smaller than zero. Furthermore, we removed all remaining data points if data was only available for one year, as we focus on trends in VA/S which cannot be identified from a single data point. Since for 2010 nearly 25% less values were available, we concluded that there were still unreported values and excluded the year 2010. In the last step, we removed all erroneous results (VA/S greater than one). Finally, we were left with 44,141 software firms and 197,012 firm-year observations in the period 2002-2009.

In this paper, we use the ratio of value added to sales as a measure for vertical integration. We do not adjust for profits, because – as became apparent from the literature review – the results from all VA/S approaches are highly correlated. Given the firm-level data, the industry-level values are calculated as the simple average over all firms. Thus, the values represent an average software company, independent of its size.

Value added and sales are readily available from the Orbis database. Value added comprises the sum of salaries, net income, interest income, income taxes and depreciation. Notably, the database only contains the value added figure for firms where all its components are available. Therefore, no U.S. firms are included in our sample, as they don't report employee salaries. This calculation of value added is similar to other approaches (e.g. [15]).

The VA/S measure has important shortcomings: Other factors than vertical integration impact the measure. Those include the position of the firm within the value chain [11] and firm profitability [18]. On the other hand, the measure is widely used and its advantages and disadvantages are well documented (e.g. [6]). All data can be derived from secondary sources [26], allowing for analyzes of large samples. Even though the measure does not capture the concept of the vertical integration entirely, there is compelling logic behind a certain causal relationship [6].

Descriptive statistics of the sample are shown in Table 3. Firm size is operationalized by using value added, because it is a better measure than the commonly used sales [33].

Table 3. Distribution of the sample firms over countries, NACE codes and firm sizes

#	Country	Firms	#	Country	Firms	#	NACE	Firms	#	Size (USD)	Firms
1	AT	114	16	IL	3	1	6190	9	1	0-100	13,149
2	AU	32	17	IS	1	2	6200	379	2	100-500	17,340
3	BE	295	18	IT	14,392	3	6201	16,352	3	500-1,000	5,123
4	CA	2	19	JP	914	4	6202	10,226	4	1,000-10,000	7,090
5	CH	9	20	KR	325	5	6203	1,070	5	>=10,000	1,439
6	CZ	666	21	LU	23	6	6209	6,369			
7	DE	2,663	22	NL	35	7	6300	10			
8	DK	6	23	NO	1,212	8	6310	1			
9	ES	8,349	24	NZ	4	9	6311	8,246			
10	FI	1,368	25	PL	497	10	6312	296			
11	FR	5,131	26	PT	2,462	11	6391	415			
12	GB	63	27	SE	4,991	12	6399	768			
13	GR	4	28	SI	152						
14	HU	200	29	SK	223						
15	IE	2	30	TR	3						

4 Results

Table 4 shows the VA/S results for the sample firms. The value added and sales figures reflect the general economic development during this period of time. For instance, overall high values can be found in the years 2002 and 2007.

The VA/S value increases considerably in the sample period by more than ten percent from the original value in 2002. The standard deviations are small, indicating a steady increase in all periods. Whereas these aggregated values show consistent results, large differences exist on individual firm-level. In fact, detailed results for individual firms show all values in the range from 0.0 to 1.0.

Table 4. Results for the entire sample

	2002	2003	2004	2005	2006	2007	2008	2009	SD	Change	Mean
Firms	12,650	14,332	20,611	24,488	26,994	31,420	34,591	31,926	4,067	19,276	29,884
Added value (in thousand USD)											
Mean	4,275	3,856	3,473	3,102	3,629	4,125	3,488	3,951	401	-324	3,659
Median	257	308	263	216	246	261	240	258	18	1	244
SD	108,867	54,274	56,608	52,202	58,785	69,457	55,257	63,208	6,787	-45,659	59,782
Sales (in thousand USD)											
Mean	10,808	9,435	8,029	7,214	8,630	9,728	8,254	9,002	931	-1,806	8,566
Median	661	786	633	517	591	629	561	591	42	-70	578
SD	286,698	109,411	111,515	95,513	114,312	131,849	109,105	121,845	13,643	-164,853	111,525
VA/S (average)											
Mean	0.4444	0.4489	0.4589	0.4629	0.4617	0.4695	0.4788	0.4884	0.0113	0.0440	0.4723
Median	0.4444	0.4467	0.4546	0.4588	0.4558	0.4653	0.4787	0.4903	0.0144	0.0458	0.4698
SD	0.2122	0.2132	0.2214	0.2232	0.2227	0.2238	0.2243	0.2232	0.0006	0.0110	0.2234

Table 5 shows detailed VA/S results for NACE codes for which at least 100 firms are available in each year. The segment 6209 ("Other information technology and computer service activities") exhibits considerably lower values than the segment 6311 ("Data processing, hosting and related activities"). While the absolute values differ, we find increasing VA/S values in all segments. The standard deviations are small, indicating a steady increase in all segments.

Table 5. Results for individual industry segments where the number of firms is at least 100 in all years. The results are sorted in ascending order by the column mean.

NACE	VA/S								SD	Change	Mean
	2002	2003	2004	2005	2006	2007	2008	2009			
6209	0.3968	0.4006	0.3984	0.4017	0.4046	0.4113	0.4310	0.4455	0.0177	0.0487	0.4112
6391	0.4472	0.4652	0.4544	0.4519	0.4332	0.4376	0.4272	0.4518	0.0125	0.0046	0.4461
6399	0.4471	0.4505	0.4616	0.4634	0.4486	0.4533	0.4605	0.4613	0.0066	0.0143	0.4558
6201	0.4433	0.4533	0.4491	0.4562	0.4577	0.4670	0.4754	0.4855	0.0141	0.0421	0.4609
6203	0.4493	0.4496	0.4626	0.4546	0.4569	0.4615	0.4781	0.4855	0.0131	0.0362	0.4623
6202	0.4539	0.4583	0.4853	0.4879	0.4835	0.4941	0.5036	0.5096	0.0197	0.0557	0.4845
6311	0.4854	0.4803	0.4893	0.4914	0.4892	0.4935	0.5006	0.5093	0.0090	0.0240	0.4924

Table 6 shows the results grouped by the countries of origin of the respective firms. Except for France, we find increasing VA/S values in all countries. Interestingly, for European firms, Scandinavian and western countries show the highest absolute values, but the lowest increase over time. The large "jump" in VA/S for Sweden from 2003-2004 seems to be an exception. There are 2,481 firms available in 2003, but only 2,111 in 2004. 909 firms with mostly low VA/S values left the sample, while 539 firms with average values were added in 2004. The standard deviation is higher than for industry segments, but excluding Sweden the differences seem to be rather small.

Table 6. Results for individual countries where the number of firms is at least 100 in all years. The results are sorted in ascending order by the column mean.

Country	VA/S								SD	Change	Mean
	2002	2003	2004	2005	2006	2007	2008	2009			
JP	0.3130	0.3097	0.3259	0.3328	0.3410	0.3571	0.3764	0.3834	0.0277	0.0704	0.3424
PL	0.3447	0.3385	0.3499	0.3589	0.3808	0.3903	0.4037	0.4086	0.0275	0.0640	0.3719
IT	0.4104	0.4152	0.4202	0.4263	0.4261	0.4367	0.4440	0.4561	0.0153	0.0457	0.4294
PT	0.4212	0.4270	0.4328	0.4434	0.4422	0.4469	0.4658	0.4878	0.0217	0.0666	0.4459
ES	0.4381	0.4395	0.4430	0.4416	0.4435	0.4571	0.4807	0.4938	0.0212	0.0557	0.4547
BE	0.4523	0.4534	0.4846	0.4748	0.4712	0.4674	0.4672	0.4681	0.0106	0.0157	0.4674
DE	0.4726	0.4828	0.4821	0.4780	0.4741	0.4758	0.4754	0.4872	0.0050	0.0146	0.4785
FR	0.5124	0.5169	0.5113	0.5079	0.5021	0.5026	0.4983	0.5019	0.0065	-0.0106	0.5067
SE	0.4099	0.4162	0.5426	0.5604	0.5635	0.5796	0.5870	0.5888	0.0744	0.1789	0.5310
FI	0.5463	0.5583	0.5591	0.5582	0.5670	0.5787	0.5871	0.5778	0.0136	0.0315	0.5666

Finally, Table 7 shows the results for individual firm sizes. Again, while absolute values vary, the VA/S values increase in all sub-samples. There is a positive relationship between size and the VA/S value. Mathematically, this is not surprising, as size is measured by value added. However, this result indicates that sales do not increase proportionally with value added. Just as in previous sub-sample results, the standard deviation is consistent, suggesting a steady increase of the VA/S value.

Table 7. Results for individual size classes. The firm sizes are defined in Table 3.

Size class	VA/S								SD	Change	Mean
	2002	2003	2004	2005	2006	2007	2008	2009			
1	0.3780	0.3780	0.3552	0.3609	0.3561	0.3748	0.3911	0.3984	0.0184	0.0204	0.3763
2	0.4299	0.4302	0.4597	0.4704	0.4720	0.4852	0.4991	0.5077	0.0164	0.0777	0.4869
3	0.4707	0.4793	0.4977	0.5069	0.5083	0.5186	0.5267	0.5358	0.0123	0.0652	0.5193
4	0.4895	0.4997	0.5197	0.5268	0.5268	0.5317	0.5380	0.5482	0.0090	0.0587	0.5343
5	0.4947	0.5061	0.5239	0.5223	0.5196	0.5255	0.5300	0.5385	0.0074	0.0438	0.5272

5 Discussion

As became apparent from the literature review, the VA/S measure is widely used as a proxy for the degree of vertical integration. Whereas the comprehensive literature review summarizes current research on VA/S, this section discusses implications from our descriptive empirical results. The VA/S values increase in the period 2002-2009. This tendency is consistent and present in the total sample as well as in all given sub-samples for individual sectors, countries and firm sizes. For countries we find that the increases in VA/S are larger for countries with lower absolute VA/S levels. Also, the results for different size classes support the results obtained from other industries, that firm size and vertical integration are positively correlated.

Overall, these results indicate that the software industry is developing towards a higher level of vertical integration. The evaluation of country results further indicates that the countries with lower degree of vertical integration are catching up. Notably, this development over time opposes other results obtained from the literature, where increasing vertical integration over time is unusual. We suggest that this might be due to the fast changing nature of the software industry: Profound technological changes open up business opportunities, spawning new business models which rely on a higher initial degree of vertical integration. This hypothesis is consistent with Stigler's hypothesis [43], but remains yet to be tested for the software industry.

Despite the overall consistency in the increase of VA/S in our sample, the variance is high on the individual firm-level. Also, many firms had to be excluded because no reasonable VA/S value could be calculated. If VA/S captured the concept of vertical integration entirely, those difficulties and variances should not appear. We also support the view found in the literature that vertical integration is a multi-dimensional concept. VA/S arguably accounts for a certain aspect of the concept. However, if the entire concept needs to be captured, further measures should be added. Especially variables specific to the software industry could yield promising results.

Furthermore, VA/S is an abstract figure. In order to explain its development, one either requires detailed information on the components that comprise the total figure, or one has to run regression analyzes. Whereas the latter is more suitable for research, practitioners who have detailed information on their companies can engage in detailed case studies. Notably, we do not provide recommendations on the optimal VA/S level. A simple regression analysis shows a highly significant impact of VA/S on firm profitability (measured as return on sales). This result is consistent with previous empirical results [20]. The impact of VA/S on firm performance in the software industry remains yet to be addressed in future research.

6 Conclusion

Major elements of a firm's strategy and business model deal with how the firm creates value and brings it to the customer. In this paper, we outlined the potential of the VA/S method based on a broad structured literature review. We then provided first empirical insights for the software industry by applying the VA/S measure.

Our sample encompasses 44,171 software firms for the period 2002-2009. For the year 2009, the mean VA/S value of an average software firm was 0.4884. The development over time shows an increasing tendency. The increase is consistent over different sub-sectors, countries and firm sizes. This suggests that the software industry is evolving towards a higher degree of vertical integration. This evolution could indicate that a higher degree than the current one is more optimal in case of the average software firm.

Researchers will find our results particularly useful as a starting point for deductive analyzes. Our literature review provides a holistic overview of the relevant literature. Given these sources, researchers can conduct similar studies including software-specific variables, thus providing us with results specific to the software industry. Practitioners can use our results as a benchmark for their own companies. As the high variance on the individual firm-level can impact comparisons in a negative way, we propose to use more detailed information on companies to analyze individual components of the aggregated VA/S value. This should produce more meaningful results on the individual firm-level.

As a limitation to our study, the development of VA/S values over time is hard to explain given its abstract nature. We would require more detailed information on the individual components of the comprising figures. As those cannot be obtained from secondary sources on such a broad dataset, we attempt to extend this study through detailed case studies. This might also shed more light on additional dimensions of the concept of vertical integration. Finally, we strongly encourage the application of the VA/S measure as a proxy in regression analyzes in software industry research.

Acknowledgments. This work was supported by the Software-Cluster and partially funded within the Leading-Edge Cluster competition by the German Federal Ministry of Education and Research (BMBF) under grant "01IC10S05". The authors take the responsibility for the contents.

References

1. Bryant, J.: Assessing Company Strength Using Added Value. Long Range Planning 22, 34–44 (1989)
2. Porter, M.E.: Competitive Advantage. Free Press, London (1985)
3. Burkhart, T., Krumeich, J., Werth, D., Loos, P.: Analyzing the Business Model Concept - A Comprehensive Classification of Literature. In: 32nd International Conference on Information Systems, pp. 1–19 (2011)
4. Cusumano, M.A.: The Business of Software: What Every Manager, Programmer, and Entrepreneur Must Know to Thrive and Survive In Good Times Aand Bad. Free Press, New York (2004)
5. McGrath, R.: Why Vertical Integration Is Making a Comeback, in HBR Blog Network. Harvard Business Review (2009)
6. Hutzschenreuter, T., Gröne, F.: Changing Vertical Integration Strategies under Pressure from Foreign Competition: The Case of US and German Multinationals. Journal of Management Studies 46, 269–307 (2009)
7. Messerschmitt, D.G., Szyperski, C.: Software Ecosystem. The MIT Press, Cambridge (2003)
8. Léger, P.-M., Yang, S.: Network Effects and the Creation of Shareholders' Wealth in the Context of Software Firm Mergers and Acquisitions. In: Proceedings of ECIS 2005 (2005)
9. vom Brocke, J., Simons, A., Niehaves, B., Riemer, K., Plattfaut, R., Cleven, A.: Reconstructing the Giant: On the Importance of Rigour in Documenting the Literature Search Process. In: Proceedings of ECIS 2009 (2009)
10. Zott, C., Amit, R., Massa, L.: The Business Model: Recent Developments and Future Research. Journal of Management 37, 1019–1042 (2011)
11. Adelman, M.A.: Concept and Statistical Measurement of Vertical Integration. In: Stigler, G.J. (ed.) Business Concentration and Price Policy, pp. 279–328. Princeton University Press (1955)
12. Barnes, I.R.: Comment on Adelman. In: Stigler, G.J. (ed.) Business Concentration and Price Policy, pp. 322–330. Princeton University Press (1955)

13. Crandall, R.: Vertical Integration and the Market for Repair Parts in the United States Automobile Industry. Journal of Industrial Economics 16, 212–234 (1968)
14. Laffer, A.B.: Vertical Integration by Corporations, 1929-1965. The Review of Economics and Statistics 51, 91–93 (1969)
15. Tucker, I.B., Wilder, R.P.: Trends in Vertical Integration in the U. S. Manufacturing Sector. The Journal of Industrial Economics 26, 81–94 (1977)
16. Bowman, E.H.: Strategy, Annual Reports, and Alchemy. California Management Review 20, 64–71 (1978)
17. Greene, B.B.: A Note on Relevant Comparisons of Corporations and Countries. American Journal of Economics and Sociology 42, 39–43 (1983)
18. Buzzell, R.D.: Is vertical integration profitable? Harvard Business Review 61, 92–102 (1983)
19. Levy, D.: Testing Stigler's Interpretation of "The Division of Labor is Limited by the Extent of the Market". The Journal of Industrial Economics 32, 377–389 (1984)
20. Maddigan, R.J., Zaima, J.K.: The Profitability of Vertical Integration. Managerial and Decision Economics 6, 178–179 (1985)
21. Levy, D.T.: The transactions cost approach to vertical integration: an empirical examination. Review of Economics and Statistics 67, 438–445 (1985)
22. Balakrishnan, S., Wernerfelt, B.: Technical Change, Competition and Vertical Integration. Strategic Management Journal 7, 347–359 (1986)
23. Cho, K.R.: The role of product-specific factors in intra-firm trade of U.S. manufacturing multinational corporations. Journal of International Business Studies 21, 319–330 (1990)
24. van Ark, B.: Comparative Levels of Labour Productivity in Dutch and British Manufacturing. National Institute Economic Review 131, 71–85 (1990)
25. Barney, J.B., Edwards, F.L., Ringleb, A.H.: Organizational Responses To Legal Liability: Employee Exposure To Hazardous Materials, Vertical Integration, and Small Firm Production. Academy of Management Journal 35, 328–349 (1992)
26. Lindstrom, G., Rozell, E.: Is There A True Measure Of Vertical Integration? American Business Review 11, 44–50 (1993)
27. Balakrishnan, S.: The dynamics of make or buy decisions. European Journal of Operational Research 74, 552–571 (1994)
28. Brush, T., Karnani, A.: Impact of Plant Size and Focus on Productivity: An Empirical Study. Management Science 42, 1065–1081 (1996)
29. Dean, T.J., Meyer, G.D.: ndustry Environments and new venture formations in U.S. manufacturing: a conceptual and empirical analysis of demand determinants. Journal of Business Venturing 11, 107–132 (1996)
30. Holmes, T.J.: Localization of industry and vertical disintegration. Review of Economics and Statistics 81, 314–325 (1999)
31. Lipovatz, D., Mandaraka, M., Mourelatos, A.: Multivariate analysis for the assessment of factors affecting industrial competitiveness: The case of Greek food and beverage industries. Applied Stochastic Models in Business and Industry 16, 85–98 (2000)
32. Sumner, D.A., Wolf, C.A.: Diversification, Vertical Integration, and the Regional Pattern of Dairy Farm Size. Review of Agricultural Economics 24, 442–457 (2002)
33. King, C., Hamman, W.D.: Assessing company strength in South Africa using value added: 1990-2000. South African Journal of Business Management 35, 39–55 (2004)
34. Nakamura, K., Odagiri, H.: R&D boundaries of the firm: An estimation of the double-hurdle model on commissioned R&D, joint R&D, and licensing in Japan. Economics of Innovation and New Technology 14, 583–615 (2005)

35. van Aswegen, N., Steyn, B.W., Hamman, W.D.: Trends in the distribution of added value of listed industrial companies – 1990 to 2002. South African Journal of Business Management 36, 85–94 (2005)
36. Nor, N.G.M., Abdullah, A.Z., Nor, K.M.: Vertical Integration, Foreign Multinationals and Stigler's Hypotheses: An Empirical Test Using Malaysian Data. Asian Economic Journal 20, 257–274 (2006)
37. Thesmar, D., Thoenig, M.: From flexibility to inssecurity: how vertical separation amplifies firm-level uncertainty. Journal of the European Economic Association 5, 1161–1202 (2007)
38. Waldenberger, F.: Growth and Structural Change in the Japanese Economy 1985-2000: An Input-Output Analysis. Asian Business and Management 6, 15–33 (2007)
39. Macchiavello, R.: Contractual Institutions, Financial Development and Vertical Integration: Theory and Evidence, University of Oxford, Department of Economics, Economics Series Working Papers: 392: Oxford (2008)
40. Bamiro, O.M., Shittu, A.M.: Vertical Integration and Cost Behavior in Poultry Industry in Ogun and Oyo States of Nigeria. Agribusiness 25, 1–15 (2009)
41. Yao, L.J., Liu, C., Chan, S.H.: The influence of firm specific context on realizing information technology business value in manufacturing industry. International Journal of Accounting Information Systems 11, 353–362 (2010)
42. Li, H.-L., Tang, M.-J.: Vertical integration and innovative performance: The effects of external knowledge sourcing modes. Technovation 30, 401–410 (2010)
43. Stigler, G.J.: The Division of Labor is Limited by the Extent of the Market. Journal of Political Economy 59, 185–193 (1951)

Introducing Software Ecosystems for Mass-Produced Embedded Systems

Ulrik Eklund and Jan Bosch

Chalmers University of Technology
Software Engineering Division, Dept. of Computer Science & Engineering
Göteborg, Sweden
{ulrik.eklund,jan.bosch}@chalmers.se

Abstract. Embedded systems are today predominantly developed with an integration-centric approach. The paper identifies the need to remove full-scale integration and process synchronisation of involved development teams. The paper presents software ecosystem as an alternative approach to develop embedded software and identifies a set of key activities for how an original equipment manufacturer can introduce an ecosystem. An example of a software ecosystem is presented for the car industry together a case which implemented some of the ecosystem platform properties.

Keywords: Embedded software, software architecture, software ecosystem, case study.

1 Introduction

The approach of developing software in an ecosystem instead of as an integrator towards the customer could provide some advantages also in the embedded domain, such as alleviating the complexity of synchronising large-scale development projects and extending the innovation base. Software ecosystems have been studied by several researchers [1,2,3]. Jansen et al. [4] presents a set of research challenges and this paper responds to the first challenge of characterisation and modelling of ecosystems for the domain of software-intensive embedded systems.

The main contribution of this paper is a method for establishing an ecosystem for mass-produced software-intensive embedded products. The method consists of a set of key activities for the original equipment manufacturer (OEM) to introduce the ecosystem and facilitate the interaction between development parties.

2 Context and Problem Statement

Many companies developing mass-produced embedded systems view software as a necessary evil rather than as a strategic opportunity and business differentiator. One reason for this is that they have extensive supplier and subcontractor

M.A. Cusumano, B. Iyer, and N. Venkatraman (Eds.): ICSOB 2012, LNBIP 114, pp. 248–254, 2012.

relationships and the cost, effort and unpredictability of the deliverables from these external partners is experienced as a major problem. The mass-produced embedded systems are typically developed with an integration-centric approach where the OEM needs to be in full control of the development of all software and synchronise the development of the involved parties.

Examples of mass-produced embedded products include vehicles, washing machines and other home utensils, and printers. We will give general examples from the automotive industry since cars are arguably the most complex product of this category, both in terms of conflicting requirements and subcontractor relationships. We define the domain of mass-produced software-intensive embedded systems by four characteristics:

- Deep integration between hardware and software for significant parts of the functionality
- Strong focus on manufacturing aspects of the product in the development (e.g. by development process gates)
- Strong supplier involvement in the form of subcontractors
- Some elements of the system realise safety-critical functionality

There are four main reasons why the integration-centric approach, is a "dead end" for many embedded domains, especially in the case of significant outsourcing: First, it is *not possible to rely on control* through processes and synchronisation of processes because external developers might not use the same process. Second, when the release cycle is imposed on software from hardware manufacturing concerns it results in "old" software applications since the lead-time of mechanical/hardware development and its industrialisation is longer than competitively desired for software. Third, feature content is growing exponentially [5], especially in the automotive domain [6]. Since this adds interdependencies if not managed the integration phase actually gets shorter since all software parts have to be finished before integration can take place. Last, heavy outsourcing of software development, often globally, goes against the need for efficient inter-team communication in integration-centric development.[7]

The conclusion is that it is necessary to move away from integration-centric development. The most sustainable alternative is the open ecosystem [7] and it will thus be further elaborated in this paper. The research question investigated is thus: *What are the key activities to establish a software ecosystem for mass-produced embedded systems?*

3 Introduction of a Software Ecosystem

The ecosystem would focus on a product or family of products of embedded devices with an open software platform. The hardware technology would be very domain specific, e.g. sensors and actuators for cars or printers. To facilitate new business opportunities and remove the burdensome synchronisation of subcontracted development teams there are two dimensions where decoupling between development parties/teams must take place and which should be supported by the ecosystem and the platform: 1) Decoupling between applications, this would otherwise make future feature growth impossible at some point. 2) Decoupling in time, i.e. all software must not join at manufacturing of the product.

A model defining the transition from an integration-centric software development to the establishment of a software ecosystem includes the following key activities for the OEM:

3.1 Choose the Ecosystem Type

There are three types of software ecosystems according to the second author [2]: Operating System-centric, application-centric, and end-user programming. An ecosystem for embedded software would start from a product family that already achieved success in the market place without the support of an ecosystem around it, and thus have the characteristics of an application-centric software ecosystem; a domain-specific application(s) deeply embedded in the product which is sold to the end customer.

3.2 Open Up the Platform

The software platform supporting the ecosystem and the applications must be deployed to each product. The platform would include an operating system, domain-specific middleware and key domain applications, sufficient to use the product and fulfil any legal and safety requirements. Many embedded products exhibit real-time behaviour so application execution must be supported by real-time mechanisms, depending on the domain. Since the software can be deployed at any time the platform and its architecture should allow development, integration and validation of feature applications independent of other applications. Each application executes in an isolated environment, with critical applications executing on dedicated hardware, and dependencies between applications are only established at run-time, for example realised by process virtualisation [8].

3.3 Establish OEM as Keystone Organisation

The OEM would have a crucial role in the ecosystem as a keystone organisation [9] since it manufactures the product that software applications will run on. The OEM is responsible for developing the ecosystem platform, at least initially. The keystone organisation should provide the stability of the ecosystem for niche developers to establish themselves by producing the systems with the embedded platform for a sufficiently long time. This allows both developers seek out cooperation with the OEM and/or establish a direct relationship between 3rd-party developers and the end customer.

3.4 Establish Business Opportunities for Developers

The reason for the customer to buy the product is the capabilities provided by domain-specific software applications utilising the hardware of the product, i.e. sensors and actuators manufacture by the OEM. The applications are provided by the OEM and by 3rd parties directly to the end customer, enabling for business opportunities not possible when all software is directed by the OEM. Technical end customers can even develop their own applications if sufficient IDE support for the platform is available. The incentive for the OEM to migrate towards an ecosystem would be to share total cost of development between parties in the ecosystem and open up the innovation base. In return the OEM provides the stability necessary for other parties.

3.5 Establish Infrastructure for Continuous Deployment of Software

The development teams deploy their applications independent of each other and independent from the platform and hardware. This is enabled by an automated infrastructure that can distribute software application to thousands of devices, each with its own software configuration. This contrasts with continuously checking in software to a central repository and build system for e.g. web applications. The infrastructure must both allow customers to enhance their product with new applications as well as allow developers to push updates of already deployed applications. To facilitate business opportunities for the external developers the infrastructure would have a marketplace for them towards the end customer. This can be provided by the keystone organisation or by already established mechanisms. The infrastructure also support necessary certification processes before deploying software to customers, processes that are demanded by legal, safety-critical or security reasons.

4 An Ecosystem in the Car Domain

Since there is no widely known software ecosystem such as the one described above it is difficult to present proven industrial cases, but we present an instantiation of the software ecosystem for the automotive domain.

A modern car is arguably the most complex mass-produced embedded system developed in terms of conflicting requirements and subcontractor structure. Software development follows the process logic of the mechanical development and the deployment of software to the customer follows the physical delivery of the product. In a software ecosystem, where software can be deployed to the product also after delivery, the platform would include vehicle software necessary to fulfil legal and safety requirements, e.g. displaying vehicle speed in a cluster display and ESP. This would make the car usable at delivery to the end-customer without further actions. All other software applications could be deployed on the vehicle en route to the customer or after delivery; it could either be the sales organisation that acquired additional software components from the OEM or 3rd parties, or the end customer. For vehicle fleets it would be possible to acquire or replace application software catering to fleet-specific needs, e.g. car-share pools or large taxi firms. Suppliers could focus on providing domain specific actuators, e.g. brakes or door locks, with middleware conforming to the platform, leaving the vehicle-level development to other parties, e.g. the OEM, or also offer those as well. Firms providing after-market solutions, including the OEM, would have unprecedented opportunities to integrate their solutions seamlessly with the OEM platform, providing better customer value than what is possible today.

AUTOSAR is a project to "establish an open industry standard for the automotive software architecture between suppliers and manufacturers." [10] The AUTOSAR architecture exhibits some of the properties in Section 3.2 [10], however the suggested methodology assumes that all integration of software components is done by the OEM [11], i.e. falls into the integration-centric development category. There are no mechanisms to support independent software deployment. Even if there is no business model prescribed by the AUTOSAR standard, it can be assumed that the closed supplier-OEM business relationship seen in the automotive domain today is preserved.

4.1 Open Infotainment Labs

The Open Infotainment Labs was a prototype of an in-vehicle infotainment system developed in cooperation between Volvo Car Corporation and EIS by Semcon, but was not intended to go into mass-production and be sold to customers. The project had two goals: First, feature development with extremely short lead-times from decision to implementation compared to present automotive industry standard, from a nominal lead-time of 1-3 years to 4-12 weeks. Second, to investigate application-based architecture open to 3rd party feature development, i.e. development not sourced or ordered by Volvo Cars, and as such form the basis for a software ecosystem around in-vehicle infotainment systems. The software platform was based on Android, which already had some desired architectural properties, such as run-time isolation of applications and an established infrastructure for continuous deployment. In addition to this the following architectural mechanisms were investigated:

- Possible app market solutions for the OEM
- Secure gateway between Android apps and vehicle-critical micro-controllers
- Domain-specific API available for Android app developers with over 50 different vehicle attributes
- Mechanisms to sign OEM-approved applications with privileges to allow interaction with critical vehicle sensors and actuators
- Models for different categories of applications, for example to prevent applications to start when driving the vehicle e.g. to minimise driver distraction
- Domain-specific resource management, in a car audio warnings have higher priority than a phone call

The prototype system was implemented in an actual car and tested by persons outside of the two development partners. It was possible for the users to tailor the system according to their individual wishes by e.g. installing their favourite web radio application from an external marketplace while in the car.

5 Related Work

Jansen et al. [1] provides two cases of software ecosystem together with a definition of ecosystem characteristics. The activities in Section 3 fall into their external scope in terms of market, technology, platform and firms.

Rohrbeck et al. [12] describes how Deutsche Telekom created an open innovation ecosystem and identifies 11 open innovation instruments. The resulting innovations range from features added to what the suppliers offer to those developed entirely at Deutsche Telekom. The focus on the paper is on innovation schemes and thus complements the activities in Section 3.

Viljainen and Kauppinen [3] describe a set of management practices for software ecosystems, together with a case from the telecom industry. They focus on the platform integrator which plays the role of keystone organisation. The activities in Section 3 can be categorised within their practice of "orchestration", but for mass-produced embedded systems.

The second author et al. [7] provides three cases of ecosystems, one of them being a company developing embedded products. The paper defines five approaches to software development from integration-centric development to software ecosystems, with criteria for when each should be successful, which provided the rationale for the ecosystem presented in this paper.

6 Conclusions

We conclude that an integration-centric development of embedded software may not be a sustainable development approach based on four reasons: Feature growth and the resulting complexity, decoupling of the software deployment cycle from manufacturing concerns, alleviate OEM integration efforts, and managing heavy outsourcing to subcontractors. Based on this we proposed a set of five key activities for the OEM to establish the software ecosystem. The ecosystem platform and its architecture are key factors to successfully allow continuous deployment of software directly from the development teams to the customer without requiring big-bang integration from the OEM. Finally we presented how a software ecosystem could look like for the car industry, and presented a case which had implemented some of the platform properties. We reviewed an automotive software architecture standard, AUTOSAR, in terms of its viability as an embedded platform for a software ecosystem in the automotive industry.

Acknowledgements. This work has been financially supported by the Swedish Agency for Innovation Systems (VINNOVA) and Volvo Car Corporation.

References

1. Jansen, S., Brinkkemper, S., Finkelstein, A.: Business network management as a survival strategy: A tale of two software ecosystems. In: Proceedings of the First Workshop on Software Ecosystems, pp. 34–48 (2009)
2. Bosch, J.: From software product lines to software ecosystems. In: Proceedings of the 13th International Software Product Line Conference. ACM (2009)
3. Viljainen, M., Kauppinen, M.: Software Ecosystems: A Set of Management Practices for Platform Integrators in the Telecom Industry. In: Regnell, B., van de Weerd, I., De Troyer, O. (eds.) ICSOB 2011. LNBIP, vol. 80, pp. 32–43. Springer, Heidelberg (2011)
4. Jansen, S., Finkelstein, A., Brinkkemper, S.: A sense of community: A research agenda for software ecosystems. In: Proceedings of the International Conference on Software Engineering - Companion Volume, pp. 187–190. IEEE (2009)
5. Ebert, C., Jones, C.: Embedded software: Facts, figures, and future. Computer 42(4), 42–52 (2009)
6. Broy, M.: Challenges in automotive software engineering. In: Proceedings of the International Conference on Software Engineering, pp. 33–42. ACM (2006)
7. Bosch, J., Bosch-Sijtsema, P.: From integration to composition: On the impact of software product lines, global development and ecosystems. Journal of Systems and Software 83(1), 67–76 (2010)
8. Smith, J.E., Nair, R.: The architecture of virtual machines. Computer 38(5), 32–38 (2005)
9. Iansiti, M., Levien, R.: Strategy as ecology. Harvard Business Review 82(3), 68–78 (2004); PMID: 15029791
10. Fürst, S., Mössinger, J., Bunzel, S., Weber, T., Kirschke-Biller, F., Heitkämper, P., Kinkelin, G., Nishikawa, K., Lange, K.: AUTOSAR - a worldwide standard is on the road. In: International VDI Congress Electronic Systems for Vehicles, Baden-Baden, Germany (2009)
11. AUTOSAR: AUTOSAR technical overview v2.2.2 (August 2008)
12. Rohrbeck, R., Hölzle, K., Gemünden, H.G.: Opening up for competitive advantage - how deutsche telekom creates an open innovation ecosystem. R&D Management 39(4), 420–430 (2009)

Controlling Lost Opportunity Costs in Agile Development – The Basic Lost Opportunity Estimation Model for Requirements Scoping

Krzysztof Wnuk[1], David Callele[2], Even-Andre Karlsson[3], and Björn Regnell[1]

[1] Department of Computer Science, Lund University, Sweden
{Krzysztof.Wnuk,Bjorn.Regnell}@cs.lth.se
[2] Department of Computer Science University of Saskatchewan, Saskatchewan, Canada
callele@cs.usask.ca
[3] AddALot, Lund, Sweden
even-andre.karlsson@addalot.se

Abstract. We present a model for estimating the final keep/cancel decision point, on a per-feature basis, for scope inclusion in a future release. The Basic Lost Opportunity Estimation Model (BLOEM), based on data from a company that uses an agile-inspired software development model, supports feature selection when the time-dependent business value estimates change as the requirements analysis progresses. The initial BLOEM validation, conducted on a set of 166 features, suggests that the model can valuable input to the feature selection process for a given release, helping to control lost opportunity costs due to feature cancellation. Limitations of BLOEM are discussed and issues for further research are presented.

Keywords: Requirements management, scope management, agile development, software business.

1 Introduction

Market-driven software development attempts to deliver the right product at the right time to the target market; time-to-market and release scheduling may strongly affect market success [1]. Threats include introducing new requirements in response to competitive pressures thereby creating a risk of feature creep negatively impacting timely (reliable) market introduction. Prior work [2] identified a pattern where features were pruned from a release only after significant (wasted) investment. These wasted efforts may negatively impact the effectiveness of requirements engineering and management activities.

Numerous prioritization techniques have been investigated and utilized to identify and select the most valuable features for the next release of a project. However, most techniques rely on accurate market value and effort estimates that can be difficult to generate early in the development process. The agile software development movement [3] attempts to increase requirements process flexibility and process

M.A. Cusumano, B. Iyer, and N. Venkatraman (Eds.): ICSOB 2012, LNBIP 114, pp. 255–260, 2012.

responsiveness to unexpected changes in scope using continuous scope updating and one-dimensional (relative) methods for cost estimation and as a substitute for real market values [4]. However, it remains unclear how long potential features should be considered within project scope when there exist a high probability that scoping decisions may need to change due to unexpected events. Finally, this methodology does not address unexpected market forces such as revolutionary technologies or patent litigation nor does it target the release date as a critical success factor for software product delivery in a market-driven context [1].

We present the Basic Lost Opportunity Estimation Model (BLOEM), a simplified version of the previously published LOEM model [5] for controlling software project lost opportunity costs. BLOEM targets processes that use a one-dimensional requirements prioritization technique such as agile software development as well as processes where accurate effort estimation is challenging [4, 6]. BLOEM attempts to control wasted effort by facilitating earlier identification of feature cancellation candidates, promoting constructive use of resources. The model enhances existing processes by providing input to the keep/cancel scoping decision.

Cost functions identified in prior work [5] are collapsed into a single return on investment calculation represented by the Value function and we expect the Value to be obtained from marketing and sales information. The simplified model can use relative or absolute values for candidate features as well as their planned release date for estimating final decision points for inclusion or rejection within a release.

2 Background and Motivation

Agile software development focuses on continuously delivering business and customer value to increase the probability of early ROI [6]. Cao *et al.* noted that agile requirement engineering practitioners uniformly reported that their prioritization is principally based on business value [7]. While prioritizing based on business value is considered a key requirements prioritization criterion [4], it doesn't decrease the temporal uncertainty as a consequence of rapidly changing markets.

To illustrate the motivation behind BLOEM we present the results of our analysis of an agile-inspired prioritization process applied to a set of features for an embedded system product line developed at a large multinational company[1]. The case company has adopted a continuous development model with continuous feasibility assessment of proposed features and a one-dimensional prioritization model for scope management of a common platform technology based product line supporting more than 10 affiliated products.

Figure 1 depicts the normalized value of the (widely varying) business priority for each of a set of features plotted against the total time that the features were in the software development process (including the requirements phase). The case company data was collected with the help of the third author, currently under contract to the case company, who ensured that the collected data was correct and meaningful. Of 166 candidate features that were considered for this software product release, 83 were

---

[1] Due to space constraints in the conference format, we present the company description at `http://serg.cs.lth.se/research/experiment_packages/BLOEM/`

withdrawn. As can be seen in Figure 1, withdrawn features had both high and low priorities (value) and were withdrawn at all times throughout the release cycle.

BLOEM's intent is to quantify the effort spent on the features in the triangle labeled "area of interest" in Figure 1 to support efficient process management. Ultimately, we want to decide to keep/cancel a feature as quickly as possible – if a feature is withdrawn, it is best to withdraw it as early as possible to minimize wasted effort.

3 The Basic Lost Opportunity Estimation Model

The BLOEM model assumes that the decision-making criteria are temporal functions, not fixed values, which facilitates their use even in dynamic situations with uncertain scoping decisions. The model is based on the market-driven requirements engineering premise that the value of a requirement is a temporal function that is sensitive to market forces and opportunities – often a feature will only have market value for a limited time. Even features that offer unique capabilities see a significant reduction in their market value when competitors catch up and offer the feature in their own products.

Total value ***V(t)*** for a feature is defined in formula (1), where t=a is feature inception (when the feature begins to have non-zero value) and t=b is when the feature ceases to have any market value. A feature is cancelled at t=c. Maintenance, as both a cost and as a revenue source, is not considered in this simplified model.

$$V(t) = \int_a^b V(t)dt \quad (1) \qquad \int_a^c V(t)dt \leq \delta \quad (2)$$

The value function will depend on the characteristics of the target market and must be estimated when applying the model.

From a management perspective we assume that features under investigation should be kept within the project scope until a defined value threshold ($\boldsymbol{\delta}$), known as the Final Decision Point (FDP), is reached. The threshold value can be unique to each feature and should be estimated per feature. High-value features (*e.g.* priority in the top 25%) could have the FDP threshold set higher than less valuable features (*e.g.* priority in the bottom 25%). Final decisions as to whether to keep (and realize the investment) or cancel (and minimize losses) are then delayed for the most valuable features while the least valuable features are canceled relatively early. The FDP can be used as to enforce a budget-like approach to the scoping management process.

We consider all canceled features to be wasted effort. However, investments in features that are canceled before the threshold are considered *controlled waste*: there is waste but it is under management control and the risk of inter-feature dependencies is held to an acceptable level. Features that are canceled after the final decision point are *uncontrolled waste* – something unexpected has happened and time or resource constraints cannot be met for this release cycle.

The flexibility required in the development process can be adjusted by changing the value of $\boldsymbol{\delta}$. The *overall impact* of a set $\boldsymbol{K}$ of withdrawn or cancelled features within a development cycle is calculated using formula 3:

$$\sum_{k=1}^{K} \frac{\int_a^b V_k(t)dt - \delta_k}{K} \tag{3}$$

4 Initial Model Evaluation

BLOEM was initially validated using a set of 166 features analyzed by the case company (depicted as dots in Figure 1). The feature status in the data set ranged from the definition phase, through implementation, to completion. During this period 87 features were canceled (dots with X's in Figure 1, several Xs overlap). The value function is defined relative to the lifespan for the feature, the period from feature inception until the feature ceases to have any market value. Two value functions were considered to observe their effects upon the results. The first function assumes a constant value across the lifespan of the feature. The second function assumes that value is normally distributed with the mean positioned at 50% of the lifespan and the standard deviation set to 1/6 of the lifespan. Under the normal value function, each

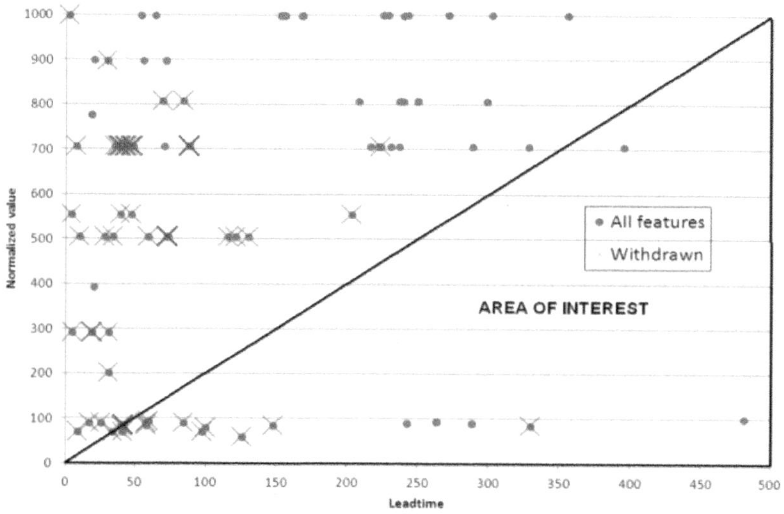

Fig. 1. Dots represent implemented features while crossed dots represent withdrawn features

feature has a very low value at the beginning of the lifespan. However, the value follows the cumulative distribution function therefore those features that exceed the FDP have much higher associated value on a per-feature basis that is realized as a loss (wasted effort) when the features are cancelled.

Results. Figure 2 depicts the results of using BLOEM with these two value functions (several data points overlap). The constant value function is represented by dots and the normal value function is represented by triangles. Because the value function is defined, in this case, to cover the entire product lifecycle, the final decision points should be only a small portion of the lifespan of the feature. The final decision points, represented by the red line in Figure 2, are set to 5% of the value function for low priority features (below 250), 10% for low-medium priority features (between 251 and 500), 20% for medium-high priority features (between 501 and 750) and 40% for high priority features (over 750). These exemplary final decision point values represent, in effect, the budget for feature scoping activities at each priority level – individual projects must set the thresholds in a contextually appropriate manner.

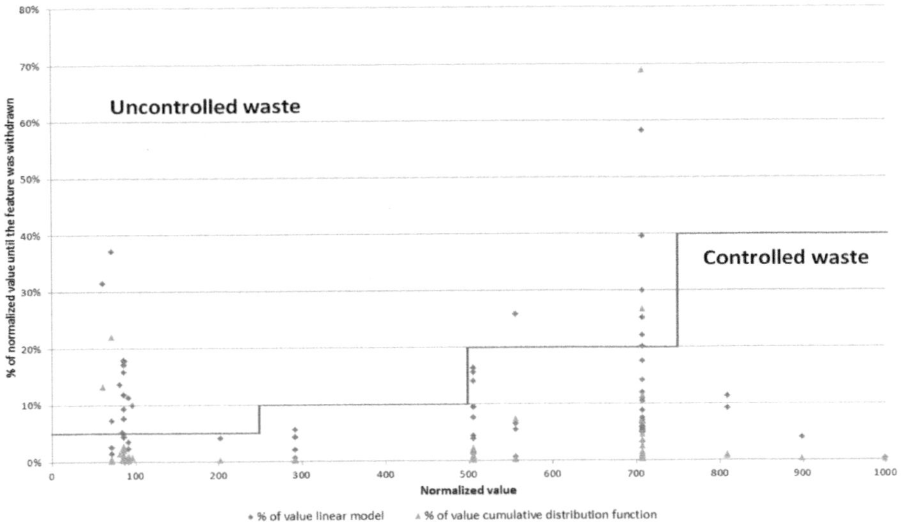

Fig. 2. Results from model validation

Discussion. Under the assumptions of the constant value function, the average *uncontrolled waste* was 10.2% of the normalized value for the 25 features that were withdrawn after their final decision point. Under the assumptions of the normal value function, the average *uncontrolled waste* was 20.3% of the normalized value for the 4 features that were withdrawn after their final decision point. The 25 features remained in the process for a cumulative 1021 days after the FDP while the 4 features remained in the process for a cumulative 75 days after the FDP. The resources expended upon these features during this period represent both direct costs and lost opportunity costs. In both cases, the overall impact of the entire feature set (kept and cancelled) was under the budget line (linear: -5.1%, normal: -37.6%) indicating that there was capacity to investigate more features within the given budget. Alternatively, the budget could have been tightened (final decision points set earlier) or fewer resources could have been allocated to the release as a whole (more features per human resource).

5 Conclusions and Further Work

The Basic Lost Opportunity Estimation Model (BLOEM) for controlling lost opportunity costs related to cancelled and withdrawn features was presented. Targeted at processes that employ one-dimensional requirements prioritization (such as agile methodologies where feature planning and roadmapping is required), its performance was investigated with an initial data set. The presented model is related to the models of investing under uncertainty described by Dixit and Pindych [8]. The analysis clearly identified opportunities to improve process efficiency within the examined data set. The costs associated with delayed feature cancellation were quantified and a budget-driven final decision point mechanism was presented as well as management guidance for interpreting the results. Preliminary discussions of the initial validation results were held with two practitioners at the case company who responded positively to the model concept and its potential for controlling lost opportunity costs.

This investigation showed that BLOEM results are sensitive to the cost function and further investigation into other cost functions is suggested to determine their utility for management decision support. For example, agile methodologies suggest a constant feature priority evaluation process – how well does BLOEM perform in such an environment? Further validation with other data sets is needed.

Regarding the validity of the obtained results, the first significant threat to validity is uncertainty as to whether or not the value functions provide proper guidelines to the management. The second main threat to validity is the fact that the study was conducted at one company and therefore the generalizability of the achieved results should be confirmed in the follow up studies.

References

1. Regnell, B., Brinkkemper, S.: Market-Driven Requirements Engineering for Software Products. In: Aurum, A., Wohlin, C. (eds.) Engineering and Managing Software Requirements, pp. 287–308. Springer, Berlin (2005)
2. Wnuk, K., Regnell, B., Karlsson, L.: What Happened to Out Features? Visualization and Understanding of Scope Change Dynamics in a Large-Scale Industrial Setting. In: 17th IEEE Int. Requirements Engineering Conference, pp. 41–50. IEEE Press, New York (2009)
3. The Agile manifesto, `http://agilemanifesto.org/` (accessed January 2012)
4. Racheva, Z., Daneva, M., Sikkel, K., Herrmann, A., Wieringa, R.: Do We Know Enough about Requirements Prioritization in Agile Projects: Insights from a Case Study. In: 18th IEEE International Requirements Engineering Conference, pp. 147–156. IEEE Computer Society, Washington, DC (2010)
5. Wnuk, K., Callele, D., Regnell, B.: Guiding requirements scoping using ROI: towards agility, openness and waste reduction. In: 18th IEEE Int. Requirements Engineering Conference, pp. 409–410. IEEE Press, New York (2010)
6. Beck, K.: eXtreme Programming Explained: Embrace Change. Addison Wesley (2000)
7. Cao, L., Ramesh, B.: Agile Requirements Engineering Practices: An Empirical Study. IEEE Soft. 25, 60–67 (2007)
8. Dixit, A., Pindych, R.: Investment Under Uncertainty. Princeton Univ. Press (1994)

Costs of Using Hybrid Cloud Infrastructure: Towards a General Framework

Oleksiy Mazhelis

University of Jyväskylä, Finland
oleksiy.mazhelis@jyu.fi

Abstract. Cloud computing infrastructure is a state-of-the-art computing as a utility paradigm, offering individuals and organizations instantly-available and scalable computing capacity. Organizations may deploy the cloud infrastructure in own data centers, as a private cloud, or use the public on-demand cloud infrastructure charged on a pay-per-use basis. The organizations may also adopt a hybrid solution, i.e. use public cloud capacity to complement the resources in the private cloud, e.g. during the periods of rapid growth in the demand. One of the important factors that affect the organizations' decisions to adopt a hybrid cloud is the total cost of acquiring and managing the infrastructure. In this paper, a general framework for cloud infrastructure cost assessment is introduced, wherein for several types of cloud infrastructure resources, the associated cost components and the factors determining these components are considered.

Keywords: Cloud computing infrastructure, hybrid cloud, cost model.

1 Introduction

Cloud computing is a state-of-the-art computing as a utility paradigm, allowing the computing and storage capacity, as well as platforms and applications built on top of them to be provided to the customers on-demand in a scalable and efficient manner [5]. The lowest-level family of the cloud computing services is the so-called infrastructure as a service (IaaS) offering the customers the baseline computing, storage, and data communication capacities, while giving them the freedom to install and run on top of this infrastructure the applications of their choice.

Cloud infrastructure can be offered by a public cloud service provider (public cloud), and charged depending on the actual usage. Alternatively, the cloud infrastructure can be deployed as a so-called private cloud, i.e. within the organization's data center(s). Finally, the organization may combine both the in-house capacity of private cloud with the resources offered by the public cloud, to form a so-called hybrid cloud [5].

Cloud infrastructure services are adopted rapidly [6]; this rapid pace of adoption can be partly attributed to the cost savings for the customers promised by the cloud services [1]. On the other hand, available evidence suggests that the unit cost of public cloud capacity is higher than that in the private cloud [7,3]. In other words, using public cloud resources only is likely to be more expensive in longer term than acquiring the needed resources up-front and managing them in-house.

M.A. Cusumano, B. Iyer, and N. Venkatraman (Eds.): ICSOB 2012, LNBIP 114, pp. 261–266, 2012.

However, the use of expensive public cloud is economically justified when the need for computing capacity fluctuates. In this case, the use of the private cloud alone often results in over-provisioning, i.e. the infrastructure resources being underutilized most of the time. The hybrid cloud gives the opportunity to increase the utilization of the private cloud resources and hence minimize the overall infrastructure costs [8,4].

The cost of the cloud infrastructure was studied in several works, where a number of factors determining whether the hybrid solution brings cost savings were identified:

- The degree of demand fluctuation [8,4] and demand growth predictability [9];
- The pricing models applied to the private and public resources [8,4];
- The communications overheads and the effect of volume discounts in the above pricing [4], as well as the expected trends in pricing [7,3];
- The net present value of money related to the expected lifetime of solution [7,3];
- The start-up costs and/or the costs of transforming the current solution towards enabling a hybrid solution [3].

As could be seen, the state-of-the-art research on the hybrid cloud costs is rather fragmented, with different research efforts dealing with individual aspects of the issue. In this paper, we aim at elaborating a generic costs framework for hybrid cloud infrastructure, where these factors are integrated. In the framework, several cost components are considered, including the cost of computing, data communications, and data storage. These cost components are categorized according to their likely effect on the overall costs, which in turn depends on whether the cost component is affected by the interaction between the private and the public clouds.

The remainder of the paper is organized as follows. In section 2, the cost components and the factors affecting them are considered. The identified cost components are classified in section 3 into three categories. Finally, section 4 concludes the paper and outlines the directions for further work.

2 Hybrid Cloud Infrastructure Cost

In this section, we decompose the costs of hybrid cloud infrastructure into cost components based on the resource whose usage incurs these costs, and consider different factors that may have an effect on the identified cost components.

An organization can allocate the workload to the private and public portions of a hybrid cloud in two ways. In case the organization deals with the workload of heterogeneous nature, the allocation of workload to the infrastructure can be based on the workload type: for instance, the tasks involving sensitive data or having carrier-grade performance requirements may be assigned to the private infrastructure, while less critical tasks tolerating occasional delays may be allocated to the public infrastructure. Alternatively, in case the workload is homogeneous, the organization may decide on where to allocate the workload on the fly, depending on the current load - e.g. by offloading the peak load exceeding the private capacity to the public cloud, and using the private infrastructure otherwise. For simplicity, in this paper we will assume the presence of homogeneous workload and hence the second type of allocation.

The cost of the hybrid cloud infrastructure can be decomposed into the cost components according to the capacity provided by the cloud and charged for. Taking the Amazon Elastic Compute Cloud (EC2, `http://aws.amazon.com/ec2/`) as an example of the cloud infrastructure offering, the cost components include the costs of computing, persistent storage, data communications, load balancing, and monitoring. The cost incurred by each component is determined by the usage patterns, the charging scheme applied, and other factors considered below.

Dependency on the demand/usage. The cost of an infrastructure capacity can be estimated as a product of i) the volume of the capacity charged for and ii) the unit cost of that capacity (taking into account the time of expected usage as well as possible reservation charges and volume discounts).

The volume of the capacity charged for depends on whether the capacity belongs to the private or to the public portions of the cloud. In the private cloud, the capacity is usually acquired up-front, configured and integrated, and then operated and maintained throughout its lifecycle. Its cost is proportional to the amount of resources acquired, and hence is proportional to the maximum demand it serves. The private cloud costs are rather independent of the actual degree of utilization (in fact, power consumption is affected by the computing load, but the effect is not dramatic [2]).

The capacity charged in the public cloud depends on how much the capacity is used. Its consumption can be measured on hourly or monthly basis, based on counting the number of virtual instances (e.g. computing capacity), on counting the volume of data (data communications and storage), or on whether the capacity is used or not during the period of interest (e.g. load balancing). As could be seen, the cost of public cloud infrastructure depends on the capacity usage patterns. The computing and data communication capacity are taken into use upon need and released as soon as the computing task or data communication is completed; the capacity usage is therefore likely to follow the peaks and drops in demand. On the other hand, the persistent storage capacity, once used, is likely to remain used for a long period of time; hence, the capacity usage is likely to exhibit eventual growth rather than fluctuations.

Time dimension. The continous growth of the computational power of hardware is likely to result in eventual decline of the prices for infrastructural resources. Indeed, Amazon cut the prices of on-demand instances by 15% in November 2009[1] and the data transfer prices by 20% in July 2011[2]. Therefore, some researchers assume the prices of public cloud infrastructure resources to decline by 15% on a bi-annual basis [3].

Similarly, the equipment procured for the private cloud is subject to price reductions, due to accelerating price-performance ratios in computing power (expressed by Moore's law), bandwidth availability (expressed by Gilder's law), and storage capacity (the GB-per-dollar ratio has been doubling every 14 months[3]).

---

[1] `http://aws.amazon.com/about-aws/whats-new/2009/10/27/announcing-lower-amazon-ec2-instance-pricing/`

[2] `http://aws.amazon.com/about-aws/whats-new/2011/06/30/aws-announces-new-data-transfer-pricing/`

[3] `http://www.mkomo.com/cost-per-gigabyte`

Besides the pricing trends, the time value of money should be taken into account when assessing the costs of both the private and the public cloud infrastructure. In particular, the net present value (NPV) of cash flow over time can be estimated [7]. Generally, the NPV analysis favors the public cloud option, due to the decaying factor applied to the future expenses as compared with the up-front costs.

3 Types of Cost Components

The contribution of the cost components above to the overall costs and their effect on the cost-efficient division between the private and the public cloud infrastructure depends on whether a cost is incurred due to the interaction between the private and public portions of the private cloud. Therefore, in this section, the costs components are divided into the categories of: i) the constant costs due to the adoption of a hybrid infrastructure, ii) the costs depending on the usage of the private or public portions of the hybrid infrastructure, and iii) the costs depending on the interaction between the private and public portions of the cloud, which are considered separately below.

Constant costs due to the adoption of a hybrid infrastructure. Belonging to this category are the invariable costs incurred due to the adoption of cloud, whose value is rather independent of the intensity of use - and hence independent of the specific division between the private and the public clouds. These costs can be exemplified with the costs of Amazon EC2 elastic load balancing or detailed monitoring service, which are charged independently on how intensely the infrastructure is used. These cost components depend partly on the maximum expected demand and the specifics of the service: for instance, given the maximum demand below a certain limit and best effort service quality guarantees, the elastic load balancing may be unnecessary.

Being independent on the usage, these costs do not affect the optimal division between the public and private cloud. Still, the presence of these costs may rise the cost of the hybrid cloud infrastructure, thereby potentially making the private or public cloud the cost-efficient solution. Thus, taking these costs into account is important.

Costs incurred due to using private or public cloud infrastructure. The costs of the components in this category, exemplified with the cost of computing capacity, vary depending on how intensively they are used. More specifically, with respect to the private portion of the infrastructure, these costs depend on the amount of capacity acquired up-front, and therefore depend on the maximum demand that the private infrastructure is expected to serve. With respect to the public portion of the infrastructure, the costs depend on the amount of capacity that has been consumed over the charging period.

These costs are affected by the split of the load between the private and the public portions of the infrastructure: the smaller the threshold demand served with the private infrastructure, the less the amount of equipment to acquire and operate in-house, the greater the portion of public infrastructure that needs to be provisioned on demand. The cost-efficient division between the private and the public portions of the infrastructure is achieved when the time of using the public infrastructure is inversely proportional to the premium charged by the public infrastructure service provider. It has two implications: i) the greater the premium, the greater the portion of private cloud infrastructure, and

ii) the greater the fluctuation of the demand, the greater the cost benefit of the hybrid cloud as compared with the fully private cloud infrastructure [8,4].

It should be noted that, whereas the computing resources are released as soon as computing task is completed, the demand for persistent storage capacity often accumulates over time. In this scenario, the storage consumption can be approximated as a monotonically increasing function of time (compare with the fluctuating demand for the computing capacity). Thus, assuming that the overall volume of storage can be predicted correctly, the cost of storage depends on the cumulative storage capacity consumed - i.e. effectively on the actual usage. It can be shown that in this case, assuming that the private and the public cloud storage capacities are acquired and charged with the same interval (e.g. monthly) and have the same unit prices, the total storage cost in the hybrid cloud stays constant independently on how storage is distributed between the private and the public infrastructure. As a result, the cost-efficiency of private vs. public storage in this case is determined by the pricing of the private and public infrastructure (including volume discounts), and the intervals between storage acquisitions.

Costs depending on the interaction between the private and public cloud. These costs depend not only on the intensity of using the private and the public infrastructure, but also on the intensity of interaction between the two. Such interaction affects, e.g., the costs of data communications and the costs of persistent data storage.

Consider first the data communication costs. Let us assume that the intensity of the interaction between the private and the public portions of the hybrid infrastructure is reflected in the volume of data transfered between them. It was found that, the greater the intensity of interaction, the greater the private portion of the hybrid infrastructure that should be acquired in order to minimize the overall costs [4].

The use of persistent storage may as well incur an interaction between the private and the public clouds. Two illustrative scenarios can be envisioned:

- *No interaction.* The service-related data is persistently stored by the private and the public clouds independently, with no replication or synchronization between the two. In this scenario, the storage costs will be incurred by the private and the public clouds independently, and will therefore belong to the second cost category.
- *Intense interaction.* The data is stored in the private cloud, and a full replica is stored also in a remote public cloud, to mitigate the risk of losing the data if stored in a single physical location. In this scenario, the interaction is rather intense, and hence the storage costs belong to the third category.

4 Conclusions

In the previous sections, the generic framework for the costs of using a hybrid cloud infrastructure has been introduced. The framework accounts for various cost components, including the costs of computing capacity, persistent storage, data communications, load balancing, and monitoring. A number of factors affecting these cost components have been identified including demand fluctuation and dynamics, the unit costs and demand elasticity of the unit prices, as well as the evolution of the above factors in time. Based on the possible effects of these factors, the cost components are classified as the constant costs, the costs depending on the usage of private or public clouds, or the costs depending on the interaction between the private and public portions of the cloud.

Among the factors affecting the costs, only the workload division between the private and the public portions of the cloud infrastructure is controlled by the organization using the cloud services, whereas the others are external variables mainly determined by the end-customers (shaping the demand) or by the cloud service providers. Therefore, the organizations using cloud infrastructure services can seek a cost-efficient solution by adjusting the workload division between the private and the public clouds.

Due to the effect of fluctuating demand, the costs of computing capacity and data communications are often minimized by using the hybrid cloud. Meanwhile, as the demand for persistent storage usually accumulates over time, the storage costs are at their minimum in case the private cloud only is used. Furthermore, since the overall storage cost is relatively independent on how the storage is distributed between the private and the public clouds, as compared with the costs of computing capacity and data communications costs, the latter largely determine the shape of the total cost function. As a result, the minimum of total cost is usually achieved by using a hybrid solution.

In future work, the proposed framework shall be extended by taking into account the growth of customer demand, caused either by the growth of customer base or by intensified usage of individual customers. The framework shall be also validated by applying it to analyzing the costs of hybrid cloud infrastructure in real-world scenarios.

References

1. CIO Magazine. Cloud computing survey. Tech. rep., CIO magazine (June 2009), `http://www.cio.com/documents/whitepapers/CIOCloudComputingSurveyJune2009V3.pdf`
2. Greenberg, A., Hamilton, J., Maltz, D.A., Patel, P.: The cost of a cloud: research problems in data center networks. SIGCOMM Comput. Commun. Rev. 39, 68–73 (2008)
3. Khajeh-Hosseini, A., Greenwood, D., Smith, J.W., Sommerville, I.: The cloud adoption toolkit: supporting cloud adoption decisions in the enterprise. Software: Practice and Experience 42, 447–465 (2011)
4. Mazhelis, O., Tyrvinen, P.: Economic aspects of hybrid cloud infrastructure: User organization perspective. Information Systems Frontiers, 1–25 (2011)
5. Mell, P., Grance, T.: The NIST definition of cloud computing. Version 15, National Institute of Standards and Technology (July 10, 2009), `http://www.csrc.nist.gov/groups/SNS/cloud-computing/` (2010)
6. Pring, B., Brown, R., Frank, A., Hayward, S., Leong, L.: Forecast: Sizing the cloud; understanding the opportunities in cloud services. Gartner Dataquest (March 18, 2009)
7. Walker, E.: The real cost of a cpu hour. Computer 42, 35–41 (2009)
8. Weinman, J.: Mathematical proof of the inevitability of cloud computing. Working paper (January 8, 2011), `http://www.joeweinman.com/Resources/Joe_Weinman_Inevitability_Of_Cloud.pdf` (last retrieved on October 28, 2011)
9. Weinman, J.: Time is money: The value of "on-demand". Working paper (January 7, 2011), `http://www.joeweinman.com/Resources/Joe_Weinman_Time_Is_Money.pdf` (last retrieved on October 28, 2011)

Strategic Success Factors in Customization of Business Software

Tobias Tauterat, Lars Oliver Mautsch, and Georg Herzwurm

Universität Stuttgart, Chair of Information Systems II (Business Software)
Keplerstraße 17, 70174 Stuttgart, Germany
{tauterat,mautsch,herzwurm}@wi.uni-stuttgart.de

Abstract. Customers often ask software vendors for business software customized to their needs and fitting into the existing application landscape. But unlike other areas of research there are just a few isolated results about the factors, which promote success of companies offering customization services for business software and which can serve as a guideline. This paper tries to overcome this weakness by presenting the results of a qualitative exploratory study conducted with German and Swiss software companies in 2011.

Keywords: Bespoke software, business software, custom software, customizable software, customization, degree of customization, expert interviews, software product management, strategic success factors.

1 Motivation

Despite actual economic and financial crises the demand for software products and related services is still growing, particularly concerning business software. [1] Software companies within this sector face an increasing (competitive) pressure within a customer dominated marketplace (see e.g. [2] and [3]). Customers are often asking for software based solutions customized to meet essential business needs and implemented into the surrounding information system of their companies to generate the benefit they expect from their investment in business software. In addition, following the generally accepted sociological megatrend of customization, [4] several studies and publications confirm the relevance of customization of (business) software products (see e.g. [5] and [6]). But unlike other areas of research for example best practices in general business management [7], [8], software development [9] or management of software projects [10], just a few isolated results exist about the factors, which promote success of companies offering customization services for business software. We call them strategic success factors.

In order to close this knowledge gap, this paper presents the results of a research project targeting on the identification and analysis of strategic success factors in customization of business software.

For the purpose of this paper customization in the context of business software will be defined as the alignment of business software to suit the individual needs, business

M.A. Cusumano, B. Iyer, and N. Venkatraman (Eds.): ICSOB 2012, LNBIP 114, pp. 267–272, 2012.

specific requirements and application landscape of customers. [11] Hereby the degree of customization can range from more or less trivial and customer-unspecific modifications to customer-specific development of bespoke software. [6]

2 Research Design

Based to the findings in chapter 1 the central research question within this research project is: "What are strategic success factors in customization of business software?" As shown before, there were no sufficient results, which could be analyzed to answer this research question. Thus, for this research project an approach has been chosen, which consists of two consecutive research subprojects to answer this question. [12] The first research subproject was to identify and analyze any kind of strategic success factors in customization of business software by a qualitative exploratory research method. This subproject has already been finished. Its research design and results will be presented within this paper. For the second subproject a quantitative research method has to be chosen, to prioritize and confirm the identified strategic success factors determined by the first subproject.

To reach the goals of subproject one, a qualitative exploratory research method, more precisely guided expert interviews have been selected and its execution was conducted in four sequent steps: Literature review; Elaboration of the interview guideline; Preparation and realization of the expert interviews; Analysis of the gathered data and clustering of the results (strategic success factors).

The literature review should help to generate new knowledge as well as confirm and refine existing knowledge within the context of customization. The results of this literature review were input for the elaboration of the guideline for the semi-structured interviews.

The interview guideline, containing different open questions, should help to semi-structure the expert interviews so that their output could provide a comparable input for the succeeding analysis of the gathered data. [13]

For these interviews the partners were selected using two criteria: First they need to work for a company that customizes business software to the needs of customers. In addition they must have strategic insights into their companies business to be able to discuss the questions regarding strategic success factors. The role of software product managers (for a description of its tasks see e.g. [14]) can be exemplary for the selected interview partners. Using an internal database of the Chair of Information Systems II (business software) at the University of Stuttgart 136 possible candidates engaged at German and Swiss software companies were identified and contacted via email and telephone. The total sample of 16 responding experts was interviewed within separate appointments of 30 till 90 minutes.

The gathered data, namely transcripts, was analyzed and structured using the method of content analysis (for a detailed description see [13]) to identify the possible strategic success factors in customization of business software. Using this systematical type of analysis 16 strategic success factors could be identified. In the last step the strategic success factors were clustered contentwise into areas. [15] Each of these areas consists of several strategic success factors, which can be seen in fig. 1.

3 Strategic Success Factors in Customization of Business Software

As mentioned in chapter two, the goal of this research subproject was to identify and analyze strategic success factors in customization of business software and not to prioritize or validate them by counting the frequency mentioned. This will be the major task for the second subproject. Although it can be stated, that some strategic success factors such as *direct contact with end users* or *identification of customization needs* had been mentioned by almost all experts and some such as *uniform software standards* or *continuous customization* just by a few ones.

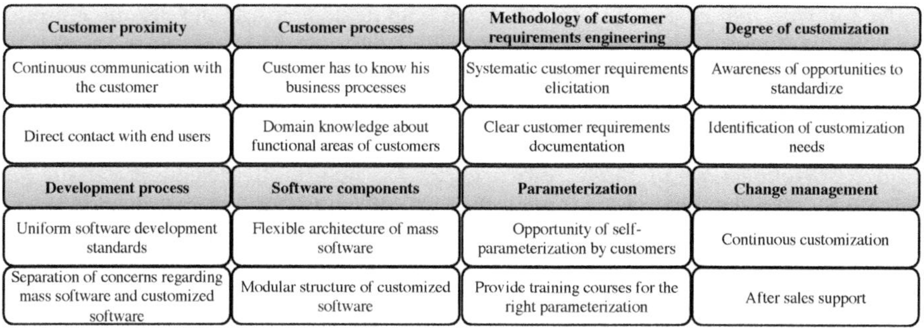

Fig. 1. Identified strategic success factors in customization of business software

3.1 Outline of the Identified Strategic Success Factors

Considering the 16 strategic success factors determined by this research project (see fig. 1), the question arises whether all of them are specific for the customization of business software. But, even though there might be success factors which are equally applicable in other domains, the question arises whether they still are of (high) importance for the customization of business software and therefore need to be mentioned or not. It can be stated that four of the identified strategic success factors are more or less specific for customization: The strategic success factors within the areas *degree of customization* and *parameterization*. The remaining twelve strategic success factors are already known from other disciplines like requirements engineering [16], software product lines [17], software engineering [18] and agile product management [19]. Because of the fact that they were explicitly named and described in the context of the customization of business software by experts they have been analyzed again and identified as important. But due to the lack of space, just a short summary of the unspecific strategic success factors will be given within this subchapter. This paper concentrates on the customization-specific strategic success factors, which will be analyzed in further detail within chapters 3.2 and 3.3.

A key area in customization of business software is the *customer proximity*. *Continuous communication with the customer* and *direct contact with end users* allows to obtain information about the business of the users more easily. In addition, the involvement of users in the customization process, the user acceptance of customized business software can be increased.

To achieve success in the context of *customer processes*, the *customer has to know his business processes*. By the detailed knowledge about his business processes he is able to define precisely what he would like to have represented within the customized business software. Having *domain knowledge about functional areas of customers* affected by the customization belongs also to this area and could help providers to simplify the correct recording and detailed analysis of the processes.

Systematic customer requirements elicitation and *clear customer requirements documentation* can help customization providers to gain knowledge about the customization needs at customers' side.

Uniform software development standards and *separation of concerns regarding mass software and customized software* can help to standardize and decouple product and customization development and subsequently increase procedure speed and quality of customization processes.

Strategic success factors dealing with the structure, characteristics and usage of customized software components can be arranged in the area *software components*. *Flexible architecture of mass software* can be helpful to design mass software inherently flexible and open, if it is used as a platform for customization and *modular structure of customized software* can support future customizations because existing modules can be reused in several software products and so the development efforts can be reduced.

Due to the longevity of business software, improvements and extensions of customizations triggered by changing customer requirements can be necessary at any later stage in time. These facts are represented by the strategic success factors *continuous customization* and *after sales support*, which were assigned to the area of *change management*.

3.2 Degree of Customization

The strategic success factors in this area build upon the interaction between the provider of business software and the future users of the customized software. This interaction should help to acquire knowledge to identify the appropriate degree of customization for the user. An appropriate degree of customization can be determined by the strategic success factors: *Awareness of opportunities to standardize* and *identification of customization needs*. The reason for a pre-determination of the degree of customization is that it should be made sure, that the supplier accepts only customization orders he is able to fulfill.

For example a supplier just offering parameterizable software will reject a request of the customer to map every single individual process within the business software. In most cases it is not possible to reach this goal with the help of parameterizable software. Therefore it would make no sense for the success of customization that this supplier realizes this type of project: He cannot fulfill the requirements of the customer and that in turn would result in the fact that the customer would rate customization as unsuccessful. For providers offering any kind of customization services, the determination of the degree of customization can also influence success of customization: It can provide the basis for the decision what kind of customized software is suitable for certain users. Customization efforts can be avoided by choosing the right type of customized software. For example code modifications might not be necessary for certain customers.

To receive an appropriate degree of customization for the user, knowledge about customer requirements and to what extent he would like to use customized software as a distinguishing feature from his competitors can be collected at the beginning of customization through communication with the user in pre-workshops or briefings. In addition it is important that the customer knows about his requirements. He already has to have some ideas in advance what he would like to have mapped with the business software and whether processes should be standardized by business software, which were not standardized before. With the help of this information the provider must be able to assess by his knowledge, what must be customized for the particular user and whether something can or should be standardized. Based on these decisions the appropriate type of customized software can be determined.

3.3 Parameterization

Two strategic success factors, which refer to a special degree of customization, the parameterizable software, could be identified by the content analysis of the expert's interviews. These are the strategic success factors, *opportunity of self-parameterization by customers* and *provide training courses for the right parameterization*. For the process of the customization, this means that the customer receives knowledge about the different possibilities for the parameterization of the referring business software. The customer learns how he can modify business software according to his special needs in an effective and efficient manner.

Opportunity of self-parameterization by customers: The idea behind self-parameterization is, that providers do not need to intervene in the customization process, because users are able to adjust their business software by their own by setting pre-defined parameters. Two types of parameters can be distinguished by the level of IT-skills needed for self-parameterization: Parameters, which should only be changed by users with focus on IT administration and adjustments, which normal end users can do without asking the IT department for advice. Examples for the first case could be structural changes of input masks or settings of application-wide security parameters. Changes of the spelling of numbers or of bank account settings can be examples for the latter case. Beside the self-evident fact that self-customization is a sales argument providers can realize staff savings by outsourcing small customizations to their customers.

Provide training courses for the right parameterization: If users want to do self-customization they have to have the necessary knowledge and skills. This specialized knowledge can be transferred to customers with the help of special training courses. Within these courses customers learn how the software can be basically customized, which specifics must be considered and which best practices exist for specific use cases. Thus the provider of the business software can influence the success of customization by offering appropriate training classes.

4 Outlook

With the results presented in this paper the first research subproject is completed. For further continuation of the research project the next step is to validate the qualitatively ascertained strategic successful factors in customization of business software by a quantitative research method through the second research subproject. This subproject has already been started. The goal of such a quantitative data acquisition is to validate the strategic success factors and thus eliminating various points of criticism of the success factor research by a high number of samples, by standardization of the questions, and by more objectivity. After the elevation and validation of the strategic success factors in customization of business software this research project can serve as input to achieve two possible goals: To put up recommendations for action and to analyze them and/or to explore the cause and effect relationship between the strategic success factors.

References

1. BITKOM e.V., http://www.bitkom.org/68301_68295.aspx
2. Messerschmitt, D.G., Szyperski, C.: Software ecosystem. MIT Press, Cambridge (2003)
3. Kilian-Kehr, R., Terzidis, O., Voelz, D.: Industrialization of the Software Sector. Wirtschaftsinformatik 49 (Sonderheft), 62–71 (2007)
4. Bidgoli, H.: The handbook of technology management. Wiley, New Jersey (2010)
5. Helferich, A.: Software Mass Customization. Josef Eul Verlag GmbH, Köln (2010)
6. Herzwurm, G.: Kundenorientierte Softwareproduktentwicklung. Teubner, Stuttgart (2000)
7. Cusumano, M.A.: Staying power. Oxford University Press, Oxford (2010)
8. Peters, T.J.: In search of excellence, Lessons from America's best-run companies. HarperCollins, New York (2008)
9. Sangwan, R., Bass, M., Mullick, N., Paulish, D.J., Kazmeier, J.: Global Software Development Handbook. Auerbach Publications, Princeton (2006)
10. Reel, J.S.: Critical Success Factors In Software Projects. IEEE Software 16(3), 18–23 (1999)
11. Reichwald, R., Piller, F.: Interaktive Wertschöpfung. Gabler, Wiesbaden (2009)
12. Creswell, J.W.: Research Design: Qualitative, Quantitative, and Mixed Methods Approaches. Sage Publications, Thousand Oaks (2003)
13. Jäger, U., Reinecke, S.: Expertengespräch. In: Baumgarth, C., Eisend, M., Evanschitzky, H. (eds.) Empirische Mastertechniken der Marketing- und Managementforschung, pp. 29–76. GWV, Wiesbaden (2009)
14. Bekkers, W., van de Weerd, I., Brinkkemper, S., Mahieu, A.: The Influence of Situational Factors in Software Product Management: Empirical Study. In: Second International Workshop on Software Product Management (IWSPM 2008), Barcelona, Catalunya, pp. 41–48 (2008)
15. Bailey, K.D.: Methods of Social Research. Free Press, New York (1994)
16. Pohl, K.: Requirements Engineering. Springer, Berlin (2010)
17. Clements, P., Northrop, L.: Software Product Lines. Addison-Wesley Prof., Boston (2002)
18. Boehm, B.W.: Seven basic principles of software engineering. Journal of Systems and Software 3(1), 3–24 (1983)
19. Thomke, S., Reinertsen, D.: Agile product development: Managing development flexibility in uncertain environments. California Management Review 41(1), 8–30 (1998)

What Information on Business Parameters Is Required by Embedded Software Developers to Do an Effective Job?

Joakim Fröberg, Stefan Cedergren, and Stig Larsson

Department of Innovation, Design and Product Development
Mälardalen University, Sweden
{joakim.froberg,stefan.cedergren,stig.larsson}@mdh.se

Abstract. Embedded software design is tightly connected to the functionality and goals of the system it is used to control. For mechatronic systems such as an in-vehicle automotive system, software developers require information on the system goals including business parameters to effectively decide on architecture and functionality. This paper presents results from an case of developing a hybrid electric drive system platform, and presents the information areas that software and system engineers do perceive as important to effectively perform design. We note that business parameters are sought for and elaborate on what information is required. We analyze what these needs are and elaborate on how to address them by using methods from the literature. We conclude that the effort of developing embedded software cannot rely on statically specified business parameters; rather these would be estimated and refined by interaction throughout the development cycle.

Keywords: Embedded software, Software architecture, Pre-Study, Product-line.

1 Introduction

Embedded software is an important part of a mechatronic system such as an automotive sub-system. It is state of practice for automotive suppliers to provide sub-systems such as transmissions, engines, or brakes for many customers by using a configurable platform product. The flexibility of software is utilized to achieve variability to reuse complex sub-systems in different applications, e.g. many vehicle models. For a hybrid electric drive system most parts of the mechatronic system is controlled by embedded software and the structure and functionality of the software is tightly intertwined with the functional architecture of the system. For software developers and architects, it is important to understand the many goals and uses of the platform in order to effectively develop the software system.

In developing any complex system, the pre-study phase is important to establish parameters such as system requirements, usage context, constraints, and optimization criteria. We have performed interviews with system developers of a hybrid electric drive system platform and elicited the information needs those practitioners consider important to succeed in developing such a system. From the results we have analyzed the challenges related to software development of a platform that enables variability, customization to accommodate a product line of drive systems.

M.A. Cusumano, B. Iyer, and N. Venkatraman (Eds.): ICSOB 2012, LNBIP 114, pp. 273–278, 2012.

1.1 A Development Pre-study of an Automotive Sub-system Platform

For a platform or product line initiative, it is critical [1] to define the requirements and content of the reusable assets and to setup the development structure to achieve goals in reuse, costs, and time-to market. It is known to be an engineering problem to perform early phases of product definitions and requirements definition, but guidance and techniques are available in textbooks e.g. [4], [6].

The life-cycle of a platform product is different from that of a 'regular' product. The development of reusable assets may involve different customers, and often company strategy, complex configuration management and quality management is involved. The value and cost of platform assets are often more complex to estimate and can depend on projected production volumes, forthcoming customers, strategy, and other dynamic factors. When designing a platform, information on how to relate to the above-mentioned sources of complexity needs to be addressed.

1.2 Case Characteristics

The case company has previously developed a customizable hybrid electric drive system intended for only a few similar heavy automotive applications. The goal of the development effort is now to offer customizable hybrid electric drive systems to a large number of customers with a wider scope of applications. Embedded software is involved in all parts of the system as well as in all system wide functionality.

The developed drive system shall accommodate the following functionalities: Re-generation of motion energy, optimized performance of motion actuators, optimized combustion engine control, productivity enhancement. The increased ability to control electric components compared to conventional automotive components provide the possibility to develop new functions that improve or optimize performance. The customers' willingness to buy and introduce such a drive system is heavily dependent on what fuel effectiveness and performance can be achieved for their particular applications. The resulting software system is layered in a structure from low-level control up to higher levels of decision-making and strategic functionality.

The drive system is intended for use in many, and yet to some extent unknown vehicles involve problems of flexibility and system boundary. The design needs variability and flexibility enough to accommodate vehicles with radically different architectures, system decomposition and design philosophy. Examples of design solutions that may well differ is paradigms for fault handling, diagnostics, and modes of operation. Design of an automotive subsystem will involve these types of complexity.

Developing a drive system platform product is to be performed at the same time and coordinated with development of several drive systems for specific applications. Platform development is inter-twined with each individual development project and provides and receives information and assets. As the development progress, more automotive applications will be considered. It is not fully known which applications are to be developed and thus needs support from the platform.

1.3 Objectives of Study

The goal of this study is to describe the information needs in terms of business parameters in a case of developing a software platform for a complex automotive system; for what purpose and why do developers need business parameters in the development effort. Moreover, the objective is to identify known methods that can be used or could be adapted to tackle the information needs in such a pre-study phase.

Previously, we did a study to propose a method to find critical information in a pre-study phase for developing a complex automotive platform [9]. Part of the result was a listing of information areas that practitioners deemed critical to be able to design the system in an effective way. Strikingly, two out of five information needs expressed by developers were related to business parameters. In this paper, we use the results from our previous study, and describe and analyze the need for business parameters for embedded software developers involved in complex mechatronic automotive systems.

The method to perform the study was based on interviews. First we examined the development effort by performing exploratory interviews with eight line managers and project managers. The interviews were structured as open discussion around what challenges are faced and what the system is to do. The answer were documented and compiled into a problem formulation document that was reviewed by the interviewees. Secondly, we analyzed the problem formulation and listed the areas where some piece of information is missing in order to effectively develop the platform. Information needs were identified in five information areas around which practitioners expressed some level of concern. We elaborate on the problem of eliciting or estimating the information by studying related literature.

2 Challenges and Information Needs

The study gave us a listing of challenges as perceived by the interviewees in the case. We compiled all challenges that were given into six different categories.

Challenge 1. Eliciting all the complex requirements of any given heavy-vehicle application. An automotive product can be used in a number of different usage scenarios e.g. transporting goods on flat ground, or lifting material in a mine.

Challenge 2. Methods and process guidance for coordinated development of multiple drive systems. The method to systematically manage the development effort is reportedly a challenge. The overall idea is to reuse assets from a common drive system platform. The decisions on what and how to develop reusable assets must be kept on a strategic level outside the individual development projects.

Challenge 3. Deciding content and system boundary of the platform. A specific problem is the problem of deciding the scope and boundary of the drive system platform. What should be developed customizable to allow reuse and adapting to many applications, and what should be developed specifically in each case?

Challenge 4. Organizing people. A model for deciding on organization seems needed.

Challenge 5. Methods to estimate scope of applications. Many vehicles are imaginable as recipients of a hybrid drive system. Knowing what application will be targeted would enable selection of systems concepts. It is expressed that it would be difficult to take design decisions without these facts as optimization criteria.

Challenge 6. Methods to estimate business criteria. The idea with reuse is to minimize development effort for subsequent uses of the same technology. Interviewees express that the criteria for how much development effort is allowed, in order to be considered business worthy must be made known in order to plan and execute platform development.

We analyzed each of the six challenges and noted what information seems needed to enable the developers to do their job effectively according to their statements. We classified the information needs into five categories:

Info need 1. System content/boundary. In order to proceed with development of a platform hybrid electric drive system, information on the functional boundary of the platform is needed. Functional content and functional interface is requested.

Info need 2. Application scope. Information on what applications are to be developed and supported by the platform in the future. This can be based on the current customer base and company strategy.

Info need 3. Business model. A business model describes the mode of performing business; what is to be sold; who is the customer. For instance it is possible to sell engineering hours, components, or up-time. Technical decisions are made, based on assumptions around what business model is going to be employed.

Info need 4. Business criteria. Information on what constraints are imposed by the business context. There is a limit to what costs and development times can be accepted in order to meet business criteria. This information is dependent on predicted production volumes, investments, level of reuse etc. These business criteria parameters are likely dynamic over time.

Info need 5. Roles & responsibility. Information is needed on roles and responsibilities involved in decision-making in the development effort.

2.1 Discussion and Related Work

We note that two out of five information needs that practitioners point out are related to business parameters. We want to elaborate the need for business parameters expressed by info need 3 and 4 above: Business model, and Business criteria.

The developers state that the business model and business criteria must be made known for them to select technical concept and corresponding software architecture and controls strategy. For example, the time and cost limits for development may disqualify expensive or time-consuming concepts. At the same time these business parameters and constraints are in fact dependent on the performance and architecture of the system. For example, a higher time and cost limit is viable if the resulting fuel efficiency is correspondingly better. We conclude that the developers demand to know business parameters as if they were static is not viable; instead the business parameters and design decisions need to be increasingly accurately specified in an interaction between the company's business and development functions. Business and technical concept must be refined in parallel and both need better methods to perform estimations of outcome. At the same time, changing business parameters is bound to cause uncertainty when developing the system, as changing requirements would do.

We look at the need for business parameters and elaborate on which information is viable to define or estimate.

Developers desire knowledge about business parameters, but at the same time, the same parameters seems unrealistic to know beforehand. So, how should either the business parameters or the technical design be done? If the range and scope of the vehicles to employ the drive system platform were known and static, there would still be the issue to decide what functional boundary of the platform is suitable. Boundary would be selected based on cost comparison between development for reuse and one-shot development. In a real case the functional scope of the product line, the system boundary, the production volume, are all dynamic parameters that are not necessarily predictable beforehand.

We would like to devise a method to elicit or estimate the information that is needed. What methods exist? System Engineering texts e.g. [3], [4], [5] propose in a too general way, how to find business context. Methods for scoping are described by both Clements and Northrop [1] and Bosch [2]. Clements and Northrop [1] offer a guide as how to perform scoping of the coming applications. In order to get a method for precise estimations it seems likely that a specific method be devised for this company. Company strategy and customers may affect the estimates.

Thornell [7] describes different modes of performing business, but there is no guidance as to how to select a business model given a set of case parameters. The explicit act of modeling [8] the business parameters may help communication. The problem seems to be complex and our interviewee's express somewhat different notions on how business parameters are understood. One solution to unify developer team notions would supposedly be to model business parameters.

In a technical note from SEI, Chastek et al. [10] describes how a production strategy for product lines connects the business strategy with a roadmap for how to develop (produce) core assets and products. However, the report shows a method and an example, and no case study using the method is presented. In the case studies done, e.g. [11] and [12], several of the information needs discussed above are addressed. However, the need for business information is neglected in these studies and need as we have seen in our study more attention. The BAPO framework, presented by van der Linden et al. [13], is a model describing different aspects of product lines including business properties. An example illustrating the use is presented [13], but no case. Future work will include applying the BAPO model to the described case and other case studies to understand if there are general conclusions that can be drawn.

3 Conclusion

First, we acknowledge that software development and the selection of software architecture are tightly connected to the goals and functionality of the mechatronic system. Late involvement of software design is bound to create a lacking estimate of engineering effort that is needed by the other roles; managers and engineers of other disciplines. When software is involved in controlling most or all parts of a system, the software functionality and architecture makes for the same type of considerations as the overall system design.

We describe the case and present what information needs was reported. Similar cases of developing embedded software for complex automotive subsystems may benefit from our guidance if the information needs seem similar. We have described some of the problems in choosing and estimating business parameters and the interaction that needs to take place between business and technical roles.

Practitioners in our case express a need for knowing business parameters in order to effectively perform software and system design. In planning and executing a development effort similar to our case, consideration should be made to business model, business criteria.

Elaborating on future work we provide pointers to some relevant literature that may aid in successfully selecting and estimating business parameters.

Recognizing that business parameters are critical in an early phase of developing a software system for control of complex mechatronics could be one key to leverage complexity in an advanced product line effort.

Acknowledgments. This work has been supported by Swedish Energy Agency.

References

1. Clements, P., Northrop, L.: Software Product Lines-Practices and Patterns. Addison Wesley (2001)
2. Bosch, J.: Staged Adoption of Software Product Families. In: Software Process Improvement and Practice, pp. 125–142 (2005)
3. Department of Defense. Systems Engineering Fundamentals. Defense Acquisition University Press (2001)
4. Sage, A.P.: Systems Engineering. Wiley Series in Systems Engineering. John Wiley & Sons (1992)
5. Kotonya, G., Sommerville, I.: Requirements Engineering. Worldwide Series in Computer Science. John Wiley & Sons (1998)
6. CMU/SEI. A Systems Engineering Capability Maturity ModelSM, SECMM-95-01, CMU/SEI-95-MM-003 (1995), `http://www.sei.cmu.edu/reports/95mm003.pdf`
7. Thornell, H.: Spetsföretag. Uppsala Publishing House (2007)
8. Weilkiens, T.: System Engineering with SysML/UML – Modelling, Analysis, Design. The MK/OMG Press (2006)
9. Fröberg, J., Cedergren, S., Larsson, S.: Eliciting Critical Information in a Pre-Study Phase of Developing a Drive System Platform for Automotive Applications, Systems Engineering and Engineering Management for Sustainable Global Development (2011)
10. Chastek, G.J., Donohoe, P., McGregor, J.D.: Formulation of a Production Strategy for a Software Product Line. Carnegie Mellon University (2009)
11. Strobl, S., Bernhart, M., Grechenig, T.: An experience report on the incremental adoption and evolution of an SPL in eHealth. In: ICSE Workshop on Product Line Approaches in Software Engineering, Cape Town, South Africa (2010)
12. Takebe, Y., Fukaya, N., Chikahisa, M., Hanawa, T., Shirai, O.: Experiences with software product line engineering in product development oriented organization. In: 13th International Software Product Line Conference, San Francisco, California (2009)
13. van der Linden, F., Bosch, J., Kamsties, E., Känsälä, K., Obbink, H.: Software Product Family Evaluation. In: SPLC (2004)

Existing System Solutions Redeployment in Remote Developing Country: Lessons Learnt from a Multi-national IT Consulting Firm

Yi Wang

Department of Informatics, University of California, Irvine, CA 92697, USA
yiw@ics.uci.edu

Abstract. As one kind of world economic shift, redeploying existing IT solutions from developed countries to developing ones now becomes common practice for many multinational IT consulting and service firms. The redeployment process may encounter many new challenges due to complexity of unfamiliar contexts with various uncertainties. Most project management literatures and best practices do not take this unique category of project into considerations, hence lead to gaps between theory and practice. This paper presents case studies on the practice of remote redeployment practices. Through analyzing collected data, we reported seven aspects that are essential for the success of these projects. The case study brings some novel results, some of them even contradict to that in textbooks.

Keywords: Redeployment in Different Country, Case study, IT Consulting.

1 Introduction

Redeployment of existing IT solution is an important type of information technology projects. In these projects, IT systems are customized and configured to fulfill the new clients needs. In recent decade, with the economy expansion in *BRIC* countries, the redeployment a mature system solution from industrialized nation to organizations in a *BRIC* country has been a common practice for many multinational IT consulting and service firms [1]. Actually, it is a form of knowledge transfer from developed countries to developing countries. Although this kind of redeployment projects brings numerous benefits (lower cost, short delivery time, etc.), many new challenges are proposed due to the radical change of contexts.

This type of IT project will keep increasing in near future. The enterprises in emergent countries have strong motivations to use successful IT solutions to improve their competitive advantages; the multinational IT service providers want to find new profit growth opportunities by leveraging their current mature solutions. In micro-level, the whole economic system will also benefit. All of these contribute to the continuous expansion of remote redeployment project market. With opportunities and challenges, summarizing best practice and developing systematic knowledge is necessary and urgent. However, as far as our current knowledge, there is no special literature addressing the project management issues on the redeployment mature

M.A. Cusumano, B. Iyer, and N. Venkatraman (Eds.): ICSOB 2012, LNBIP 114, pp. 279–284, 2012.

project in remote developing countries. Current project management literatures (e.g., [2, 3, 4]) on IT consulting/service project are generally context-free. The results (guidelines or best practices) are often generated in developed economies or pure outsourcing project. There is a huge mismatch between the continuous increase of remote redeployments and the relative few serious researches and practice reports.

This mismatch presents many research opportunities. For example, in the mature market, business practice and IT may not quite interfere each other in large extent, hence, IT project management practitioners does not need to care much about the prior [6]. However, the situation in developing market is quite different (e.g. less-skilled staffs, hybrid social and business environment). Therefore, it is suspicious whether the conventional wisdoms or best practices on redeployment still applicable. Besides, the system solutions may also not ready for the local needs, arising problems that never encounter in its original context.

Empirical results grounded by real world cases will bring more understandings on how the redeployments are executed in specific different contexts (in our study, a remote country). Some related study includes [6, 7, 8]. To achieve this goal, we report a multiple-case study design and findings in this paper. Our study consists of four different cases, covering the air transportation, banking, manufacturing, and public medical service industries. The major contributions of this study is as follows:

1. The study demonstrates the uniqueness of redeployment existing system solution in a remote developing country and provides first-hand evidences.

2. The findings summarized in this report enhance the understandings on the redeployment existing IT systems in a remote developing country. We identify the major factors that require special attentions in project management.

3. The findings of case study would bring further research benefits for replication and extension. It also can be the checklist for future project management practices.

2 Research Design

The target IT consulting firm is AITC, which is one of the leading IT consulting firms, running business in more than 100 countries. Its project process passed *CMMI* level-5 certification. In China, it has around 800 IT consultants with 10 regular subcontractors working for it (in 2009). It has been implemented over 700 projects since 2000. In most cases, its consultants work on clients' sites with clients' IT staffs together. Many of projects use solutions that are introduced from developed markets such as Canada or United States. In AITC, its organizational structure takes Matrix structure. Project team is often more dynamic than traditional functional-based team.

AITC's project evaluation system has four levels, from failed project to highly successful project. In fact, there is no project has been evaluated as "*Failed*" due to unspoken company politics. But there are about 10% projects being labeled as "***Problematic***" ones, which is the second worst level. We believe people can learn more from failures rather than successes. We chose four cases from them. The clients of them belong to four different industry sectors, making the case studies achieve high representativeness. We followed the standard multi-case study procedures in [9, 10]. For each case, we interviewed some key project staff. We had 3-5 interviews for each project. In total, we got 17 interviews (30-60 min. each).

3 Description of Selected Case

3.1 Alpha

Project Alpha was a business transformation project for a medium size public listed consumer bank to improve their performance through implementation a distributed banking system. After some preparations (requirements, design, evaluation), AITC team selected the Core-Banking system. The Core-Banking system was developed in United States and widely adopted by many middle size banks. It has been proved as a mature and successful business application. The project included both hardware (mainframes) and software solutions.

The alpha project was scheduled for 12 months (06/2008-05/2009) with 1-year free of charge maintenance provided by AITC and its subcontractor. In the initial stage, everything was pretty good: no hardware delay, successful pilot system. The original system only needed some minor revisions such as localization, UI changes. However, after most of branches deployed it, problems occurred. In the first two weeks of maintenance, nearly 100 times of out of service was recorded. The problem was identified as the high volume of transactions. Firstly, SICB is located in a province whose population is near 90 million (≈1/3 of U.S.' population). It has around 0.1 billion accounts, which exceeds the system burden in busy periods. Another problem is the habit of China account holders; they more tend to visit the branches to finish their transactions rather than using ATMs. The pre-sale and design team only considered the turnovers and profits scale. Obviously, it needed fundamental revisions to the system. It is impossible for current maintenance team. Considering the high *sunk cost*, SICB refused to give up, and threatened to put AITC into court. Finally, AITC had to organize another team (32 developers) to decentralize the system into 3 distributed data centers to balance load. 7 months extra efforts spent on it, and AITC also have to give 2 new servers to SICB for free. This project leads around 6,000,000CNY (nearly 0.9 million USD) loss to AITC. We also examines the documents of this project, we found the number of total identified bugs was still quickly increasing which means the system was not suitable for release. Final delivered system was still in high risk. It is very likely that some problems would occur sooner or later.

3.2 Beta

Project Beta is a Health Information System (HIS) project for a major public hospital (CPH for short) in Shanghai. This project was planned for 8 months. The HIS system was initially developed by AITC's US branch. This system (CMC) has been deployed in over 20 public medical service organizations. All stakeholders thought this was a simple project. The small contract reflects the optimistic attitudes.

The first major problem was caused by the differences on public hospital operations between United States and China. In China, public hospitals run both medical service and drug business, while U.S. hospital mainly focus on the prior. The original system does not provide enough support to the later although it performs very well in EMR. To track this problem, the project team had to develop a *"brand-new"* drug sales management system. To make the new developed system compatible to the original system, 6 months (equals to 3/4 of whole planned schedule) used to testing and revision. However, things were not ended. In China, there is a social norm that giving a small sum (around 200-500 USD) of money ("*Hongbao*" in Chinese) to the doctors who take charge of a treatment or surgery. Generally, the doctor will give a part of this money to the hospital. The hospital wanted the system has some functions to manage this money. But this kind of "gray income" is very ambiguous in law. Although it only needs to alter a small part of original system, this made the project team into a dilemma. If following the requirements, the project team may engage in some illegal action. If not, the client might refuse to accept the system and delay the payment. After consulting some legal experts, AITC agreed to deliver this function with official declaration for all possible legal responsibilities exemption issued by CPH. The project manager told us it would be finished in next 3 months.

3.3 Gamma

Gamma project aimed to develop a Kiosk system for one of China largest and busiest international airports (SIA). The Kiosk system provides self check-in service and real-time data collection and consistency checking. The project used a system developed by an AITC R&D lab in Canada. The system has been certified by the IATA and deployed in many North America Airports. The project team consisted of eight AITC consultants and three employees from subcontractor. The project contained two phases: the first phase was for hardware customization (Kiosks); the second phase was for system development and deployment. One consultant and two employees of subcontractor would take charge of following system maintenances and supports.

One of the major functions of the Kiosk system is to provide demographics to the airport for tracking traveler flow and other data analysis. However, the data it provided was different from the actual data reported by the airlines companies. It was sure that the numbers reported by the airline companies were right. The maintenance team had to go through all related source code but also found no problems. They also invited an expert team from Canada to Shanghai to identify this problem. And finally, they knew the data variance was caused by one China's unique air regulation which is "the international connected passenger ticket should be counted once rather than twice or more". The Kiosk counts the number purely according to how many boarding passes are printed, thus, makes the number is higher than the actual data. After identified the problem, the project team started to rewrite some source code. Some core source code had to be rewritten by the Canada colleagues, because no one in project team (even in the whole AITC China) knew CORBA well and the current license does not allow core source code changing. Although the problem finally solved, the maintenance budget was severely overspent due to the traveling cost and manpower. Besides, most revision code was not fully tested (budget problem), and the design of data collection modular was changed without an architect.

3.4 Delta

Delta project aims to develop an Automobile Parts Procurement Platform for a Local major auto manufacturer (SHV). Thanks to high market expansion, China's local auto producers have resources and willingness to using IT technology and process redesign to optimize their procurement. AITC has a lot of experience to build such kind of systems. It provided services to most of major auto manufacturers. This project is different from above 3 because there is no a ready full built system directly for deployment. The project team needed to build a new web based procurement portal by reusing the components developed in other similar projects. The power distribution in SHV is highly centralized. The CTO is the only person who has decision-making power. Both the IT staff and the consulting team were asked by him to alter the system and design every day although most of them are unnecessary or even bring damages to the system. During the whole project process, the chief architect changed three times. One AITC's senior executive had to direct contract SHV to solve every conflict.

Meanwhile, SHV was under a significant structure changes for acquisition of a company located in another city (around 300 km away). The project team did not know this in advance, for SHV must keep it as secret for stock regulations reasons. SHV asked the project team to redesign the whole system and to support multi-location logistic and stock management while keeping the smooth of the whole procurement process. Many prior efforts immediately became useless. The project team, even senior executive who takes charge of this project did not dare to say "NO" to SHV, for SHV is one of the biggest and most powerful clients of AITC China. Over 10 projects for SHV were running during that time. The company also cannot bare any failure in SHV, which may lead to significant damages to AITC China's business. The project team had to change their designs and implementations. Even the development team does not know which will be the final design. The client (SHV) also does not know what they want exactly. This project has been severely delayed. It has no apparent sign that it would finish in near future.

4 Findings

Table 1. Summary of main features of 4 cases

		Alpha	**Beta**	**Gamma**	**Delta**
Project Attributes	*Industry*	Banking	Medical	Air Trans.	Auto
	Est. Effort: *Actual:*	Medium Heavy	Small Small	Medium Heavy	Heavy Heavy
	*Duration** *(Planned/Actual)*	12/19	8/9	6/10 (2nd Phase)	18/29
Factors Involved	*Staffing*	✔	✔	✔	**
	Law and Reg.	**	✔	✔	✔
	Domain Know.	✔	✔	✔	✔
	Technology	✔	**	✔	✔
	Sys. Flexibility	✔	✔	✔	✔
	Org. Culture	✔	✔	**	✔
	Social Eco.	✔	✔	**	✔
	Moral Hazard	✔	✔	✔	✔
Project Status	*(At 03/2010)*	Finished	On-going (Delayed)	Finished	On-going (Delayed)

Notes: * in months. ** does not to indicate that there is no effect of these factors, but only show this effect is not significant for a specific project.

We summarized the main points of each case in table 1, with seven constructs extracted from collected data. They are *Staffing, Law and Regulation, Domain Knowledge, Technology, System Flexibility, Organizational Culture, Social Ecology, and Moral Hazard.* We map them to each project. Due to the page limitation, we have no enough space to discuss them with their implications. For more detailed discussion about them, please refer our technical report on: `http://goo.gl/P0Y3x`.

5 Conclusions

With the quick economic development in emergent economies, the remote redeployment project market will keep expanding in predictable future. Given the importance of these projects, it is necessary for project management research domain put more effort on it. But the current situation is not positive enough. There has been an obvious research gap between industrial practices and project management researches. Researches are not ready to provide guidelines to practitioners.

To address this research gap, we studied four typical remote redeployment projects in China. Each one represents an important industry sector. Our results suggest seven major factors influence the process of remote redeployment. The study provides some possible research directions and useful implications to the remote deployment practitioners. Our ultimate goal is to improve remote redeployment efficiency and effectiveness in complex new context full of uncertainties. For future studies, we plan to conduct a large sample survey to further verify our results, and replicate this study in some other contexts to examine the generalizability of our results.

References

1. International Data Corp. Application Development Software (2007)
2. Demirkan, H., Nichols, J.: IT Services Project Management: Lessons Learned from A Case Study in Implementation. Intl. J. of Pro. Org. and Manag. 1(2), 204–220 (2008)
3. Napier, N., Keil, M., Tan, F.B.: IT Project Manager's Construction of Successful Project Management Practice: A Repertory Grid Investigation. Info. Sys. J. 19(3), 255–282 (2007)
4. Wysocki, R., MGray, R.: Effective Project Management: Traditional, Adaptive, Extreme, 3rd edn. Wiley (2003)
5. Besner, C., Hobbs, B.: Project Management Practice, Generic or Contextual: A Reality Check. Project Management Journal 39(1), 16–33 (2008)
6. Djavanshir, G.R., Agresti, W.W.: IT Consulting: Communication Skills Are Key. IT Professional 9(1), 46–50 (2007)
7. Ratakonda, K., Williams, R., Biscegia, J., Taylor, R., Graham, J.: Identifying trouble patterns in complex IT services engagements. IBM J. of Res. and Dev. 54(2), 184–192 (2010)
8. Wang, Y.: An Exploratory Investigation on Refactoring in Industrial Context. In: Bomarius, F., Oivo, M., Jaring, P., Abrahamsson, P. (eds.) PROFES 2009. LNBIP, vol. 32, pp. 185–198. Springer, Heidelberg (2009)
9. Yin, R.K.: Case Study Research: Design and Methods (Applied Social Research Methods), 3rd edn. SAGE Publications (2002)
10. Easterbrook, S., Singer, J., Storey, M.-A., Damian, D.: Selecting Empirical Methods for Software Engineering Research. In: Guide to Advanced Empirical Software Engineering, Section III, pp. 285–311. Springer (2008)

The Evolving Structure and Function of Commercial Open Source Software Ecosystems

Donald Wynn, Jr.

University of Dayton,
300 College Park Drive, Dayton, OH 45066
dwynn1@udayton.edu

Abstract. Commercial open source software firms depend on an ecosystem consisting of individuals and organizations to develop and support the necessary source code, services, and delivery conditions. The structure and function of this ecosystem, as a social system and technological platform, evolves based on its membership composition and the ensuing differentiation and integration of these members' contributions. Based on an explanatory case study, we conclude that researchers and practitioners can benefit from an increased attention to these composition and interactions within a given software ecosystem.

Keywords: Software Ecosystems, Open Source Software.

1 Introduction

Contemporary software firms depend on a variety of consultants, service providers, and other partners to develop, integrate, deploy, and maintain a given enterprise software application. Each of these actors contributes services and/or products which are combined with the contributions by others to ultimately provide a portion of the net benefits available to the end-users. Software firms typically rely heavily on the creation of a network of complementary vendors and developers to provide software development, service provisioning, and other components of the 'whole product' associated with the development and commercialization of a given software application or platform. We refer to this network of participants surrounding a given application as a software ecosystem. In the current paper, we apply the software ecosystem concept as a means of developing an understanding of the evolving structure and function of a commercial open source software project. Commercial open source software (OSS) firms are characterized by the use of an open source licensing strategy combined with the use of commercial-grade development and service provisioning models [1]. These firms capitalize on several advantages of both traditional proprietary software firms and the newer open source model and have arguably become a dominant model for open source software development [2]. Using an explanatory case study approach, we develop a conceptual model based on to examine the evolution of a commercial open source software ecosystem and establish guidance on future research efforts in the area of software ecosystems.

M.A. Cusumano, B. Iyer, and N. Venkatraman (Eds.): ICSOB 2012, LNBIP 114, pp. 285–290, 2012.

2 The Ecosystem Concept in Ecology and Software

The concept of an ecosystem can be used as a metaphor to discuss various phenomena within social, organizational, and technological contexts. An organizational ecosystem can be described as a system of participants and resources that interact to meet the needs of the various participants. Several authors have used the ecosystem concept as a metaphor to discuss various phenomena within an organizational context. Moore [3] defines an ecosystem as "an economic community of interacting organizations and individuals – the organisms of the business world." Further, he states that these organisms "co-evolve capabilities around a new innovation." Iansiti and Levien [4] focus on the strategic management of different members in an ecosystem, particularly the keystone, defined as the dominant member of the ecosystem (e.g. Microsoft). Recently, several researchers have proposed similar definitions specifically for software ecosystems (See Table 1).

Table 1. Software Ecosystem Definitions

"The set of software solutions that enable, support and automate the activities and transactions by the actors in the associated social or business ecosystem and the organizations that provide these solutions." [6]
"A set of actors functioning as a unit and interacting with a shared market for software and services, together with the relationships among them." [7]

Metaphorically, a software ecosystem suggests an open system of various types of participants, a flow of energy and materials within and across a given boundary, and an emergent perspective that supersedes that of lower-level units. Consistent with these definitions, we define a software ecosystem as the components of the social system surrounding a given technological platform, including the users, developers, entrepreneurs, investors, and third-party service providers, and the interactions among them. The interactions among these actors and their coordinated contributions result in the products, services, and delivery conditions which provide the net benefits available for stakeholders to appropriate. We can translate this definition into a conceptual model consisting of the specific classes of actors in a given software ecosystem, along with the various products and services they provide. By identifying the interactions among them, this model highlights the structure and function of an ecosystem. Our goal in this paper is to use this conceptual model to gain an understanding of the evolution of an open source-based software ecosystem from its founding through growth and maturity.

3 Case Study Methodology and Site Description

We employed an explanatory case study methodology to investigate a commercial open source firm and the partners, investors, and service providers which combined their efforts to provide an enterprise-class software platform.[1] When we began

[1] The name of the firm and interviewees are not disclosed due to confidentiality agreements.

studying this ecosystem, it had been in existence for approximately five years and had experienced phenomenal growth in its developer and user communities. At its zenith, the ecosystem was composed of hundreds of partner firms and individuals, engaging in the development and maintenance of the source code as well as the provisioning of related services such as support, training, and integration. This ecosystem growth was paralleled by the central firm, which grew from a single developer into a large firm employing over 150 people in the United States and across the world.

To collect data, we conducted 19 semi-structured interviews with individuals throughout the ecosystem, including senior officers and other employees of the commercial OSS firm, external developers, end users, analysts, and service providers. We also collected secondary data from publicly available news reports, analyst studies, and message boards. We relied on a template coding scheme that included both theory-driven and inductively-derived codes [9]. Inductive codes were generated from evolving insight about the ecosystem's participants, resource and capital flows, and functional outputs, and modified or added as necessary. Reliability was tested by comparing the coding efforts of an additional coder to those of the author, and revising the scheme until coding matches exceeded 80% .

4 Case Narrative

The evolution of this particular ecosystem can be characterized by the distinct increase in the number and type of components present in the ecosystem, as well as changes in the role and interactions among these components. As larger numbers of actors contribute to the ecosystem, each with different production functions and consumption requirements, a richer set of exchange relationships and capital paths was established to match the increasingly complicated interdependencies. We can view this evolution in three loosely delimited stages: early, growth, and maturity. Each stage lasted approximately 2 years, culminating in the acquisition of the software firm by a larger commercial firm.

In the early stage, the key goal is not only to produce a working version of the software product and to attract more developers, but to sell the vision for the organization [3]. In the current study, the open source software project underlying the OSS ecosystem was founded by a software engineer who wanted to write a specific software tool based on his own interests in the technology. Two early decisions shaped the future of this project. First, he opted to release the code as an open source project in order to attract more contributors. Second, he also decided to build an service business around the platform, using some of the revenues to support developers involved in the open source project. The project was initially successful in attracting participants, including system administrators, users of the tool itself, and several developers (several of whom were essentially hired as employees).

However, the service firm went out of business due to an inability to obtain investment funds to continue operations. The hired developers were suddenly unemployed, many discontinuing their participation altogether. However, the software and the open source community surrounding it survived because it was held separately from the ASP business and was therefore not directly affected by the failure of a business operating within the boundaries of the ecosystem. Those participants who were attracted by the features of the software's architecture and source code, as well as the expertise and relationships inherent in the community, had not been expecting direct financial returns from their contributions so a lack of financial capital was not a significant detraction. These developers were able to carry on and continue building an application which was capable of providing the desired level of performance. They were also the initial service providers from which the revenues were generated. Because of the survival of the OSS community and the resultant community needs, the founder was able to create a new business revolving around training and documentation services. The components present in the early stage are shown in white in Figure 1.

Within a couple of years, the project and corresponding ecosystem had gained significant traction to entice a significant numbers of developers and users, growing to approximately 150,000 downloads per month. Although service revenues were growing substantially, the conservative strategy of funding the company from revenues and not taking on additional funding or debt put a cap on the firm's growth. Much of this changed as several seasoned executives were hired to manage and transform the operational and strategic aspects of the business. Based on the counsel of these executives, the firm enacted a number of initiatives which increased the flow of capital into the ecosystem. At the core of this strategy was the establishment of partner relationships to handle much of the non-scalable customer support requirements, enabling the firm to focus on development and third-level support, which carries dependable revenues and higher margins. Additionally, OEMs (original equipment manufacturers) and ISVs (independent software vendors) were signed to contracts to embed the firm's software into their products.

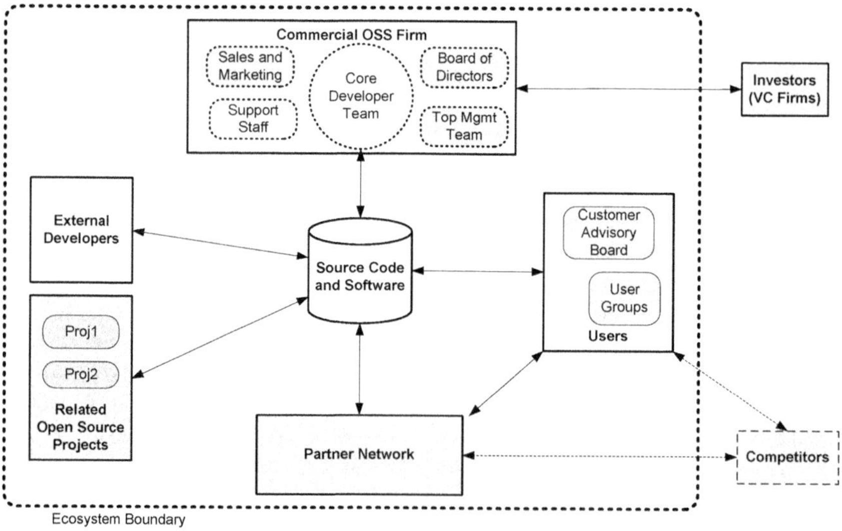

Fig. 1. Ecosystem Structure: Early Stage (white) and Maturity (shaded)

The firm obtained venture capital funding to ensure its stability. The firm also acquired several complementary open source projects by hiring the developers running them. In so doing, the firm was able to increase the number of contributors participating in the ecosystem surrounding their products while increasing its control over the future direction of these projects. For the newly hired developers, the acquisition of their projects enabled them to spend more time on development while leaving much of the administration to the POS firm. As a result of these initiatives, the firm was transformed from a small startup with a conservative, non-scalable business model to a viable corporation with stable, predictable revenues.

Figure 1 shows the changes in structure as the current ecosystem reached maturity, with participants arriving since the earliest stages of the ecosystem shown shaded accordingly. The evolution of the ecosystem results in larger numbers of diverse contributors, each with different production functions and consumption requirements. As a result of this rapid growth, the ecosystem achieved a critical mass and a very diverse, complex set of exchange relationships and increasingly complex interdependencies among the components of the ecosystem.

The firm's success also attracted larger competitors interested in the apparent profits available in this particular niche market. This heightened competitive pressure was a key factor in the firm's decision to be acquired by a larger firm. Following this acquisition, many of the members of the ecosystem and the relationships among them survived, albeit in a modified form as additional members and relationships were available through the acquiring firm's original ecosystem.

Table 2. Evolution of Ecosystem Composition by Stage

	Early	**Growth**	**Maturity**
Developers	Founder and developers from the community.	Core developers hired by the firm; growing external community.	Hired developers & leaders from acquired projects.
Users	Early adopters of the technology	First enterprise customers and OEMs as support options appear.	More enterprise customers as support options and reputation increase.
Service providers / Partners	Some developers hired to handle user requests.	Formal channel structure attracts large firms as partners.	Wide range of internal & external service providers
Mgmt Team	Founder only.	Experienced managers hired from outside firm	Management team evolves using VC firm contacts.
Investors	Funded by founder and financial partner.	Funded from revenues.	VC funding.
Competitors	Proprietary firms, but ignored by OSS firms.	Several other OSS firms move into the market.	Larger competitors entered the open source market.

5 Conclusion and Future Research

As the composition and diversity of the ecosystem's membership evolved (as shown in Table 2), along with the integration of contributions and inducements among the members, so do the capabilities and the stability of the ecosystem as a whole. To the extent that the conversion, production, and transportation of various types of capital, resources, and information among the members of an ecosystem are sufficient to encourage sustained contributions, the ecosystem is likely to be able to sustain itself. Thus, we conclude that both researchers and practitioners can benefit from an increased attention to developing and monitoring the changing membership and interactions within a software ecosystem.

Future researchers seeking to expand upon these findings may be able to expand upon these models by examining individual flows at a lower level of aggregation. Also, these findings may be replicated across other types of open source or proprietary software firms, or different software types (e.g. mobile application platforms). In much the same way as ecology depended upon a large number of individual studies focused around the ecosystem concept, the combination of a large number of studies across multiple platforms and industries may lead to a more complex, yet useful model of software ecosystems. It is our hope that the current study contributes to this effort.

References

1. Watson, R., Wynn, D.E., Boudreau, M.-C.: JBoss: The Evolution of Professional Open Source. MISQ Executive 4(3), 329–341 (2005)
2. Watson, R., Boudreau, M.-C., York, P., Greiner, M., Wynn, D.E.: The Business of Open Source. Comm. of the ACM 51(4), 41–46 (2008)
3. Moore, J.B.: The Death of Competition: Leadership and Strategy in the Age of Business Ecosystems. HarperCollins, New York (1996)
4. Iansiti, M., Levien, R.: The Keystone Advantage: What the New Dynamics of Business Ecosystems Mean for Strategy, Innovation, and Sustainability. Harvard Business School Press, Boston (2004)
5. Messerschmitt, D.G., Szyperski, C.: Software Ecosystem: Understanding an Indispensable Technology and Industry. MIT Press, Cambridge (2003)
6. Bosch, J.: From Software Product Lines to Software Ecosystems. In: 13th International Software Product Line Conference, San Francisco, CA (2009)
7. Jansen, S., Brinkkemper, S., Finkelstein, A.: A Sense of Community: A Research Agenda for Software Ecosystems. In: 31st International Conference on Software Engineering (2009)
8. Popp, K., Meyer, R.: Profit from Software Ecosystems. Books on Demand, Norderstedt (2010)
9. Boyzatis, R.E.: Transforming Qualitative Information: Thematic Analysis and Code Development. Sage Publications, Thousand Oaks (1998)

Differentiation in Freemium: Where Does the Line Lie?

Davide Semenzin, Edwin Meulendijks, Wilbert Seele, Christoph Wagner, and Sjaak Brinkkemper

Utrecht University
Department of Information and Computing Sciences
Princetonplein 5, 3584CC, Utrecht, Netherlands
{d.semenzin,e.meulendijks,w.j.seele,c.wagner1}@students.uu.nl,
s.brinkkemper@cs.uu.nl

Abstract. As the freemium business models is becoming a prominent success in the online software market, companies are challenged with the question of how to design freemium pricing schemata. This study investigates 17 freemium companies to help understand which features should be made available for free and which shouldn't. It is observed that the free-premium transition is typically marked by a significant increase in the privileges, access to value-creating gap-filling features.

1 Introduction

In the context of Software Product Management the problem of identifying and implementing an efficient pricing strategy is regarded as "one of the most critical decisions that a firm can make in the launch of a product." [1] A new pricing approach that leverages on customer-value has emerged under the name of *freemium*; companies adopting it provide a combination of products or services where one item is provided for free, and the complimentary item is sold at a price. Anderson [2] defines this business model as having "*a free version, which is made available to anyone who wants it in the hope that some users will then choose to upgrade to the premium version*" [2]. In particular, a premium version includes "advanced features, functionality, or related products and services" [3]. Pujol [4] defines freemium as a business model containing two "softly connected" (coupled) products or services. Niculescu and Wu [5] distinguish three forms of freemium models: feature-limited freemiums and time-limited freemiums, as well an hybrid form of these models which had the characteristics of both. Across all these instances comes the need for a differentiation strategy (DS) [4] between the free and the paid service.

1.1 Freemium and Pricing

Three differention strategies can be pursued: by quantity, by feature or distribution; in either case, there exists a distinction between the core of free features (FC

M.A. Cusumano, B. Iyer, and N. Venkatraman (Eds.): ICSOB 2012, LNBIP 114, pp. 291–296, 2012.

- Free Core) and the one of paid services (PC - Premium Core). This is as an instance of the general pricing problem of mediating between maximising revenues (pay for every service) and maximising attractiveness (give out everything for free); in the words of [6], the key is to create the right mix of features to segment out the people who are willing to pay, but without alienating the users who make up your free audience. We conducted a case study research on freemium-based success stories in order to determine whether there are shared characteristics among the two sets (PC and FC) in relation to the specific business, and what they may be. Hence the research question for the present study is: "*What are the differentiating features of a software product that mark the transition in the freemium pricing strategy of being free to collecting a premium?*

2 Research Approach

We adopted Bekkelund's [3] three-step set-up as a methodology to selecting cases in order to perform Qualitative Content Analysis (QCA). This approach was selected because it has proven to be fit and useful in researching within the specific domain, as the original paper was also about freemium. Due to the specific nature of QCA[1], this paper entails a subjective interpretation of the information shared from the chosen companies (we are assuming only one product per company).

First, a comprehensive set of cases that use the freemium model was assembled. A prerequisite for selecting a company is that it shared "extensively shared information" [3] about its freemium pricing model. Search engines were used to find suitable cases. Secondly, all cases found through the previous step were classified according to their relevance to the research at hand. Appendix 2 shows this list. It includes the product or company name, as well as an evaluation (Likert-5) of:

- accessibility of information (measured as the ease of access to the information on pricing on the website and its clarity);
- amount of information available (length of the information page, number of related pages, amount of details provided per pricing option, presence and number of use figures);
- whether the free and premium price models are easily comparable (i.e. if premium features are upgraded or added).

The third step merely constitutes executing the selection and compiling the final list. To improve the replicability of this research, current URLs of the case websites from which we extracted the information are provided.

We then classified the information on individual features along the free or premium and core or non-core axes. Whereas the definition of the terms free and premium is trivial ([4] offers a comprehensive overview), the one of core or non-core is not: we define *core features* as those features that scope the core business, and *non-core* as the features (such as "no ads" or an enhanced customer

[1] "A research technique for making replicable and valid inferences from texts (or other meaningful matter) to the contexts of their use" [7].

service) that are part of a value-adding package, but independent from the specific business undergoing analysis. This categorisation allowed us to measure and evaluate different products on a number of uniform metrics, e.g. feature names and limitations. For each company we also noted the free core package name, and what the core limitation were, qualitatively where possible. The paid core functionalities were listed per premium level, as products sometimes have often more than two-tiered plans. Non-core features were treated similarly, except for the "no advertisement" option, which constitutes a dimension of its own due to its strategic relevance. We classified each company with a 0 for advertisement in the premium version, 1 for no advertisement in the premium, and 2 for no advertisement in the free version to begin with.

2.1 Freemium Case Categories

In selecting the business cases we observed a remarkable number of different pricing structures, however, from the list of companies we had gathered some categories emerged, and the ones we found suitable and then selected for this research fall into the following four: cloud storage, music players, presentation tools and image sharing. This categorisation stemmed from the consistent nomenclature found throughout the research material (companies self-description, profiles, reports, etc.), and its rationale is to give a well-rounded account of the use of freemium in modern consumer applications.

- **Cloud Storage**: these products offer an online, syncronised and virtualised storage space with eventual consistency among data replicas. Dropbox rose to become a major player in the segment, with a market share of 14 percent as of Q4 2011 [8], only three years after the first release (October 2008).
- **Music players**: streaming services such as Spotify, last.fm or Grooveshark are redefining the end-user experience of personal music, leveraging on vast song libraries, ubiquity and personalisation.
- **Presentation tools**: cloud-based tools offer similar presentation design capabilities as desktop programs such as Microsoft PowerPoint or Apple Keynote, along with the advantages of cloud storage and social sharing features. A notable product is zoom-presentation software Prezi, which has proven a successful alternative to slide-based presentation tools.
- **Image sharing**: these services offer the possibility to upload and share images and videos. The largest player in this segment is Flickr, with 51 million registered members [9] as of 2011.

3 Results

Overall Trends. Observing the table in Appendix, a number of behaviours and patterns are immediately evident. Similarities are numerical to begin with: there is a significant overall price agreement among competitors, both in absolute terms (typically between 3 and 50 USD per month, absolute average: 11.12USD, average of entry premium: 8.89USD), and relatively to each premium level in the same segment; it is noteworthy how the growth of privileges (i.e. number and quantity of premiums) and prices is typically linear among levels of premium, whereas in all the measurable cases examined, the gap between the free package and the first level of premium was always at least one order of greatness. Prices grow linearly with privileges, allowing for an easy-to-understand schema, which in fact rarely contemplates more than two levels of premium (freemium is as much of a pricing strategy as it is a marketing tool), the exception typically being cloud storage services - that can afford a four-tier schema as a result of the simplicity of the priced good, as observed in Figure 3. In our sample the average number of premium levels was measured at 2.05 per vendor; storage products had an average of 3.0, opposed to the average of 1 in the case of image processing and 2 in the case of music players and presentation tools, confirming the theoretical stances.

Cloud Storage. Unlike the general trend that dictates up to two and only rarely three levels of premium, in the segment of cloud storage all vendors offer *at least* two levels of premium, and very similar numbers both in the prices and the size associated. As stated previously, the peculiarity of these services is a distinctively clear relationship between the price and the goods purchased: it is in fact mono-dimensional, contemplating only the actual storage space. Few to no extra perks are associated with the premium levels. All these factors contribute to a very uniform landscape. As noted before, there seems to be agreement on the fact that the difference between free and premium is at least one order of magnitude, whereas premium versions grow in a linear fashion. It was found that the average price-per-unit (uniformely Gigabytes) was 0.17USD, with a standard overall deviation of only 0.08USD, confirming the stability of the price-per-unit ratio. There is a steady pattern of linear evolution in prices distribution, which remains constant tier by tier and almost identical among competitors. This specific structure allows also for an extensible pricing model, free to scale up as per market request.

Music Players. In the cases at hand, there was a considerable gap between the free and the premium offer (10 vs. 730 hours per month, still one order of magnitude), whereas there was virtually none in the premium versions, which are in fact differentiated by perks such as mobile access, desktop clients and offline playback. The core product alone seems to be not enough to attract users to transition to premium; the pricing schema seems to support the stance that said main product has low marginal costs [3], allowing the company to focus instead on value creation outside the core feature. The extras are in fact very similar from one another, indicating alignment in the market and suggesting that all companies intend to leverage on a continuous, all-around user experience, actively trying to fill any gap (mobile applications "fill the gap" when the user is away from the computer, local cache when the user is offline, etc.) in users' lives that is left without music. A dramatic example of this strategy is represented by Grooveshark, a website that gives out the core music streaming service for free with no limitation whatsoever. Consistently within the sample, companies that run music players try to capitalise on the free segment by means of ads; Spotify efforts in this sense are particularly noteworthy, as the desktop application grew to become an all-round advertisement platform. In this context it is worth remembering how previous research in freemium models highlights that "the majority of users likely have no intention of ever becoming a customer" and that "it only makes sense to seek ways to benefit from and monetize their usage of the system. [?].

Presentation Tools. Inheriting the legacy of complex end-user programs, presentation tools offer a variegated landscape of options for personalisation and are typically advanced software products. As a result, it is far more difficult than it was in previous cases to establish a clear relationship between price and goods billed. A common metric used by vendors to advertise the distinctions among premium levels is storage space, which is significant because it carries another clear indication in support of the stance that successful freemium models charge support features, but not the core service the company is providing, no matter how sophisticated. Instead, along with a linear increase in storage space, premium levels focus on providing customer care and other non-core services aimed at conveying a more complete user experience. In the case of Prezi, a perk associated with the first paid transition is private storage; in this case it is interesting to notice how the free usage exploits the social layer, forcing non-paying customers to share all their presentations in the local community.

Image Sharing. Image sharing services appeared on the internet market significantly earlier than any of the other categories here examined; they have historically served the double purpose of remote storage and social sharing beacons, and their pricing strategy has to be understood in light of this bi-faceted nature. For instance, it is evident from the table that Flickr's preemium price represents a notable exception in comparison to the other services listed, being priced as much as three times the most expensive of the other services. What justifies a difference this dramatic? We argue an answer is to be found both in the overall product quality (Flickr is, under any possible metric, a much larger and complete product than any of the other competitors listed), as well as in the sharp focus Flickr has adopted in addressing the social and storage capabilities. It is, in other words, not just the quality of execution that makes up for the price, but it is also the precise focus on which execution efforts are conveyed. It is evident that imaging services offer typically only one level of premium, associated with limitless storage space and non-core perks and a mixed use of ads. In this context, the transition between the free and the paid core is once again marked by an increase in the main resource of one order of greatness or more. This applies to the core service (image upload) but not necessarily to additional services such as video uploads.

4 Conclusions and Further Work

Two significant observations can be drawn from the sample taken into consideration. The first finding suggests to make as much of the core service available for free as possible, with respect to keeping marginal cost per user as low as possible. The second observation is that differentiated freemium services create premium value by introducing extra features in the paid package, and that the precise focus on which of these extra features execution efforts are conveyed is mission-critical.

The main limitation of this study is identifiable in a very scoped sample size which purposely left out many other categories of online products or services using freemium (e.g. games, communication tools, one-click uploaders) Further leads for research include investigation of these categories as well, larger data set and trans-category comparisons and study of failure cases.

References

1. Harmon, R., Raffo, D., Faulk, S.: Value-based pricing for new software products: strategy insights for developers. In: Portland International Conference on Management of Engineering and Technology, Seoul (2004)
2. Anderson, C.: Free: The past and future of a radical price. Hyperion, New York (2009)
3. Bekkelund, K.J.: Succeeding with Freemium. Thesis (MSc.), NTNU School of Entrepreneurship (2011)
4. Pujol, N.: The Mind Share Market: The Power of an Alternative Currency. CreateSpace, unknown (2011)
5. Niculescu, M., Wu, D.J.: When Should Software Firms Commercialize New Products via Freemium Business Models? Under Review (2011)
6. Chen, A.: How to create a profitable Freemium startup, `http://andrewchenblog.com/2009/01/19/how-to-create-a-profitable-freemium-startup-spreadsheet-model-included/`
7. Krippendorff, K.: Content analysis: An introduction to its methodology. Sage Publications, Beverly Hills (2004)
8. OPSWAT: Security Industry Market Share Analysis, `http://www.opswat.com/sites/default/files/OPSWAT-market-share-report-december-2011.pdf`
9. Flickr company information sheet, `http://advertising.yahoo.com/article/flickr.html`

Definition of Open Data Services in Software Business

Yulia Tammisto[1] and Juho Lindman[2]

[1] Aalto University School of Economics,
P.O. Box 21220,
00076 Aalto
yulia.tammisto@aalto.fi
[2] Hanken School of Economics,
P.O. Box 479,
00101 Helsinki, Finland
juho.lindman@hanken.fi

Abstract. New software businesses are extending the software industry via private enterprises that build new and innovative services on top of Open Data (OD) sets released by government and public bodies. What are the tenable value propositions and income-generating mechanisms for these private enterprises and what are the new opportunities for service development? This paper combines conceptual and empirical investigations of OD definition to clarify the benefits open data sets hold for service development.

Keywords: Open data, open data definition, open data services.

1 Introduction

The prevailing wisdom is that new services and novel businesses can be created by opening up the data archives collected by government [3, 4, 9, 13]. Contrary to popular belief, releasing the data may provide value to society rather than limiting the archives to within its organizations. Organizations may create new ways to capture the benefits of this new value in the ecosystem by building new services. This is why also entrepreneurs push for OD policy initiatives related to government data sets. Opening of data for public use also provides a variety of new market opportunities for start-ups and other small companies.

However, it remains unclear what the term OD in this sense actually entails. We position our study in the field of research (see for example, [15]) that recognizes similar confusion as related to any new ICT innovations (some previous examples [15] of other novel technologies including case tools, intranet, and open source [12]. Furthermore, the confusion does not have to be considered only negative. Ambiguity of the exact meaning of OD may help a movement, a new process, or a tool to grow a usage base. This diffusion of innovation happens when consultants and business press are charting the business interest and potential, the demand in their customer organizations, and also, at the same time, defining the legal and commercial implications of the wide range

M.A. Cusumano, B. Iyer, and N. Venkatraman (Eds.): ICSOB 2012, LNBIP 114, pp. 297–303, 2012.

diffusion of the said phenomenon [15]. In short, both constructing meaning and building legitimate use for the new ICT innovation characterized by the term 'Open Data' in the industry. However, such ambiguity may also hinder the adoption by confusing some of the actors who might benefit from it, especially if the legal and commercial implications of opening the data remain unclear.

To summarize, we investigate a gap in the research literature related to defining the term OD in a way that would be both informed by relevant research and take into account how the term is currently applied in business. We address this issue by posing two research questions: one about the meaning of the term and the other about the arguments given to its benefits. The first question is: *What is open data*? The second question is: *What are the legitimizations for data openness*?

Our data set includes both small and large companies operating in the Finnish software sector to simplify the legal environment, but we posit that similar characteristics of the OD definition are likely in other legal contexts. We also note that there are political issues related to the OD definition, but we limit them outside the scope of this paper and focus on service development in commercial context.

2 Open Data Service as Software Business

According to the Open Knowledge Foundation [13], data can be called open if it can be, "freely used, re-used and redistributed by anyone without legal, technical or social restrictions." How the data is published determines its potential for re-use (for example, how well-structured the data is [1]). To improve data's usability, develop a service on the top of it one needs to convert it into open and re-usable format. This conversion requires resources and involves a number of technical challenges [2].

Latif et. al [10] provide one classification role in linked data publication that can be applied to both corporate entities and non-corporate actors, i.e.: persons, enterprises, associations, and research institutes. The adapted version of this classification and brief descriptions of the roles is as follows:

1. Raw Data Provider (or Data Provider) possesses and provides any kind of data;
2. Linked Data Provider (or Data Service Provider) possesses the expertise to convert the raw data into linked data machine-readable format;
3. Data Application Provider (or Application Developer) possesses the expertise to develop applications, visualizations, and mash-ups – all kinds of human-readable outputs, on top of data and linked open data.
4. End Users are persons who consume the data in human-readable format, not raw or unstructured data.

How to build a solid business model [6]? Latif et al. [10] offers a starting point for charting the roles of open data value chain and the service providers' business models. Building service-based business models on top of public good includes challenges [17, 18]. Open source [5] and innovation studies [11] identify different processes related to inbound acquisition and outbound data sharing/data publication.

The processes identified above describe the movement of resources (such as data) from an internal organizational environment to external and vice versa. Organizations can apply these approaches to generate and capture value by offering their internal assets externally, or by making use of external assets internally. Moreover, different third party organizations can build their businesses by helping to implement these processes.

3 Empirical Analysis

In order to answer our research questions about the meaning and benefits offered by Open Data, we chose several OD service providers and their customers for explorative interviews. The interviews were semi-structured and centered around the phenomenon of OD and elements of business models related to OD. Interviewees shared their perception of OD from their own business perspectives. To conduct the interviews and perform the analysis we applied an interpretive approach, as described by Klein and Myers [8].

Most of the respondents are from Finland and work for companies that build services on top of OD (Service Providers), or are the employees of the client companies of OD service providers (Data Providers). We conducted a total of 16 interviews including 5 sessions with small data service providers, 5 sessions with large data service providers, 5 sessions with a large data provider, and 1 session with a small data provider. Among interviewees there are CEOs, project managers, consultants and developers who deal with OD services in their companies.

4 Findings and Discussion

Coming back to the research questions: *What is open data*? and *What are the legitimizations for data openness*? our research indicates that the views on openness as well as views on the data varied between respondents from the different organizations. Interviewees also expressed a variety of opinions on how OD could be applied in their organizations. This points out that there is indeed a certain tension between policy documents surrounding OD and the empirical realities in the companies that actually build the services.

Talking about data openness some interviewees referred to externally open data – freely available for everyone. Others referred to internally open data – data that is only accessible by employees of an organization that provided this data. Another characteristic of OD that was frequently mentioned by interviewees was the technical format of open datasets. A number of interviewees distinguished several data formats or stages of data development. These formats correspond to the classification of roles in linked data development processes.

As expected, interviewees expressed distinctive opinions on what OD is technologically, legally etc. The two alternate opinions to this question, as expressed by the interviewees are: (1) data is open when it is published publicly (over the internet), and (2) data is open when it is distributed freely within one organization or a network of organizations (intranet or extranet). Results show a clear transition: the archives that were previously unused or closed within an organization or certain part of the organization are now being opened either to the public or to some particular networks, communities. In both situations, whether the data is available for everyone or just for several units of the same organization, the interviewees referred to it as OD. Moreover, many interviewees pointed out that the term OD is more about the process of application than about the opening of the data set itself.

OD can bring benefits when the data is opened and applied internally (within an organization or a network of organizations): *"It might be surprisingly big that an organization that opens its data might develop an internal tool, because the data from different departments, units will be available for use, then sharing of the data and collaboration between departments would become much easier. When the data is available it provides inter-operability between the departmental systems and it has a potential to change dramatically the way organizations work today."*

This also applies when data is opened externally (publicly): *"I think the added value comes from having more clever people look at it [data]. They [data providers] don't know how to deal with their data. In their case the added value comes from outsiders being more apt at doing that."*

During the analysis phase, we compared the ways of using data that is open internally to data that is open externally. As a result of this comparison we found substantial similarities between the ways of using internally and externally open data and consequently found similarities between corresponding aims of using OD. For example, the following aims of using OD to increase visibility of performance and assets, increase transparency, change organizational structures, and express organizational identity were similar as they involved improving the communication within an organization (in the case of internally OD) or society (in the case of externally OD). Table 1 contains an outcome of the comparison of why and how internally and externally open data is used.

Table 1. Compilation of interviewees' opinions on why to use internally and externally OD

Aims of using Internally Open Data	Aims of using Externally Open Data	Similarity
Increase visibility of performance and of assets	Increase transparency	Improve communication
Change organizational structures	Express organizational identity	
Change public sector	Benefit from combination of many datasets	Improve decision-making
Commercial use	Enable external contribution to service development and provision	Develop and provision new services
	Boost the economy	Create economic value

Accordingly, (on an organizational or internal level), an organization opens data internally to improve internal communication and decision-making, to support internal service development internally and expects monetary return on these activities. On a societal or external level, a national government publishes its datasets to improve communication between different organizations within society and to provide entrepreneurial minds opportunities to develop new services and grow the economy. Consequently, OD turns out to be a process that can appear on different levels of organization or society.

Interviewees distinguished different OD formats. OD service providers referred to three stages of data development, namely: raw data, linked data, and applications built on top of the data. All the interviewed data providers recognized two data formats: 1) raw data – "the data as it is" or as it was collected and 2) various data applications (services built on the top of data, data visualizations, and mash-ups). Some data provides also identified linked OD format, or, *"semantically enriched open data."* Each data provider decides which format to choose. The framework that reflects how interviewed data service providers and their clients perceive different data formats is presented in Table 2.

Table 2. Interviewees' views on OD technical formats

Format	Readability	Examples
Raw data	Neither machine-, nor human-readable data	CSV files that are contained in data providers' databases.
Linked open data	Machine-readable data	A rather technical concept that consists of 5 rankings [1] - requirements that should be fulfilled in order to call the data – linked open data.
Applications build on the top of data	Human-readable data	Applications, visualizations, mash-ups that are easier to comprehend than large rows and columns of data.

Based on empirical analysis OD service providers differentiate OD according to the level of its technical development. In terms of OD usability or applicability, "Raw data" is the hardest to apply. It takes a professional to first scrape it and convert into a machine- or human-readable representation of the original data set. "Linked open data" is easier to handle from a professional point of view, but still is not understandable for an inexperienced user. The last data format, "applications" is basically a user interface that allows regular users to clearly comprehend the content of the dataset that it was built upon.

5 Conclusion

There are several perceptions on what the phenomenon of OD implies. The classifications of these perceptions that we found are following: the degree of data openness (internal vs. external) and OD technical format (raw data, machine-readable data, and human-readable data).

Some people call the data that is available internally within one organization open. Others argue that only the data that is available for everyone externally can be called open. Both name a number of benefits that their version of OD that provide. In case of internally open data those benefits apply to an organization where the data was opened, such as improving internal communication and organizational performance. When talking about data open for everyone or externally OD people refer to national scale benefits like increasing transparency and boosting economic development (see 2). Consequently, the benefits of OD are expected to occur within the system where the data was opened whether it is an organization or a nation.

The entities and different actors can open their data externally or internally to pursue various goals and improve organizational processes. Some organizations may adopt a completely open model by making their data open externally - for example, non-profit organizations that collect statistics on particular area like government agencies and cultural institutions. Others can consider opening their data internally, for example, to increase interoperability between different departments or organizational network members. Also, both approaches may be applied simultaneously, when some parts of data are released only for internal use and others are available to everyone.

OD technical format is related to data usability. The more technically developed the data, the easier it is for the not-versed user to exploit it. Consequently, raw data is the hardest format to use and applications are the easiest way to get the information out of an original dataset. From this perspective we logically assume that the OD's capability to achieve expected benefits of its usage (listed in Table 1) correlates with OD format. By choosing and maintaining an appropriate OD format a data provider encourages OD usage thus increases its chances to improve communication, decision-making, develop and provide more services, and create economic value either at organizational or national level.

References

1. Berners-Lee, T.: Linked Data Design Issues (July 2006), http://www.w3.org/DesignIssues/LinkedData.html
2. Bizer, C., Heath, T., Berners-Lee, T.: Linked Data – the Story So Far, to appear. In: Heath, T., Hepp, M., Bizer, C. (eds.) Special Issue on Linked Data, International Journal on Semantic Web and Information Systems (IJSWIS), http://linkeddata.org/docs/ijswis-special-issue
3. Data. Gov: Data, http://www.data.gov/about
4. European Commission: Open data An engine for innovation, growth and transparent governance. In: COM, vol. 882, Brussels, Belgium (2011)

5. Fink, M.: Business and Economics of Linux and Open Source. Prentice Hall, New Jersey (2002)
6. Halb, W., Stocker, A., Mayer, H., Mülner, H., Ademi, I.: Towards a commercial adoption of linked open data for online content providers. In: Proceedings of I-SEMANTICS the 6th International Conference on Semantic Systems, Graz, Austria (2010)
7. Huijboom, N., Van den Broek, T.: Open Data: an International Comparison of Strategies. European Journal of ePractice 12 (March/April 2011), http://www.epractice.eu/files/European%20Journal%20epractice%20Volume%2012_1.pdf
8. Klein, H.K., Myers, M.D.: A Set of Principles for Conducting and Evaluating Interpretive Field Studies in Information Systems. MIS Quarterly 23(1), 67–94 (1999)
9. Kuk, G., Davies, T.: The Roles of Agency and Artifacts in Assembling Open Data Complementarities. In: Proceedings of Thirty Second International Conference on Information Systems, Shanghai, China (2011)
10. Latif, A., Saeed, A.U., Hoefler, P., Stocker, A., Wagner, C.: The Linked Data Value Chain: A Light Weight Model for Business Engeneers. In: Proceedings of I-SEMANTICS 2009 International Conference on Semantic Systems, Graz, Austria, pp. 568–575 (2009)
11. Lichtenthaler, U.: Open Innovation: Past Research, Current Debates, and Future Directions. The Academy of Management Perspectives 25(1), 75–93 (2011)
12. Lindman, J., Rossi, M., Marttiin, P.: Open Source Technology Changes Intra-Organizational Systems Development – A Tale of Two Companies. In: Proceedings of European Conference of Information Systems, Pretoria, South Africa, pp. 7–9.6 (2010)
13. Open Knowledge Foundation, http://okfn.org/, http://www.opendefinition.org/okd/
14. Somus (Social media for citizens and public sector collaboration) project – final report (January 2011), http://www.vtt.fi/inf/pdf/publications/2011/P755.pdf
15. Swanson, B., Ramiller, N.: The Organizing Vision in Information Systems Innovation. Organization Science 8(5), 458–474 (1997)
16. Van de Ven, A.H., Johnson, P.E.: Knowledge for theory and practice. Academy of Management Review 31, 802–821 (2006)
17. Vargo, S.L., Lush, R.F.: Evolving a services dominant logic. Journal of Marketing 68, 1–17 (2004)
18. Von Hippel, E., Von Krogh, G.: Open Source Software and the 'Private-Collective' Innovation Model: Issues for Organization Science. Organization Science 14(2) (March-April 2003)

Benefits of Software Renting in Cloud Business

Arto Ojala

University of Jyväskylä
arto.k.ojala@jyu.fi

Abstract. In the new era of computing, software can be sold and delivered as a cloud service, and software renting has become a strategic tool to compete in the market. In this multi-case study, software renting was found to help the case firms to (i) differentiate themselves from competitors; (ii) increase their competitive advantage by making the software available for a larger customer group, and (iii) decrease the price of software by using centralized software delivery and maintenance.

Keywords: Software renting, cloud computing, cloud business, SaaS.

1 Introduction

Software renting may give more economic benefits than other revenue models [1]. However, although software renting is becoming more frequent in the new era of computing, in which software is delivered via the Software-as-a-Service (SaaS) model, little is known about the advantages of software renting. In addition, most of the existing literature on software renting uses analytical approaches to analyze the benefits of software renting [1, 2, 3, 4]. I acknowledge the importance of these studies, but see a need for real-life cases in elucidating the strategic reasons that drive software firms to rent their software applications, in preference to the other revenue models available (see e.g. [1]).

The rapid growth of cloud computing has opened up new possibilities for software renting. In the SaaS model, the software is hosted in the data center of a service provider or third party, and delivered to customers via the Internet as a service. Since the software is used as a service, without physical installation in the customer's computers, SaaS is well suited to software renting. However, as noted by Armbrust et al. [6], most of the studies focusing on cloud computing have looked at the benefits from the customer's point of view, neglecting the possible benefits for the software vendor. In addition, there have been calls for a better understanding of revenue models in the software business in general [5, 8, 9], and especially in relation to software renting [1, 2, 4]. From these considerations, this study contributes to current knowledge in the following ways: (i) it reveals some of the competitive advantages of software renting from the software vendor's point of view, with reference to the competitive theory of Porter [10, 11] and (ii) it builds on previous work using analytical approaches in relation to software renting [1, 2, 3, 4]. The research question addressed in study is: What are the benefits of software renting?

M.A. Cusumano, B. Iyer, and N. Venkatraman (Eds.): ICSOB 2012, LNBIP 114, pp. 304–309, 2012.

2 Literature Review

2.1 Cloud Computing and SaaS

In cloud computing, users obtain access to computing resources, storage space, and software applications via the Internet as a service. Cloud computing includes three service layers. These consist of (i) Infrastructure as a Service (IaaS), which provides computation and storage capacity, (ii) Platform as a Service (PaaS), which provides software development tools plus an application execution environment, and (iii) SaaS, which provides applications on top of PaaS and IaaS [6, 13, 16]. Thus, cloud computing refers to the provision of computing capacity, storage capacity, and applications as a service across the Internet.

The data center hardware and software forming a "cloud" can be divided into a public cloud, a private cloud, and a hybrid cloud. In a public cloud, a software vendor uses his/her own or a third party's cloud infrastructure (data center) to offer SaaS for customers on demand. A private cloud involves the customer's internal data center, with the software being installed and used in a centralized manner within the organization; in this case the software is not made publicly available [6, 14]. In the case of a hybrid cloud, a firm using a private cloud may, for example, offload part of the workload onto a public cloud, and in that way acquire more computing capacity [14].

SaaS refers to the provision of software applications over the Internet. Hence, customers have online access to the software when it is needed instead of having it permanently installed on their own computers. SaaS also ensures that the latest version of the software is in use without the continuous installation of updates. In addition, because the software is executed on a service provider's server, it frees users from worrying about the technical specification of the computer or the data storage capacity [13, 15, 16].

2.2 The Economics of Renting

Renting is a widely studied topic in economics literature [7, 12]. Flath [7, p. 247] defines renting (or leasing) as "a contractual arrangement for trading the rights to temporary use of an object, but not the right to all possible future use." Thus, in a rental agreement, a customer does not get the full ownership rights over the object rented, as distinct from ownership following purchase. However, there are always trade-offs between the benefits of full ownership and those of "partial ownership" – i.e. renting. From the customer's point of view, these benefits are related to the characteristics of the product and the time period needed for usage of the product. In the words of Flath [7, p. 249], "The shorter is one's expected tenure of use of a good, the greater are the transacting cost gains to his leasing it rather than purchasing it outright."

In software rental, the customer pays a negotiated subscription fee. There is a time limitation such that the software license is for a fixed period, irrespective of usage [6]. Choudhary et al. [1] list four reasons why the customer may rent software in preference to buying it, as follows: (i) the software is for use in a short-term project,

(ii) a customer may simply want to gain experience of using the software, (iii) a customer wants to test and evaluate the usability of the software, or (iv) a customer wants to avoid negative network externality. Choudhary et al. [1] also found that software renting benefited both the software vendor and the customer by providing cost savings for customers, with higher profits also for software vendors. In a subsequent study, Choudhary [2] has argued that software renting also increases the quality of the software. Software renting lessens the customers' need to have their own IT personnel and IT infrastructure. This decreases the total cost of ownership and reduces hidden costs. According to Waters [15], the hidden costs in traditional software licensing can increase a firm's IT budget by as much as 80 percent.

2.3 Software Rental as a Competitive Strategy

Renting can be seen as a strategy to compete in the market on the basis of the positive impact of the rental on switching costs. According to Porter [11, p. 81] "switching costs are fixed cost that buyers face when they change suppliers." Switching costs arise, for instance, when a buyer changes to an alternative product, with the buyer then being obliged to train employees to use the product. In his study, Choudhary [2] found that in software renting, switching costs are relatively low, and this makes it easy for customers to change a software vendor if the quality or functionality of the software is not at the appropriate level.

Low switching costs in software renting may also increase the negotiating leverage of customers. The negotiating leverage of customers is also higher if the products are highly standardized. In this case, customers can always find an alternative product, and they can invite suppliers to tender against each other [11]. The threat of substitutes may also impact on software rental as a strategic choice. A substitute is a product that "performs the same or a similar function as an industry's product by a different means" [11, p. 84]. The threat of a substitute is high if a new product offers better value at a more attractive price than the older one. Rivalry among existing competitors impacts on prices. According to Porter [11], rivalry may decrease prices, for example (i) if the products are similar and there are low switching costs for customers, or (ii) if the product is perishable.

3 Methodology

The research method selected for this study should be able to cover human actions, enable the in-depth investigation of the complex phenomena, and capture cause-and-effect relationships. With all this in mind, I used a multiple case study methodology similar to the approaches presented by Eisenhardt [17] and Yin [18].

The research setting for this study consisted of five software firms (see Table 1) who acted as SaaS providers. I used multiple sources of information to gather data on each case firm. The main form of data collection was in-depth interviews. Altogether, 23 semi-structured open-ended interviews were conducted for this study. In addition to the face-to-face interviews, telephone and e-mail communication was used to collect further information, and to clarify inconsistent issues if necessary. In the data collection, I also used many types of secondary information such as press releases, websites of the firms, brochures, etc. to collect the kind of information that could validate the data gathered in the interviews. The method utilized in the data analysis was content analysis. The analysis of the case data consisted of three concurrent flows of activity [19]: (i) data reduction, (ii) data displays, and (iii) conclusion-drawing/verification.

Table 1. Overview of the case firms

Firm	Year of establishment	Product	Target industry
Firm A	1998	Planning and optimization software for telecom operators	Telecom operators
Firm B	2000	Gaming platform and content	Game players
Firm C	2006	Risk management software	Bank and financing sector
Firm D	2008	Entitlement management software	Large and medium-sized corporations
Firm E	2006	Interactive 3D sales software	Furniture industry

4 Findings

The benefits to the case firms relating to software renting were mainly based on (i) the technical factors that made software renting cost-effective for a software provider and consequently for its customers, (ii) competitive advantages, in so far as software renting and SaaS were seen as forming a new way to sell the product, (iii) the low investment costs for customers in the rental model, and (iv) the positive network effect brought about by software renting. The interviewees from firms A, B, D, and E commented that in technical terms, SaaS brings several advantages to both the software provider and the customer, especially if the software is used in a public cloud. From the point of view of the software providers (firms A, D, and E), the SaaS model was seen as having achieved cost savings, as the software firms do not need to install the software on each customer's Intranet separately. It also decreases possible traveling costs related to installation, implementation, and after-sales support.

Other benefits of the SaaS model included centralized development, maintenance, and expandability. This meant that the case firms knew that the customers were using the same version of the software, and by means of the public cloud, the case firm were able to bring in new options that were visible to all their customers immediately. These technical features consistently brought cost savings to the case firms. It made it possible to offer the software at a lower price in the rental mode than in the traditional licensing mode. In addition to cost savings, customers benefited from better scalability of the software, increased computing power and storage capacity, better flexibility, ease of use, and so on.

The case firms saw the SaaS and software renting as a new way to offer and deliver software products to their customers. They also anticipated that traditional licensing would disappear from the market in the future. The software firms were keen to follow the developments in the field, differentiate themselves from their competitors, and take advantage of the possibilities offered by SaaS and software renting.

All the case firms emphasized that the rental model was attractive to customers because of low initial investments. This made purchasing decisions much easier for the customer, bearing in mind the high investment costs associated with the traditional licensing fee. Hence, renting became a particularly attractive option for smaller customers who lacked a budget for costly licenses. In practice, this meant that in the rental model, customers were able to purchase the software without having to make special budgeting arrangements, undertake long decision-making processes, or apply for the approval of top management. All this implied more attractive pricing for the customer than with traditional licensing, and the possibility of cost savings. Interviewees from firms A, C, D, and E commented that software renting also enabled them to bring the product more quickly to the market. Smaller customers were able to buy it, and this helped the case firms to acquire good market visibility rapidly, thereby achieving a positive network effect.

5 Discussions

The findings of this study indicate that the benefits of software renting derive from both technical advantages and competition strategies. First of all, software rental through the public cloud made software renting easier from a technical point of view, since the firms could use centralized delivery of software to their customers. Centralized software delivery and maintenance decreased the transaction costs and brought savings. This method also protected their products against perishability (see [11]), as the case firms were able to update new versions of the software in a centralized manner.

Secondly, software rental and SaaS gave competitive advantages to the case firms. By using a suitable combination of the new revenue and delivery model, they were able to differentiate themselves from other competitors and to offer something new to the customer. Thus, software renting and SaaS can be seen as a substitute for the old licensing model. This is in line with Porter's [11] notion that substitutes gives competitive advantages if they perform the same task within a lower price range than the original.

Thirdly, software renting made the case firms' products available for smaller customers, who would not have been able to pay for the software by the traditional licensing method. This method also provided added value to customers in terms of flexibility. Shifting capital investment onto operational costs enabled them to start using the software without special budgeting, or without having to obtain the approval of top management. This increased the case firms' competitive advantage, since they were now able to widen their customer segment from large corporations to small and medium-sized firms. In addition, software renting made it possible for customers to predict the actual costs of the software.

6 Conclusions

This study contributes to research on benefits of software renting in the following respects: (i) it validates and expands on earlier work related to software renting by providing empirical support for their economic models, (ii) it reveals the competitive advantages related to software renting from the software vendors' point of view, in contrast to previous research focusing mainly on the benefits to customers, and (iii) it contributes to knowledge of software renting in cloud computing, bearing in mind that cloud computing constitutes a new strategic tool for the delivery of software products.

References

1. Choudhary, V., Tomak, K., Chaturvedi, A.: Economic Benefits of Renting Software. Journal of Organizational Computing and Electronic Commerce 8(4), 277–305 (1998)
2. Choudhary, V.: Comparison of Software Quality Under Perpetual Licensing and Software as a Service. Journal of Management Information Systems 24(2), 141–165 (2007)
3. Gurnani, H., Karlapalem, K.: Optimal pricing strategies for Internet-based software dissemination. Journal of the Operational Research Society 52(1), 64–70 (2001)
4. Varian, H.: Buying, Sharing and Renting Information Goods. The Journal of Industrial Economics 48(4), 473–488 (2000)
5. Ferrante, D.: Software Licensing Models: What's Out There? IT Professional 8(6), 24–29 (2006)
6. Armbrust, et al.: A view of cloud computing. Communication of the ACM 53(4), 50–58 (2010)
7. Flath, D.: The Economics of Short-term Leasing. Economic Inquiry 18(2), 247–259 (1980)
8. Huang, K.-W., Wang, M.: Firm-Level Productivity Analysis for Software as a Service Companies. In: Proceedings of the ICIS (2009)
9. Sainio, L.-M., Marjakoski, E.: The logic of revenue logic? Strategic and operational levels of pricing in the context of software business. Technovation 29(5), 368–378 (2009)
10. Porter, M.: How Competitive Forces Shape Strategy. Harvard Business Review 57(2), 137–145 (1979)
11. Porter, M.: The five competitive forces that shape strategy. Harvard Business Review 86(1), 78–93 (2008)
12. Bulow, J.I.: Durable-Goods Monopolists. Journal of Political Economy 90(2), 314–332 (1982)
13. Hugos, M.H., Hulitzky, D.: Business in the Cloud: What Every Business Needs to Know About Cloud Computing. John Wiley & Sons, Inc. (2011)
14. Louridas, P.: Up in the Air: Moving Your Applications to the Cloud. IEEE Software 27(4), 6–11 (2010)
15. Waters, B.: Software as a service: A look at the customer benefits. Journal of Digital Asset Management 1, 32–39 (2005)
16. Ojala, A., Tyrväinen, P.: Developing Cloud Business Models: A Case Study on Cloud Gaming. IEEE Software 28(4), 42–47 (2011)
17. Eisenhardt, K.M.: Building theories from case study research. Academy of Management Review 14(4), 532–550 (1989)
18. Yin, R.K.: Case study research: Design and methods. SAGE Publications, CA (2009)
19. Miles, M.B., Huberman, A.M.: Qualitative Data Analysis: An Expanded Sourcebook. Sage Publications, California (1994)

Author Index